IDENTITIES

AND

INEQUALITIES

EXPLORING THE INTERSECTIONS OF RACE, CLASS,
GENDER, AND SEXUALITY

DAVID M. NEWMAN
DePauw University

Boston   Burr Ridge, IL   Dubuque, IA   Madison, WI   New York
San Francisco   St. Louis   Bangkok   Bogotá   Caracas   Kuala Lumpur
Lisbon   London   Madrid   Mexico City   Milan   Montreal   New Delhi
Santiago   Seoul   Singapore   Sydney   Taipei   Toronto

The *McGraw-Hill* Companies

 Higher Education

Published by McGraw-Hill, an imprint of The McGraw-Hill Companies, Inc., 1221 Avenue of the Americas, New York, NY 10020. Copyright © 2007 by The McGraw-Hill Companies. All rights reserved. No part of this publication may be reproduced or distributed in any form or by any means, or stored in a database or retrieval system, without the prior written consent of The McGraw-Hill Companies, Inc., including, but not limited to, in any network or other electronic storage or transmission, or broadcast for distance learning.

This book is printed on acid-free paper.

4 5 6 7 8 9 0 FGR/FGR 0 9

ISBN-13:   978-0-07-312406-3
ISBN-10:   0-07-312406-0

Editor in Chief: *Emily Barrosse*
Publisher: *Phillip Butcher*
Sponsoring Editor: *Sherith Pankratz*
Marketing Manager: *Dan Loch*
Developmental Editor: *Rebecca Smith*
Production Editor: *Leslie LaDow*
Manuscript Editor: *Jan Fehler*
Designer: *Preston Thomas*

Photo Research Coordinator: *Brian J. Pecko*
Art Editor: *Ayelet Arbel*
Production Supervisor: *Tandra Jorgensen*
Media Project Manager: *Nancy García*
Composition: *10.5/13 Aldus by GTS-India*
Printing: *45# New Era Matte by Quebecor, Fairfield*

Cover images: © Jon Shireman/Getty Images/The Image Bank.

Credits: The credits section for this book begins on page 367 and is considered an extension of the copyright page.

Library of Congress Cataloging-in-Publication Data

Newman, David M., 1958-
   Identities and inequalities : exploring the intersections of race, class, gender, and sexuality/
   David M. Newman.
      p. cm.
   Includes bibliographical references and index.
   ISBN 978-0-07-312406-3
   ISBN 0-07-312406-0 (alk. paper)
      1. Equality–United States. 2. Group identity–United States. 3. Prejudices–United States. 4. Discrimination–United States. 5. Differentiation (Sociology) 6. Social classes–United States. 7. Race awareness–United States. 8. United States–Social conditions–21st century. I. Title.

HN90.S6N45 2006
305'.0973–dc22   2005044393

The Internet addresses listed in the text were accurate at the time of publication. The inclusion of a Web site does not indicate an endorsement by the authors or McGraw-Hill, and McGraw-Hill does not guarantee the accuracy of the information presented at these sites.

www.mhhe.com

FOR MY MOM

David M. Newman is currently Professor of Sociology at DePauw University in Greencastle, Indiana. He received his Ph.D. in sociology from the University of Washington in 1988. He teaches courses in deviance, mental illness, family, social psychology, and research methods and has won teaching awards at both the University of Washington and DePauw University. He has published numerous articles on teaching and has presented several research papers on the intersection of gender and power in intimate relationships. He has authored two textbooks, *Sociology: Exploring the Architecture of Everyday Life* (and co-edited an accompanying anthology) and *Sociology of Families*. When not hunkered down in his third-floor office, he enjoys running, swimming, and arguing with his teenage sons.

CONTENTS

CONTENTS

I'm a regular visitor to the fitness center at my university's physical education building, which is open to people in the local community as well as people affiliated with the university. An interesting mixture of individuals is often there: professors, students, deans, secretaries, artists, UPS truck drivers, insurance salespeople, restaurateurs, farmers, construction workers, ministers, retirees, and so on. The locker-room conversation typically includes laments about the dismal play of local sports teams, complaints about the weather, and advice on the best way to strip old wallpaper, hit a nine-iron out of the rough, or get rid of backyard moles. Certain professors predictably drone on about lazy students, too many exams to grade, an unfair administration, and so on.

To be honest, such topics bore me, so I usually do more eavesdropping than talking. Every once in a while, though, a person from the local community will try to engage me in casual chitchat. Since I began writing this book about a year ago, I've had the same conversation five or six times, with only minor variations:

> *Other person:* So, David, how are your classes going?
>
> *Me:* Actually I'm not teaching right now. I'm on sabbatical.
>
> *Other person:* Sabbatical, huh? Must be nice, having a vacation, not having to work for months.
>
> *Me:* [sounding annoyed] It's not a vacation! I work harder on sabbatical than I do when I'm teaching.
>
> *Other person:* Sorry. Sorry. So what are you working on that's keeping you so busy?
>
> *Me:* I'm writing a book.
>
> *Other person:* Oh yeah? Impressive. What's it about?
>
> *Me:* Inequalities.

I realize that such a one-word description is completely insufficient, but it's an effective way to conclude the discussion on the spot. Most people have responded with unpersuasive expressions of interest ("Hmm, that sounds . . . um . . . nice."), sarcasm ("Fascinating! But if you don't mind, I'll wait for the movie version."), or vacant, deer-in-the-headlights stares. A couple of brave souls have plunged past this conversational dead end, though. A soybean farmer said he wasn't aware that I was a math teacher. The owner of a local pizza joint suggested that if I wanted to sell more copies I should use some obscure science-fiction space alien's name in the title. A guy I'd never seen before complained that his own impoverished state—due to chronic unemployment—was recently made worse by the fact that his wife left him. The ex-mayor asked if I'd help him find a publisher for a book he wants to write. Even colleagues from other departments at the university have managed to convey their disinterest or downright disapproval:

> *Other professor:* What kinds of inequalities are you referring to?
> *Me:* Social inequalities. Race, class, gender, and sexuality mostly.
> *Other professor:* What do *you* know about social inequality? You're a white, male college professor for crying out loud!

Secretly, I have wished that I was writing about something a little more concrete and a little less threatening, like the history of calculators or an illustrated coffee-table book about lawn furniture.

Writing a book—whether it's a children's book, a romance novel, or a sociology textbook—is a daunting task. Writing a book about a hot-button topic upon which everyone has an opinion, and usually a strong opinion, is absolutely fearsome. Social inequality is not just an academic subject, described and explained dispassionately during a semester-long college course. It is a way of life with real and sometimes dangerous consequences. It touches people directly, whether we're talking about their physical well-being, the availability of economic and educational opportunities, their access to political decision makers, their interactions with the law, the way other people communicate with them, or the prestige and power their group has in society. Some people want to deny the existence of inequality, hoping that if we simply say it doesn't exist, it will disappear; others wear it as a moral badge, making it a part of everything they do and say.

People's reactions to the topic of inequality are influenced by, among other things, whether they are harmed by it or benefit from it. Those who are members of groups that have historically been disadvantaged by social inequality—namely ethnoracial and sexual minorities, women, and poor people—are understandably sensitive (perhaps even angry) about their position. Although they may be appreciative that their problems are being written about at all, many believe that they have a vested interest in how inequality is portrayed in books like this one. Some may even feel that the topic is private property that cannot be fully understood by outsiders. At the same time, some people from disadvantaged groups are sick and tired of talking about inequality. They see no value in perpetuating a dialogue of despair and hopelessness, preferring to see themselves as masters of their own fate and not victims of it.

On the other hand, those who have been historically privileged by social inequality—namely, Whites, men, heterosexuals, members of the middle and upper classes—sometimes become defensive when the subject of inequality is raised. They seem to assume that any talk of it will lead to their advantages being confiscated.

So you can see that the task of writing a book about race, class, gender, and sexuality is a formidable one. Ironically, however, my locker-room experiences have reinforced the importance of writing about this topic. A lot of people never get past sound bites and superficial rhetoric to develop a deeper and more useful sociological understanding of social inequality. It's my hope that this book will help you look at the issue with greater clarity.

IDENTITIES AND INEQUALITIES

Though we call attention to them to greater or lesser degrees, all of us have a race, a sexual orientation, an ethnic heritage, a gender, and a class status. All of these characteristics—not to mention religion, family membership, age, intellect, sense of humor, physical attractiveness, and so on—combine to determine our identities, or who we are. But we live in a society that places dramatically different values on the various component categories of these identifiers. So at the same time that race, ethnicity, gender, sexuality, and social class combine to construct our identities, they also determine our place in society, or the inequalities that affect us. Our identities dictate our chances for living a comfortable life; our access to valued economic, educational, or political resources; the likelihood of being seen positively or negatively by others; and our susceptibility to victimization, either by crime or by illness.

For over a century, sociology has outpaced other disciplines in describing and explaining the ways in which race, class, gender—and more recently sexuality—determine people's experiences and their access to important life chances. These concepts are the bread and butter of our discipline. You'd be hard-pressed to find a sociologist who would deny the everyday influence or intellectual importance of these features of social life. No sociology course (or textbook) worth its salt would totally ignore the impact of race, class, gender, or sexuality. Our scholarly books and journals are filled to the brim with theoretical and empirical work that to some degree incorporates these concepts.

That's not to say that all sociologists agree about the everyday influence of these factors or even how they're best defined. Are they personal traits or social groupings? Are they micro-level phenomena best examined as private lived experiences, or are they macro-level elements of culture best examined from the institutional perspective of the social structure? Are they primarily characteristics of difference or characteristics of inequality? As someone who has taught sociology courses for close to 20 years, my answer to these questions is an unequivocal, shoulder-shrugging "I dunno." I think they are all of these things, simultaneously. They exert their influence on our lives at both the very personal and the very structural levels. They are the fundamental elements of our self-concepts and public identities, but they also shape the contours of our society and determine the history and quality of our lives.

Given the ubiquity of race, class, gender, and sexuality in our teaching and their popularity in our scholarship, it might seem . . . well . . . rather stupid to write yet another book about them. But as I combed through the scores of books that I have on the topic, I noticed that something was consistently missing. It seemed to me that the vast majority of books in this area treat race, class, gender, and sexuality as independent concepts, often occupying entirely separate sections of the book. That approach would be relatively useful if people were just male or just Asian or just heterosexual and nothing else or if people embraced the same identity in every situation throughout their entire lives. But that's not the way most people define themselves or experience everyday life. In fact, the determination of our identities is always a little like ordering from a menu in a Chinese restaurant: We select one item—or sometimes more than one item—from column A, column B, column C, and so on and then we mix everything together on our plate. The meal is not simply three or four or five separate and mutually exclusive dishes, but a delightful mélange of our various selections. And the next time we order Chinese food, we may come up with a different combination of flavors.

So this book emphasizes the confluence of those four key social identifiers—race, class, gender, and sexuality—from the perspective of individuals embedded in particular cultural, institutional, and historical contexts. I attempt to move away from the common "if it's week three, it must be gender" approach to a more integrated examination of how these four elements work together (or for that matter, in opposition) to form people's social identities and experiences with inequality.

Another complexity that cropped up as I was writing this book is that it's nearly impossible to account for—let alone explain—the experiences of everyone. It became clear early on that it would be impossible to address every possible combination of every race, class, gender, and sexual category. Instead, I've tried to consistently examine the experiences of people at all levels of the continuum of inequality. Too often sociologists focus on those who veer most obviously from the dominant groups: poor people, women, people who are members of non-white ethnoracial groups, homosexuals. I feel it is important to examine race, class, gender, and sexuality as variables with many constituent categories and not as single attributes. This book explores the experiences of white people as well as people of color; men as well as women; the wealthy and the middle class as well as the poor; heterosexuals and bisexuals as well as homosexuals. It is about privilege as well as disadvantage, "otherness" as well as similarity, invisibility as well as visibility.

Trying to accomplish this balancing act hasn't been easy. And at the risk of giving away the punch line too soon, the overall message about inequality is not particularly uplifting. Although, as a society, we've made tremendous strides in acknowledging the problems some groups face and in improving their lives, we still face imbalances, injustices, and disadvantages. But perhaps by grappling with the sociological theories, research, and insight that inform this book, you will come to think of yourself and others as complex beings whose multifaceted identities offer both challenges and opportunities.

THE BOOK'S WRITING STYLE

Because so much of what you will read in this book is derived from research conducted by professional social scientists, it has the potential to seem rather cold and distant. So I have chosen to write this book in a style that I hope is simultaneously informative, accessible, and entertaining. I have tried to avoid mystifying jargon wherever possible. At the same time, I have tried not to oversimplify the material. In short, I have tried to write the way I speak (hopefully with all my grammatical gaffes edited out). I truly believe that sociology has a great deal of useful information to offer, which people need to know simply in order to understand how their lives intersect with the social structure, and that a comfortable writing style helps to get that information across.

Each chapter begins with a small snippet of everyday life—often taken from my own personal experiences—to show you how the information contained in that chapter applies to understanding our personal lives. Indeed, the book is peppered with such everyday examples, sometimes taken from contemporary headlines and sometimes taken from the experiences of people just like you and me.

Moreover, you'll notice that the book is written primarily in the first person. I have purposely chosen to write the book this way to remind you that it comes from a real individual (me) who often struggles just like you to understand how and why things happen. I know it's heresy for an author to admit deficiencies in knowledge, but I am not so arrogant as to believe that I know everything about everything. Most of the questions that crop up in a book about social identities and inequalities do not have easy, clear, straightforward answers. Most of the time, the answers are frustratingly complex or even unanswerable. But that shouldn't stop us from asking them.

The first-person format of the book also serves as a reminder that as a real human being, I have beliefs, assumptions, biases, and values that I bring with me to every situation I encounter—including book writing. This book is about social inequalities because I believe that although we can debate their causes, educational, legal, political, cultural, and economic imbalances exist and create serious problems for some people while creating enormous advantages for others. That's not meant to be a blanket condemnation of those at the top or a blanket absolution of responsibility of the "downtrodden." Instead, it is my belief, based on the evidence that I have seen (and present in this book), that the way people are defined and treated in society—both by others and by the larger institutions that govern everyday social life—is not fixed and inevitable. In some ways, things are better than they once were; in other ways, they're worse. Sometimes people deserve the problems they bring upon themselves; other times they truly are the victims of circumstances that are largely beyond their control. Sometimes people who are advantaged are generous and helpful; other times they're callous and exploitative.

My purpose in this book is not to persuade you to believe exactly what I believe or adopt the same perspective on things that I have. On the contrary, my hope simply is that by reading this book you will begin to take a critical look at your life in relation to others and to the society in which you live. Some of what you will read will make you nod in agreement; some of it will make you angry and frustrated. But all of it will make you acknowledge and, I hope, examine your own beliefs, your own values, and the assumptions you make about others who are different from you.

THE BOOK'S ORGANIZATION

This book is organized as simply as possible. It's divided into two parts that, from the title, should be quite obvious. Part 1, *Identities*, examines the origin and utility of the concepts of race, class, gender, and sexuality. It focuses primarily on the nature of difference, the historical construction of these identifying concepts, the ways they are culturally presented and reflected in language and media, and the ways they are learned and incorporated into our personal identities. Where do our ideas about race, class, gender, and sexuality come from? How are they defined? How do we balance the features that make us different from others with those that we have in common? How do we learn to be a member of a particular gender, race, class, or sexual group and come to see ourselves accordingly?

Part 2, *Inequalities*, draws on the information in Part 1 and examines the everyday and institutional consequences of race, class, gender, and sexuality, paying particular attention to their relationship to social inequality. This part explores issues of prejudice and discrimination at the individual level and in the context of important social institutions: health care, the criminal justice system, and economics. The final chapter examines the future of inequalities, paying particular attention to movements for social change.

To highlight the importance of examining the connections between race, class, gender, and sexuality, a feature called "Intersections" appears throughout the book. These features focus on specific areas of research or interesting social phenomena that illustrate the important combinations of two or more social identifiers. The goal is to enhance your appreciation of the importance of looking at race, class, gender, and sexuality collectively rather than separately. These sections cover such topics as mothering, single parenthood, bullying in high school, the history of childbirth, weight concerns, the death penalty, and workplace discrimination.

At the end of each chapter is an exercise titled "Investigating Identities and Inequalities" that will allow you to go outside the classroom and systematically observe some aspect of social identity and inequality. Some of the exercises require that you survey other people in order to gain some insight into their firsthand experiences. Others ask you to venture into your own past or into common social settings—businesses, local neighborhoods, hospitals—to examine the features that perpetuate social inequalities. I believe that learning is most effective and meaningful when it is active, not passive. These exercises are designed to bring you face-to-face with the everyday experiences of identities and inequalities from the perspective of both individuals and the social institutions they inhabit.

MY CREDENTIALS

As I alluded to earlier, I am male. I am white. I am heterosexual. I suppose I am middle class, though significant portions of my life would be better characterized as working class. Although I am a member of a religious minority, most people would say that I'm comfortably situated at the advantaged end of all the important dimensions that determine social privilege. What, then, can I possibly say about the intersections of race, class, gender, and sexuality and their contribution to the construction of social inequalities? What do I know about being the victim of subtle and wanton discrimination?

Some of you might think that my traits immediately disqualify me from writing this book. But although I can't truly know what it feels like to be a woman, an immigrant, a member of a racial minority, a homosexual, or a desperately poor person in this society, I do know what it feels like to have a gender, race, sexual orientation, and class standing. These characteristics are not invisible to me.

I went to college in San Diego, California, not that far from the Mexican border. At the time, my parents lived in the Los Angeles area, about a two-hour drive north up Interstate 5. I made this drive a couple of times a month throughout college. Fifty miles or so north of San Diego along the freeway was an Immigration and Naturalization Service checkpoint. Northbound traffic was required to slow down so INS officers could visually inspect the vehicles to see if any of the riders might be in the country illegally. Suspicious cars were instructed to pull over for a more thorough inspection. In the four years I made that drive, I never experienced any problems at this checkpoint. I was always waved through by a smiling INS officer and allowed to go on my merry way. That is, except for the one time a dark-skinned friend of mine (whose grandparents had come to this country from Pakistan) made the drive with me. Instead of being waved through as I expected, we were pulled over and the car searched. I was asked nothing. He was asked a series of intrusive questions about why he was traveling to L.A., why he was in the country, and how long he planned to be here. Eventually we were allowed to leave, but not before he got a serious dose of humiliation and I learned a lesson about the unequal treatment people receive because of the color of their skin.

This experience made me realize that being a member of privileged social categories means that I have a special obligation to understand the systems of privilege and inequality that exist in this society. I have spent my entire academic life in the pursuit of this understanding, and I have spent my entire life as an adult citizen seeking ways to redress the disadvantages that others suffer. Now it is my privilege to be in a position to share some of what I've learned about inequality in this book. I hope it helps you to understand how your own identities—whatever they may be—shape your experiences and how you can use your knowledge of inequality to shape a more just society.

ACKNOWLEDGMENTS

Just as I started writing this book, I was invited to participate in a panel discussion with a few colleagues from other departments on the process of writing. In addition to me, there was a fiction writer, a psychologist, and a historian. We talked about how we write, why we write, when and where we write, and so on. Although our specific tastes and styles were quite different, we all had some things in common. When the topic came to the role of other people in the writing process, however, I broke ranks and stated rather bluntly that writing is as solitary an act as there is. When push comes to shove, I pointed out, it's just the author, alone with her or his keyboard, who's responsible for organizing a dense body of knowledge and creatively presenting it in a way that makes grammatical and substantive sense to the reader.

But that's not to say that others don't play a role. Indeed they do. Anyone who's written a book knows full well that books are always collective ventures. We get editorial help from some people and substantive help from others. Some people pitch in with the mundane responsibilities of everyday life to free us up to write. And the indebtedness we feel toward them is genuine and deserved. As weird and paradoxical as it sounds, the solitary act of writing cannot be accomplished without the help of other people.

That said, let me acknowledge the people who managed to effectively avoid annoying me as I wrote this book. First, let me thank Becky Smith, my longtime editor. Becky has provided editorial guidance on every book I've written. Other than me, no one on the planet is more familiar with my writing tendencies and quirks. Becky often knows what I'm going to write before I write it. It makes for interesting conversations sometimes, but it also means that the process is as effective and efficient as possible. I am forever indebted to her assistance and insight.

ACKNOWLEDGMENTS

My sincere thanks to Sherith Pankratz at McGraw-Hill for taking a chance on this book and providing useful guidance during its final stages. I'd also like to thank Leslie LaDow, Jan Fehler, Sheri Gilbert, Preston Thomas, and Brian Pecko for their work on the project.

In addition, thanks to the following instructors who provided valuable comments and suggestions in their reviews of the book:

Todd E. Bernhardt, Broward Community College
Nelson E. Bingham, Earlham College
Michelle J. Budig, University of Massachusetts
Jan Buhrmann, Illinois College
Philip N. Cohen, University of California–Irvine
Rachel L. Einwohner, Purdue University
Elizabeth B. Erbaugh, University of New Mexico
Dona C. Fletcher, Sinclair Community College
Sarah N. Gatson, Texas A&M University
Tom Gerschick, Illinois State University
Suzanne Hopf, University of Louisville
Judith A. Howard, University of Washington
Shayne Lee, University of Houston
Larry Lovell-Troy, Millikin University
Peter Meiksins, Cleveland State University
Seth Ovadia, Towson University
Michael P. Perez, California State University–Fullerton
Craig T. Robertson, University of North Alabama
Sergio Romero, University of Montana
Theodore C. Wagenaar, Miami University
Janelle Wilson, University of Minnesota–Duluth
Idee Winfield, College of Charleston

Several colleagues provided suggestions and "raw data" along the way. Rebecca Upton was especially helpful in providing many anthropological examples. Others at my university, including Eric Silverman, Nancy Davis, Kelley Hall, and Bruce Stinebrickner, provided additional useful information. Our departmental administrative assistant, Krista Dahlstrom, was invaluable in helping with the compilation of the bibliography, a difficult and time-consuming task.

Lastly, let me express my deepest gratitude to my wife, Elizabeth, and my two sons, Zachary and Seth. I am fully aware that having an author for a spouse/father is no picnic. They don't know sociology from a hole in the ground, but they put up with me, graciously, supportively, and without (much) complaint.

IDENTITIES AND INEQUALITIES

Identities

How would you respond if someone asked, "Who are you?" Would you respond differently if this person asked, "*What* are you?" Both questions ask us to reveal our identities, but the second is particularly likely to probe our *social* identities, the group memberships by which we define ourselves in relation to others.

Our social identities consist of a myriad of different components. Some mark us as unique, distinct from anyone else on the planet. Others connect us to larger communities of people, giving us a sense of group membership and perhaps even collective pride. In Part 1, we will explore the nature and development of our social identities, especially race, class, gender, and sexuality. ■

CHAPTER 1

Differences and Similarities

September 11, 2001, was a watershed day in American history. Thousands of people lost their lives in the attacks that occurred that morning, and thousands more have died in the ensuing military actions in Afghanistan and Iraq. The events of 9/11 changed the political, social, economic, and ideological course of the nation like perhaps no other moment in our history. Many of us talk about that day as one of those punctuating historical flashes that clearly demarcates the "before" and "after" of our lives and our society.

To varying degrees, all of us have seen the common and previously unexamined rhythm of our daily lives altered. If you regularly travel by plane, for instance, you've no doubt seen alterations in your flying behaviors—from the clothes you wear and the way you pack your luggage (easily accessible for security inspections) to the preflight time you allot for proceeding through various checkpoints. Perhaps you follow political developments abroad more closely than you did prior to 9/11. If you're like me, you might still feel a queasy nervousness when watching pre-2001 films set in Manhattan, hoping that casual shots of the World Trade Center towers won't appear in the background, conjuring up those recognizable feelings of sadness and lingering disbelief. At the linguistic level, terms like "homeland security," "ground zero," "terrorism," "Taliban," "Osama," and "weapons of mass destruction" have entered our collective, everyday vocabulary.

What's especially important about 9/11 and its aftermath for present purposes—namely, a book on race, class, gender, and sexual identities and inequalities—is that it serves as a symbol of the common ways that Americans have always thought about themselves and others. I remember a discussion in one of my courses the day after the attacks in which a student remarked that this catastrophe, like other national catastrophes before it, would inevitably bring out the absolute best and absolute worst in us as a society and as a people. She was right. In the days and weeks following the attacks, strangers came together like never before to weep, to grieve, to share in the collective pain of this tragedy. People began to look out for one another in unprecedented ways. Communities mobilized to take care of their own. People began to feel a sense of solidarity, a shared anguish, motivated in part by a swelling anger directed outward against the perpetrators of such a dastardly deed. We were one. No matter what our ethnic, racial, religious, or class background or where we fell on the political spectrum, we were in this thing together. Getting angry at the slow driver in front of you on the highway or fretting over the fact that your local grocery store was out of your favorite brand of ice cream didn't seem worth it anymore. All those trivial annoyances that once drove us to distraction were no longer significant. After all, there were more serious issues to worry about.

And yet there was an unmistakable and predictable darker side that also emerged as a result of these attacks: a hideous unmasking of our deep-seated hatreds and prejudices. In the weeks following 9/11, individuals who looked "Arab" or "Middle Eastern" were beaten up on the street or taunted in their schools. Mosques were vandalized. Some people found themselves stopped and interrogated by law enforcement officials because they fit a stereotypical terrorist profile. Old friendships were disbanded; lives were destroyed. To this day, anyone whose apparent ethnicity even remotely resembles that of the people responsible for the attacks is subjected to telltale signs of suspicion: angry stares, apprehensive whispers, interpersonal withdrawal. Recently, a white colleague in another department was describing to me the intense scrutiny he was subjected to when crossing the border from Canada to the United States. When he finished, he quipped, "Yeah, but if I was Arab American, I'd have been there for hours and they probably would have strip-searched me!" Though he meant his remark as a joke, there was certainly some truth to his contention that people from particular ethnic groups do not enjoy the same interactional privileges as members of other groups. The fact of the matter is that his coloring would always serve as a protective coat of armor against others' suspicions.

In fearsome times and in the interests of feeling safe and secure, the things that mark us as different take on added relevance, outshining all the things that we might have in common. Easily visible distinctions become the chief criteria for determining who is with us and who is against us, who is trustworthy and who is suspect, who is harmless and who is dangerous. Out of a mistaken belief that those who are different pose the greatest risk to personal well-being, some people secretly and not-so-secretly long to surround themselves with others who are "like me."

Sadly, 9/11 wasn't the first time that we let our differences divide us, and it probably won't be the last. A quick glance back in time reveals that virtually every minority group in this country—be it racial, ethnic, religious, sexual, gender-based, or class-based—has had or continues to have its own historical moment of persecution:

- After centuries of mistreatment and forced relocation of Native Americans, the Dawes Allotment Act of 1887 granted parcels of reservation land to individuals rather than to particular tribes. It was believed that if individuals owned their own land, adopted white clothing and ways, and were responsible for their own farms, they would gradually lose their Indian-ness and be assimilated into the white population.
- From 1619, when the first black slaves arrived, to 1865, when the 13th Amendment was ratified, outlawing slavery, millions of African Americans endured the hardships of forced servitude. After emancipation, they continued to be brutalized through the practice of lynching and other forms of violent intimidation.
- In the mid-19th century, war with Mexico and westward expansion redrew national boundaries, enabling white settlers to freely move into lands previously inhabited by Mexicans.
- In the late 19th and early 20th centuries, several laws, such as the Chinese Exclusion Act, the Scott Act, and the Geary Act, barred

Chinese immigrants from entering the country and stripped those already here of many of their legal rights.

- Early 20th-century immigrants from Ireland, Italy, Greece, Poland, Russia, and other Eastern European countries were subjected to varying degrees of hostility and discrimination. Business owners routinely prevented individuals from these groups from applying for jobs that were open to other Whites. The National Origins Act of 1924 established quotas on immigrants from southern and Eastern Europe.
- During the Great Depression of the 1930s, poor refugees from Oklahoma who moved westward in search of work were exploited, beaten, and forced to live in shantytowns known as "Hoovervilles."
- Japanese Americans (and some non-Japanese Asian people) were forcibly relocated from their homes to high-security internment camps after the bombing of Pearl Harbor and our entry into World War II.
- Employed women—who were told that it was their patriotic duty to work in factories during World War II—were vilified in the press when the war ended and were portrayed as destroyers of their families.
- In many areas of the country today, openly gay men and women still risk occupational discrimination, political hostility, and outright violence.

In short, in our 230 year history, the tension between similarity and difference—what brings us together and pushes us apart—has been the hallmark of the American experience. We take great pride in the fact that we are a nation of immigrants, welcoming people of different races, religions, and nationalities who have come here throughout the years to make a better life. And yet the responses to people who are different are often tension, distrust, and hostility. In this chapter, we'll look at this phenomenon from a **sociological perspective**—a way of examining everyday social life that emphasizes the interplay between societal forces and personal characteristics—in influencing people's thoughts, actions, feelings, judgments, and interactions. Why do people distinguish between "us" and "them"? Are some aspects of difference more desirable than others?

SIMILARITIES AND DIFFERENCES IN EVERYDAY LIFE: DRAWING LINES

As a rule, I hate clichés. I recently told my 18-year-old son, who was preparing a speech for his high school commencement ceremony, that if he used any clichés (like "Today we embark on a life's journey filled with exciting new challenges" or "Follow your dreams, reach for the stars, and be all that you can be"), I'd disown him. But clichés always have some kernel of truth to them. Take "no two people are exactly alike," for instance. Obviously, no two people could ever be exactly alike. Walk down a bustling city street someday, and you'll no doubt see an eye-popping assortment of human sizes, shapes, skin colors, and ages. Spend time getting to know the people you see and you'll unearth a vast range of different mannerisms, life experiences, attitudes, values, ideas, tastes, likes, dislikes, and so on. Your faith in clichés would soon be restored: *No two of us are exactly alike!*

But let's imagine what the world would look like if we take that trite statement to an extreme conclusion. What if no two people were alike in any way? What if we shared *absolutely nothing* with anyone else—no physical characteristic, no personality trait, no life experience? Imagine that every single person was a different sex, a different age, a different race, and that no two people had the same educational experiences, the same relationships with parents, the same birth order, or the same socioeconomic status. No two people prayed to the same god, spoke the same language, told time the same way, obeyed the same laws, enjoyed the same music, or found the same food tasty. Life would be utterly chaotic and unmanageable. In this imaginary world, meeting someone for the first time would be like meeting a new life form from another planet. You wouldn't be able to place them into any sort of existing social category. You wouldn't be able to draw on your past experiences with people who possess similar characteristics. You could assume *nothing* about anyone you meet. You could draw on no commonalities.

So, obviously, there are some limits to the applicability of this little cliché. Obviously, there's something more to this society than 300 million completely unique individuals living in the same geographic region of the world. It turns out that we actually have quite a bit in common with other Americans. We're not clones, of course, but we do share membership in particular categories. With some people, we have a gender in common; with others, a sexual orientation, a race, an ethnicity, a religion, or a social class.

Although at times it's to our advantage to recognize and celebrate our individual uniqueness, at other times it's the similarities that provide us with the comfort of knowing that there are "people like us." Perhaps you've attended a festival devoted to the collective expression of pride in your ethnic group. If you're Irish, you're lucky enough to have a whole day devoted to your heritage: St. Patrick's Day. Or maybe you've been in a different city and attended a religious service at your religion's local church, synagogue, or mosque and felt reassured by the fact that these strangers share your spiritual beliefs and know the words to your favorite hymns and prayers. Or maybe you've had the experience of traveling somewhere far away and meeting someone who happens to hail from your hometown. You may not even know this person, but right away you're likely to feel a connection, a bond that's reinforced by talk about neighborhoods, restaurants, and landmarks that only someone from that town could appreciate.

If you think about it, the fact that 300 million of us in this society are able to live together in a reasonably stable way most of the time is possible only because we have many things in common that we can easily count on. You can assume, for instance, that as you pull up to a traffic light, the driver approaching the intersection to your right shares an understanding of what a red light or green light means. In fact, your life depends on it! You can assume that upon initiating a handshake with someone you've just met, this person won't slap or spit on your extended hand but instead will hold it for a second and release it. Indeed, our everyday lives depend on literally thousands of these taken-for-granted bits of information that we assume others understand as we do. These things are so common, so immediately understood, that we don't have to think about them.

We come to appreciate commonalities when we're faced with situations in which we can't assume that "everybody knows that." If you've ever traveled to a foreign country, for instance, you probably felt some disorientation when you first arrived. Some of the confusion could no doubt be attributed to not knowing the language well enough to read street signs or ask people for directions or order from a restaurant menu. But you probably quickly realized that you lacked more than just an understanding of the vocabulary. You lacked knowledge of the common, taken-for-granted assumptions of everyday life. You didn't share the rules, the unspoken code of behavior that people with common cultural understandings live by and don't have to think about. To some degree, we experience these differences when we come into contact with other groups in our own society.

The trick to living in a society where people differ on some social dimensions but share others is finding a way to balance the things that make us dissimilar with the things that make us alike. At what point, for instance, does pride in our heritage or ethnicity become exclusionary and maybe even threatening to those who don't belong? Wearing a large crucifix or displaying a Confederate battle flag on one's car may be expressions of pride that hold people of a particular community together, but they can also evoke extreme emotions in others who don't share those beliefs or sentiments and who may even feel threatened by them.

Deciding when, where, and with whom to highlight certain differences is a constant struggle of social life. Some distinguishing features are, of course, more important than others. We don't attribute importance to differences in eye color or foot size or whether people have earlobes or not. But differences in race, gender, social class, and sexuality carry enormous cultural, historical, and institutional weight in this society.

At times, differences are considered positive. For instance, when it comes to food, music, or art, we tend to enjoy the diverse palette of ethnic influences. Neighborhoods acquire the label "desirable" or even "upscale" if they have an abundance of "ethnic" restaurants from which to choose or some trendy shops offering collections of ethnic-themed goods different from what one finds at a generic shopping mall. These kinds of differences aren't threatening. Instead, they're safe because they give us an opportunity to taste another way of life without actually having to live it.

Other differences don't have the same cachet, however. Distinctive lifestyles associated with a lack of wealth or income, for example, don't have quite the aura of exotic desirability that ethnic differences can sometimes have. Poor or working-class people may wear clothes, eat food, or engage in leisure activities that distinguish them from, say, middle-class people. But these differences are not choices that are an expression of pride; they're ways of life that represent limited or nonexistent opportunities to live differently. Poor people have a different diet than wealthier folks because they can't afford anything else. We don't hear people talk about going for "poor people's food take-out." Indeed, any sort of celebration of poverty "fashion" or "cuisine" would probably strike most people as cruel and insensitive. Moreover, the lifestyles of poor or working-class people are sometimes seen as a direct threat to the interests of wealthier people, as when a trailer park is feared to bring down the "property values" of an adjacent middle-class neighborhood.

"CLASSIFIED" INFORMATION: FORMING IMPRESSIONS

Humans have a profound tendency to define, classify, and categorize. Among the ways they apply this tendency is to sort themselves and their fellow humans into groups. Every human society—from the simplest to

the most complex—has a means by which members differentiate themselves from one another.

People begin defining, differentiating, and ranking things early on.
When children are first learning to talk, they begin to understand that
tangible objects fall into broad distinct categories: Apples and oranges are
"fruits," Chihuahuas and Great Danes are "dogs," Fords and Toyotas are
"cars," and so on. They also learn that these categories can be distinguished from other categories: Fruits are different from vegetables, dogs
are different from cats, and cars are different from trucks. Eventually, they
learn that people can also be categorized and differentiated. As they get
older, children spend a huge chunk of their lives ruthlessly making
"us/them" distinctions and then ranking people in terms of those distinctions. In fact, making such judgments is probably the defining feature
of social life in American elementary, junior high, and high schools. Even
as early as the third grade, children develop sophisticated ways of including some and excluding others that result in a clearly identifiable power
hierarchy among nine-year-olds (Adler & Adler, 1998). Young people typically go beyond the most obvious types of distinctions (gender, race, religion, age, grade level) to more specific lifestyle traits and labels, such as
jocks, burnouts, nerds, skaters, metal-heads, punks, Goths, preps, straight-
edgers, gangstas, and so on.

When obvious distinguishing characteristics aren't available, young
people will invent them. When I was in my early teens growing up in
southern California, two broad groups—surfers (who tended to be Anglos)
and low-riders (who tended to be Latinos)—dominated social life at my
junior high school. The labels originally derived from specific recreational
activities: surfing and driving cars that sat low to the ground. But one
didn't have to surf or have a driver's license to be a member of either
group. The labels were simply shorthand for making broad distinctions that
sometimes—but not always—paralleled ethnic and social class differences.
The two groups rarely interacted and fights were not uncommon. The
creation and maintenance of such boundaries provided the interpersonal
landscape upon which everything else in school seemed to be built: friendship, romance, achievement, popularity, safety, and so on.

Eventually, we come to realize that the categorical cliques that are so
central to our lives during the teen years are based on rather superficial
information—what a person wears, what kind of music a person listens
to, what slang terms the person uses, and so on. But other criteria remain
important throughout our lives. Indeed, we never stop defining group
boundaries in terms of countries, regions, religions, generations, races,

sexes, classes, political groups, families, and so on (Epstein, 1997). We all know the powerful role that these differentiating characteristics play in everyday life.

Indeed, we regularly illustrate the importance of this information every time we meet people and immediately draw inferences about them based on a quick assessment of their membership in particular social groups. We learn—from others, from past experiences, from the media— the cultural significance in this society of being male or female, Asian or African American, upper class or working class, gay or straight. For instance, if all you know about someone you meet for the first time is that she's female, you might initially assume that she's probably more compassionate, more nurturing, and less aggressive than if this person were male. Likewise, if all you knew about a person was that she is in her late 60s, you might conclude that she is close to retirement, enjoys the "oldies" radio station, and goes to bed at a decent hour. Imagine arriving for college the first day and learning that your roommate is of a differ-ent race and comes from a different state or, for that matter, a different country. Think about all the inferences you'd make about this person even before you meet her or him. "She's Asian? I bet she'll be studying all the time." "He's from Texas? Well, I guess that means I'm doomed to a steady dose of Tim McGraw on the CD player." "She's originally from France? She probably smokes cigarettes and will complain about how American fast food is destroying French culture."

Of course, these sorts of conclusions can never (or should never) be final. Forming impressions and expectations of others on such a tiny amount of information will never be completely accurate. Certainly, we don't want to admit that our interchanges with others depend on that per-son's sex or race or whatever. But, whether we like it or not and whether it's fair or not, we always begin social interactions with these kinds of cul-turally defined ideas about how people in certain social groups are likely to act, what their values might be, and what we think their tastes are. These initial assumptions save us the energy of having to start from scratch in forming impressions of every single person we meet.

The importance of this distinguishing information is especially con-spicuous when it is missing. When I was in college, I paid my way by working as an "expediter" in a company that sold airplane and machine parts (nuts, bolts, fittings, O-rings, and so on). An expediter is the person whom customers call when their orders don't arrive on time. Needless to say, no one who called me was ever in a particularly good mood; some were downright furious because the delayed delivery of a part (which, of course, they blamed me for) frequently meant a plane was idle on the ground or important cargo was not being delivered. If we didn't have the part in stock, I would then contact the manufacturer to see why there was a delay and when our customer could expect to receive the parts in question. I quickly discovered that the best way to get positive information that I could then pass on to my irate customer was to joke around and be nice and friendly with the sales rep at the manufacturer. I spent a great deal of time developing these telephone relationships.

After a few weeks, I noticed that the content of my friendship-building conversations depended on whether I was talking to a man or a woman. I saved my arcane sports references and metaphors for male contacts and described my latest culinary creations only to my female contacts. Several months into the job, though, my contact person at one of our major manufacturers left the company to be replaced by someone named "Chris." My first conversation with Chris was stilted and awkward. It wasn't that Chris was unfriendly or incompetent. It was that I didn't know if Chris, a gender-ambiguous name to begin with, was a man with a somewhat high voice or a woman with a somewhat low voice. I became conversationally disoriented because I was too busy listening for gender cues. Part of me was ashamed that I could be so superficial as to be unsettled by not knowing the sex of the person on the other end of a phone line. I was a sociology major in college at the time and was taking a class called "Gender and Society" in which I came to appreciate issues of differential treatment and inequality. I had even begun to announce to my friends that I was a feminist. In another setting, I might have embraced the ambiguity, but I had a job to do here and Chris wasn't helping. So I was also a little miffed. At some level, I expected Chris to provide the requisite gender information that would have made my interactions and my task easier. The fact that the ambiguity created so much difficulty for me attests to the crucial role that such commonplace distinctions play in our everyday interactions with others.

VARIATION BETWEEN GROUPS, VARIATION WITHIN GROUPS

When thinking about the implications of race, class, gender, and sexual diversity for people's everyday experiences, there is a tendency to focus on the differences that exist *between* groups (for instance, between men and women, between working-class people and upper-class people, between heterosexuals and homosexuals, or between African Americans and Whites). This emphasis on between-group differences can obscure both the differences that exist among individuals *within* groups as well as the similarities that exist between individuals who belong to different groups. It may be trendy to talk about men and women as being from different planets, but such a conclusion overshadows the fact that they are much more alike than they are different. Similarly, if you're white, it's tempting to view African Americans, Latino/as, Asians, and Native Americans as homogeneous communities with shared values, interests, and behaviors, even though there is tremendous within-group variation. In Chapter 3, we will examine how this tendency is reflected in our racial language—for instance, using the term "Asian" to lump together a variety of groups with very different languages, cultures, and immigrant experiences.

At the individual level, the tendency to overlook within-group variation can have important consequences. Students of color at predominantly white universities, for example, often report that their white fellow students and even their white professors look to them in class to provide a "minority perspective" on particular issues (Feagin, Vera, & Imani, 2000). Similarly, the thoughts, beliefs, and actions of a lone female executive in a predominantly male company may be taken by her male co-workers as typical of all women (Kanter, 1977). The assumption underlying such experiences is that members of a particular group are alike or at least similar; therefore, one individual can be a spokesperson for an entire race or gender.

Curiously, when we think of our own group—be it based on race, ethnicity, gender, class, or sexual orientation—we're more inclined to highlight or at least pay heed to the diversity of individuals. We're loath to make generalizations about our own group because we know, from first-hand experiences with fellow members, that we don't all believe the same things, act the same way, or speak with a singular voice.

I teach at a private liberal arts university in the Midwest. My students are predominantly white (though this is changing), and many come from wealthy families. As a way of introducing the topic of race in the introductory course I teach, I ask my students to list the features that they think are typical of African American families. When they're finished compiling that list, we do the same for Latino/a families, and then for Asian families. I don't filter or modify their lists. I simply record on the board what they mention. They have little trouble identifying these traits, even though they're often quick to point out that many of the items on the lists are stereotypes that they, themselves, don't believe. Some of the stereotypical characteristics they mention are positive (for instance, Asian families are supportive and tight-knit); others are distinctly negative (for instance, African American families are weak and prone to instability). The lists they amass are usually long.

I then ask them to list the traits that typify white families. Here the discussion usually grinds to a screeching halt. They have tremendous difficulty with this question. I don't come to their rescue. I let them struggle. After a while, some version of the following conversation inevitably ensues:

> *Student:* "What kind of white family are you talking about?"
> *Me:* "What do you mean?"
> *Student:* "Well, there are too many kinds of white families and it'd be impossible to generalize."
> *Me:* "OK, what kinds of white families are there?"
> *Student:* "Some white families are poor and they're different from rich families."
> *Me:* "Uh-huh. Go on."
> *Student:* "Some white families are very religious and others aren't. Also they might be of different nationalities, live in different parts of the country. You know, they're all different. There's no way you can come up with common traits."
> *Me:* "You're absolutely right! [The student usually beams with pride at this point for being a good sociologist.] But why didn't you ask me what kind of African American family or Latino family or Asian family I had in mind when I asked you to characterize them? Surely there are rich Asian and poor Asian families. There must be religious Latino and nonreligious Latino families out there. There are African American families that live in big cities and others that live on farms."

My point in these discussions is not to humiliate my students or put them on the spot. Instead, it is to illustrate how our relative perspectives determine our perceptions of between-group and within-group diversity. These mostly white students were flummoxed by the question because of the obvious diversity they saw in the category "white families." Being a member of a majority racial group conferred on them the privilege of thinking about their "whiteness" in terms of individuality and not in terms of common traits. Yet, when considering other groups, they were more inclined to form broad generalizations, even though there's just as much within-group diversity among African American, Latino/a, and Asian families as there is among white families. They soon realize that it's misleading to try to ignore these within-group differences to talk about all African Americans, all Latino/as, all Asians, or all Whites as if they were homogeneous groups. For that matter, it would be misleading to discuss all heterosexuals, all poor people, or all men as if they all looked alike, acted alike, and believed the same things.

THE POWER OF "NORMALITY": ALL DIFFERENCES ARE NOT CREATED EQUAL

To "vary" is to "deviate" or to "depart" from what is expected. Variations fall outside the typical. When musicians talk about variations on a theme, they imply that there is a main, core composition from which other works diverge. The same goes for human difference. Terms like "diversity" and "variation" imply that there is a standard way of being from which others deviate. When most of us think of diversity, it's easier to think of examples of the "variations" than of the things they vary from.

If you were to thumb through some of the most popular sociology textbooks on American families that are on the market today, you'd notice that most of them contain a chapter called something like "Family Diversity" or "Family Variations." Typically, these chapters will have a section devoted to "African American families," "Latino families," "Asian families," "same-sex families," and "poor families." Occasionally, there is a small discussion of white "ethnic" families (for instance, Italian, Irish, Jewish, or White Anglo-Saxon Protestant families). But rarely is there a chapter or section in such books devoted simply to "white families." Why not? The answer, of course, lies in what is and what isn't considered normal in a society. White families are simply "families." In the absence of a modifying racial or ethnic adjective, they're the default option. White families are assumed to be ordinary and regular. Consequently, they need no explaining, no special chapter devoted to their striking differences. Whether or not their actual characteristics match the idealized images people have of them, they are the benchmark against which all other family forms are described and judged (Smith, 1993).

In a racially imbalanced society like ours, whiteness, in general, is the yardstick against which "non-white" racial groups are evaluated. Likewise, "middle-class," "heterosexual," and "male" are also the taken-for-granted standards of class, sexuality, and gender. Each year, the U.S. Bureau of the

Census publishes its *Statistical Abstract*—a compendium of population statistics covering all aspects of social life. The index of this massive document contains entries for "Women," "Poverty," "Black population," "American Indians," "Asian and Pacific Islander population," and "Hispanic origin population," but none for "Men," "Middle class," or "White population."

Listen to how one social psychologist describes the universal male standard of normality:

> Men and women are not simply considered different from one another, as we speak of people differing in eye color, movie tastes, or preferences for ice cream. In almost every domain of life, men are considered the normal human being, and women are "abnormal," deficient because they are different from men. Therefore, women constantly worry about measuring up, doing the right thing, being the right way. It is normal for women to worry about being abnormal, because male behavior, male heroes, male psychology, and even male physiology continue to be the standard for normalcy against which women are measured and found wanting. (Tavris, 1992, pp. 16–17)

Consider also the current debate over legalizing same-sex marriage (see Chapter 7 for a lengthier discussion of this issue). When the state of Massachusetts began issuing marriage licenses to same-sex couples in 2004, it marked the first time in our history that a state granted gay and lesbian couples full legal recognition of their relationships. More than just a symbolic gesture, such recognition comes with many rights and privileges typically accorded heterosexual married couples, such as coverage on spousal insurance policies and inheritance rights. While many people viewed this action as a positive step forward in the movement for civil rights, notice how it reinforces the idea that the standard of intimacy toward which people are presumed to want to aspire is a distinctly heterosexual model: monogamous marriage. In fact, a small but vocal contingent of homosexuals has been critical of the amount of attention that has been devoted to the movement to legalize same-sex marriage, fearing that such action would subordinate the uniqueness of gay or lesbian culture to the mainstream heterosexual ideal of intimacy.

Indeed, the cultural and media representation of every aspect of romance invariably presumes a world in which men are sexually attracted to women and vice versa. Think of the flurry of magazine and TV advertisements we're subjected to in the weeks prior to Valentine's Day. Outside of gay and lesbian publications or neighborhoods, you'd be hard pressed to find ads that don't depict men and women embracing, gazing longingly into each other's eyes, buying each other expensive jewelry, or enjoying the Sunday paper together in bed in their pajamas. Furthermore, the heterosexual standard is even apparent in academic scholarship. A mountain of space is devoted to articles on why people become homosexual, but few researchers bother to ask the question: Why or how do people become heterosexual?

The fact that we make assumptions about what's normal may seem insignificant, but it is at the root of much social conflict. If different categories of people were arranged horizontally—that is, with all groups considered normal and all aligned on the same level—there'd be no problem. We'd all simply be part of a "vast cultural smorgasbord" (Anderson, 2001). However, in all societies, such distinctions tend to be arranged vertically, resulting in a ranking of groups. In every society, some people make the rules and others must live by those rules; some are granted the right to make important decisions and others must endure the consequences of those decisions; some enjoy everyday privileges that provide comfort and stability and others lack such privileges and experience constant struggles in their lives as a result. It's no surprise then, given the historical arrangement of power relations in this society, that the standard of social comparison continues to be white, heterosexual, middle-class, and male. These differences determine access to resources, future goals and aspirations, and overall life chances. Systems of difference are always associated with systems of power and privilege (O'Brien, 1999).

Indeed, groups with significant social power typically have the luxury of remaining unexamined. For people who identify themselves as African American, Latino/a, Asian, and Native American in this society, race may be the pivot around which the rest of their lives circles. For Whites, race is something they rarely have to think about. It's a characteristic that other groups have. In Chapter 5, we'll see how such racial "invisibility" creates and reinforces positions of authority and dominance. Similarly, men in this society have the luxury of living in a society where gender inequality is typically seen as a "women's issue." Like most people in dominant positions, men are largely unaware of the small and large advantages the social structure provides them. The same is true for middle- and upper-class individuals and for heterosexuals. In examining the roles that race, class, gender, and sexuality play in determining an individual's position of privilege or disadvantage in society, it's important to note that these factors can often conflict, even within the same person.

The complex intersections of privilege are apparent in this sociologist's memoir:

> As the first and, for a while, only child of upper-middle-class, Orthodox Jewish parents growing up in New York City, race and class privilege came easily to me, but it was gender that has always been problematic. I understood in some vague way that it would have been preferable had I been born a boy. . . . At another time and in another place, perhaps, my parents would have found the birth of a *girl* child so burdensome that they would have simply abandoned me or sold me into marriage as an infant. . . . But I was fortunate; I was born into a family that did not have to choose which of its children to feed and clothe, or which would receive medical treatment and which would die from neglect. In this respect, a potential fate for others of my gender was mitigated by my class. (Rothenberg, 2000, pp. 9–10)

Similarly, a white lesbian enjoys social advantages because of her race but disadvantages because of her gender and sexuality. Black lesbians face disadvantage on three levels. As one author puts it, "Heterosexual privilege is usually the only privilege that black women have. None of us have racial or sexual privilege, almost none of us have class privilege, maintaining 'straightness' is our last resort" (quoted in Collins, 1990, pp. 195–196).

STRATIFICATION, POWER, AND PRIVILEGE

It doesn't take being on the wrong end of "normal" to know that people categorize others in comparison to themselves, make judgments about those others, and then act toward them on the basis of those judgments. From there, it's just a short step to understanding that inequality is woven into the fabric of all societies through a structured system of **stratification,** the ranking of entire groups of people that perpetuates unequal rewards and life chances. Just as geologists talk about strata of rock that are layered one on top of another, the "social strata" of people are arranged from low to high.

Stratification systems can be based on a variety of different dimensions and statuses. Sometimes groups of people are ranked on the basis of what sociologists call ascribed statuses. An **ascribed status** is a social identity or position that we obtain at birth or develop into involuntarily as we get older. Race, sex, ethnicity, religion, and family status (that is, the identity as someone's child or grandchild) are all usually considered ascribed statuses. As we age, we enter an ascribed identity called "teenager," followed by "middle-aged person," and ultimately "old-timer." We can try to hide our "membership" in these positions (by wearing a toupee or buying a more youthful wardrobe), and sometimes people go to great lengths to change their ascribed status (as when individuals have sex-reassignment surgeries), but for the most part, ascribed statuses aren't positions we choose to occupy. An **achieved status,** in contrast, is a social position or identity we take on voluntarily or earn through our own efforts or accomplishments, like being a student or a spouse or a sociologist.

Of course, the distinction between an ascribed and an achieved status is not always obvious. Some people become college students not because of their own efforts but because of their parents' influence. In theory, you can choose to identify with any religion you want, but chances are that the religion with which you identify is the one your parents belong to. But some people decide to change their religious membership later in life. More importantly, sex, race, ethnicity, and age may be ascribed statuses, but they have a direct effect on our access to desirable or affluent achieved identities.

All societies past and present use ascribed and achieved statuses to create some form of stratification, although they may vary in the degree of inequality between strata. Most Western societies today rely on social class and socioeconomic status as the primary criteria by which individuals and groups are stratified. **Socioeconomic status** refers to the prestige, honor, respect, and power associated with different social class positions in society (Weber, 1970). Socioeconomic status is obviously influenced by wealth and income, but it can also be derived from achieved characteristics, such as educational attainment and occupational prestige, and from ascribed characteristics, such as race, ethnicity, gender, and family pedigree. For instance, high school teachers have much higher occupational prestige than carpenters, plumbers, or mechanics (Davis & Smith, 1986), even though teachers usually earn substantially less. Organized criminals may be multi-millionaires and live in large estates, but they lack prestige and honor—and therefore socioeconomic status—in mainstream society.

THEORIES OF INEQUALITY

For well over a century, sociologists have been trying to figure out why societies are unequal and stratified. Let's take a brief look at the two main groups of theories regarding stratification: structural-functionalism and

conflict theories. These groups of theories differ dramatically in their conclusions about the role of stratification in human societies.

Structural-Functionalism According to **structural-functionalism,**
society is a complex system composed of various parts, much like a living organism. Just as the heart, lungs, and liver work together to keep an
animal alive, so, too, do all the elements of a society's structure work
together to keep society alive. From this perspective, if an aspect of social
life does not contribute to social order and ultimately to society's survival—that is, if it is dysfunctional—it will eventually disappear. Things
that persist, even if they seem to be harmful, unfair, or disruptive, must
persist because they contribute somehow to the continued existence of
society (Newman, 2004).

So how can society benefit in the long run from inequality? Societies
are made up of a variety of different roles that people must fill in order
for society to function. In complex, modern societies, these roles are allo-
cated through a strictly defined division of labor. If the tasks associated
with all social positions in a society were equally pleasant, were equally
important, and required the same talents, who got into which position
would make no difference. But structural-functionalists argue that it does
make a difference. Some occupations, such as teaching and medicine, are
more important to a society than others and require greater talent and
training. Society's dilemma is to make sure that the most talented people
perform the most important tasks. One way to ensure this distribution of
tasks is to assign higher rewards—better pay, greater prestige, more social
privileges—to some positions in society so that they will be attractive to
the people with the necessary talents and abilities. Those who rise to the
top are seen as the most worthy and deserving, because they're the ones
who can do the most good for society (Davis & Moore, 1945).

The functional importance of a position is not enough to warrant a
high place in the stratification system, however. If a position is easily
filled—even if it is vital for society's survival—it need not be heavily
rewarded (Davis & Moore, 1945). For instance, there is perhaps no more
important occupation in a society than trash collection. Imagine what our
society would be like without people who remove our trash. Not only
would our streets be clogged with litter, but disease would be rampant and
our collective health and longevity would suffer in the long run. But
garbage collection is neither prestigious nor considered worthy of high
salary. Why not? According to the structural-functionalist perspective, it
is because we have no shortage of people with the skills needed to collect

garbage. And it doesn't take much training to learn how to dump people's trash. Physicians also serve the collective health needs of a society. But because of the intricate skills and extensive training needed to be a doctor, society must offer rewards high enough to ensure that qualified people will want to become one.

According to structural-functionalism, then, inequality is inevitable and necessary. Societies have to assign different levels of importance to different positions. They can't all be equal. And we all benefit in the long run when our most qualified members fill our most important positions. So it's appropriate that certain "important" people earn a lot and accumulate a lot. If we take the functionalist argument to its logical conclusion, then there should be a direct correlation between the average salaries of a given occupation and its importance in society.

But a quick look at the salary structure in our society reveals obvious instances of highly rewarded positions that are not as functionally important as positions that receive smaller rewards. Our best-known actors, filmmakers, comedians, rock stars, and professional athletes are among the highest-paid people in U.S. society, earning millions of dollars each year to entertain us. You might say that boxers, singers, movie stars, and baseball players serve important social functions by providing the rest of us with a recreational release from the demands of ordinary life. However, society probably can do without another CD, adventure movie, or pay-per-view prizefight more easily than it can do without competent physicians, scientists, computer programmers, teachers, or even trash collectors.

Furthermore, what this perspective overlooks is the fact that stratification can be unjust and divisive, a source of social disorder (Tumin, 1953). The argument that only a limited number of talented people are around to occupy important social positions is probably overstated. Many people have the talent to become doctors. What they lack is access to training. And why are some people—women and racial and ethnic minorities—paid less for or excluded entirely from certain jobs (see Chapter 8)? Finally, when functionalists claim that inequality and stratification serve the needs of society, we must ask, Whose needs? A system of slavery obviously meets the needs of one group at the expense of another, but that doesn't make it tolerable.

In a class-stratified society, those individuals who receive the greatest rewards have the resources to make sure they continue receiving such rewards. Over time, the competition for the most desirable positions will become less open and less competitive—less a function of achievement than ascription. In such circumstances, the offspring of "talented"—that is, high-status—parents will always have an advantage over equally talented people who had the bad sense to be born into less successful families.

Conflict Theories Structural-functionalism has been criticized for accepting existing social arrangements without examining how they might exploit or otherwise disadvantage certain groups or individuals within the society. The **conflict perspective** addresses this deficiency by viewing the structure of society as a source of inequality, which always benefits some groups at the expense of other groups. Social inequality is neither a necessity nor a source of social order. Instead, it is a reflection of the unequal distribution of power in society and is a primary source of conflict, coercion, and unhappiness.

According to perhaps the most famous conflict theorists, Karl Marx and Friedrich Engels (1848/1982), stratification ultimately rests on the unequal distribution of resources—some people have them, others don't. Important resources include money, land, information, education, health care, safety, and adequate housing. The "haves" in such an arrangement can control the lives of the "have nots" because they control these resources and are ultimately the ones who set the rules. According to this perspective, a system of stratification allows members of the dominant group to exploit those in subordinate positions as consumers, renters, employees, and so on, thereby reinforcing their own superiority over others. Hence, stratification virtually guarantees that some groups or classes of people (those who have less) will always be competing with other groups or classes (those who have more). The fundamental proposition of this perspective is that stratification systems will always serve the interests of those at the top and not the survival needs of the entire society.

Marx's original theory was, in essence, a wholesale critique of capitalism. **Capitalists**—those who own the means of producing the goods and services society needs, and to whom others must sell their labor in order to survive—have considerable influence over what will be produced, how much will be produced, who will get it, how much money people will be paid to produce it, and so forth. Such power allows them to control **workers**—who neither own the means of production nor have the ability to purchase the labor of others. Hence, capitalists control other people's livelihoods, the communities in which people live, and the economic decisions that affect the entire society. Marx and Engels supplemented this two-tiered conception of class by adding a third tier, the petite bourgeoisie, which is a transitional class of people who own the means of production but don't purchase the labor power of others. This class consists of self-employed skilled laborers and businesspeople who are economically self-sufficient but don't have a staff of subordinate workers.

Rich and politically powerful individuals—who not coincidentally tend to come from advantaged gender and ethnoracial groups—frequently work together to create or maintain privilege, often at the expense of the middle and lower classes (Phillips, 2002). What the conflict perspective gives us that the structural-functionalist perspective doesn't is an acknowledgment of the interconnected roles that economic and political institutions play in creating and maintaining a stratified society (Newman, 2004). In such a structure, the rich inevitably tend to get richer, to use their wealth to create more wealth for themselves, and to act in ways that will protect their interests and positions in society.

You'd expect constant attempts by those at the bottom to transcend their lowly status and seek control over limited resources. But such revolutions rarely occur in human societies. Why not? Marx and Engels argued that those in power have access to the means necessary to create and promote a reality that justifies their exploitative actions. Their version of reality is so influential that even those who are disadvantaged by it come to accept it. They called this phenomenon **false consciousness.** False consciousness is crucial because it is the primary means by which the powerful classes in society prevent protest and revolution. As long as large numbers of poor people continue to believe that wealth and success are solely the products of individual hard work and effort rather than of structured inequalities in society—that is, believe what in the United States has been called the American Dream—resentment and animosity toward the rich will be minimized and people will perceive the inequalities as fair and deserved (Robinson & Bell, 1978).

Marx's theory was based on 19th-century economic systems. In his time, the heyday of industrial development, ownership of property and control of labor in a capitalist system were synonymous. Most jobs were either on farms or in factories. It made sense to lump into one class all those who didn't own productive resources and who depended on wages from others to survive, and into another class all those who owned property and paid wages. However, the nature of capitalism has changed a lot since then. Today a person with a novel idea for a product or service, a computer, and a telephone can go into business and make a lot of money. Corporations have become much larger and more bureaucratic, with a long, multilevel chain of command. Ownership of large companies lies in the hands of stockholders (foreign as well as domestic), who often have distant connections or even no connections at all to the everyday workings of the business. Thus, ownership and management are separated. The powerful people who run large businesses and control workers on a day-to-day basis are frequently not the same people who own the businesses.

With these changes in mind, some sociologists have revised Marx's original argument. For instance, sociologist Erik Olin Wright and his colleagues (Wright, 1976; Wright, Costello, Hachen, & Sprague, 1982; Wright & Perrone, 1977) have developed a model that incorporates both the ownership of means of production and the exercise of authority over others. The capitalist and petite bourgeoisie classes in this scheme are identical to Marx and Engels's. What is different is that the classes of people who do not own society's productive resources (Marx and Engels's worker class) are divided into two classes: managers and workers.

Wright's approach emphasizes that class conflict is more than just a clash between rich people and poor people. Societies have, in fact, multiple lines of conflict—economic, political, administrative, and social. Some positions, or what Wright calls "contradictory class locations," fall between two major classes. Individuals in these positions have trouble identifying with one side or the other. Managers and supervisors, for instance, can ally with workers because both are subordinates of capitalist owners. Yet because managers and supervisors can exercise authority over some people, they also share the interests and concerns of owners. During labor disputes in professional sports, for example, coaches often struggle with the dilemma of whether they represent the interests of the owners or the players (Newman, 2004).

Other sociologists have criticized Marx's exclusive reliance on economic factors to explain inequality. The early 20th-century sociologist Max Weber (1970) identified two other sources of inequality—prestige and power—in addition to the control of property, wealth, and income. **Prestige** is the amount of honor and respect people receive from others. Class position certainly influences prestige, but so can family background, physical appearance, intelligence, and so on. **Power** is the ability to influence others and to pursue and achieve one's own goals. Wealth, prestige, and power usually coincide, but not always. Sometimes groups with little if any wealth have managed to have their voices heard and have exerted a powerful influence on more advantaged groups. In 2004, for example, cooks, housekeepers, and bellboys went on strike at four San Francisco hotels. Two days later, workers were locked out of 10 other hotels. The strike eventually spread to nearby Monterey. The actions of these low-wage laborers discouraged visitors from coming to the Bay Area and had an enormous effect on the local economy.

Recently, the conflict approach to social inequality has expanded even further by incorporating race, ethnicity, and gender. For instance, workers of color may share a class location with Whites, but as you'll see in Chapter 8, the lower wages that working-class ethnoracial minorities earn as well as their concentration in particular low-paying occupations double their vulnerability to exploitation (Feagin & Feagin, 2004). Furthermore, as long as workers see their primary adversaries as other workers who are competing with them for scarce jobs (such as immigrants or members of other ethnoracial minorities), their anger will be directed toward one another and not "upward" against those in positions of power. Indeed, research has shown that downward mobility (Silberstein & Seeman, 1959) and the rapid influx of new ethnic groups into a community (Bergesen & Herman, 1998) are associated with higher levels of ethnic hostility, conflict, and backlash violence. One might conclude that it is in capitalists' best interest to foster ethnoracial divisions among the working class, thereby preventing them from unifying and taking advantage of their numbers to seek a more equitable division of resources.

Another variety of the conflict perspective that has become particularly popular among sociologists in the last several decades is the **feminist perspective.** Feminist sociologists focus on gender, more so than class or socioeconomic status, as the most important source of conflict and inequality in social life. They argue that in nearly every contemporary society, important social institutions—education, economy, politics, religion, family—are controlled and dominated by men. Men use a variety of methods—including violence, exploitation, and other forms of discrimination—to reinforce their dominance. Consequently, women have less power, influence, and opportunity than men do. In families, for instance, women have traditionally been encouraged to perform unpaid household labor and child care duties whereas men have been free to devote their energy and attention to earning money and power in the economic marketplace. Women's lower wages when they do work outside the home are often justified by the assumption that their paid labor is secondary to that of their husbands. But as women in many societies seek equality in education, politics, career, marriage, and other areas of social life, their activities inevitably affect the broader structure of society.

Early forms of feminist thinking were often criticized for ignoring race and class and trivializing the experiences of poor women and women of color. So more recent feminists (sometimes called "gender rebellion feminists" [Lorber, 1998]) focus on the complex connections between inequalities based on sex and gender and inequalities based on race, ethnicity, social class, and sexuality. By looking at the intersections among these varieties of difference, we can see what all disadvantaged segments of society have in common and how they're unique (Collins, 2004).

CULTURAL CAPITAL

Racial, gender, class, and sexual differences and similarities are an enormously powerful predictor of life chances and access to important social resources. Sociologists use the term **cultural capital** to refer to the status characteristics that can determine a person's social opportunities. For instance, many top universities reserve a certain number of positions for "legacies," applicants whose parents are alumni of that institution. Family name, in this case, can serve as a form of cultural capital. In a society that values physical appearance, beauty is also cultural capital that can be exchanged for economic advantage. Research indicates that "attractive" people are assumed to possess other positive qualities, such as a pleasing personality, high intelligence, and success in interpersonal relationships (cited in Ruane & Cerullo, 1997). Likewise, membership in advantaged gender, ethnoracial, and sexuality-based groups can serve as cultural capital as well, as illustrated by the historical preference for white, male, heterosexual employees over women, people of color, and homosexual or transgendered individuals.

The more privileged one's status, the larger one's endowment of cultural capital. In Chapters 5 through 8, I will examine the biological, political, educational, and economic imbalances that result from the cultural capital that people amass by virtue of their membership in certain groups.

CONCLUSION

This brief introductory chapter hints at several key themes that will percolate through the remainder of this book. In what ways are we different from one another? How are we the same? Is similarity or difference more important in our everyday lives? Are all differences inevitably associated with inequality? How is inequality constructed and reinforced in our everyday lives? How is it embedded in our language, our culture, and our social institutions? In addressing these general questions, I will pay particular attention to the key social characteristics that we use to differentiate ourselves from others: race (and ethnicity), gender (and sex), sexuality, and social class. No characteristics are as influential as these in determining our identities, our life chances, and the shape of our social institutions.

In any book that focuses on identities and inequalities, the use of particular terminology to refer to dimensions of social identity carries significant cultural and political weight. People often choose words carefully when referring to themselves. However, there is no consensus about the acceptability or unacceptability of particular terms. And the term of choice in one decade may fall out of favor in the next. Thus, my choice of words in this book inevitably runs the risk of offending some readers sometimes. But in the interests of consistency, I will use the terms *sex* and *gender* when referring to girls/boys, women/men, and femininity/masculinity. I will use the terms *race*, *ethnicity*, and *ethnoracial* when examining the lives of people who identify themselves as Asian American, Native American, Latino/a, African American, and White. When I talk about *minority groups*, I will be referring not to statistical minorities but to groups that have historically been disadvantaged in this society because of their race or ethnicity. And I will use the terms *sexuality* or *sexual orientation* when discussing people's erotic identities (homosexual, heterosexual, bisexual, and so on).

In addition, I will make the argument that race, class, gender, and sexuality are not biological givens but are, to a large degree, social constructions. Hence, when I refer to members of particular groups (for example, "heterosexuals," "lesbians," "Whites," "Asian Americans," and so on), I am talking about those people who identify themselves as members of these groups. The first step in exploring the intersections of race, class, gender, and sexuality is respecting the way that individuals define themselves.

[**INVESTIGATING IDENTITIES AND INEQUALITIES**
Identity inheritance: Climbing up (or down) your family tree]

The concept of cultural capital is important because it shows that social advantage and disadvantage do not emerge from differences in material wealth alone. Indeed, cultural capital consists of all the social assets that lead to differences in material wealth. Any characteristic, possession, or identifier that can be exchanged for economic gain can be considered a form of cultural capital. Often, people are unaware that they even have these "non-economic" forms of capital. Take, for instance, a person's family heritage. Wealthy parents often endow their children with reputations, connections, and knowledge that will aid them as they grow up. Sometimes simply inheriting a family name is enough to provide economic, educational, and political advantages. Poor parents are less able to pass on such cultural capital to their children and instead are likely to leave their children a legacy of disadvantage that they must fight to overcome.

To understand how cultural capital is handed down from generation to generation, construct your own family tree. Go as far back into the past as you can. You may need to ask your parents, grandparents, and other older relatives about long-deceased ancestors. Face-to-face interviews are better, but you may have to conduct your interviews over the phone or via e-mail. If family artifacts are available (for example, old letters, diaries, photographs, home movies/videos, heirlooms, and so on), use them for insight into the identities and lives of your ancestors.

You may focus on one side of your family or both sides. If there have been remarriages in your family, try to obtain information on the various familial branches.

For each person in the tree, identify the primary occupation and the highest level of education she or he achieved. Look for patterns in family members' experiences that are linked to race, ethnicity, culture, gender, social class, and religion. It would be helpful to determine how your family first came to the United States. If some of your ancestors lived their whole lives in another country, you can examine how their experiences and achievements differed from those of your ancestors who immigrated to the United States or those who lived here their entire lives.

Can you detect a pattern of upward or downward mobility in your family? Have relatives from previous generations attended college? Did any attend the college you presently attend? Has some career legacy been handed down from generation to generation? For instance, has a family business, dwelling, or tract of property stayed in the family across generations? How do the occupational and educational paths of men and women differ in your family?

Now examine how your family history has influenced your own life. What sorts of ideals, values, beliefs, and traditions do you think you've "inherited" from members in previous generations? How do your own career aspirations compare to those of your ancestors? If you have or expect to have children, what are your career and educational aspirations for them?

After a thorough examination of your family experience, ask yourself this question: Does your family tree support the contention that cultural capital is "hereditary"?

CHAPTER 2

Manufacturing Difference
The Social Construction of Race, Class, Gender, and Sexuality

Donald McCloskey received a Ph.D. in Economics from Harvard in 1970. He's been a professor of economics at several prestigious universities, including the University of Rotterdam, the University of Chicago, and the University of Iowa. In his career, McCloskey has written numerous influential books and articles; he is an internationally renowned economic historian. Married, with two children, his life appeared to be the great American success story. What his friends and colleagues didn't know, though, was that from age 11, Donald had been a part-time cross-dresser, outfitting himself in women's clothing a couple of times each week. Other than that, he said, "I was normal, just a guy" (McCloskey, 1999, p. xiii).

In 1994, at the age of 52 and after 30 years of marriage, Donald came to the conclusion that wearing women's clothing wasn't enough. He wanted to *be* a woman. So over the span of the next three years, he underwent hormone replacement treatments, electrolysis to remove facial hair, facial plastic surgery, and ultimately genital surgery to transform his male body into a female one. Today, Donald McCloskey is Deirdre McCloskey, a Distinguished Professor of Economics at the University of Illinois–Chicago.

Deirdre's story is important not because it's rare or bizarre but because of what it says about how we all view, define, and take for granted the nature of sex and gender. Even though she knew she could never be like other women, her female identity was endorsed as others began to take her sexual appearance for granted:

> After [three years], I found to my delight that I had crossed. Look by look, smile by smile, I was accepted. That doesn't make me a 100 percent, essential woman—I'll never have XX chromosomes, never have had the life of a girl and woman up to age fifty-two. But the world does not demand 100 percents and essences, thank God. . . . Gender is not in every way "natural." "Feminine" gestures, for example, are not God's own creation. . . . The social construction of gender is, after all, something a gender crosser comes to know with unusual vividness. She does it for a living. (pp. xiv–xv)

Gregory Williams is also a successful academic. He has earned five degrees (including a law degree) and holds three honorary degrees. He is currently the president of City College of New York. Like Deirdre McCloskey, Gregory also crossed a boundary—but not voluntarily.

He was born in Virginia in the late 1940s, a time when racial segregation was a reality in the United States. He spent his days in Whites-only schools, movie theaters, and swimming pools. Then, when he was 10 years old, his parents divorced. His father was awarded custody and decided to move back to his hometown of Muncie, Indiana. On the way there, Mr. Williams gave Gregory and his other son, Mike, some startling news: Once they reached Indiana, they could no longer be white. He explained to his bewildered sons that their paternal grandmother was black and that this fact made them black too. "Life is going to be different from now on," he told them. "In Virginia you were white boys. In Indiana you're going to be colored boys. I want you to remember that you're the same today that you were yesterday. But people in Indiana will treat you differently" (Williams, 1995, p. 33).

Gregory initially refused to believe his father's news, but his perceptions quickly began to shift:

> [F]or the first time, I had to admit Dad didn't exactly look white. His deeply tanned skin puzzled me as I sat there trying to classify [him]. Goose bumps covered my arms as I realized that whatever he was, I was. I took a deep breath. I couldn't make any mistakes. I looked closer. His heavy lips and dark brown eyes didn't make him colored, I concluded. His black, wavy hair was different from Negroes' hair, but it was different from most white folks' hair, too. He was darker than most Whites, but Mom said he was Italian. . . . [But when] I glanced across the aisle to where he sat . . . I saw my father as I never had seen him before. . . . Before my eyes he was transformed from a swarthy Italian to his true self—a high-yellow mulatto. My father was a Negro! We were colored! After ten years in Virginia on the white side of the color line, I knew what that meant. (Williams, 1995, pp. 33–34)

From that moment on, Gregory's life was a difficult struggle to learn to be black. He was rejected by black and white children alike. Members of his own extended family—aunts, uncles, and cousins—resented him because he looked white. And each day brought a new predicament about his "proper place." As he got older, dating became especially difficult. Because he was considered black, he wasn't supposed to date white girls. But because he *appeared* white, the community couldn't tolerate seeing him with black girls. Despite all the obstacles, however, Gregory went on to a successful career as a lawyer and a professor and came to accept and embrace his multiracial identity. In the process of his "crossing," he learned the importance of racial constructions in everyday life.

Both Deirdre's and Gregory's stories feature transformations and triumphs. Both of them have climbed to the tops of their professions despite enormous obstacles that few of us will ever have to face. But what makes their stories interesting and important is what they tell us about what are widely believed to be the most fundamental, biological, and permanent elements of personhood: sex and race. Deirdre made a conscious decision to alter her physical body so that it would align with an inner sense of femaleness that she had harbored for decades. Gregory's transformation was different. His body didn't change at all, but the way others perceived, defined, and treated him did. And that was enough to make him question and ultimately change a racial identity he had taken for granted for as long as he could remember. Their stories challenge some of our deepest assumptions about self, identity, and the way the social world is ordered.

In this chapter, I will examine the key sources of our personal identities—not only race, ethnicity, and gender, but also social class and sexuality. Which, if any, of these identifiers exist as objective entities in nature? Which are human creations that emerge within particular cultural and historical contexts? Do the boundaries that separate different sexes, classes, races, or sexualities ever change? And how do our identities reflect the intersections of race, ethnicity, class, gender, and sexuality?

PERSPECTIVES ON IDENTITY

Identities are the definitional categories we use to specify, both to ourselves and to others, who we are. They are social locations that determine our position in the world relative to other people. At times, we purposely call attention to them, through how we dress, walk, and use language, whom we choose to associate with, perhaps even where we live. At other times, though, people ascribe identities to us, whether we want them to or not. If you're openly gay, for example, others may react to your sexuality as the primary definition of who you are regardless of your wishes, thereby rendering other components of your identity—such as gender, race, and class—insignificant.

We all possess multiple identities, be they based on race, ethnicity, religion, gender, class, sexuality, occupation, education, family, or some other aspect of our background. At any given moment, certain identities might overshadow the others. For instance, if you suddenly find yourself in a crowd of people of a different race than yours, that feature of your identity will no doubt become quite salient to you. When circumstances change, though, a different characteristic is likely to emerge as the most noticeable feature of your identity.

Few of us spend much time thinking about how we acquire our identities. It's simply who we are. But people like Deirdre McCloskey and Gregory Williams force us to question things that usually remain unquestioned. What makes a person male or female? Is it their genitals? Deirdre's story raises the possibility that maybe our sex is ultimately a matter of self-perception and self-definition. For most of her adult life, her body was genetically, anatomically, and physiologically male. But in her mind, she was a woman. So she had her body changed—first hormonally and then surgically. She couldn't change her chromosomes, though, so could she ever really be female? She may now look female and be visually classified by others as female, but can she be a complete woman without having experienced childhood, adolescence, puberty, and early adulthood as a female?

Likewise, what determines if you're black or brown or white? Is skin color all there is to it? Recently a colleague of mine was shopping in a department store and noticed a display of 3-foot-tall singing Santa Claus dolls lined up in a row. They were all identical except for one, whose face was black. But because none of that Santa's other facial features were different, this doll looked not like a black St. Nicholas but like a white person whose face had been painted black. So is it the size and shape of one's eyes, nose, lips that determine racial identity? Hair texture? How about speech patterns or mannerisms? Does race reside permanently in our genes, or is it something so tenuous that it can be changed simply because others begin to label and treat us differently? If Gregory had moved back to Virginia while he was still young, would he have changed back into a "white" person?

Let's not stop there. What makes a person heterosexual or bisexual or homosexual? Is erotic activity with someone of the same sex, the opposite sex, or both sufficient to determine sexual identity? Does such contact have to lead to an orgasm? Can a person be homosexual or heterosexual without ever engaging in sexual activity with another person? Can sexual orientation change, like Gregory's race, when a person's social situation changes, or is there something more permanent to it? Suppose Donald McCloskey was involved romantically with a man both before and after his transformation into Deirdre. You might characterize them as homosexuals before, but would they still be afterward? Or would they now be a heterosexual couple, with the same rights, privileges, and cultural recognition that other heterosexual couples enjoy?

Finally, how do you know if you're "upper class," "middle class," or "working class"? Is the size of your paycheck or checking account all that matters? What about your occupation? Your educational attainment? Maybe your class identity is based on less measurable things like taste, refinement, sophistication, or family pedigree. Is class standing linked to other identifiers like race or ethnicity? Is it easier or more difficult for members of certain ethnoracial groups to claim membership in the upper class? Are we quicker to assume other ethnoracial groups are of the lower classes?

All these questions are hard to ask and even harder to answer. How you answer them depends in part on the basic perspective that influences your view of individual differences. It's common to see individuals as having a fundamental essence that may, at times, be disguised, hidden, or misinterpreted but never actually changed. But if you look hard enough, you will see instances in which the social environment has indeed changed an individual's true identity.

ESSENTIALISM

To most people, the boundaries that divide people into different sex, race, class, and sexual orientation groups are obvious and reflect who people truly are. A person *is* a female, *is* an Asian American, *is* a heterosexual, *is* middle class. This way of thinking, known as **essentialism,** focuses on what are believed to be universal, inherent, and unambiguous "essences" that distinguish one group from another. It doesn't matter what people call these categories or how they react to them; these categories have a concrete truth that exists independently of people's judgments or definitions. From an essentialist perspective, people's definitions and labels can change, but an individual's essence always exists.

Like most kids, when I was little I thought that dolphins were fish. I don't know much about the history of biology, but I'd venture to guess that for centuries, other people must have thought the same thing. Dolphins look like fish, move like fish, and smell like fish. Eventually, some smart aquatic zoologist discovered their "true" essence: Dolphins weren't fish at all; they were mammals. Soon this conclusion became part of the taken-for-granted truth of science. It wasn't that dolphins underwent some overnight anatomical alteration that abruptly changed them from fish to mammals. Instead, we humans had mistakenly labeled them in the first place. The "mammalness" of dolphins had always resided and will always reside in their nature, whether people call them fish or birds or cucumbers.

Is essentialism similarly at work when it comes to the ways that humans are classified? Consider sexual orientation. An essentialist view of sexual orientation might argue that people are homosexuals or heterosexuals, just as people have a certain blood type or a certain height. But what would an essentialist say about the heterosexual who "becomes" homosexual later in life? To the essentialist, this person has always been in actual fact homosexual. She or he may have lived the life of a heterosexual, but one is either inherently heterosexual or inherently homosexual, and the act of coming out as a homosexual can negate an entire life of heterosexual activity up to that point (Fausto-Sterling, 2000).

Believing in the essential reality of these categories has important implications. When race, class, gender, and sexuality are seen as innate, individual characteristics rather than locations in larger systems of inequality, group differences in behaviors or traits tend to be explained by group members' essential natures (Hollander & Howard, 2000). Once these differences are assumed to be inherent and natural, they can be used to justify unequal treatment and maybe even subordination of one group by another. For instance, men and women are clearly biologically different in some ways. But if you believe that those innate differences determine other differences (for instance, that men are more aggressive and less nurturing than women simply because they're men), then it becomes justifiable to encourage or even require them to occupy the social positions for which they are "naturally" best suited (such as management and decision-making positions) and exclude them from domestic work and child care, activities for which they are "ill-suited" by nature.

CONSTRUCTIONISM

An alternative to essentialism is **constructionism** (also known as the *social construction of reality* perspective), which argues that what we "know" to be real and essential is always a product of the culture and historical period in which we live. Categorical distinctions based on race, class, gender, and sexuality are human creations and don't exist independently of our ideas about them and responses to them. We may be quite sure that an objective reality independent of us exists out there, but constructionists argue that what we believe to be "real" (and what we call that reality) is always a matter of human definition and collective agreement—in other words, is a reality that is socially constructed.

From this perspective, "mammals" as a class of creatures don't exist in nature. People determined that certain organisms that meet a particular set of criteria (including nourishing their young with milk, having skin that is more or less covered with hair, and being warm-blooded) could be grouped together as mammals. Organisms that meet some but not all the criteria may be mistakenly classified. Dolphins, for instance, are hairless creatures that live in the ocean (usually that means the creatures are fish). But they are also warm-blooded and nourish their young with milk, so we've decided to call them mammals. If we ever decided to change the criteria of "mammalness," dolphins might once again fall into a different category. Similarly, a few years ago, a panel of medical experts decided to lower the cut-off point that defined "healthy" blood pressure. Overnight, 45 million once-healthy Americans became unhealthy (cited in Newman, 2004). It wasn't that they suddenly got sick. Social criteria changed, and thus so did their health status.

Understanding race, class, gender, and sexuality as socially constructed human identifiers requires that we take into consideration the following points (Weber, 1998):

- *Identifiers depend on context.* Although race, class, gender, and sexuality have existed throughout most of history as ways to differentiate among individuals, their meanings constantly change as a result of economic, political, and ideological trends and events. Their meanings vary not only across time but across different societies and even different regions within the same society. The meanings of race, gender, class, and sexuality, therefore, are fluid, socially or politically determined, and historically or culturally specific.

- *Identifiers tend to make us think in terms of opposites.* We have a tendency to identify people in "either/or" terms—as white or black, rich or poor, man or woman, heterosexual or homosexual. It is a short step from these dichotomies to identifying one member of each pair as good and the other as bad, one moral and the other immoral, one worthy and the other unworthy. Thinking in terms of "either/or" dichotomies also reinforces the view that these identifiers are permanent fixtures in all human societies, a biological imperative.

- *Identifiers reflect social rankings and power relations.* Race, class, gender, and sexuality are not simply individual traits. They are systems of dominance and power that determine where and how important resources like income, wealth, and access to education and health care are distributed. The status of one group is always defined in terms of its relations to other groups:

  There can be no controlling males without women whose options are restricted; there can be no valued race without races that are defined as "other"; there can be no owners or managers without workers who produce the goods and services that the owners own and the managers control; there can be no heterosexual privilege without gays and lesbians who are defined as "abnormal". (Weber, 1998, p. 20)

- *Identifiers have both psychological and structural meanings.* Race, class, gender, and sexuality have meaning at the level of individuals' lived experiences as well as the level of communities and social institutions. Sociologists often look at national trends and broad economic indicators to describe the relative status of particular groups. But these societal-level trends are always felt by individuals where they work, where they live, and where they form and maintain close, personal relationships (Newman, 2004).

Constructionism taken to its extreme might lead you to conclude that race, class, gender, and sexuality have no reality independent of our definitions. The famous sociologists William Thomas and Dorothy Thomas (1928) once wrote, "If [people] define situations as real, they are real in their consequences" (p. 572). What they meant was that we respond to situations and events in our lives on the basis of the meaning we attach to them. Their essential reality, if it exists at all, is irrelevant. If you were an American living in the 1950s, chances were pretty good that you would have defined the Soviet Union as our country's most dangerous national threat. Hence, it's likely that if you had the chance to meet a Soviet person, perhaps as a tourist, you might have responded to this person as the treacherous individual you anticipated he or she would be. You might have looked at her or him with suspicion, cut conversations short, withdrawn from social interaction, avoided eye contact, and so on. It wouldn't have mattered whether or not this person really was dangerous. The fact that you defined her or him that way would have been sufficient to affect your behavior—and the Soviet person's behavior as well. Indeed, such perceptions of distrust—on both sides—characterized U.S.-Soviet relations for the better part of the 20th century.

At a societal level, then, the Thomases are right: our collective definitions of reality are what matter. But what about the individual level? We live in a society that often says we can do what we want and be what we want as long as we don't hurt others or infringe on their rights. Such a cultural value implies that perhaps how we identify ourselves is solely a matter of individual determination. But you're probably well aware that for some aspects of our identity, those choices are limited. You may have seen a delightful old movie from 1979 called *Breaking Away*. In it, an Indiana teenager who dreams of becoming a professional bicycle racer proudly announces to his parents one day that he is Italian (the family *isn't* Italian). Pretty soon, he's singing along to recordings of Verdi and Puccini operas and saying things like "grazie," "buon giorno," and "ciao, genitori" to his chagrined parents. The humor in this aspect of the film derives from our understanding that, although there's no law against it, one cannot simply ignore personal history and physical reality and declare oneself to be a different nationality—or, for that matter, a different gender, race, social class, or sexuality. Individuals may play an important role in coordinating and giving meaning to definitions of reality in their every-day lives, but their ability to define these classifications on their own is always limited. We're all born into a preexisting society in which the cri-teria for determining difference have already been constructed and have largely become a taken-for-granted part of social institutions and belief systems. More important, some individuals and groups—those with more power, prestige, status, wealth, and access to high-level decision makers—can be more influential in defining difference than others. "He who has the bigger stick has the better chance of imposing his definitions of reality" (Berger & Luckmann, 1966, p. 109).

It's important to emphasize that, although the social construction of differences is a collective enterprise, it can be enormously consequential for individuals. Placement into a racial, gender, class, or sexual category is a powerful predictor of life chances and access to important social resources, as the discussion of the concept of cultural capital in Chapter 1 explains. But keep in mind too that because these categories are socially constructed, they are changeable.

DEFINITIONS OF DIFFERENCES AND IDENTITIES

From the time we're small children, we are exposed to cultural messages that teach us that our lot in life is not fixed. In principle, we are all capa-ble—as long as we have the requisite energy, drive, and ambition—to improve our situation. It's up to us to "be all we can be." A recent Pew Center poll of 38,000 people in 44 countries found that the United States had the lowest percentage of citizens who agreed with the statement "Suc-cess in life is pretty much determined by forces outside of our control" (cited in Leland, 2004). And yet we receive other messages that seem to suggest quite the opposite. More often than not, our race/ethnicity, our gender, our sexual orientation—all powerful markers of our identity—are portrayed as exclusively or at the very least primarily a product of bio-logical factors over which we have little if any control. Certainly there's some truth to this contention. Men and women are different anatomi-cally. People who identify themselves as members of different racial groups do possess certain distinguishable physical characteristics. The per-petuation of the species does depend on reproductive imperatives linking males and females that appear to be universal, natural, and perhaps even instinctual. But these obvious biological realities are not sufficient to explain the means by which human societies construct and define social differences. Let's take a look at how sociologists define race, class, gender, and sexuality. Although one of the themes of this book is that in people's lived experiences these elements of identity work in combination and not independently, it is useful at this point to define these concepts separately.

RACIAL/ETHNIC IDENTITIES

To most people, **race** is a category of individuals who share common inborn biological traits, such as skin color; color and texture of hair; and shape of eyes, nose, or head. It is widely assumed that people who are placed in the same racial category share behavioral, psychological, and personality traits that are linked to their physical similarities. But sociologists typically use the term **ethnicity** to refer to the nonbiological traits—such as shared ancestry, culture, history, language, patterns of behavior, and beliefs—that provide members of a group with a sense of common identity. Whereas ethnicity is thought to be something that we learn from other people, race is commonly portrayed as an inherited and permanent biological characteristic that can easily be used to divide people into mutually exclusive groups.

The concept of race is neither as natural nor as straightforward as this definition implies, however. Some people who consider themselves "white," for example, may have darker skin and kinkier hair than some people who consider themselves "black." In addition, some groups have features that do not neatly place them in one race or another. Australian Aboriginals, for instance, have black skin and "Negroid" facial features but have blond, wavy hair. The black-skinned !Kung of Africa have epicanthic eye folds, a characteristic typical of Asian peoples. It turns out that there may be as much or more biological variation within so-called races as there is between them. In addition, since the earliest humans appeared, they have consistently tended to migrate and interbreed. Some surveys estimate that at least 75% of U.S. Blacks have some white ancestry (cited in Mathews, 1996). The famous naturalist Charles Darwin (1871/1971) wrote that despite external differences, it is virtually impossible to identify clear, distinctive racial characteristics. Indeed, there is no gene for race—no gene that is 100% of one form in one racial group and 100% of a different form in another racial group (Brown, 1998).

That is not to say that race has absolutely no connection to biology. Geneticists have known for quite a while that some diseases are not evenly distributed across racial groups. The overwhelming majority of cases of sickle-cell anemia, for instance, are people of African descent; it is rare among non-Hispanic Whites (BlackHealthCare.com, 2003). Hemochromatosis, a disorder that causes the body to absorb too much iron, is virtually absent among Asian peoples from India and China but occurs in 7.5% of white Scandinavians (Wade, 2002). But no disease is found exclusively in one racial group. Furthermore, it's unclear whether these differences are due solely to some inherited biological trait or to the life experiences and geographic/environmental location of certain groups historically.

Certainly there are physical differences between people who identify themselves as members of different races. But it's our collective imagination that organizes, attaches meaning to, and perhaps alters the meanings of those differences. If we didn't think that differences between black, white, red, yellow, and brown were relevant in some way, we wouldn't see those differences. When I began graduate school in the early 1980s at the University of Washington, I served as a teaching assistant for a large Introduction to Sociology course. One day a student in the class, who was born in Vietnam and spent most of her childhood there, came to my office to discuss the day's lecture on race. She had been a small child in Vietnam during the war and had come into contact with many American soldiers. When she came to this country, she was astonished to find that we make such a big deal about differences between black Americans and white Americans. "In Vietnam," she said to me, "all Americans were the same race. Yeah, some had darker skin than others, but that didn't matter to us. Some were taller than others too. Some were fatter than others. It didn't matter. To us, they all looked alike. We saw them all as Americans."

The Social Construction of Race and Ethnicity What ties people together in a particular racial group is not a set of shared physical characteristics—because there aren't any physical characteristics shared by all members of a particular racial group—but the shared experience of being identified by others as members of that group (Piper, 1992). During the process of growing up and creating an identity for ourselves, we learn three important things: the boundaries that distinguish group members from nonmembers, the perceived position of the group within society, and whether membership in our group is something to take pride in or be ashamed of (Cornell & Hartmann, 1998). These lessons reflect what the prevailing culture defines as socially significant (American Sociological Association, 2002). We decide that particular physical traits will be the primary markers of boundaries between groups. We invent these categories and they become socially significant to the extent that they're used to organize experiences, to form social relations, to evaluate others, and to determine social rankings and access to important resources (Cornell & Hartmann, 1998). In other words, race is a social construction.

Evidence of the socially constructed nature of racial identity appears in the shifting boundaries between racial categories. In apartheid South Africa during the 1970s and 1980s, for instance, wealthy potential investors or powerful government representatives from China, Japan, and Korea presented a problem. South Africa desperately needed the infusion of foreign capital. But Asians were considered "colored" and therefore were of subordinate status according to South African racial rankings. So the South African government created a category of "honorary white" for rich, powerful Asians (Hu-DeHart, 1996). Less affluent Asians—such as immigrant laborers from China—remained "colored." In Brazil, as people climb the class ladder through educational and economic achievement, their racial classification changes, as illustrated by popular Brazilian expressions such as "Money whitens" or "A rich Negro is a white man, and a poor white man is a Negro" (Marger, 1994, p. 441). Even though Puerto Rico is a U.S. territory, conceptions of race there are markedly more fluid than they are in the states. Race is seen as a continuum of categories, with different shades of color as the norm and as a classification that can change as one's socioeconomic circumstances change (Rodriguez & Cordero-Guzman, 2004).

The ways in which particular groups are racially classified can change over time too. In the 19th century, undesirable immigrant groups were often considered "Negro." Newspaper cartoons, for instance, frequently depicted Chinese immigrants as having African features. Such portrayals were attempts to transfer anti-black prejudice to the Chinese, rendering their condemnation more tolerable (Pieterse, 1995). See if you can tell what immigrant group these late 19th-century characterizations refer to:

- This is a race . . . of utter savages. For not merely are they uncouth of garb, but they also let their hair and beards grow to outrageous length . . .
- I am haunted by the human chimpanzees I saw along that hundred miles of horrible country.
- [They are] more like tribes of squalid apes than human beings.
- [They are] the sons and daughters of generations of beggars. . . . They themselves are the missing link between the gorilla and the Negro. (all quoted in Shanklin, 1994, pp. 3–4)

It might surprise you to learn that the group seen so negatively was the Irish. In the 19th- and early 20th-century United States, certain white,

European ethnic groups—Irish, Italians, Jews—were thought to be non-white and inferior. As recently as the mid-20th century, many restaurants, clubs, and hotels actively restricted Jews from entry. In the Southern United States, Italian children were sometimes forced to attend black schools (Lee, 1993). Irish, Jews, and Italians only came to be seen as "white" when their large-scale immigration from Europe ended in the 1920s, thereby diminishing fears about an overflow of allegedly racial inferiors (Lee & Bean, 2004). Once they were considered "white," they entered the mainstream culture and gained economic and political power (Brodkin, 2004; Bronner, 1998). Many sociologists are quick to point out, however, that these white ethnic groups were never subjected to the same type of historical systematic bigotry as Blacks or Native Americans, making their eventual societal acceptance easier (Lieberson, 1980).

In short, racial categories are not natural, essential categories. Instead, they are created, inhabited, transformed, applied, and destroyed by people (Omi & Winant, 1992). Moreover, they often emerge from political, economic, and ideological struggles. Many historians of race argue that racial classifications didn't exist until white European settlers began confronting people of different colors for the first time (Shoemaker, 1997). For instance, the appearance of slavery as an economic institution in 17th-century Colonial America coincided with the emergence of specific racial identities. All Africans, no matter what their specific ethnicity, were now "black." Not only did this term mask the diversity of cultural backgrounds among people of African descent, it also maximized the perceived differences between "black" Africans and "white" Europeans. By the 18th century, the "black-white" distinction had become more important than the "Christian-pagan" distinction as the primary justification for seizing the land or controlling the labor of others.

Racial identity isn't imposed only on vanquished or enslaved peoples by European conquerors, however. Evidence from slave narratives suggests that black slaves used the term "white" to refer to people of any color who owned property (Roediger, 1998). Some southeastern American Indian groups used the terms "red men" or "red people" before they had contact with European settlers. The Choctaw word for Indian is *hatak api homma*, a combination of *hatak* (man) and *homma* (red) (Shoemaker, 1997). However, they could not prevent Whites from co-opting "red" and using it as a derogatory label for all Indians. By the 19th century, "red man" and "redskin" had become dehumanizing racial slurs.

The fluid, socially constructed nature of race can be seen in historical changes in the categories used by the U.S. government in its decennial population censuses (Lee, 1993). In 1870, there were five races: White, Colored (Black), Mulatto (people with some black blood), Chinese, and Indian. White people's concern with race-mixing and racial purity led to changes in the social rules used for determining the status of mixed-race people, particularly in the South. This concern is reflected in the race categories of the 1890 census. Eight races were now listed, half of them applying to black or partly black populations: White, Colored (Black), Mulatto (people with three-eighths to five-eighths black blood), Quadroon (people who have one-fourth black blood), Octoroon (people with one-eighth black blood), Chinese, Japanese, and Indian. In 1900, Mulatto, Quadroon, and Octoroon were dropped, so that any amount of "black blood" meant a person had to be classified as "black." In 1910 and 1920, Mulatto returned to the census form, only to disappear for good in 1930. Between 1930 and 2000, some racial classifications (such as Hindu, Eskimo, and Mexican) appeared and disappeared. Others (Filipino, Korean, Hawaiian) made an appearance and have stayed ever since. Individuals filling out the 2000 census form had a wide array of racial categories from which to choose: White, Black, American Indian or Alaska Native, Asian Indian, Chinese, Filipino, Japanese, Korean, Vietnamese, Native Hawaiian, Guamanian or Chamorro, or Samoan.

Racial/ethnic categories in the U.S. Census still exhibit a fair amount of arbitrariness. For instance, you may have noticed that there is no "Asian" category; instead, Asian Americans must choose a specific nationality. However, "Blacks" and "Whites" do not have the opportunity to indicate their nation of origin. You might have also noticed that Latino/a is not included in the list of races on the latest census form. With the exception of the inclusion of "Mexican" in 1930, Spanish-speaking people have routinely been classified as "white." But because Latino/as can be members of any race, "Hispanic origin" is now considered by the Census Bureau, although it is characterized not as a race but as an ethnicity.

This way of thinking has not been received well by all Latino/as. About 42% of the Latino/a respondents to the 2000 census refused to identify themselves by any of the racial categories on the census form. So many Latino/as chose this option that "some other race" is now the fastest-growing racial category in the United States (Swarns, 2004b). Most self-identified Latino/as come from racially mixed backgrounds. Even within the same family, one sibling may look "black" by typical American standards while another looks white and a third looks in-between (Navarro, 2003).

The way the government decides to draw these "color lines" is not trivial. The appearance and disappearance of particular racial labels reflect

the visibility and value of certain groups in this society. And on a practical level, a great deal depends on the official system of racial categorization: anti-discrimination statutes, property and voting rights laws, health
and education statistics, legislative redistricting, and social policies such as
affirmative action. Racial information from the census is used by a variety of federal agencies, including the Departments of Commerce, Education, Justice, Labor, and Health and Human Services. The issue can be so
divisive that some jurisdictions have tried to do away with racial classifications altogether, arguing that they have become so imprecise that
they've lost all meaning and utility.

Multiracial Identities As recently as 1990, mixed-race people who identified themselves on the census form as "black-white" were counted as black;
those who wrote "white-black" were counted as white (Lee, 1993). Most
multiracial people have experienced being arbitrarily assigned a racial identity by a school principal or an employer that may differ from the identity
of other members of their families or may differ from their own identity
in other settings. The dramatic growth in the number of multiracial children has upset these traditional views of racial identity, however. In 1992,
the U.S. Bureau of the Census reported that for the first time in history
the number of biracial babies increased at a faster rate than the number of
single-race babies (Marmor, 1996). And more and more people of mixed
racial heritage are refusing to identify themselves as one race or another.

In the mid-1990s, these individuals began lobbying Congress and the
Bureau of the Census to add a multiracial category to the 2000 census.
They argued that such a change would add visibility and legitimacy to a
racial identity that has heretofore been ignored. Some argued that a multiracial category might soften the racial lines that divide the country
(Stephan & Stephan, 1989). When people blend several races and ethnicities within their own bodies, the divisiveness of race is reduced, thereby
holding out the promise of a biological solution to the problem of racial
injustice (White, 1997).

Not everyone thought such a change would be a good idea, though.
Many civil rights organizations objected to the inclusion of a multiracial
category (Farley, 2002). They worried that it would reduce the number
of U.S. citizens claiming to belong to long-recognized minority groups,
dilute the culture and political power of those groups, and make it more
difficult to enforce civil rights laws (Mathews, 1996). Job discrimination
lawsuits, affirmative action policies, and federal programs that assist minority businesses or that protect minority communities from environmental

hazards all depend on official racial population data from the census. Furthermore, people who identify themselves as biracial or multiracial are sometimes perceived by members of racial groups as sellouts who avoid discrimination by taking advantage of the confusion their mixed identity creates (L. O. Graham, 1999).

In the end, the civil rights organizations won. For the 2000 census, the government decided not to add a multiracial category to official forms. Instead, it adopted a policy allowing people, for the first time, to identify themselves on the census form as members of more than one race. The new guidelines specify that those who check "white" and another category will be counted as members of the minority group (Holmes, 2000). Data from the 2000 census, some of which are depicted in Exhibit 2.1, show that 2.4% of the population—or close to 7 million people—identify themselves as belonging to two or more races (U.S. Bureau of the Census, 2002). As you might expect, most of the people choosing this option are young (Lee & Bean, 2004). People under the age of 18 were more than twice as likely as people over 18 to identify themselves as belonging to more than one race (Jones & Smith, 2001). The changes in the census form illustrate that politics, not biology, is the determining factor when it comes to determining racial identity.

Some sociologists caution, however, that the Census Bureau's method of measuring multiracial identity—checking two or more race categories—does not adequately reflect the way people personally experience race. The National Longitudinal Study of Adolescent Health, which contains information on the racial identity of a nationwide sample of over 11,000 adolescents, shows that the way people racially classify themselves can be fluid, changing from context to context (Harris & Sim, 2002). For instance, almost twice as many adolescents identify themselves as multiracial when they're interviewed at school as when they're interviewed at home. Furthermore, nearly 15% expressed different racial identities across different settings. This research is important because it shows that the census data on multiracial identity don't necessarily account for everyone who self-identifies as multiracial in everyday situations.

CLASS IDENTITIES

Social class refers to a group of people who share a similar economic position in society based on their wealth and income (Newman, 2004). Class standing directly influences cultural capital and people's ability to attain higher education, their access to well-paying jobs, and the availability

Exhibit 2.1: Multiracial Identification

Percentage of Americans who checked at least one additional racial category in the 2000 census

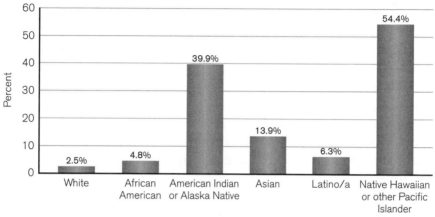

Age and racial identification reported in 2000 census

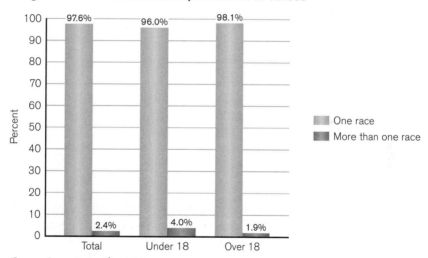

(Source: Jones & Smith, 2001)

of adequate health care. Of the four key components of identity and inequality—race/ethnicity, social class, sex/gender, and sexuality—class is no doubt the one that is least likely to be attributed to innate biological or anatomical traits. Few people would argue that social class is an anatomical identity we're born with. It would seem downright silly to talk about a "social class gene" or the anatomical underpinnings of income and wealth.

Nonetheless, in societies that stratify people on the basis of a **caste system,** socioeconomic status is determined at birth and considered unchangeable. Traditionally, in South Asia, for example, one's caste determines lifestyle, prestige, and occupational choices. Ancient Hindu scriptures identified a strict hierarchy consisting of elite priests, warriors, merchants, artisans, and untouchables who were so lowly they were actually considered to be outside the caste system. Untouchables were restricted to occupations dealing with the bodies of dead animals or unclaimed dead humans, tanning hides from such dead animals and manufacturing leather goods, and cleaning up the human and animal waste in traditional villages that have no sewer systems. In addition, they were once required by law to hide from or, if that wasn't possible, to bow in the presence of anyone from a higher caste. They were routinely denied the right to enter Hindu temples or to draw water from wells reserved for members of the higher castes, who feared they would suffer ritual pollution if they touched or otherwise came in contact with an untouchable (hence the term).

Things are changing somewhat. In India, laws have been passed that prohibit caste-based discrimination. Urban Indians are less strict about caste boundaries than rural Indians. Members of the poorest Indian castes are now voting and joining political parties in record numbers. In fact, more untouchables (or Dalits as they prefer to be called) vote than members of the upper caste (Dugger, 1999). But the caste system still exists in practice and continues to serve as a powerful source of stratification and oppression.

According to Human Rights Watch (2001), over 250 million people worldwide—including the Dalits in India, Nepal, Bangladesh, Sri Lanka, and Pakistan; the Burakumin in Japan; the Osu in Nigeria; and certain groups in Senegal and Mauritania—continue to suffer severe caste discrimination, exploitation, and violence. Caste imposes massive obstacles to their full attainment of civil, political, economic, and cultural rights.

How Do Americans Determine Class Standing? In U.S. society, we believe that the boundaries between class levels are more permeable than they are in a caste system. There are no legal barriers to **social mobility**—the movement of people or groups from one class level to another. Theoretically, anybody, no matter how humble their beginnings, can climb the class ladder. Yet even in an achievement-based class system like ours, where social standing is assumed to be a consequence of one's own actions and accomplishments, class standing is typically intertwined with and therefore inseparable from race and gender, which are perceived by many people as fixed and biologically based.

Many contemporary American sociologists have a rather essentialist view of class, compiling information on "objective," measurable factors such as annual income, wealth, occupation, and educational attainment to determine class standing. The **upper class** (the highest-earning 5% of the U.S. population) is usually thought to include owners of vast amounts of property and other forms of wealth, major shareholders and owners of large corporations, top financiers, rich celebrities and politicians, and members of prestigious families. The **middle class** (roughly 45% of the population) is likely to include college-educated managers, supervisors, executives, small-business owners, and professionals (for example, lawyers, doctors, teachers, and engineers). The **working class** (about 35% of the population) typically includes industrial and factory workers, office workers, clerks, and farm and manual laborers. Most working-class people don't own their own homes and don't attend college. Finally, the "poor" (about 15% of the population) consist of people who work for minimum wages or are chronically unemployed. They are sometimes referred to as the **lower class** or **underclass.** These are the people who do society's dirty work, often for very low wages (Newman, 2004).

Despite the apparent straightforwardness of these criteria, the boundaries between classes tend to be unclear and highly subjective. Part of the reason for this lack of clarity is that in our everyday lives class is not so much a reflection of numbers and statistics but a matter of the way people talk about themselves and others. Indeed, there is often a disconnect between people's own class identity and that imposed on them by others. Consider the difficulties encountered by one researcher trying to study people's class identities:

> The vast majority of Americans think of themselves as "middle class." There is also the folk lexicon of subdivisions of this category—"upper middle," "lower middle," and just plain "middle." . . . The term "lower middle class" is very much disliked by those who might be so categorized, apparently because of the presence of the word "lower." . . . The plain "middle class" is the most slippery category. It is either used as the modest self-label for the upper middle class . . . or it is the covering label for the lower middle class. . . . Either way there is almost no "there" there; to be plain middle class is almost always to be "really" something else, or on the way to somewhere else. At the same

> time, the "middle class" is the most inclusive social category;
> indeed almost a national category. . . . It is everybody except the
> very rich and the very poor. (Ortner, 1998, p. 8)

People think of their own social-class identity not just in economic
terms but, more importantly, in moral and cultural terms (Lamont, 1995).
Moral boundaries between the classes consist of assessments of such qualities as honesty, integrity, work ethic, and consideration for others. Cultural boundaries are identified on the basis of education, taste, manners,
and understanding of "high" culture. In other words, class resides as much
in how people talk, the way they dress, and the books, movies, and music
they prefer as it does in how much money they make. For instance, when
used in everyday conversation, "lower class" is more likely to be a synonym for lack of intelligence and taste than an assessment of one's income.

Class distinctions often go beyond upper-class snobbery and distaste
for the lifestyles of "lower" classes. People at the top often blame those
in the lower socioeconomic classes for their own condition (for example,
"Poor people are lazy and just don't want to work and that's why they're
in distress"). Such perceptions are an effective means of shifting responsibility away from the larger structural factors that contribute to class
inequality—which can be tied to race, ethnicity, and gender—and toward
individuals in the lower classes themselves. When seen this way, economic
suffering is not a by-product of entrenched social circumstances but is
instead a consequence of individual deficiency.

But perceptions of class differences don't always favor those at the
top. Consider, for instance, the 2004 presidential election. Both of the
major candidates—George W. Bush and John Kerry—were extremely
affluent and came from families of privilege. But their class identities were
judged quite differently. Even though many of the policies he advocated
were designed to help those in the lower classes, Kerry was seen by many
as an East Coast elitist with a condescending air, who windsurfed, read
esoteric novels, and spoke French. Bush, on the other hand, even though
many of his policies protected the interests of wealthy individuals and
corporations, was seen as the simple, rural, plain-spoken Texas good ol'
boy, who was more comfortable chopping wood than debating philosophy.
The outcome of the election reflected the triumph of perceptual class distinctions over economic ones. Kerry received his strongest support from
people with college educations in cities with populations over 500,000
(Connelly, 2004). Although it was still the case that wealthier people
tended to vote Republican, Bush's reelection was fueled by the votes of a

very different constituency: religious, rural, blue-collar Americans with-out college degrees. These individuals are likely to view "upper-class" peo-ple with disdain and suspicion.

Who Is Poor? Although legislators and politicians are fond of talking about what they're doing or what they intend to do for the "middle class" or the "working class," the federal government has no official mechanism for determining class boundaries. The one exception is the identification of who is and who isn't poor. But the designation of the cut-off point between poverty and non-poverty is somewhat arbitrary and therefore quite controversial.

The **poverty line** identifies the amount of yearly income a family requires to meet its basic needs. Those who fall below the line are con-sidered officially poor; those above the line are not poor. In 2004, the offi-cial poverty line for a family of four—two parents and two children—was an annual income of $19,157. The line is based on pretax money income only and does not include food stamps, Medicaid, public housing, and other noncash benefits. The figure varies according to family size and is adjusted each year to account for inflation. But it doesn't take into account geographical differences in cost of living.

The poverty line is established by the U.S. Department of Agriculture and for decades has been computed from something called the Thrifty Food Plan (Newman, 2004). This plan, developed in the early 1960s, is used to calculate the cost of a subsistence diet, which is the bare nutri-tional minimum a family needs to survive. This cost is then multiplied by 3, because research at the time showed that the average family spent one-third of its income on food each year. The resulting amount was adopted in 1969 as the government's official poverty line. Even though the plan is modified periodically to account for changes in dietary rec-ommendations, the formula itself and the basic definition of poverty have remained the same for about four decades.

Many policymakers, sociologists, and concerned citizens question whether the current poverty line provides an accurate picture of people's basic needs in the United States. Several things have changed since the early 1960s. For instance, today food costs probably account for only one-sixth of the average family's budget, because the price of other things, such as housing and medical care, has inflated at much higher rates than the price of food (Cloward & Piven, 1993). In addition, there were fewer dual-earner or single-parent families in the past, meaning that fewer fam-ilies had to pay for child care at that time. In short, today's families have many more expenses and therefore probably spend a greater proportion of their total income on nonfood items. The consequence is that the official poverty line is probably set too low today and therefore underestimates the extent of poverty in this country.

Deciding who is and isn't officially poor is not just a matter of semantics. A needy family making slightly more than the poverty line may not qualify for a variety of public assistance programs, such as housing benefits, Head Start, Medicaid, or Temporary Assistance for Needy Families. As a result, their standard of living may not be as good as that of a family that earns less and therefore qualifies for these programs. Life slightly above the poverty line can be precarious. When nothing out of the ordinary happens, people can manage. But paying for an unexpected event—a sickness, an injury, the breakdown of a major appliance or automobile—can send them into poverty. Imagine being a poor single mother with a sick child. One trip to the doctor might cost an entire week's food budget or a month of rent. Dental work or an eye examination is easily forgone when other pressing bills need to be paid. If she depends on a car to get to work and it breaks down, a few hundred dollars to fix it might mean not paying the electric bill that month and having less money for other necessities. When gasoline prices skyrocket—as they did in 2005—many poor families find that they have to cut down on food purchases so they can afford to drive to work.

Because of such situations, the U.S. Bureau of the Census is now experimenting with a new formula for determining the poverty line that would more accurately reflect contemporary spending patterns. Instead of simply using a subsistence food budget as the basis for the definition of poverty, this new formula would also consider expenses for housing, health care, transportation, utilities, child care, and personal expenses. It's estimated that this revised poverty line would be about $2,000 higher for a family of four than the current one, or roughly $21,500.

Raising the official poverty line by $2,000 would have a dramatic effect on the number of people defined as officially poor. But don't expect the poverty line to be redefined anytime soon. The resulting increase in the poverty rate not only would bring obvious political costs to whatever administration happens to be in office but would certainly cause a demand for increased spending on social welfare programs—something few people in government these days are willing to consider.

GENDER IDENTITIES

When discussing gender in my Introduction to Sociology course, I often pose this question to my students: "How do you know if a person is male or female?" After some giggling and eye rolling, someone will always mention the obvious: "Females have an XX chromosomal configuration and males have XY." I then reply, "Can you see a person's chromosomes? No, I didn't think so. So what visual information do you use to make this determination?" They then proceed to identify what they consider to be socially relevant markers of maleness and femaleness: Women have long hair, men have short hair; women have high voices, men have deep voices; women have wide hips and breasts, men have broad shoulders and facial hair; women wear dresses, men wear pants; and so on. I challenge every response: "Can a woman have a deep voice?" "Can a man wear a dress?" "Can a man have breasts?" "What about women who have their breasts surgically removed? Do they stop being women at that point?" Eventually a bolder student will say something like "men have penises; women have vaginas." Setting aside the obvious problem (that is, unless we live in a nudist colony, we usually don't see people's naked crotches when we first meet them), I then ask, "Can a man not have a penis and still be a man? A few years ago, a woman cut off her abusive husband's penis with a kitchen knife while he was asleep and threw it into a nearby field. Did he stop being a man at that moment?" The discussion typically evolves into a frustrating mess at this point.

Some of my students' anguish may be due to the fact that they, like most people, tend to confuse sex and gender. **Sex** is typically used to refer to the biological markers of maleness or femaleness. These indicators can be chromosomes (XX for female, XY for males), sex glands (ovaries for females, testes for males), hormones (more estrogen than testosterone for females, more testosterone than estrogen for males), internal sex organs (uterus for females, prostate gland for males), external genitalia (vagina for females, penis for males), reproductive capabilities (pregnancy and lactation for females, impregnation for males), germ cells produced (eggs for females, sperm for males), or secondary physical characteristics (wide hips and breasts for females, facial hair and low-pitched voice for males).

Gender, on the other hand, designates the psychological, social, and cultural aspects of masculinity and femininity (Kessler & McKenna, 1978). People are not born with a gender; they cultivate it over time as they learn the cultural expectations associated with being a boy or a girl, a man or a woman. While conceptions of biological sex are fairly consistent (although, as we'll see, not universal), conceptions of gender vary enormously. What it means to be male or female, how you're supposed to look, and the things you're expected to do by virtue of being labeled male or female are entirely dependent on the societal, historical, and even the familial context in which you live. Sex may be a status ascribed to us at birth, but gender is something that we achieve through the process of conforming to (and reinforcing) broader cultural expectations.

Most of us assume that sex and gender, if not perfectly synonymous, are at least closely intertwined with one another. Based on a visual inspection— either of ultrasound images prior to birth or a quick glance at a newborn's genitals at the moment of birth—a baby is proclaimed as male or female and from that moment embarks on a lifetime journey within the confines of male or female cultural expectations. The official detection of a penis means that the baby will be assigned a "male." He'll be identified by others as male, be provided with male clothes, male toys, and so on. Ultimately, he'll come to think of himself as a male. Likewise, babies with vaginas will be designated as female and will be expected to look and act in the culturally acceptable ways we associate with the category "female."

People commonly see gender (the social) as an outgrowth of sex (the biological) (Epstein, 1988). Since sex is assumed to be rooted in biology, it's tempting to see it as "natural," which is to say, given, fixed, and determined (Stanley, 2002). Behavioral or personality differences between males and females are therefore seen as natural too. It would be silly to argue that there is absolutely no connection between sex and gender or that there are no biological or physical differences between males and females. But what's important is how we perceive and respond to the differences. Even biological predispositions aren't completely free from social influence. The members of a society can decide which sex differences ought to be amplified and which can and should be ignored.

Gender Roles: Doing Gender Early on, children begin to acquire knowledge about gender through socialization (see Chapter 4). What they learn are the gender rules that allow them to be perceived as masculine or feminine. Simply having knowledge of these rules does not in and of itself make a person feminine or masculine. To accomplish that, they must "do gender" appropriately and continuously through everyday social interaction (West & Zimmerman, 1987). That means behaving in ways that are considered gender appropriate. For girls and women in the United States, it means things like not burping in public, sitting "ladylike," paying attention to appearance, wearing makeup and jewelry. For boys and men, it usually means things like being assertive, not overtly displaying certain emotions, and not nurturing others, especially other adults.

It is impossible not to do gender. We might not do it well, or we might do it in culturally inappropriate ways, but if we try not to display or do gender at all, others will do it for us (Newman, 2004). For instance, sociologist Betsy Lucal (1999) describes what it's like to be a woman, identify as a woman, but be mistaken for a man because she doesn't bear the traditional markers of femininity:

> I am six feet tall and large-boned. I have had short hair for most of my life. . . . I do not wear dresses, skirts, high heels, or makeup. My only jewelry is a class ring, a "men's" watch (my wrists are too large for a "women's" watch), two small earrings (gold hoops, both in my left ear), and (occasionally) a necklace. I wear jeans or shorts, T-shirts, sweaters, polo/golf shirts, button-down collar shirts, and tennis shoes or boots. . . . I prefer baggy clothes, so the fact that I have "womanly" breasts often is not obvious (pp. 786–787).
>
> Each day, I experience the consequences that our gender system has for my identity and interactions. I am a woman who has been called "Sir" so many times that I no longer even hesitate to assume that it is being directed at me. I am a woman whose use of public rest rooms regularly causes reactions ranging from confused stares to confrontations over what a man is doing in the women's room (p. 781).

According to Lucal, while she can choose not to "do" traditional femininity, she cannot choose not to "do" gender. Others will always attribute one or the other gender; it just so happens they often make a misattribution. But for Lucal, as with most of us, gender is a significant part of her identity, and she is deeply embedded in the gender system:

> I am not to the point of personally abandoning gender. . . . I do not want people to see me as genderless as much as I want them to see me as a woman. . . . I would like to expand the category of "woman" to include people like me. . . . I do identify myself as a woman, not as a man or as someone outside of the two-and-only-two categories. (pp. 793–794)

The enormous cultural and historical variation in the ways in which men and women are expected to appear and behave attests to the fact that gender is not innate. Genders are fluid. They can overlap (as when certain women are more aggressive or more skilled at math than certain men) and they can vary by degree (some men are extremely masculine, others mildly masculine).

The Sexual Dichotomy Although some might grant that gender can be shaped by our social surroundings, the typical assumption is that sex is not. Indeed, we live our lives under the taken-for-granted belief in the essential reality of a sexual dichotomy. The **sexual dichotomy** is the division of sex into two categories: male and female. These categories are considered to be biologically determined, permanent (you are what you're born with), universal (males are males and females are females whether one lives in Botswana or Boston, in the 15th century or the 21st century), exhaustive (everyone can be placed into one of the two categories), and mutually exclusive (you can only be one or the other sex; you can't be both). Casual references to the "opposite" sex reinforce the taken-for-grantedness of the sexual dichotomy. "Opposite" implies that there can be nothing in-between.

If you think about it, our entire culture is built around a sexual dichotomy. We have separate clothing sections for men and women, separate public bathrooms, separate hygienic products, separate sections in the bookstore, separate dormitory floors, and so on. The sexual dichotomy, in short, is assumed to be in the nature of things. After all, don't we need two sexes in order for the species to procreate?

But upon closer inspection, the essential reality of the sexual dichotomy begins to break down. Transsexuals like Deirdre McCloskey clearly challenge the idea that male and female are permanent biological characteristics. The impermanence of sex received official recognition of sorts when the International Olympic Committee's Executive Board approved a proposal to allow transsexuals to compete in the 2004 Athens Olympics. Athletes who had undergone sex reassignment surgery—either male-to-female or female-to-male—were eligible to compete as long as their "new" sex had been legally recognized and it had been at least two years since their surgery. Shortly afterward, the Ladies European Golf Tour enacted a similar policy, allowing a 37-year-old Danish transsexual to play in a professional golf tournament.

But the transsexual experience doesn't challenge other elements of the sexual dichotomy, chiefly its assumption that there are two and only two sexes. Deirdre did not want to be considered a third, intermediate sex. She wanted to be a woman, in a very traditional, run-of-the-mill sense. In a documentary film called *You Don't Know Dick*, a female-to-male transsexual, in response to questions from incredulous friends who are having a hard time understanding her desire to become a man, firmly says, "I don't want an alternative lifestyle. I want to be a man."

Some features of the sexual dichotomy, however—namely mutual exclusivity, exhaustiveness, and universality—are challenged when we examine sex categories cross-culturally. Throughout human history and across all societies, certain people have transcended the categories of male and female. They may be born with anatomical/genital configurations that are ambiguous. Or they may simply choose to live their lives in ways that don't conform to existing gender expectations associated with their sex. How societies respond to these individuals says a great deal about the cultural ideologies and values systems that underlie assumptions about sex and gender.

In traditional Navajo culture, for instance, one could be identified as male, female, or *nadle*—a third sex assigned to those whose sex-typed anatomical characteristics were ambiguous at birth (Lang, 1998). Physically normal individuals also had the opportunity to choose to become nadle if they so desired. The gender status of nadle is simultaneously masculine and feminine. They are allowed to perform the tasks and take up the occupations of both men and women. Far from being stigmatized, the Navajo regarded nadle as bringing luck and prosperity. They were said to "know everything"—a reference to the fact that they knew both the masculine and the feminine (Lang, 1998).

Similar institutionalized sex/gender variations have been documented in Tahiti (the *mahu*) and among the Lakota Sioux (the *wintke*). For the Chuckchi of Eastern Siberia, a biological male child with feminine traits gradually transforms into a "soft man." Although he keeps his masculine name, he is expected to live as a woman (Williams, 1992). Among the Yumas of the American Southwest, *kwe'rhame* are biological women who pass for men, dress like men, and marry women. *Hwames* among the Mohaves are biological females who don't menstruate (or who hide their menstruation) and take on some of the activities associated with men. But even though they marry women, they aren't accepted as full-fledged men. *Hwame* is a sex category distinct from male and female. Indeed, the Mohaves also have a fourth gender, *alyha*, which refers to biological men who possess feminine traits (Williams, 1992).

As in most societies, in Hindu India, male/female and man/woman are viewed as natural categories whose essential characteristics set them in opposition to one another. Nonetheless, Indians also acknowledge many sex/gender variants and changes. The most visible and culturally institutionalized variants are the *hijras*. Hijras are born as men, but by choice they have their genitals surgically removed. Unlike male-to-female transsexuals in the United States, this surgery transforms them not into women but into hijras. By all appearances, they look like women. All aspects of their gender—their clothing, hairstyle, gestures, voice, facial expressions, manner of walking—are all distinctly feminine. They take on feminine names and use female kinship terms—like *sister, aunt,* and *grandmother*—in their relationships with others. They only have sex with male partners. But although they are "like" women, they are not women. Their mannerisms are often exaggerated, and their sexual aggressiveness contrasts with the submissive demeanor of ordinary Indian women. They often use vulgar and abusive speech, which is likewise deviant for Indian women. But the main reason they're not considered women is that they don't have female reproductive organs and therefore cannot bear children.

Because reproduction is seen as such a key determinant of sexual identification in Hindu India, some biological females who voluntarily renounce reproduction are not considered women. Around puberty, a girl who rejects marriage (and thus sexuality and reproduction) can decide to become a *sādhin*. The decision is irreversible. Sādhins commit to celibacy for life. They cut their hair short and wear men's clothing. But like hijras, they are neither men nor women. Despite their male appearance, they remain socially women in many ways. They are allowed to engage in masculine tasks—like plowing, sowing crops, and herding sheep—but they also do women's work. They smoke water pipes and cigarettes—distinctly masculine behaviors—but don't attend funerals, something that is specifically a male prerogative (Nanda, 2003).

In these examples, we can see the tension between essentialism and constructionism. An essentialist would view these "intermediate" sexes as ways societies integrate biologically "abnormal" individuals into mainstream, everyday life. Note how such an approach still maintains that there are essentially only two sexes. Constructionists, on the other hand, would emphasize how these examples show that the reality of sex and gender is constructed differently in different societies. The existence of third or fourth sexes/genders implies that they constitute part of a culturally constructed reality that recognizes statuses apart from "man" and "woman" (Lang, 2003).

Intersexuals and Biological Ambiguity   When it comes to sex identification in U.S. society, physical ambiguity has historically been treated from an essentialist perspective. For instance, consider the traditional reaction to **intersexuals,** individuals in whom anatomical sexual differentiation is either incomplete or unclear. They may have the chromosomal pattern of one sex but the external genitalia of another, or they may have both ovaries and testicles. Experts estimate that about 1.7% of all babies born have some form of intersexuality, meaning that they are born with sexual organs that don't completely fit into standard sex categories (Fausto-Sterling, 2000). However, intersexuality is usually defined by biologists as a combination of the two existing categories and not as a third, fourth, or fifth category unto itself.

People born with genitals that are visually ambiguous are considered victims of birth defects. Moreover, the diagnosis of intersexuality is commonly framed as a tragedy that could doom a child to a life of abnormality, persecution, and "freakhood" if not properly managed (Fausto-Sterling, 2000). Advanced surgical, hormonal, and chemical technologies are deployed as soon after birth as possible to "fix" the anatomy so as to establish consistency between it and the social label. About 90% of intersexuals who undergo "corrective" surgery are designated as female, because creating a vagina is considered surgically easier than creating a penis (Angier, 1997b).

An increasingly vocal group of intersexuals protests that many of the surgical techniques used to "fix" their genitals are mutilating and potentially harmful. They cite cases of people with ambiguous genitals being robbed of any sexual sensation in the attempt to surgically "normalize" them—that is, give them the outward physical appearance of either a male or a female. The founder of the Intersex Society of North America eloquently summed up her organization's frustration: "They can't conceive of leaving someone alone" (quoted in Angier, 1997a, p. A10).

The medical profession has difficulty leaving these individuals alone because to do so would undermine our culture's dichotomous and essentialist understanding of sex. Intersexuals "exist on the margins and borders of society," forced to "pass" as normal in order to remain hidden in the "official ideology and everyday commerce of social life" (Herdt, 1994, p. 17). The drastic surgical intervention that ensues is undertaken not because the infant's life is threatened but because our entire social structure is organized around having two and only two sexes. The sexual dichotomy in our culture is so essential to our way of life that those who challenge it are considered either crazy people or cultural heretics who are being disloyal to the most fundamental of biological "facts." To suggest that the labels "male" and "female" are not sufficient to categorize everyone is to challenge a basic organizing principle of social life.

SEXUAL ORIENTATIONS

Related to sex and gender, of course, is **sexual orientation**—which indicates the sex for whom one feels erotic and romantic desire. Like all the elements of identity I've discussed so far, conceptions of sexual orientation (or **sexual identity**) are historically and culturally bound. Of course, the claim that sexual orientation is socially constructed does not necessarily mean that it is a learned behavior with no inherent genetic, hormonal, or physiological correlates. Instead, saying that sexual orientation is socially constructed means that our ideas about what sexual orientation is and how people are labeled and categorized are a matter of human definition influenced by cultural and historical processes. Hence, it is impossible to understand the nature of sexual orientation and the means by which we classify ourselves and others without taking into consideration the broader sociocultural context in which sexuality in general exists.

Heteronormativity American culture is considered **heteronormative**— that is, a culture where heterosexuality is accepted as the normal, taken-for-granted mode of sexual expression. Social institutions and social policies reinforce the belief that sexual relationships ought to exist between males and females. Cultural representations of virtually every aspect of intimate and family life—dating, sex, marriage, childbearing, and so on— presumes a world in which men are sexually and affectionately attracted to women and women are attracted to men (Macgillivray, 2000). In competitive figure skating, for example, the "pairs" competition always consists of women partnered with men (Wildman & Davis, 2002). Adolescent women seeing a gynecologist for the first time can expect to be given information on birth control, highlighting the assumption that they will have sex with men, it's just a matter of when.

While I was writing this chapter, I came across an issue of *CosmoGirl* magazine. A column giving sexual advice to teenage girls caught my eye. A 17-year-old from Kansas wrote in and asked, "I've never had an orgasm. Is something wrong with me?" The columnist replied:

> Absolutely not. Lots of women don't experience orgasm until they're in their twenties—after they have had more experience with guys and feel more comfortable with their bodies. ("Your most private," 2004, p. 111)

Another young woman, who worried about becoming sexually active, was given this advice:

> If you're scared to have sex, it might be because you're not emotionally ready or you haven't found the right guy yet. ("Your most private," 2004, p. 111)

Notice in both of these responses that the default assumption is that sexual concerns—as well as their solutions—are heterosexual in nature. The advice these young women are given to overcome their difficulties is to pursue relationships with men.

In a heteronormative society, heterosexuals are socially privileged because their relationships and lifestyles are affirmed in every facet of the culture. Such privilege includes having positive media images of people with the same sexual orientation; not having to lie about who you are, what you do, and where you seek entertainment; not having to worry about losing a job because of your sexual orientation; receiving validation from your religious community; being able to marry and adopt children; and being able to join the Boy Scouts or serve openly in the military (Macgillivray, 2000, p. 304).

"The Closet" It would not be surprising, against such a cultural backdrop, that some people whose sexuality places them outside the heteronormative lines of acceptability would choose to keep this component of their identity hidden. Indeed, since the 1950s, the "closet" metaphor has played a prominent role in gay life in the United States. Traditionally, remaining "in the closet" has been a life-shaping strategy of concealing one's sexual identity in order to avoid interpersonal rejection and social discrimination. The closet has been a rational and understandable response to the typical treatment afforded gays and lesbians in the workplace, in the criminal justice system, in families, and in everyday encounters with others.

Ironically, although people have remained in the closet in the belief that it would make life easier, such identity concealment can be extremely stressful and effortful, often evoking feelings of shame, guilt, and fear. It is not simply about denying and suppressing a potentially stigmatizing identity but instead involves close attention to every aspect of one's life in order to avoid detection:

> The closeted individual closely monitors his or her speech, emotional expression, and behavior in order to avoid unwanted suspicion. The sexual meaning of the things . . . and acts . . . of daily life must be carefully read in order to skillfully fashion a convincing heterosexual identity. (Seidman, 2004, p. 31)

The ever-present threat of being "outed," or forced to publicly acknowledge homosexuality, has long served as a means of social control, keeping homosexuals silent and invisible.

Over the past several decades, however, homosexuality in the United States has itself emerged from the cultural closet. As you'll see in more detail in Chapter 3, positive media and cultural images of homosexuality are more common today than ever. Gay men and lesbians are freer than ever to live outside "the closet." But they still must navigate social institutions that maintain heterosexual privilege. Sociologist Steven Seidman (2004) interviewed 30 homosexuals of different races, classes, genders, and ages and found that, for the most part, they saw their homosexuality as natural and positive. They integrated it into their daily lives. Few of them seemed particularly concerned about sexual suspicion or outright exposure when making important decisions about love, work, friends, and other social activities. But they weren't completely open about their sexual identity either. They tended to conceal their homosexuality in specific situations or with specific people. To Seidman, this type of periodic closeting marks a noteworthy shift from the life-altering closet of the past. As he puts it, "there's a huge difference between concealing from an uncle or a client and marrying or avoiding certain occupations in order to pretend to be straight" (p. 8).

The experience of the closet and the consequences of "coming out" are influenced by other components of social identity. For instance, working-class individuals, no matter what their sexual orientation, expect to turn to aunts, uncles, cousins, or siblings for financial help at some point in their lives. They can never take material well-being for granted. So for working-class gays and lesbians, being estranged from relatives as a result of exiting the closet carries the threat of losing an important source of economic and emotional support. In contrast, middle-class gays and lesbians have more options. Because of the high value placed on individualism, they can anticipate some degree of separation from their families and the communities in which they were raised. In addition, they have the economic wherewithal to support themselves if they become alienated from their families as a result of coming out.

Men and women also differ in the way they manage and conceal their sexual identities. For men who remain in the closet, simply appearing strong and masculine is usually enough to lead to the presumption that they're heterosexual and to confer the full measure of social authority and privilege given to men in our society. For lesbians, however, a traditionally feminine appearance may mark them as "straight," but it also situates them as subordinates to men. The traditional trappings of femininity do not carry the same status, authority, and economic advantage that masculinity carries in this society. Closeted lesbians who wish to be strong, assertive, and authoritative risk exposure, and straight women who do likewise risk being labeled as lesbians. As Seidman writes:

> This is a dilemma that [homosexual] men don't experience. Men who claim masculine power are rewarded as men, and as presumptively straight; women who claim the same privileges associated with masculinity are gender rebels and risk stigma and social harm. (p. 50)

Decisions about concealing or publicly expressing homosexual identities are, of course, private matters that depend on the individual's circumstances. In a society that is built by, for, and around the interests of heterosexuals, however, such decisions are always influenced by larger structures of power and privilege, especially the willingness of employers and the legal system to tolerate homosexuality.

The Complexity of Sexual Identity Because of its connection to procreation, we tend to think of heterosexuality as a socially acknowledged category of sexual orientation that has always existed. Certainly the earliest humans engaged in sexual intercourse with members of the other sex. If they didn't, none of us would be here today. But heterosexuality as a distinct and identifiable lifestyle and as an element of one's identity didn't exist until quite recently in human history. People in the distant past named and organized their sexual activities in ways that are quite different from the ways we do today (Katz, 2003).

In the time of Plato, for instance, people didn't have a notion of two distinctly different sexual appetites allotted to different individuals. They simply saw various ways of experiencing sexual pleasure (Foucault, 1990). Although anal sex between two men was considered a punishable sin, colonial Americans had no concept of homosexuality or heterosexuality as a personal condition or identity. In the mid-19th century, same-sex romantic relationships among middle-class individuals—in which women and men expressed passionate longings for emotional and physical intimacy—were common and unremarkable. A man or a woman could write of desire for a loved one of the same sex without raising suspicions about sexual orientation (D'Emilio & Freedman, 1988).

The word "homosexuality" first appeared in print in 1869, when a German legal reformer sought to change existing anti-sodomy laws (Fausto-Sterling, 2000). The earliest use of the word "heterosexual" as a noun in the United States was in an 1892 medical journal that defined it as a person who was attracted to members of both the same sex and the opposite sex (Katz, 2003). Eventually, the word acquired its contemporary meaning: sexual attraction to members of a different sex. So those who had sexual relations with members of their own sex became "homosexuals." Medical writers eventually used this term to stigmatize same-sex relations as a form of sexual perversion. Men and women could no longer openly express affectionate desire for a loved one of the same gender without causing a stir.

You'll notice in this brief history that, as we saw with sex and gender, sexual orientation is commonly viewed in dichotomous terms: one is either homosexual or heterosexual. Our culture's fondness for either-or sexual categories was challenged in the 1940s, when Alfred Kinsey published a report arguing that sexual orientation lies along a continuum, with "exclusively heterosexual" at one end of the scale and "exclusively homosexual" at the other. An "exclusive heterosexual," for example, is someone who has never had physical or psychosexual responses to individuals of his or her own sex. In between the two extremes are various gradations of sexuality, suggesting that people could be "bisexual" or "predominantly" heterosexual or homosexual.

Kinsey and his colleagues found that only 50% of the white males they studied identified themselves as "exclusively heterosexual" and only 4% identified themselves as "exclusively homosexual" (Kinsey, Pomeroy, and Martin, 1948). The rest fell somewhere between the two endpoints. When they focused on overt, physical sexual contact since adolescence, they found that 37% of men had had some homosexual experience that ended in orgasm. For women, the percentage was 13% (Kinsey, Pomeroy, Martin, & Gebhard, 1953). These percentages are significantly higher than the percentages of people who identified themselves as exclusively homosexual. In a more contemporary national survey, many more people reported homosexual desire and behavior than reported homosexuality or bisexuality as their main sexual identity (Michael, Gagnon, Laumann, & Kolata, 1994). About 3% of the men surveyed identified themselves as gay, but 9% had had sex with a man since puberty. Among women, less than 2% identified as lesbian, but about 4% had had sex with another woman since puberty.

Note that these researchers all recognized that sexual orientation cannot be measured solely in terms of sexual activity. An individual might be sexually aroused by homosexual fantasies but have had only heterosexual physical encounters. Such a person would fall somewhere in the middle of Kinsey's continuum. More recently, Fritz Klein (1990) has argued that sexual orientation is even more complex. Not only does it lie on a continuum but it can change across time along several different dimensions: sexual attraction, sexual behavior, sexual fantasies, emotional preference, social preference, hetero/homosexual lifestyle, and self-identification. Sexual behavior and lifestyles vary from day to day and year to year.

Indeed, "being" homosexual (or bisexual or heterosexual, for that matter) always consists of more than simply physiological attraction toward or sexual activity with members of a particular sex. People's desire to identify with a particular sexual orientation is always, in part, influenced by the costs and benefits of doing otherwise. Bisexuality, for instance, has until recently existed on the margins of the homosexual community, leading many bisexuals to hide their sexual identity:

> Being bi isn't a derogatory term at all . . . but that is not how I choose to identify. There are too many "queer" marches and events that only include lesbians and gays; bi and transgender people are peripheral. That's always the vibe I've gotten, and perhaps that is partly why it was so easy to say "I'm a lesbian. . . ." (quoted in Markowitz, 2000, p. 24)

The case of bisexuality raises an important sociological point about the social construction of sexuality. Categories of sexual orientation are not fixed, immutable, or mutually exclusive. People's sexuality can change during the course of their lives. In the case of bisexuality, these changes could be a consequence not of a profound identity epiphany but of the fluctuating availability of male or female sexual partners during certain periods of one's life. Ironically, when a person's erotic attractions change— say, a lifelong lesbian marries a man and has children—others often invoke an essentialist frame, saying perhaps that she was really straight all along. Conversely, people might contend that a woman who leaves her husband to begin a relationship with another woman was always a lesbian but is just now acknowledging that fact. To a constructionist, however, it may be just as correct to say that this person's sexual identity has changed along with the circumstances of her life.

Intersections
Identities on the Borderlands

It would be tempting to see race, class, gender, and sexuality as four influential, but independent, characteristics that separately influence people's identities. But it's the intersections and interactions among these factors that are useful in explaining why people are the way they are and do the things they do. Race, class, gender, and sexuality operate concurrently in every social situation. At the societal level, they're embedded in every social institution. At the individual level, our location along the confluence of all these dimensions helps form our lives and our identities as well as our opportunities and experiences (Weber, 1998). On some dimensions, we may be in dominant groups; on others, we may be subordinate. People might find themselves in positions of power sometimes (say, because they're male or white) but at other times find themselves in positions of disadvantage (because they're working class or homosexual). It's difficult, therefore, to argue that all disadvantages are the same or all victims of oppression are equally oppressed. Recognizing that every one of us benefits in some respects and suffers in others is important in fully understanding the impact of identities and inequalities in everyday life.

Some individuals face disadvantage on three or more dimensions. For instance, the intersections of race, class, and gender are particularly obvious to poor, black women. As far back as the late 19th century, black women argued that the concern with newly emancipated black men getting their rights eclipsed any concern for their rights (Weber, 1998). In addition, ideals of masculinity and femininity that emerged during the 19th century never included all men or women. The assumption that women were best suited to the domestic sphere where they would take care of the home and nurture children was an ideal that rarely extended to poor women of color, who have always participated in the paid labor force in higher numbers than white, middle-class women (see Chapter 8). Indeed, the feminist movement of the 1970s and 1980s was roundly criticized for excluding race and class in its attempts to shed light on the oppressive consequences of gender inequality alone.

Race, ethnicity, and class are so deeply interwoven in American culture that it may ultimately be impossible to pull them apart. For instance, "Jewishness" may be an ethnic or a religious category, but it is also conceptually inseparable from "middle classness" (Ortner, 1998). Nonetheless, many sociologists believe that it is important to examine the relative influence of race/ethnicity and social class on people's lives. Upwardly mobile people of color often find it difficult to leave their pasts behind and frequently feel caught between their poor ethnoracial communities of origin and the affluent communities where they now live (Feagin, 1991). They sometimes conclude that it's simply easier to keep these two facets of their lives separate. As one affluent black architect put it:

> It's like I have to be two different people. . . . It can just be easier to let my two parts stay apart. . . . I don't want people feeling uncomfortable around other people because they don't talk the same

language, or do the same things or anything like that, so I'd just as soon keep them apart. . . . I got my peers from work and that environment, business and professional, the movers and the shakers, and my peops from way back when I used to run around in the streets like a wild man. (quoted in Jackson, 2004, p. 267)

Furthermore, middle-class and affluent African Americans still face discriminatory treatment in their everyday public encounters—ranging from closer scrutiny in stores to police harassment (see Chapter 5). As a result, even African Americans who've seen their socioeconomic standing improve have become discouraged about whether the "American Dream" applies to them (Hochschild, 1995). Other sociologists, like William Julius Wilson (1980), have argued that class may be a more important determinant of social and political status than race. Wilson cites the fact that African Americans have become polarized into an educated, upwardly mobile middle class and an economically destitute underclass. These two groups have very different ideologies, perceptions of social justice, and overall outlooks on life.

The ascription of sexual labels can also be influenced by one's membership in other identifying categories. For white homosexuals, sexual orientation is the identifier that most distinguishes them from the dominant white population and culture. Their sexual orientation, therefore, may take on greater importance for them than it does for black homosexuals, who live with an added layer of difference from the dominant group because of their race. In addition, gay men and lesbians of color often feel excluded both from their ethnoracial communities and from the gay world as well (Nagel, 2003). An examination of attitude surveys over the past 30 years reveals that African Americans are more disapproving of homosexuality than other groups are (Lewis, 2003). Not surprisingly, black homosexuals, especially men, are less likely than white homosexuals to be openly gay (Boykin, 1996). Certainly there are overtly gay black men, but many—perhaps even the majority—still lead secret lives. They are, as one author puts it, "products of a black culture that deems masculinity and fatherhood as a black man's primary responsibility—and homosexuality as a white man's perversion" (Denizet-Lewis, 2003, p. 30).

Faced with the sometimes volatile and destructive combination of racism and homophobia, many gay black men reject gay culture and live their lives on the "down low," or on the DL. Most of them date or marry women and engage in sexual activity with men they meet anonymously at bathhouses, in parks, or over the Internet. While some of these men participate peripherally in mainstream gay culture, they are not known as gay by their colleagues or families. Even DL men who say they prefer sex with men are adamant that the gay label doesn't apply to them. They identify themselves first and foremost as black, which is taken to be synonymous with being masculine. Indeed, masculine appearance is an effective defense against accusations of homosexuality because of widespread stereotypes that equate homosexuality with effeminate men.

The costs of being both black and gay can be steep. As one black man on the DL put it:

> If you're white, you can come out as an openly gay skier or actor or whatever. It might hurt you some, but it's not like if you're black and gay, because then it's like you've let down the whole black community, black women, black history, black pride. You don't hear black people say, "Oh yeah, he's gay, but he's still a real man. . . ." (quoted in Denizet-Lewis, 2003, p. 31)

Many black gay men also tend to avoid condoms and HIV testing. Recently the DL culture has come to the attention of a worried public health community that attributes the increasing prevalence of HIV/AIDS among African Americans at least in part to these men, who have unprotected anonymous sex and then pass the virus to their unsuspecting wives and girlfriends. African Americans make up less than 13% of the population in the United States, but according to the Centers for Disease Control (2003a), they account for over half of all diagnoses of HIV/AIDS. Moreover, a third of young, urban black men who have sex with other men are HIV-positive, and 90% of them are unaware of their infection. Since 2001, about two-thirds of women with newly diagnosed HIV infections have been black (cited in Denizet-Lewis, 2003).

In short, the combinations of race, class, gender, and sexuality have complex effects on people's lives. We cannot understand the way people define themselves and others and the way different groups are situated in the larger society unless we look at the intersections among race, class, gender, and sexuality. Thus, throughout the remaining chapters of this book, I've highlighted some of these intersections.

CONCLUSION

We've seen in this chapter that cultural and historical ideas about race, class, gender, and sexuality can be just as influential in determining people's identities as biology is. That is not to say that biology has no role. It simply means that our ideas about the contribution of genes, hormones, or anatomy ebb and flow with shifting political and cultural tides. What's important, for our purposes, is not so much whether race, class, gender, and sexual identities have biological underpinnings but how we, as a society, come to define and value the relative contributions of biology and culture. Biology needn't be destiny. We can choose to rely on skin color or genital configuration as the primary means by which we make "us-them" distinctions. Or we can choose to downplay these traits and treat them with the same nonchalance that we treat eye color, hair color, or the shape of a nose or chin.

As long as people continue to believe that race differences or gender differences are rooted in nature, however, they will continue to accept social inequalities as natural. It's easier to justify women's lower wages in the workforce, for instance, if the cultural assumption is that they are innately less competitive and ambitious than men. It's easier to segregate members of particular racial or ethnic groups into occupations that involve tedious manual labor if the cultural assumption is that they are biologically built to tolerate such conditions.

In the following chapter, I will extend these ideas about the socially manufactured nature of difference to show how it is perpetuated through everyday language and represented through important media imagery.

[INVESTIGATING IDENTITIES AND INEQUALITIES]
A sociological treasure hunt: The artifacts of identity

Because we live in a society that is built upon acquisition and consumption, components of identity are frequently reflected in the commercial objects of our physical environment. We tend to leave a visible trail of who we are for others to notice, whether it's in our fashions, our possessions, or our living spaces. Messages about identity pervade everyday public space as well. If you look closely enough, you will notice that we are surrounded by visual images of gender, racial, ethnic, class, and sexual identity, even in those objects that are designed to symbolize other things.

For this exercise, you will go on a sort of sociological treasure hunt. Your task is to walk around your campus and, if possible, the surrounding community noting and describing the consumer products, public objects, and other visual artifacts that present or reinforce images of race, ethnicity, religion, gender, sexuality, or social class. Some might be blatant (for instance, a store that sells T-shirts with "Black is Beautiful" or "Gay Pride" emblazoned on them). But others may be much subtler (for instance, the assumption of heterosexual romance that underlies advertisements for wedding rings or the gender assumptions behind detergent advertisements depicting women as the ones who do household laundry). The experience would work best if you use a camera—preferably a digital one so photos can be seen immediately—to record the images you discover. Because this assignment is meant to focus your attention on the everyday objects of material culture, avoid photographing other people. If possible, visit areas that you know very well. One of the important features of the gender, class, race, and sexual messages that are expressed or assumed in cultural objects is that they become so commonplace that we rarely notice they're there.

For each of the images you've collected, describe what you think it symbolizes about race, class, gender, or sexuality (or some combination of these identifiers). Do these images tend to support stereotypical conceptions? Are they designed to evoke feelings of pride or shame? Are they meant for group members or non-group members? At a societal level, why are these messages important? What influence do you think such images have on people's attitudes, perceptions, and behaviors?

CHAPTER **3**

Portraying Difference
Race, Class, Gender, and Sexuality in Language and the Media

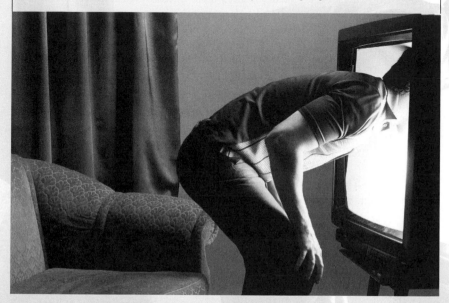

've spent the last 15 years or so living and teaching in a small town in rural west central Indiana. It's not a very diverse community, and it's in a fairly poor county. But living in a small town does have its advantages. It's relatively safe. Things are close by. The cost of living is manageable. This town is probably no different from the thousands of other small towns that dot the American countryside.

Because I had lived in large urban centers most of my life, the lethargic pace of life and the howdy-neighbor demeanor of the residents took some getting used to initially. The first time a stranger asked me, "Wasn't that you I saw running out on Albin Pond Road last Thursday at 7:45 in the morning with a blue windbreaker on?" I was taken aback. But by the 10th time you hear comments like that, it's not so creepy anymore. So I

71

should have been prepared when, on a mid-December shopping trip to the local supermarket not long after we'd moved to town, a smiling checker with a green and red felt elf hat leaned over the cash register, lowered her glasses, and asked my then-three-year-old son: "So, what are you going to ask Santa to bring you for Christmas?"

Now, you wouldn't think that such a friendly question during the holiday season would be particularly bothersome. From Thanksgiving to late December, such questions from retail employees to customers' children are as commonplace as flashy Christmas lights, piped-in renditions of "Jingle Bell Rock," and package-laden shoppers trudging through department stores. For a month every year, "Merry Christmas and Happy New Year!" temporarily replaces "Good-bye!" "Come back real soon!" or "Have a nice day!" as the courteous farewell of choice.

But I'm a sociologist and I tend to pick things apart, looking for deeper meaning. So let's take a closer look at my friendly checker's innocent but powerfully presumptuous question:

- The *asking for* part. First, she assumed that my son requests specific gifts on holidays. In some families, where children are taught to be appreciative of any gift, such a blatant show of materialism might be frowned upon. You know, "it's better to give than to receive" and all that.

- The *Santa* part. Second, she assumed that my son not only knew who Santa Claus is (so much so that she only had to use his first name in her question) but that he also knew what Santa is: the gatekeeper of goodies who breaks into people's homes once a year to bring them stuff. I know of many parents who struggle to dispel the myth of Santa Claus from their children's minds at very early ages.

- The *Christmas* part. Finally, the presumption that was the most obvious—but also the most disquieting—was simply that my son celebrated Christmas. In my family, we don't, in fact, celebrate Christmas. Although my children have a mixed religious/ethnic heritage and we frequently spend Christmas Day with Christian relatives, we've never had a tree, sung carols around the fireplace, or hung colorful lights in our house.

Even at age three, my son had seen enough TV commercials to know that Christmas had something to do with gifts and that Santa Claus was involved somehow. But beyond that, he was a little short on the specifics.

I knew that his puzzled look and awkward silence when the checker asked her question weren't going to cut it. So I had to quickly decide if I would correct her mistake or just smile, nod, and say something like, "Well, he hasn't asked for anything *yet*, but I'm sure he'll think of something. You know kids. And a Merry Christmas to you too." I opted for the latter strategy.

When I got home, I seethed. Mostly I was mad at myself for not calling out the checker's mistake. As a sociologist interested in the role that language plays in constructing and reflecting social reality, I understood that even small talk has deeper implications. Even though Christmas hasn't been a strictly religious holiday for some time, routine questions about Santa reflect the assumption that one is or should be Christian. Because we apparently didn't seem religiously "exotic" in any way to the checker, she didn't even think to ask, "Little boy, do you celebrate Christmas?" before proceeding to her Santa question.

The importance of language in creating and reinforcing perceptions of difference often lies more in what's not said than in what is. The fact that she didn't feel the necessity to ask him if he celebrated Christmas showed that Christianity—like whiteness or maleness or heterosexuality or middle-class status—has the privilege in everyday discourse not to be named. This privilege is not only found in small rural towns. It pervades society.

In this chapter, I will explore the cultural expression of images of difference. How are social differences—and ultimately, inequalities—portrayed in everyday communication? To answer this question, I will look first at the powerful role of language in highlighting identity and shaping social reality. I will then examine the equally powerful role of information and entertainment media in creating and reinforcing culturally dominant images of race, class, gender, and sexuality.

SYMBOLS AND LANGUAGE

We live in a social world in which our everyday interactions are mediated through symbols. A **symbol** is something used to represent or stand for something else (Charon, 1998). It can be a physical object (like an engagement ring standing for betrothal), a characteristic or property of objects (like a pink triangle standing for the gay community), a gesture (like a thumb pointed up standing for "everything's ok"), or a word (like the letters *d-o-g* standing for a particular type of household pet).

Symbols are powerful social constructions. They are created, modified, and used by people through their interactions with others. We concoct them and come to agree on what they should stand for. Our lives depend on such agreement. Imagine how chaotic automobile travel would be, for example, if we didn't all agree that green stands for "go" and red stands for "stop."

Symbols don't bear any necessary connection to nature. They're rather arbitrary human creations. There's nothing in the natural properties of "greenness" that automatically determines that it stands for "go." We could have decided long ago that purple polka dots mean "go". It wouldn't have mattered as long as we all learned and understood this symbol.

Even though symbols are arbitrary, they can evoke powerful emotional responses. All Americans know, for example, that a piece of cloth with red and white horizontal stripes and a blue square in the upper left corner containing 50 white stars symbolizes our nation. There's nothing particularly precious about the physical properties of the cloth itself. It's not as if it's woven of gold or platinum threads. It is simply a piece of cloth. An American flag can even be made out of paper or plastic. The value of this object comes from its symbolism, not from its material characteristics. When most Americans see the flag, they don't see the physical object; they see only the symbol. They respond to it as if it were the nation it represents. They may pledge their allegiance to it, treat it with ritualized respect, cry when it's raised after an Olympic victory, respond with anger when it is mistreated, and even risk their lives on the battlefield to protect it.

Not surprisingly, although symbols can evoke feelings of solidarity and unity, they can also be used to separate, intimidate, and evoke hostility. Take, for instance, a different piece of cloth: the Confederate battle flag. To some, it is a proud symbol of Southern heritage. To others, though, it is a painful reminder of slavery and segregation, and it has been appropriated by racist hate groups like the Ku Klux Klan. According to the Southern Poverty Law Center, more than 500 extremist groups use the Confederate battle flag as one of their symbols (cited in Brunner, 2004). In the past decade or so, controversies have arisen over the policy in some Southern states of flying the Confederate battle flag along with the U.S. and state flags over their statehouses. In 1993, three African American lawmakers in Alabama won a lawsuit that forced the governor to stop flying the Confederate battle flag over the capitol dome. In 1996, a white Kentucky teenager was killed for having a Confederate flag flying from his pickup. He, and the African American teenagers arrested for his murder, became symbols themselves in the cultural war across the South regarding the Confederate flag. To be sure, it is more than just a piece of colored cloth.

Perhaps the most important kind of symbol is language. Words— whether spoken or written—form the basis for virtually all our experiences. We communicate with words. We form relationships with words. We think to ourselves with words. We imagine our futures and record our pasts with words. Indeed, cultures and civilizations would be impossible without symbols, of which language is the most important type. Just like physical objects that function as symbols (such as flags), language can evoke powerful emotions, even in the absence of the thing to which the words refer. I had a friend in college who would become visibly shaken and depressed when he heard or read his ex-girlfriend's name. Indeed, by simply vocalizing certain words and putting them together in meaningful sentences, I can, if so inclined, make you happy, sad, frightened, angry, or sick to your stomach.

In Chapter 2, you learned about the differences between essentialist and constructionist perspectives. To an essentialist, what we call something is irrelevant. What is important is the inherent reality, which transcends human judgments and labels. But to a constructionist, what we choose to call something or someone is a crucial component of everyday life because these labels simultaneously shape social reality and reflect it. The way we use words to define ourselves and others reveals broader cultural values and inequalities and also perpetuates them.

SLURS

The most obvious way that words create and enforce social inequalities is through verbal slurs and affronts. Every conceivable racial, ethnic, national, religious, disability, body type, gender, or sexual group has at one time or another been subject to its own set of derogatory terms. About 1,200 ethnic-slur names alone have appeared in scholarly annals that record the existence of these words in the English language over time (Allen, 1990). In class- and fashion-conscious British society, for example, non-educated, ill-mannered suburban delinquents with poor taste in clothing have recently become a popular target of linguistic ridicule. As their cultural undesirability has grown, so too have the number of slurs applied to them:

> Scots call them *neds* . . . , while Liverpudlians prefer *scallies* . . . ;
> *Kev* is common around London. . . . Other terms recorded from

various parts of the country are *janners* (from Plymouth), *smicks, spides, moakes,* and *steeks* (all from Belfast), plus *bazzas, scuff-heads, stigs, skangers, yarcos,* and *kappa slappers.* . . . The term that has become especially widely known . . . , at least in southern England, is . . . *chav.* (Quinion, 2004, p. 1)

Even if we don't use them, most of us learn slurs at fairly young ages, and we quickly come to understand the kinds of strong feelings that both motivate their usage and determine recipients' responses to them. The old playground retort to teasing, "Sticks and stones may break my bones, but names can never hurt me," sounds like a positive and comforting position to take in the abstract, but it provides little solace in actual confrontations. The power of slurs stems from the realization that they are not simply personal insults. They always reflect broader cultural and political themes.

Often slurs become more pejorative when they are applied to people who are not even members of the group identified by the slur. Any male high school coach or military drill sergeant knows that the best way to whip his men into an aggressive frenzy is to call them *girls.* Likewise, among heterosexual adolescents, homophobic name calling (*queer, fag, dyke*) is one of the most common modes of bullying and coercion in school (Thurlow, 2001).

The damaging effect of some offensive slurs is amplified when applied to non-members. Take the word *bitch.* Originally a non-insulting noun meaning female dog, *bitch* eventually came to apply to a malicious, spiteful, and domineering woman. It eventually expanded past its ties to femaleness and became a verb—meaning to complain or grouse about something. Later on, it acquired meaning as a term for any subordinate, male or female (as in "You're my *bitch*"). And when combined with the word *slap,* it became a street reference for a manner of hitting someone into submission. In some circles, *bitch* is now used almost neutrally as a synonym for a female partner, and it is even embraced by some women as empowering (for example, popular T-shirts for young women that say "100% American Bitch"). It's even used as an attempt to be cute, as when groups of female knitters call themselves "Stitch 'n Bitch." Nevertheless, it can be doubly insulting when used as an epithet against men (You're acting like a little *bitch*!"). Not only is their character being demeaned, but their masculinity is as well.

The meanings of slurs change as society changes. Negative ethnoracial terms, for instance, can evolve over time both in their connotations and in the context in which they're used (Allen, 1990). Words may become more derogatory or less derogatory as the status of a particular group changes. The words *Negro* and *colored*, for example, were once common references used for and by African Americans. In time, the terms became pejorative and a variety of others rose to take their place—Black, Afro-American, African American.

Interestingly, though, a sense of group identity can sometimes be derived from the retention of derogatory terms. For instance, in the 1960s and 1970s, Americans of Mexican descent embraced the term *Chicano/a*— at the time a disparaging term implying lower-class status—and turned it into a symbol of pride and a rejection of ethnic assimilation (Martinez, 1998). One of the most powerful anti-discrimination organizations in the United States, the National Association for the Advancement of Colored People (NAACP), retains the word *Colored* in its title both as a reminder of past oppression and as a symbol of its commitment to the advancement of all people of color. Similarly, other words, like *queer, redneck,* and *nigger,* have undergone a process of "inversion" whereby they have been in a sense repossessed by the groups that were originally targets of these hostile slurs. Today, they may be used either in a friendly fashion or as badges of honor or pride.

Of course, the desire to repossess such terms varies along generational lines, with older members of certain groups less inclined to embrace a derogatory label of the past. Young hip-hop artists defiantly claim their right to use the word *nigger* whenever they wish. When pronounced differently—*nigga*—it becomes a term of endearment. For older people, however, who may recall a time when people fought and died over the word, it is likely to retain its sting (Waxman, 2004b).

Furthermore, any positive connotations derived from such terms are available only to those within the particular group in question. When uttered by outsiders, the words are still slurs. In 2004, a white public safety commissioner in Minnesota was forced to resign after admitting that he had used the word *nigger* once 12 years earlier in a court deposition (B. Williams, 2004). In a 2003 episode of the popular HBO sitcom *Curb Your Enthusiasm*, an African American hip-hop singer warmly refers to Larry David, the white, middle-aged star of the show, as "my nigger." The term is meant not as an insult but as a sign of clubby friendship. The painfully unhip Larry beams with pride at the reference because it marks him, at least temporarily, as a sort of "honorary" black person. Of course, the process of inversion is not applicable to terms that were never slurs in the first place. Larry's attempt to reciprocate by addressing his new African American friend as "my Caucasian" lacks the same in-group cachet and historical resonance. Indeed, the word *nigger,* perhaps like no other, has evoked such an enormous range of intense emotions (it's been called the "nuclear bomb" of racial epithets) that its historical usage is the subject of a book (Randall Kennedy's *Nigger: The Strange Career of a Troublesome Word* [2002]) and a recent documentary film (*The N Word*).

THE LANGUAGE OF DIFFERENCE

The importance of understanding the relationship among language, definitions of difference, and inequality goes beyond blatant insults and slurs. Shifts in the usage of language as well as in reference terms and connotations often parallel changes in the social stature of particular groups. Let's take a look now at some of the linguistic issues relevant to gender, race, ethnicity, and sexual orientation.

Gendered Language As you saw in Chapter 2, we live in a society built upon dichotomous distinctions between boys and girls, men and women, and masculine and feminine. Such distinctions are particularly noteworthy in the content and usage of language. Although English is not so grammatically gendered as, say, French or Spanish, gender pervades the language in obvious ways, such as the inclusive male pronoun *he,* the generic *man* in referring to both genders, and other common terms, such as *chairman, brotherhood, fellowship, founding fathers, man-made,* and *man-to-man defense.* Such linguistic expressions either render females invisible or make them appear as exceptions. Indeed, only when referring to inanimate objects is the female pronoun *she* used in such a manner, as when applied to cars and boats.

The priority of men in society and in the language is further reinforced when female versions of certain words are created as extensions of existing male terms, either by adding an *ess* or *ette* (for example, host*ess,* steward*ess,* major*ette*) or by using the words *lady, female,* or *woman* as noun modifiers (for example, *woman* lawyer, *female* engineer, the University of Tennessee *Lady* Volunteers). Even non-gendered words like *congressperson, waitperson,* or *spokesperson* imply that the individual being described is female. The fact that these titles are modifications of traditional male terms buttresses the cultural belief that the occupations in question are still men's domain, with women being exceptions to the rule. There's no need to call a man a *male* engineer or a *male* doctor, because the terms *doctor* and *engineer* already imply a male occupant.

Our gender-biased vocabulary also reflects and perpetuates underlying societal beliefs about the relative roles of men and women. To *mother* a child is to nurture, coddle, and protect that child; to *father* a child is simply to fertilize an egg. Similarly, a *governor* is an elected official who acts as the head of a state; a *governess* is one who cares for other people's children. In common usage, a *master* is one who rules over others; a *mistress* is a woman with whom a man has an extended extramarital affair (Richardson, 2004).

The movement for gender equality has always included battles over language. Clearly, there is greater sensitivity to the power of gender-biased terms than ever before. For instance, the term *Ms.*—invented 40 years ago to give women a term that does not reveal marital status, akin to the male *Mr.*—is now a common word in the language. Nowadays, most people consciously avoid gender-biased terms or are at least aware of broader implications of their usage. Many organizations routinely provide guidelines to their members on how to avoid gender-biased terminology.

Recently, some people have attempted to challenge the gendered nature of language in a more fundamental way. The term *transgendered* has gained in popularity among those who place themselves outside the conventional male/female dichotomy. It is purposely a somewhat ambiguous term that can refer to people who change their bodies to fit their gender (that is, "transsexuals"), who move across genders without altering their genitals, or who claim no gender at all (Kessler & McKenna, 2003).

Ethnoracial Language Language is especially volatile in the area of race and ethnicity. Here, words always reflect the relative cultural value of particular groups. Consider the connotations of the words *black* and *white*. Good guys in old western movies wore white hats, and the bad guys wore black hats. *White lies* are small, insignificant, and harmless. But *black magic* is dark and ominous. A *black eye* and a *black mark* are symbols of shame. To *blackball* is to ostracize or exclude socially. The *black sheep* of the family is an embarrassment to his or her relatives. Among the definitions of *black* in *Webster's New Universal Unabridged Dictionary* are "soiled and dirty," "thoroughly evil," "wicked," "gloomy," "hopeless," "marked by disaster," "hostile," and "disgraceful." The definition of *white*, in contrast, includes "fairness of complexion," "innocent," "favorable," "fortunate," "pure," and "spotless." The pervasive "goodness" of white and "badness" of black affects children at a very young age and can provide white children with a false sense of superiority (Moore, 1992).

Ethnoracial labels carry important political significance. For instance, *American Indians, tribal nations, Indian tribes, indigenous nations, Fourth World peoples, Native American peoples, Aboriginal peoples, First*

Nations, and *Native peoples* are all terms that are used to refer to indigenous people living in the continental United States (Wilkins, 2004). Officially, the government still uses the term *Indian.* What constitutes an "Indian tribe," though, is a matter of some contention. The extension of federal recognition by the U.S. government to a tribal nation is the formal acknowledgment of the tribe's legal sovereign status. The Department of the Interior's Bureau of Indian Affairs currently recognizes over 560 tribal governments (Wilkins, 2004). In the past, "recognition" simply meant an acknowledgment that a tribe existed. But by the 1870s, "recognition" began to be used in a more formal sense to describe a political relationship between a tribe and the U.S. government. In this sense, recognition means that a tribe is entitled to some privileges (for instance, documented tribal nations are exempt from most state tax laws) but also certain limitations and obligations (Wilkins, 2004). In the 1950s and 1960s, more than a hundred tribes and bands had their "recognized" status terminated, rendering their members ineligible for the benefits and exemptions they had enjoyed up to that point.

On an individual level, the determination of who is an "Indian" is also linguistically complicated. Congress uses a variety of criteria for determining whether one can be labeled an "Indian," including having a certain percentage of "Indian blood," belonging to a federally recognized indigenous community, living on or near a reservation, and being a descendant of a tribal member. The government uses something called a "certificate of degree of Indian blood" to determine whether or not a person is an "Indian" and therefore eligible for federal programs and services (Wilkins, 2004).

In addition to words that are direct references to particular groups, some words that seem not to be ethnoracial at all are, at times, used as code words for particular groups. For instance, in some circles, *New Yorker* is still used as a code word for Jews. Likewise, euphemisms such as *culturally deprived, economically disadvantaged, inner city, urban,* and *underprivileged* sound race-neutral, but they are commonly used to refer to poor black and Latino/a Americans. An examination of the 1995 Louisiana gubernatorial election revealed that the white candidate's discussion of the crime problems in particular *inner-city* neighborhoods (by which everyone knew he meant minority neighborhoods) subtly symbolized his racial attitudes, appealed to many white voters, and thereby contributed to his victory over a black candidate (Knuckey & Orey, 2000).

Sexual Language The politics of language is especially important for people whose sexual practices and identities fall outside what is considered normative sexuality. Terms used to refer to people outside the sexual mainstream have throughout history expressed moral, spiritual, legal, or psychiatric condemnation.

Self-labeling at the individual level can also be seen as a political act of sorts. The distinction, for example, between *gay* and *lesbian* emerged from concerns among women that the word *gay*, despite common usage, technically applied only to men. Within the past 10 years, the word *queer* first became a reclaimed epithet and since has become a term applied not only to homosexuals but to any marginalized sexual minority (Zwicky, 1997). As sexual categories expanded in the interests of inclusion, terms became unwieldy and were consequently shortened either to abbreviations (such as *lesbigay*) or to acronyms: LGB (lesbian, gay, and bisexual) or, more recently, GLBTQ (gay, lesbian, bisexual, transgendered, queer). Notice that the shifting terminology has nothing to do with essential changes in the nature and configuration of the group and everything to do with political pressures from subgroups.

As much as we come to think of self-labels as crucial monikers of identity, they are always context- and audience-specific. Whether someone refers to herself or himself as *gay, homosexual, bisexual,* or *queer* may very much depend on the person to whom that individual is speaking and the nature of the interaction:

> Even when I was . . . by inclination and behavior bisexual, I spoke of myself as gay in most public contexts, preferring to ally myself with those whose orientation was entirely toward members of their own sex rather than risk being seen as some sort of straight person. (Zwicky, 1997, p. 25)

On the other hand, labels for heterosexuals in our heteronormative society bear little of the political weight and delicacy that labels for sexual minorities bear. In fact, the term *straight* emerged not as a result of some movement of the "heterosexual community" to establish a collective identity and political presence, but as a catch-all antonym to all labels for people with a different sexual orientation (Murphy, 1997).

THE USE OF LANGUAGE TO CONCEAL VARIATION

While linguistic terminology—whether imposed from without or embraced from within—marks groups as different, it can also be used to gloss over relevant internal variation, thereby lumping together disparate groups with different languages, cultures, religious beliefs, and histories.

For instance, the 560 or so Native nations recognized by the government as "Indian" have widely divergent cultures, languages, and histories. "Latino/as" may speak the same language, but Mexicans, Puerto Ricans, Cubans, Nicaraguans, Venezuelans, and others have dramatically different histories, dialects, and immigration and citizenship experiences. People of Asian descent have rarely thought of themselves as a single racial group. Korean, Japanese, Chinese, and Filipino Americans may all be considered "Asian," but each group has its own language, religious beliefs, and history (Espiritu, 2004). To some, even the term "African American," which is widely considered to be a positive racial label, glosses over the thousands of ethnic groups, class interests, and indigenous religions that exist on the continent of Africa. And of course, terms like "White," "Caucasian," and "Anglo" also conceal enormous cultural, geographic, religious, and economic diversity.

Panethnic labels—general terms applied to diverse subgroups that are assumed to have something in common—have historically been used by people outside those groups for the sake of convenience. But they have the effect of perpetuating the notion that the dominant group matters most. I remember watching television coverage of the Olympic marathon race a few years back and being struck by the announcer's consistent reference to the runners in the lead pack as "the Africans." These runners hailed from such diverse countries as Tanzania, Ethiopia, and Kenya. Yet referring to them as "the Africans" reduced them to a single entity and gave the impression that since they were all "African," they were conspiring to compete against the non-African runners. Hence it didn't really matter which African country was victorious.

Panethnic labels aren't always negative. In fact, some people argue that political power can emerge from adopting a panethnic identity and creating a common heritage among diverse groups. In this sense, the imposition of the label "Asian," for instance, becomes a symbol of the collective experience of discrimination, intolerance, exploitation, and perhaps even violence at the hands of non-Asians in the larger society (Espiritu, 2004). A study of Chinese American and Korean American college students found that the shared experience of being stereotyped as "nerdy" and being made to feel like outsiders led most of them to seek comforting friendships with other Asian students, no matter what their specific ethnic heritage (Kibria, 2004).

Group identity and political power are also reflected in the tendency toward hyphenation, especially among ethnoracial minorities (Asian-American, Native-American, Mexican-American, Italian-American, and so on). The use of a hyphenated label is a function of a group's degree of or desire for **assimilation,** the process by which members of minority groups alter their ways to conform to those of the dominant culture. One of the fundamental goals of U.S. society has always been the ultimate absorption of groups into mainstream society. Yet the goal of a fully assimilated society has never been realized. Many people are forced to or choose to retain connections to their ethnic or racial heritage. Indeed, **multiculturalism,** unlike assimilation, emphasizes the importance of maintaining those cultural elements that give us variety and make us different from one another. For many groups, moving away from assimilation and toward multiculturalism means adopting a hyphenated ethnoracial identity. Some have argued, for instance, that the movement from "Negro" to "Black" and then to "African-American" as the racial label of choice marked a rejection of the idea of assimilation—symbolized by the middle-class "Negro" aspiring to assimilate into mainstream white culture—in favor of pride in the differences from mainstream culture (Spencer, 1994). But the notion of ethnic hyphenation doesn't mean that all ethnoracial qualities are valued equally (Alexander, 2001). For groups that are socially marginalized, subordinated, or repressed, it can be a stigmatizing reminder of difference.

THE DIFFERENCES OF LANGUAGE

Given the strong human desire to emphasize difference over similarity, it is not surprising that one of the chief interests of sociologists who study language is whether or not particular groups have their own distinct language, dialect, or vocabulary. Certainly, we can use a person's accent to determine whether she or he is from Brooklyn, Chicago, or Atlanta. If certain groups are considered cultures unto themselves and maintaining identifiable boundaries between "us" and "them" is a key concern, then it would make sense that they too would have a unique way of communicating with fellow members—in addition to a unique lifestyle and unique norms and values. For instance, do you think you could tell the difference between someone defined as "upper class" and someone defined as "working class" simply by listening to their accents and vocabularies?

One object of this sort of sociological inquiry has been whether or not certain language patterns are common to historically disadvantaged groups. For example, over 60 years ago, the folklorist Gershon Legman (1941) published a glossary of terms that he purported were used exclusively by male homosexuals. Some words disappeared; others, like *drag* and *straight*, have entered the mainstream vocabulary. In the 1960s, sociologist Rose Giallombardo (1966) published a glossary of close to 300 terms used by lesbians in prison. In it, she describes an elaborate system of named kin and sexual relationships among the inmates.

Today, linguists talk about a "code," known variously by such terms as "gayspeak," "lgb talk," "queerspeak," "gay English," and "lavender language" (Kulick, 2000). One author describes communication patterns among homosexuals as the "language of risk," meaning that because of continuing fears about condemnation or discrimination, closeted gays and lesbians often develop ways of speaking that camouflage their identities (Leap, 1996). For example, they may use genderless pronouns to describe a partner or strategically maintain silence on certain issues to allow people to maintain default assumptions about heterosexuality. However, others (for example, Queen, 1997), argue that gay men and lesbians do not represent a single unified group and therefore cannot have a common language.

Gender differences in language use have occupied even more scholarly attention. In the 1990s, Deborah Tannen (1990) popularized the idea that men and women have dramatically different linguistic styles. She likened male-female differences in conversation and the use of language to cultural differences. She went so far as to argue that women and men frequently experience miscommunication with one another on a par with the sorts of miscommunications that can sometimes hinder interactions between people of different ethnic groups or nationalities.

But some researchers (for example, Kollock, Blumstein, & Schwartz, 1985) argue that certain gender-typed conversational behaviors actually reflect power differences rather than gender differences. Linguistic tendencies typically attributed to men—like interrupting, being nonresponsive, and controlling topics of conversation—are best understood not as cultural differences between men and women but as a consequence of power imbalances between men and women. Each of these tactics is a way of preventing others from contributing to the conversation. To be silenced in such a way is to be rendered invisible (Lakoff, 1995). Similarly, the common belief that women's speech tends to be more emotionally expressive than men's reflects the deeper cultural belief that women are the ones who are supposed to tend to relationships (Lakoff, 1973). Unfortunately, one of the consequences of disclosing a great deal of information about yourself or openly showing your emotions is that it makes you less powerful (P. M. Blau, 1964). By linguistically overexposing themselves—something they are taught to do as a way to build and tend to relationships—women perpetuate the preexisting power differences between them and men.

Some ethnoracial groups, of course, do actually speak a different language. The issue for them is not so much whether their unique language exists but where and when it should be spoken. People for whom English is a second language have historically faced pressure within the larger society to abandon their native tongue. A Mexican American woman recalls such pressure from her childhood:

> I remember being caught speaking Spanish at recess—that was good for three licks on the knuckles with a sharp ruler. I remember being sent to the corner of the classroom for "talking back" to the Anglo teacher when all I was trying to do was tell her how to pronounce my name. "If you want to be American, speak 'American.' If you don't like it, go back to Mexico where you belong." (Anzaldúa, 2003, p. 450)

To some people, the desire on the part of certain groups to retain their native languages poses a threat to American society. According to U.S. English, Inc. (2004), a law declaring English as our official national language—something that this organization supports—would require that official government business at all levels be conducted solely in English. This includes all public documents, records, legislation, and regulations, as well as hearings, official ceremonies, and public meetings. Twenty-seven states currently have official English-only laws on the books.

At an even more fundamental level is the question of what constitutes a language. In 1996, the Oakland, California, School Board set off a nationwide controversy when it proposed that Ebonics (a dialect of American English closely related to southern forms of black speech) be recognized as the primary language of African American students. The move was based on the assertion that the continued use of black vernacular accounts for the high proportion of Blacks in remedial education and high rates of black unemployment (Williams, 1997). The board encouraged teachers to familiarize themselves with Ebonics so they could communicate better with their black students. Supporters felt that African American children have a right to be taught in their "primary language." Opponents—many of whom were black themselves—claimed that the policy would merely elevate slang to the status of a language, thereby damaging the reputation of the school district and hurting African American students in the long run.

THE BATTLE OVER "POLITICAL CORRECTNESS"

Few terms in the English language are as polarizing as "political correctness." It is commonly used to refer to efforts to rectify, through the use of language, real or alleged discrimination. Sometimes, "political correctness" takes the form of euphemistic terms for members of particular ethnic, racial, religious, gender, sexual, and ability groups. Other times, it is a more grammatical matter, as in the avoidance of exclusive language (for instance, using terms like "*man*kind," "fresh*men*," or "chair*man*" to refer to people of all sexes). In addition, it might also be exhibited in the refusal to point out that particular groups are overrepresented in certain undesirable activities, such as crime and unemployment ("Political correctness," 2004).

Since language is the vehicle through which groups are separated, denigrated, and stratified, so-called political correctness actually represents an attempt to give voice to or increase the visibility of groups that have been marginalized in society. Consider the flare-up over the use of Native American names and images as sports mascots (Braves, Chiefs, Indians, Redmen, Blackhawks, Warriors, Fighting Sioux, Redskins, Aztecs, and so on). Some people argue that such names and mascots flatter indigenous people because they emphasize strength and bravery. They claim that the use of these terms is no different than the use of other ethnically inspired team names—Vikings, Fighting Irish, Celtics—and therefore shouldn't be interpreted as derogatory (Eitzen & Baca Zinn, 2003). Nonetheless, caricatures of Native Americans that would not be tolerated if they portrayed other racial or ethnic groups are institutionalized in school, university, and professional sport teams and then distributed by local, national, and global media outlets (Strong, 2004). As one author put it:

> Can you imagine if they called them the Washington Jews and the team mascot was a rabbi leading them in [the song] "Hava Nagila," fans in the stands wearing yarmulkes and waving little sponge torahs? (quoted in Eitzen & Baca Zinn, 2003, p. 462)

Does such imagery act as an obstacle to equal cultural recognition and full societal participation, or is it trivial and inconsequential because it's "just a name"? The words "Indian" or "Chief" or "Seminole" or "Ute" aren't necessarily insulting or derogatory. But when the words are accompanied by simplistic and stereotypical symbols of the group's culture—rubber tomahawks, feather headdresses, war paint, or activities such as dances and chants—used in the context of a sporting event, their meaning becomes trivialized. Furthermore, "honoring" these groups by emphasizing aggression and violence overshadows other cultural features, such as cooperative social relations, democratic tribal structures, and environmental sensitivity and protection.

Critics often frame the movement to eliminate the insensitive use of minority groups' names as a misguided attempt to sanitize the language. They typically point, mockingly and derisively, to such awkward alterations as "person with mobility impairment" instead of "cripple," "intellectually challenged" instead of "mentally retarded," and "vertically challenged" instead of "short."

Concern with the potentially harmful impact of language is most visible these days on some college campuses that have enacted "speech zone" policies, e-mail policies, or "diversity statements" that ban things like "offensive or uncivil speech," "intolerant expression," or "hostile viewpoints" (Silverglate & Lukianoff, 2003). Such policies typically attempt to prevent and, if need be, punish speech that directly denigrates or threatens members of certain groups or creates a "hostile environment." My university, for example, prohibits the inappropriate treatment of members of the campus community based on race, ethnicity, sex, religion, sexual orientation, veteran status, gender identity, or disability. Inappropriate treatment could mean slurs, epithets, abusive language, derogatory nicknames, taunts about cultural observances, or threatening or offensive e-mail or voice-mail messages.

An organization called the Foundation for Individual Rights in Education is committed to abolishing all such "speech" codes on college campuses. To this and other similar organizations, any attempt to limit the speech of anyone, no matter how offensive, is an attack on the Bill of Rights and the doctrine of free speech, which is traditionally a core value in universities. Their web site states:

> At almost every college and university, students deemed members of "historically oppressed groups"—above all, women, Blacks, gays, and Hispanics—are informed during orientations that their campuses are teeming with illegal or intolerable violations of their "right" not to be offended, as if these individuals were not capable of living with freedom and the values of the Bill of Rights. At almost every college and university, students are presented with long lists of offices to which they should submit charges of such verbal "harassment," with promises of "victim support," "confidentiality," and "understanding" when they file such

complaints. What an astonishing expectation to give to students: the belief that, if they belong to a protected category, they have the right to four years of never being offended. (Foundation for Individual Rights in Education, 2004, p. 1)

The debate over policies derived to reduce the stigmatizing and alienating consequences of particular forms of speech will not be settled here. No one wants to have all their thoughts and utterances tightly scrutinized. The free exchange of ideas does require that everyone be willing to at least hear what others have to say, no matter how distasteful. Some well-meaning professors say they're reluctant to raise controversial issues or use humor in their classes for fear of being tagged as "racist," "sexist," or "homophobic."

In the end, though, the issue of "political correctness" is less about the appropriate use of particular words than it is about the socially constructed nature of reality and the relationship between language and social inequality. It pits the rights of people to speak their minds no matter what against the rights of people who are the direct or indirect targets of such remarks. It's not a simple issue. However, when only the most extreme examples are presented to the public under the blanket accusation of "political incorrectness," actual instances of assaultive speech, threatening e-mails, degrading images, and verbal harassment directed toward marginalized groups are belittled. Those who are subjected to such verbal aggression experience real consequences, ranging from fear, humiliation, and discouragement to difficulty breathing, nightmares, hypertension, and, in rare cases, suicide (Matsuda, 1993). When some students must operate under the burden of painful or exclusionary symbols or words, their opportunities to learn and their ability to compete fairly are constrained.

MEDIA REPRESENTATIONS OF DIFFERENCE

As you're well aware, people develop and communicate images of and attitudes toward race, class, gender, and sexuality through language and their interactions with others. But messages of difference don't emerge solely from interpersonal conversations. One of the chief sources of information about difference is the media. Boundaries between "us" and "them" are often constructed or reinforced through literature, television, film, and video games.

Although whiteness, maleness, heterosexuality, and middle-class status pervade television and film, they are rarely the subject of specific attention. One of the luxuries of taken-for-grantedness is that these categories don't require positive media depictions for their advantaged positions in society to be reinforced. So the media portrayals that have received the most scholarly attention are of groups typically defined as "other": people of color, homosexuals, women, and, to a lesser degree, the lower and working classes. These depictions are often one-dimensional. For example, media portrayals of ethnoracial minorities have historically focused on working-class and poor people.

GENDER IN THE MEDIA

By and large, the media—especially the electronic media—are dominated by men. On television, all major network evening news anchors are white men, as are the most popular late-night talk-show hosts. In key behind-the-scenes roles like creators, producers, directors, writers, editors, and directors of photography, men outnumber women four to one. This percentage has remained virtually unchanged over the past four years (Media Report to Women, 2003). In 2004, Sofia Coppola became the first American woman to be nominated for Best Director at the Academy Awards and the first woman of any nationality to actually win. Such an imbalance in productive and creative control means that what we see in theaters and on television is likely to reflect men's perspectives.

The media are an important purveyor of information about gender. They promote stereotypes of masculinity and femininity, not only by choosing which kinds of men and women to portray but also by choosing which kinds of stories and programs to run. For example, television networks like Lifetime, Oxygen, and WE (Women's Entertainment) openly and proudly devote their programming to women and women's "issues." In theaters, so-called women's movies are designed to appeal to traditionally female interests, such as deep communication, emotional bonding, intimate relationships, and motherhood. On the other hand, television networks for men, such as the Men's Channel and Spike TV, offer shows such as *Hunting Adventure, Outdoor Quest, Tough Truckin', Horsepower TV,* and *Paintball 2xtremes*. And you can bet that films identified as "men's movies" will contain little emotional introspection and plenty of gore, fast cars, and explosions.

Children's Exposure to Gender in the Media Media representations of gender reach children very early in their lives. Children's books, for instance, teach youngsters what is expected of girls or boys in their culture. In the early 1970s, Lenore Weitzman and her colleagues studied the portrayal of gender in popular U.S. preschool books (Weitzman, Eifler, Hodada, & Ross, 1972). They found that boys played a more significant role in the stories than girls by a ratio of 11 to 1. Boys were more likely to be portrayed in adventurous pursuits or activities that required independence and strength; girls were likely to be confined to indoor activities and portrayed as passive and dependent. Despite some improvement in the number and characterization of female characters (Williams, Vernon, Williams, & Malecha, 1987), gender stereotypes remain prevalent in children's books (Peterson & Lach, 1990). Furthermore, in spite of publishers' guidelines, elementary school reading textbooks still primarily portray males as aggressive, argumentative, and competitive (Evans & Davies, 2000). In fact, even children's books that are characterized as "nonsexist" portray gender-stereotypical personalities, domestic chores, and leisure activities. What's particularly striking about "nonsexist" books is that their response to gender inequality usually involves female characters taking on characteristics and roles typically associated with males. They rarely, if ever, portray male characters adopting female traits (Diekman & Murnen, 2004).

Media images of males and females have a strong influence on children's perceptions and behaviors (Good, Porter, & Dillon, 2002). For instance, children who watch a lot of television are more likely to hold stereotypical attitudes toward gender, exhibit gender-stereotyped characteristics, and engage in gender-stereotyped activities than are children who watch little television (M. Morgan, 1987; Signorielli, 1990). In one study, girls who did not have stereotypical conceptions of gender to begin with showed a significant increase in such attitudes after two years of heavy television watching (M. Morgan, 1982).

These effects are not surprising given the programming that children encounter. A study of 41 Saturday morning cartoons found that male characters are more likely than female characters to occupy leadership roles, act aggressively, give guidance to or come to the rescue of others, express opinions, ask questions, and achieve their goals. In addition, males are more likely to be portrayed in some kind of recognizable occupation, whereas females are more likely to be cast in the role of caregiver (Thompson & Zerbinos, 1995).

As video games have grown in popularity, they've attracted increasing attention for their demeaning portrayal of women. Most video games are designed by males for other males. Female characters are often provocatively sexual, scantily clad, and voluptuous. The developers of one game, *BMX XXX*, were forced to add clothing to their topless female riders after major retailers refused to carry the game. Many games portray female characters as prostitutes and strippers, who are frequent targets of violence at the hands of psychopathic male characters. In *Duke Nukem 3D*, the player is awarded bonus points for shooting naked, bound prostitutes and strippers who plead "Kill me!" In *Grand Theft Auto 3*, players can beat prostitutes to death with baseball bats after having sex with them (Media Awareness Network, 2005). The gender messages in such games may have a detrimental effect both on boys' attitudes toward girls and women and on their conceptions of appropriate male behavior.

Television commercials perpetuate powerful stereotypes as well. In an analysis of over 500 U.S. and Australian commercials targeting children, boys were more likely than girls to be depicted in dominant and active roles (Browne, 1998). Girls tended to be portrayed as shy, giggly, and passive. The differences were less pronounced in Australia, however, which has a more active movement to counter gender stereotypes in the media. Such images are not trivial, given that U.S. children watch over 20,000 TV commercials a year.

Gender stereotypes can be found in prime-time commercials as well. One study of 944 characters in commercials found that men are more likely than women to be employed, while women are more likely than men to be shown as spouses or parents. Commercials for a popular brand of peanut butter still contain the tag line "Choosy mothers choose Jif," reinforcing the expectation that mothers are the primary caretakers of their children. In addition, women are more likely than men to appear in commercials for products used in the home; men are more likely than women to advertise products used outdoors (Kaufman, 1999).

Media-Reinforced Femininity Even the most casual glimpse at the portrayal of modern women in U.S. advertising, fashion, television, music videos, video games, and films reveals a dual stereotype (Sidel, 1990). On the one hand, we see images of the successful woman of the 21st century: the perfect wife and mother, the triumphant career woman. Like the high-powered female politicians, lawyers, and doctors we're likely to see on television these days, she is outgoing, bright, attractive, and assertive.

At the same time, though, we continue to see the stereotypical image of the "exhibited" woman: the seductive sex object displayed in beer commercials, magazine advertisements, video games, prime-time sitcoms, and soap operas. Perhaps the most memorable media event of 2004 was the exposure of Janet Jackson's breast during halftime of the Super Bowl, although many viewers may have missed it because they had tuned into the "Lingerie Bowl" on pay-per-view TV—a halftime "game" between teams of underdressed actresses and models. The media coverage of female athletes also tends to focus on physical appearance and sexual attractiveness (Shugart, 2003). The image of soccer player Brandi Chastain peeling off her jersey after making the penalty kick that won the United States the 1999 World Cup got more media attention than the team's victory itself. Anna Kournikova became the highest-earning player in women's tennis in the late 1990s without ever having won a major tournament. According to a *Sports Illustrated* story on her, "a hot body can count as much as a good backhand" (quoted in Dowd, 2000, p. 19).

More generally, television continues to present stereotypes that show women as shallow, vain, and materialistic characters whose looks overshadow all else. Popular reality TV shows, like *Extreme Makeover* and *The Swan*, perpetuate the belief that without beauty (attainable through plastic surgery), women are doomed to a life of heartache and failure. Dating-themed shows like *Average Joe* and *The Bachelor* go one step further, reinforcing the belief that sexual charm and physical attractiveness are lures that women can use to attract men. The "sex object" is the most dangerous media image of all because conventional physical beauty is a woman's only attribute: "Women are constantly exhorted to emulate this ideal, to feel ashamed and guilty if they fail, and to feel that their desirability and lovability are contingent upon physical perfection" (Kilbourne, 1992, p. 349).

Aside from the occasional powerful female character—like Xena the Warrior Princess or Sydney Bristow on the popular TV show *Alias*—the portrayal of women on prime-time television also remains rather traditional and stereotypical. Despite the fact that women make up a majority of the population, most characters on prime-time television are male (D. Smith, 1997). Although fewer women are portrayed as housewives than in the past, men are still more likely than women to be shown working outside the home (41% of male characters versus 28% of female characters). Women express emotions much more easily and are significantly more likely than men to use sex and charm to get what they want. An analysis of 18 prime-time television situation comedies found that female characters are significantly more likely than male characters to receive derogatory comments about their appearance from other characters. These comments are typically reinforced by audience laughter (Fouts & Burggraf, 2000).

Unfortunately, the image of beauty presented by the exhibited woman is artificial and largely unattainable. For instance, researchers at Johns Hopkins University compiled data on the heights and weights of Miss America pageant winners between 1922 and 1999. They found that the weights of these women have been steadily decreasing, reaffirming the cultural value of thinness (Rubinstein & Caballero, 2000). Recent winners have had a height-to-weight ratio that places them in a range of what the World Health Organization defines as "undernourished."

It's not surprising that women internalize these media messages. A study of Canadian girls between 10 and 14 found that 30% of them were currently trying to lose weight (McVey, Tweed, & Blackmore, 2004). And perhaps as many as two-thirds of all American high school girls are either on a diet or planning to start one (cited in Thomsen, Weber, & Brown, 2002). Dieting has become so common among young women that some researchers now believe that what was once considered disordered eating behavior is now considered "normal" adolescent eating. Ultra-thin, media-driven standards of beauty continue to be an ideal that many young women are willing to starve themselves to attain. By conservative estimates, 1 in 10 young U.S. women today has a serious eating disorder (National Institute of Mental Health, 2001).

Media-Reinforced Masculinity The overall portrayal of men in film and on television is much harder to pinpoint and has been the topic of considerably less research than the portrayal of women. Because of men's advantaged position in society, they needn't be named. When they are named, accurate portrayals of masculinity are virtually nonexistent. Instead, we're likely to find highly traditional stereotypes or negative portrayals in the form of gross caricatures. For decades, the quintessential Hollywood leading man was square-jawed, rugged, not particularly chatty, violent when necessary, and unemotional (think of Keanu Reeves, Vin Diesel, and Arnold Schwarzenegger). That type hasn't disappeared completely. But today it exists side by side with a new generation of leading men who are considerably more thoughtful, sensitive, and emotionally available (for instance, Tobey Maguire, Orlando Bloom, Jake Gyllenhaal) (Waxman, 2004a).

The traditional tough guy image has also given way to a less complimentary image: that of men as dumb and clueless. But far from being demeaning and destructive, these images have the luxury of being harmlessly humorous. Making fun of masculinity—like making fun of heterosexuality or of white people—bears little, if any, of the cultural and historical weight that accompanies stereotypical portrayals of women and other disadvantaged groups. It is not uncommon for men in prime-time comedies to be depicted as rude, crude, sex-crazed, sexist, childish, egotistical, and stupid. For instance, the popular "Joey" character on the now-defunct series *Friends* was a dim-witted womanizer who had trouble pronouncing multisyllabic words and ate steak with his fingers. But such a character faced little risk of being interpreted as a representative of all men. His dullness and bravado were sweet. We could laugh at Joey, knowing full well that he was a caricature. "As long as men are in power, they are the one group that television can ridicule without fear of reprisal" (Gates, 2000, p. 35).

Another case in point is the popular Comedy Central program *The Man Show*. This show purposely elevates stereotypical masculinity to laughable heights. Each week, the two hosts tutor a studio audience of predominantly young men on what "real men" should think and do. These lessons inevitably merge with stereotypically degrading depictions of women—such as buxom bikini-clad women called "Juggies" jumping on trampolines. The gender messages are so raunchy and juvenile, though, that they seem cartoonish, unreal, and, in the minds of producers, harmless. Indeed, it's hard to tell whether stereotypical masculinity is being lampooned or celebrated.

RACE AND ETHNICITY IN THE MEDIA

As you saw in Chapter 2, race is a social construction. Hence, it's not surprising that one of the most influential sources of information about race in this society is the media. Nor should it be surprising that the dominant white culture prevails and is taken for granted. The films and shows and other entertainment products they create tend to reflect white sensibilities and assumptions. Ethnoracial minorities tend to be underrepresented in television, film, popular magazines, and advertising (Croteau & Hoynes, 2000).

Yet minority ethnoracial images are immensely popular with young people around the world. For instance, youth in Europe and Asia can be seen trying to emulate rap and hip-hop fashion, music, and demeanor. Latino/a musicians enjoy tremendous crossover appeal. Because of their global reach, American media images of African American and Latino/a pop culture have greatly increased the visibility of these ethnoracial groups worldwide.

In the early years of film and television, ethnoracial minorities were largely absent. Even black, Asian, Native American, and Latino/a characters were usually played by white actors. By the 1960s and 1970s, however, television programs began featuring more African Americans and, to a lesser extent, other ethnoracial groups (Croteau & Hoynes, 2000). Representation continued to increase throughout the 1980s and 1990s, but it has since leveled off or even dropped slightly. According to the Screen Actors Guild (2002), in 2001, 22% of all television and movie roles went to African American, Latino/a, Asian, or Native American performers, down from 23% in 2000. For Latino/as, the number of primary or recurring television roles dropped by a third (Children Now, 2001).

The number of prime-time, predominantly black television shows reached its peak in 1997, when there were 15 such series. Today there are only six. And all of these are comedies. No predominantly black dramatic series has ever succeeded on network television (Moss, 2001). A report by the Screen Actors Guild found that more than half of all black actors on prime-time television appear on all-black, or mostly black, comedy shows ("Limited black slots on TV," 2000).

Television viewership remains segregated along racial lines too. In 2003, the five most popular television shows among African American viewers were *Bernie Mac, The Parkers, One on One, Girlfriends,* and *My Wife and Kids* (Initiative Media North America, 2003). All of these shows had predominantly black casts. Among white viewers, these shows ranked 94th, 131st, 134th, 132nd, and 54th, respectively. *Friends,* the number one show among white viewers that year, ranked 91st in African American homes.

As in the case of gender, media images play a significant role in the creation and maintenance of ethnoracial stereotypes. Consider the biased images of certain ethnic groups that have historically been served up on television: the savage Indian, the Italian Mafioso, the fanatical Arab terrorist, and so on. Asians are frequently depicted as camera-wielding tourists, scholastic overachievers, or sinister warlords. Latino/as have historically been cast as "Latin lovers," "banditos," "greasers," or "lazy good-for-nothings" (Reyes & Rubie, 1994). Common media stereotypes often reflect the intersections of race, ethnicity, class, and gender, as in the depiction of poor, black women as "welfare queens," wealthy Jewish women as "princesses," and poor Latino men as drug pushers. Recent reality shows, like *The Apprentice, Survivor,* and *The Real World,* have begun portraying black female participants as arrogant, pushy, or overly aggressive.

Stereotypical depictions are not limited to the entertainment media. For instance, an analysis of a random sample of television news shows aired in Los Angeles and Orange Counties in California revealed that

Whites are more likely than African Americans and Latino/as to be portrayed on television news as victims of crime. Conversely, African Americans and Latino/as are more likely to be portrayed as lawbreakers than as crime victims (Dixon & Linz, 2000). Another study found that although people of color appear regularly in prime-time TV commercials, they usually appear as secondary characters. Furthermore, the nature of their depiction differs compared to that of Whites. Whites are more likely to appear in ads for upscale products, beauty products, and home products. People of color, in contrast, are more likely to appear in ads for low-cost, low-nutrition products (like fast foods and soft drinks) and in athletic or sports equipment ads (Henderson & Baldasty, 2003).

Most researchers of race and the media argue, though, that, in general, images of ethnoracial minorities have improved over time. When people of color did appear in early Hollywood films, the language of race was apparent in such images as the familiar servant/slave figure: dependable and loving in a simple childlike way, like the devoted "Mammy" character in such films as *Gone with the Wind* (Hall, 1995). Chinese servants and Indian sidekicks in old westerns could fall into this category as well. But while devoted and naive, the stereotypical servant/slave was also unpredictable and unreliable, susceptible to "turning nasty" at any moment. Another common early image was the clown. As an entertainer, the clown's job was to put on a show for others. While sometimes depicted as being physically graceful, the darker side of the clown image was that he or she need not be taken seriously.

Early television images didn't fare much better. Shows of the 1950s, like *Amos 'n Andy* and *The Beulah Show*, depicted Blacks as either lazy buffoons, opportunistic crooks, or happy, docile servants. But by the 1970s, *Sanford and Son, Good Times, What's Happening,* and the other so-called ghetto sitcoms were trying to represent African Americans more positively. They showed slums and housing projects as places where people could lead happy, loving, even humorous lives.

When U.S. society itself could not achieve social reform through civil rights, television solved the problem by inventing symbols of black success and racial harmony (Gates, 1992). Shows such as *Julia* or *I Spy* in the 1960s; *Roots* and *The Jeffersons* in the 1970s; *Benson, A Different World,* and *The Cosby Show* in the 1980s; *The Fresh Prince of Bel-Air, Family Matters,* and *Moesha* in the 1990s; and *Gideon's Crossing, Jamie Foxx, Bernie Mac, The Parkers, My Wife and Kids, Malcolm & Eddie,* and *Kevin Hill* in the 2000s seemingly overcame these harmful racial stereotypes by depicting Blacks as strong, smart, and successful.

In addition, popular shows with predominantly white casts, such as *CSI: Crime Scene Investigation, ER, Boston Public,* and *Law & Order,* began portraying successful black characters. Indeed, the number of multi-ethnic television series increased 59% between 2000 and 2002 (Freeman, 2002). These shows have played an unmistakable role in showing that Blacks and Whites often share the core values of U.S. culture.

Although the mainstream media have seemingly grown more sensitive to stereotypical images, controversial depictions continue to emerge. Critics have charged, for instance, that many of the recent portrayals of African Americans on television and in video games continue to reflect some of the negative stereotypes of the 1950s. Working-class and poor African Americans—especially men—still may be depicted as menaces to society, involved in such activities as crime, gang violence, drug use, homelessness, and general aimlessness (Gray, 1995).

SEXUALITY IN THE MEDIA

To the casual outside observer, it might appear that U.S. society is becoming "homosexualized." Consider the popularity of the makeover reality show *Queer Eye for the Straight Guy* (and its spinoff, *Queer Eye for the Straight Girl*). In each episode, a team of five gay men "dedicated to extolling the simple virtues of style, taste and class . . . transform a style-deficient and culture-deprived straight man" in five areas of his life: fashion, food and wine, interior design, grooming, and culture (Bravo.com, 2004). Recently, the *New York Times* ran a front-page article in its Styles section with the title "The Subtle Power of Lesbian Style." According to the author, as a result of increased visibility in film and on television, lesbians have become a powerful presence in fashion. The coolness is evident in clothes that are "hip and sexy tough; vulnerable and imposing" (Trebay, 2004, p. 9-1). Although homosexuality may have become somewhat trendy, the content of media depictions remains stereotypical— "effeminate" men and "butch" women.

Not surprisingly, when it comes to media depictions of sexual orientation, those that are most noteworthy are portrayals of gays and lesbians. One would be hard pressed to think of a movie or a TV show that explicitly emphasizes and purposely draws attention to representations of "heterosexual lifestyles" or "the heterosexual community." Instead, the plots of practically every movie and TV show routinely revolve around taken-for-granted heterosexuality in one form or another. As with other forms of power, those shows and films that do consciously call attention to heterosexuality often portray it in ways that are so excessive as to be harmless. For example, in virtually every teen-oriented film, youthful male heterosexuality is depicted for laughs as lustful, insatiable, and uncontrollable.

Although the depiction of openly gay characters has been intermittent, American television has featured a wide array of gay characters over the years ("American Television," 2004). Early on, such characters were depicted as unstable villains or suspects in crime shows (Hantzis & Lehr, 1994). In sitcoms, they were usually minor characters. In the 1970s, openly gay and bisexual characters began appearing on popular sitcoms like *All in the Family, The Mary Tyler Moore Show, Barney Miller,* and *Soap.* But more commonly, homosexuality was presented as an implied—and stigmatized—identity. A continuing theme on the popular 1970s show *Three's Company,* in which a man pretended to be gay in order to share an apartment with two women, was dialogue between the man, Jack Tripper, and his homophobic landlord that relied on references to Jack's purported gay tendencies and on epithets like "Tinkerbell."

When not depicted as stereotypically effeminate, gay characters were often presented as victims. The film and television portrayal of homosexuality in the late 1980s and early 1990s often went hand in hand with depictions of or thinly veiled political statements about HIV/AIDS (Gross, 1994). In 1993, the film *Philadelphia* won acclaim for its portrayal of the discrimination faced by a sympathetic lead character with AIDS, played by Tom Hanks. Indeed, the first television documentaries and movies that dealt with HIV/AIDS shaped the way the public perceived the disease and its victims. In so doing, the media helped foster the impression that HIV/AIDS was a "gay disease" (Netzhammer & Shamp, 1994).

The 1990s brought unprecedented openness regarding homosexuality, although most depictions of homosexual people were one-dimensional caricatures. In 1994, PBS aired the controversial gay-themed miniseries *Tales of the City,* which featured frank language, nudity, and sexual situations. In the mid-1990s, same-sex weddings appeared on shows like *Northern Exposure, Roseanne,* and *Friends.* The Carter Heywood character on the sitcom *Spin City* was one of the first regularly appearing "normal queers," a gay man who was not mincing and flamboyant ("American Television," 2004).

Perhaps the watershed moment for gays and lesbians on television was the April 1997 "coming out" of Ellen DeGeneres's character on her show, *Ellen.* After months of media speculation as to the actress's own sexual orientation, her character's coming out was met with praise from the gay and lesbian community. Ironically, much of the humor and appeal of this show up to this point derived from the subtle references and "Is she or isn't she?" atmosphere surrounding Ellen's character. Hence, after this monumental declaration, the show's popularity waned, and it was soon canceled.

In the 2000s, the number of gay-themed television shows (such as the popular *Will & Grace*) and openly gay characters on other shows is at an all-time high, though in truth most of them are on cable, not commercial, networks. In 2004, MTV unveiled plans to begin airing Logo, the first channel designed specifically for gay and lesbian viewers. But despite their growing media presence and influence, one subtle but powerfully stereotypical theme remains: that gays and lesbians are either extremely or at least moderately preoccupied with sex. David and Keith, the openly gay, interracial couple on the HBO show *Six Feet Under,* have professions and everyday lives that aren't about sex, but many of the plot lines that include these characters focus on their sexual appetites, activities, and problems. The openly gay character Stanford Blatch on *Sex and the City* seemed to be able to talk only about sex and the physical attractiveness of men. Such portrayals reinforce the perception that homosexuality is first and foremost about sex. Heterosexual couples on TV and in film typically are granted a wider array of interests, concerns, and life experiences that needn't be linked to eroticism.

Gay men and lesbians are especially vulnerable to the power of images, perhaps even more than racial minorities and women are. The producers of TV shows and films have, over the years, become sensitive to the blatant stereotyping of these groups. But the traditional stereotyping of homosexuality—effeminate men, masculine women—is more likely to be tolerated than the stereotyping of other groups. As one author puts it, gays and lesbians "are . . . the only group . . . whose enemies are generally uninhibited by the consensus of 'good taste' which protects most minorities from the more public displays of bigotry" (Gross, 1995, pp. 63–64). Furthermore, while the media are increasingly likely to include diverse portrayals of other "minority" groups (for instance, not depicting all African Americans as poor), images of homosexuality remain rather narrow. Most gay and lesbian characters are white, and virtually all of them are comfortably middle class.

SOCIAL CLASS IN THE MEDIA

Social class pervades the media. The for-profit nature of the commercial media guarantees that class concerns will link advertisers, producers, and audiences. Consider, for example, the tendency for newspapers to reduce circulation in order to increase profits:

> Newspapers receive about two-thirds of their revenue from advertisers, not readers; therefore, they must be sensitive to advertiser needs in order to stay in business. In turn . . . advertisers want to reach only readers with enough disposable income to buy their products. . . . To sell advertising space at a premium, newspapers want to improve the demographic profile (in terms of average household income) of their readership. They can do this in two ways: Attract more affluent readers, and/or get rid of poorer readers. (Croteau & Hoynes, 2000, p. 215)

The comfortable middle classes and the affluent upper classes have always been a mainstay in the popular media as well. Indeed, the society that is usually portrayed on television is considerably wealthier than the society in which we actually live. Whether their lives are depicted with a hint of desirous envy (as in *The OC*) or playfully caricatured as snooty blue bloods (for example, Lorelei's parents on *The Gilmore Girls*), the very wealthy have been a surefire hit among television viewers for decades. The HBO documentary *Born Rich* featured interviews by producer Jamie Johnson (heir to the Johnson & Johnson pharmaceuticals company fortune) of 10 of his fellow wealthy inheritors. MTV aired the eight-episode *Rich Girls*, in which designer Tommy Hilfiger's daughter and a friend fight boredom with self-indulgent shopping trips. Recently, reality shows have jumped on the "If they're wealthy, people will watch" bandwagon. NBC's *The Apprentice* tantalizes its contestants with snippets of the exorbitantly wealthy lifestyle of its star, Donald Trump—helicopter rides, polo matches, visits to his luxury apartment (Stanley, 2005).

Conversely, even though most working adults in the United States have manual, unskilled, or semiskilled jobs, poor and working-class people typically are depicted in minor roles (Parenti, 1996). A study of prime-time network television series between 1946 and 1990 found that in only 11% of the series were heads of households portrayed as working class—that is, holding occupations as blue-collar, clerical, or semiskilled service workers. Middle-class families were featured in 70% of the shows (Butsch, 1995). When working-class or poor people are shown, the depiction is often either unflattering or pitying. The blue-collar heads of households that have existed on prime-time television throughout the years are typically portrayed as dumb, immature, or irresponsible buffoons. *The Honeymooners, All in the Family, Married with Children*, and *The Simpsons* are the most famous examples. Films such as *Saturday Night Fever, Working Girl, Good Will Hunting*, and *8 Mile* portray working-class men as macho exhibitionists (Ehrenreich, 1995). On confrontational television talk shows such as *Jerry Springer* and *Judge Judy*, the odd personal problems of working-class guests are displayed for the condescending amusement of viewers. The reality show *Extreme Makeover: Home Edition* often depicts desperately needy families being "saved" with a new house designed and built by the show's cast.

It's difficult, if not impossible, to separate the images of working-class people from the images of gender or race/ethnicity. For instance, many of the earliest sitcoms on American television were constructed around working-class ethnic communities (Cornell & Hartmann, 1998). *The Goldbergs* was a 1950s comedy about a working-class Jewish family in the Bronx; *Mama* was about Norwegian immigrants in San Francisco; *Life with Luigi* was about Italian immigrants in Chicago. Later on, shows like *Sanford and Son* (a black father and son living in the Watts section of Los Angeles) and *Chico and the Man* (Mexicans living in Los Angeles) continued this tradition.

One enduring media image that reveals a great deal about attitudes toward both class and race is the "white trash" stereotype. White trash culture began as the maligned lifestyle of poor and working-class rural Southern Whites but soon became a metaphor for all that is tacky, unsophisticated, ignorant, or excessive—"from the darker aspects of racial politics and the Ku Klux Klan, feuding, incest, and the cult of the Rebel, to country music, faith-healing and snake-handling, and the phenomenon of Elvis veneration" (Sweeney, 2001, p. 144). The white trash aesthetic has been featured in factual as well as fictional media. For instance, the news media's depiction of former President Bill Clinton—who was commonly referred to as "Bubba" even while in office—often focused on his Arkansas roots, good ol' boy carousing, love of junk food, and his turbulent childhood that included protecting his mother from his drunken and abusive stepfather. The filmmaker John Waters once said that white trash is "the last racist thing you can say and get away with" (quoted in Friend, 1994, p. 24).

The white trash culture is often portrayed through condescending humor. Movies like *Joe Dirt* and *Dukes of Hazzard*, and television shows like Comedy Central's *Blue Collar TV* depict the low-brow lifestyles of working-class white folk as consisting of comedic preoccupations with hunting, a lot of beer-drinking, and a fondness for NASCAR. In 2003, the

Fox network offered *The Simple Life*, which documented the travails of hotel heiress Paris Hilton and her wealthy friend Nicole Ritchie (daughter of singer-songwriter Lionel Ritchie) as they adjusted to life on an Arkansas farm. At a time when the income and wealth gap between the very rich and the very poor grows dangerously wide (see Chapter 8), the mismatch between their upper-crust sensibilities and the uncultured lifestyles of their hosts was played each week for laughs. But at whose expense? Did the show lampoon poor, rural folk? Or did it contrast the vapid stupidity of these pampered women with the noble "salt of the earth" straightforwardness of their poor counterparts as a clever social critique? What was painfully obvious in this particular show was that the discomfort that the two stars felt living in cramped quarters, navigating the shabby decor, or tending to uncooperative farm animals was, in the end, transitory. Their experience of poverty was a temporary game, a playful—and ultimately escapable—walk on the other side of the socio-economic street.

In the news media, stories about poor people tend to be quite rare. When the news media do turn their attention to the poor, the portrayals are often negative or stereotypical, as when local TV stations run the usual human interest stories about the "less fortunate" in soup kitchens and homeless shelters during Thanksgiving and Christmas. More detailed stories about poor people tend to focus on welfare cheats, drug addicts, street criminals, and aggressive panhandlers.

A reversal of the tendency to denigrate the poor and working class (but one that may be equally inaccurate) is the portrayal of poverty as righteous and wealth as inherently corrupt. Wily servants turning the tables and outwitting their complacent and pompous bosses has been a theme in comedic books and films for decades. Recent movies like *Down to Earth, Maid in Manhattan, Sweet Home Alabama*, and *Mr. Deeds* depict working-class characters as heroic, a counterpoint to the depiction of wealthy characters who are greedy, mean, and small-minded.

Usually, however, the media tend to focus much of their favorable attention on the concerns of the wealthy and the privileged. Television air time is filled with advertisements for luxury cars, cruise vacations, diamond jewelry, and other things that only the well-to-do can afford. If you take a peek at the "Style" section of a large metropolitan newspaper, you'll likely find a focus on high-priced fashion, designer home furnishings, costly vacation spots, investment opportunities in foreign real estate, expensive restaurants, and etiquette for lavish, formal dinner parties. The news media also devote a significant amount of broadcast time and print space to daily business news and stock market quotations (Mantsios, 1995), even though only about half of U.S. families own any stock at all (National Center for Policy Analysis, 2000). Some cable television networks report exclusively on stock market issues. International news and trade agreements are reported in terms of their impact on the business world, not on ordinary working people.

The media also regularly provide information on individuals who have achieved extraordinary success. We receive regular reports about the multimillion-dollar contracts of professional athletes, film stars, and TV personalities. *People* magazine devotes an entire issue each year to a detailed description of the expensive gowns and tuxedos celebrities wear on Oscar night. Society pages and gossip columns keep those in the upper class informed of one another's doings and entice the rest of us to admire their achievements.

The mass media clearly shape how people think about each other and about the nature of society. By celebrating the lifestyles of the upper and middle classes, the media create the impression that the interests and worries of the well-off are, or should be, important to everyone. Consequently, class differences and conflicts are concealed or rendered irrelevant.

CONCLUSION

This chapter has been about naming groups of people in order to highlight difference, both in everyday conversation and in media portrayals. Our ideas about race and ethnicity, class, gender, and sexuality are both created and reinforced in everyday discourse and in the media.

Reconsider the supermarket checker I described at the outset of this chapter. She is not an anomaly. Her question about what Santa was going to bring to my son for Christmas is repeated thousands of times throughout our society every December, and similarly presumptuous questions are asked at many other times and in many other situations. The supermarket checker represents the way that our deepest routine beliefs drive our daily interactions with other people.

Linguistic conventions and media images that contain such default assumptions reinforce the differentness of people whose membership puts them on the religious, ethnic, racial, or sexual periphery. In short, the act of naming is never socially neutral. The extent to which certain identities can or must be named—both in everyday conversation and in media portrayals—is inversely related to power in this society. Those who need not be named or depicted—who need no modifying adjective or who need no film or television show to inform viewers of their "way of life"—are those who wield the authority to define themselves and others.

[**INVESTIGATING IDENTITIES AND INEQUALITIES**]

But I play one on TV: Media portraits of race,
gender, and sexuality

Adisturbing feature of racial, ethnic, gender, sexual, and class identity is that many of our beliefs and attitudes about people from other groups are formed without any direct contact with members of those groups. The media—most notably, television—play a significant role in providing the public with often inaccurate and oversimplified information that indirectly shapes attitudes. As you've seen in this chapter, the stereotypical media depictions of people who have historically been the least powerful in society—namely, women, homosexuals, and ethnoracial minorities—have received a lot of attention. But even though men, heterosexuals, and Whites dominate television and movies, their presence remains rather taken for granted and unexamined.

To compensate for this lack of attention to the dominant groups, your assignment in this exercise is to observe over the span of a week several prime-time television shows whose prominent recurring characters are from the following groups: Whites, men, and heterosexuals. Try to include both comedies and dramas. Avoid "reality" shows. For each show you watch, record the proportion of regular characters who are white, who are heterosexual, or who are male out of the total number of regular roles. Is the ethnicity or religion of these characters ever made clear on the show? If so, how? You may also want to note the proportion of white, heterosexual men on these shows.

Pay particular attention to the way these characters are portrayed. Examine their mannerisms, their occupations (if applicable), their apparent socio-economic status, their dialogue, and their appearance (hairstyle, clothing, and so on).

Do these characters conform to common stereotypes associated with Whites, men, and heterosexuals? How frequently do these characters refer to their own whiteness, maleness, or heterosexuality? Do the plots of the shows revolve around what you might consider "racial," "gender," or "sexual" themes? That is, how often does the issue of race, ethnicity, or sexual orientation come up during the course of the show?

Did you notice any characters who act or appear in ways, or are employed in occupations, you'd consider "non-traditional" (for instance, a man working as a nurse or a white person working as a domestic servant)? Describe how these "non-traditional" portrayals deviate from more stereotypical character-izations. Are they treated positively or negatively on the show? Do charac-ters make references to these depictions? Are they the source of conflict or humor? How might this type of depiction ultimately affect public perceptions of race, gender, and sexuality?

Interpret your observations sociologically. What are the implicit messages communicated by the portrayal of whiteness, maleness, and heterosexuality? Would this assignment have been easier or more difficult if you were asked to analyze the portrayals of women, homosexuals, and ethnoracial minori-ties? Explain. Based on your observations, what can you conclude about the relationship among power, invisibility, and media imagery?

CHAPTER 4

Learning Difference
Families, Schools, and Socialization

When I was in my first year of graduate school, I became friends with a couple who were the parents of twins—a boy and a girl. My friends were self-defined feminists. Although they realized that they couldn't raise their children in a completely genderless fashion, they did everything they could to try to minimize gender-specific child rearing so that both children had the same opportunities, were exposed to the same expectations, and received the same type of parental encouragement.

Just before the children's fourth-birthday party, the parents decided to buy each of them the same gender-neutral gift. You could bet that there wouldn't be a Barbie doll, a toy stove, a cap gun, or a football helmet within 20 miles of that party. They settled on a big box of multicolored geometric shapes and blocks made out of firm foam rubber. The shapes were safe, easily manipulable for little hands, and could be used for creating just about anything a kid's imagination could concoct.

The day of the birthday party arrived. I wasn't a parent yet myself at the time, so I watched the proceedings like an anthropologist visiting a different culture for the first time. The children began opening their presents. Legos. Stuffed replicas of Bert and Ernie from *Sesame Street*. More Legos. A video of *101 Dalmatians*. Apparently, the other parents had gotten the message and had managed to avoid gender-specific gifts. The twins seemed genuinely pleased when they opened their parents' gift, fondling the vibrant, multihued cones, spheres, cubes, blocks, and pyramids with glee.

After cake, the adults lingered in the backyard as the kids went off to play somewhere. All seemed well. After a while, though, the twins' mother got up and went to check on the kids. A couple of minutes later, she returned, ashen-faced. "I can't believe it! They've divided themselves up!" she cried. "The boys are in one room and the girls are in another." That didn't seem so bad to the rest of us. "Well . . . there's more," she said, in a tone that was equal parts grief, exasperation, and embarrassment.

When she went to check on the children, she first went to her son's room. As she approached, she could hear the sounds of little boys making machine gun and explosion noises with their mouths. Horrified, she walked in and found her son "aiming" a purple foam-rubber rectangle at another boy and "shooting" him. "I killed you! You're dead!" he screamed. The other boy, unshaken by the news, replied, "If I'm dead, you're dead too!" as he "shot" back with a red foam-rubber cone.

Deflated by the sight of her son using her wonderful gender-neutral gift as a weapon, she ventured over to her daughter's room. She heard no shooting or killing sounds. Instead, she found her daughter and another little girl sitting in separate corners of the room, caressing, cooing to, and rocking their geometric shapes to sleep. "Mommy wants baby to nap now," she heard her daughter whisper to the yellow sphere she had wrapped in a blanket and was now cradling in her arms.

I lost track of this couple not long after the birthday party, so I don't know how the "trauma" affected either the parents or the children. My guess is that the twins turned out just fine. Yet this incident reveals a great deal about the process by which children learn who they are. As much as parents would like to believe that they can completely control how their children develop their identities, their influence is, in fact, limited. On their developmental path, children acquire information from a variety of sources—books, television, video games, the Internet, toys, teachers, other children, other children's parents, strangers they see on the street. Sometimes, this information aligns with the messages conveyed by parents; other times, however, this outside information contradicts and maybe even eclipses parents' messages.

What my friends didn't want to acknowledge was that "becoming" a girl or a boy—or an African American, a Latino/a, a heterosexual, a homosexual, a member of the middle class, or whatever—never occurs in a social vacuum. The development of gender, ethnoracial, class, and sexual identities is always a joint social production that includes intimates as well as others outside the immediate family. It is always influenced by broader economic, political, and religious concerns. My friends thought they could "create" their children in an image of their choosing. They didn't stand a chance.

Although learning about one's race, one's class, one's sexuality, or one's gender takes place throughout our lives and in a variety of settings, this chapter will focus on the lessons we learn in our families and those we learn in schools, through interactions both with teachers and with peers. In addition, since we don't live our lives *just* as a member of a particular race, gender, class, or sexual orientation, this chapter will examine how the intersection of these phenomena affects the way we learn our identities.

IDENTITY SOCIALIZATION IN FAMILIES

In previous chapters, you've seen that social reality is not an inherent feature of the natural world but is instead a human creation, established in a process of ongoing social interaction. We create, re-create, confirm, or change our social identities every time our actions, appearances, thoughts, perceptions, and values are taken as reflective of or in contrast to what others expect of us. Just as our ideas about the nature of difference and the meanings of race, ethnicity, sex, gender, social class, and sexuality are socially constructed, so too are the individuals who constitute these groups.

One of the fundamental tasks facing any society is to create members whose values, behaviors, attitudes, and perceptions correspond to those deemed by that society as appropriate. This task is accomplished through the process of **socialization,** the way that people learn to act in accordance with the rules and expectations of a particular society (Newman, 2004). It's the means by which people acquire important skills and knowledge. One of the most crucial outcomes of the socialization process is the development of a sense of self. How does one become a male or a female; a white person or a Native American; a working-class individual or a member of the upper classes; a heterosexual or a homosexual? I'm not talking here about inheriting a particular biological/anatomical/genetic identity. Nor am I talking about earning a certain amount of money that objectively puts one over a particular socioeconomic threshold. Instead, I'm talking about how we learn to think, act, and perceive ourselves as members of particular groups and how we incorporate those perceptions into our personal identity.

LEARNING GENDERS

One of the most important aspects of identity that people must learn is gender. Distinctions along sex/gender lines are the cultural, institutional, even architectural foundations of everyday life. Its importance as a shaper of our social experiences is beyond debate. What is debatable, though, is where gendered traits and behaviors come from.

Biological Predispositions Certainly, at a basic level, our sexual anatomy has something to do with our gender identity. Sociologist Richard Udry (2000) studied 351 adult women whose pregnant mothers had been entered in the Child Health and Development Study between 1960 and 1969. Regular specimens of amniotic fluid were taken from these women and recorded. Hence, Udry could determine the levels of hormones his sample of women were exposed to before they were born. He found that those women who were exposed to higher levels of testosterone as fetuses exhibited more "masculine" traits and behaviors as adults than women who were exposed to lower levels of testosterone. He found these differences even in women whose own mothers had strongly encouraged them to be "feminine" as children. He concluded from this finding that biological predispositions can limit the effects of gender socialization.

Some researchers have attempted to uncover the biological under-pinnings of gender by examining differences in the behaviors of male and female newborns and infants. For instance, one study found that con-sistent sex differences in the achievement of fundamental developmen-tal milestones (smiling, sitting up without support, crawling, walking, and so on) appear within the first year of life, early enough to make cul-tural or environmental influence unlikely (Reinisch, Rosenblum, Rubin, & Schulsinger, 1997). The researchers argue that boys tend to reach these milestones earlier than girls, biologically predisposing them to be more independent and directive later on and predisposing girls to be more warm, nurturant, and interested in relationships with others. They acknowledge that some of these differences may result from factors in the postnatal environment. But because the differences appear so early, they attribute most of the effect to genetic, hormonal, or prenatal influences.

Others, however, have argued that even at so early an age, a wide variety of factors other than biology can affect physical development, such as how much parents encourage the child and how much opportunity a child has to learn these activities (Carli, 1997). For example, in some African cultures where mothers actively teach their babies to crawl, children reach this milestone significantly earlier compared to children raised in cultures where crawling is not taught (Super, 1976). Likewise, in the United States, giving infants practice in sitting or stepping can accelerate the age at which they learn these abilities. In fact, children who enter the crawling stage of development when the weather is cold tend to begin crawling later than children who enter this stage during the warmer months (Benson, 1993).

Using biology to explain gender differences later in life is also the subject of much debate. For instance, sociologist Steven Goldberg (1999) argues that because male rule and male dominance seem to characterize the vast majority of human societies, this gender difference must be rooted in evolutionary biology. However, anthropologists have identified noteworthy exceptions. The famous anthropologist Margaret Mead (1963) studied three cultures in New Guinea in the 1930s:

- Among the mountain-dwelling Arapesh, both men and women displayed traits we in the West would commonly associate with femininity: cooperation, passivity, sensitivity to others. Mead described both men and women as being "maternal." These characteristics were linked to broader cultural beliefs about people's relationship to the environment. The Arapesh didn't have any conception of "ownership" of land, so they never had aggressive conflicts over possession of property.
- South of the Arapesh were the Mundugumor, a group of cannibals and headhunters. Here, both men and women displayed traits that we in the West would associate with masculinity: assertiveness, emotional inexpressiveness, insensitivity to others. Mundugumor women, according to Mead, were just as violent, just as aggressive, and just as jealous as men. Both were equally virile, without any of the "soft" characteristics we associate with femininity.

- The Tchambuli, the third culture Mead observed, did distinguish between male and female traits. However, their gender expectations were the opposite of what we expect in Western societies. Women were dominant, shrewd, assertive, and managerial; men were submissive and emotional and were seen as inherently delicate.

Mead's work is important because it shows that definitions of the "natural" tendencies of men and women aren't necessarily universal. The vast majority of societies may be dominated by men, but the fact that there are exceptions, no matter how rare, shows at the very least that biological predispositions, if they exist at all, can actually be overcome by culture.

Gender Training Because gender-typed expectations are so ingrained, parents are often unaware that they are treating their children in accordance with them (Goldberg & Lewis, 1969; Will, Self, & Datan, 1976). In one study, 30 first-time parents were asked to describe their recently born infants (less than 24 hours old). Those with daughters described them as "tiny," "soft," "fine-featured," and "delicate." Sons were seen as "strong," "alert," "hardy," and "coordinated" (Rubin, Provenzano, & Luria, 1974). A replication of this study two decades later found that U.S. parents continue to perceive their infants in gender-stereotyped ways, although to a lesser degree than in the 1970s (Karraker, Vogel, & Lake, 1995). For instance, a colleague of mine gave birth to a daughter several years ago. When I saw her the day after the baby was born, she described her daughter as looking like a "little China doll." Recently, she gave birth to a boy whom she immediately described as "handsome."

Researchers have also found subtle differences in the ways parents communicate with their sons and daughters. For instance, parents are more likely to talk about sadness with daughters than with sons; they're more likely to talk about anger with sons than with daughters (Adams, Kuebli, Boyle, & Fivush, 1995). Parents also tend to engage in rougher and more interactive physical play with infant sons than with infant daughters and use different pet names, such as "Sweetie" versus "Tiger" (MacDonald & Parke, 1986; Tauber, 1979). In one study, all mothers—whether they eschewed common gender expectations or were more traditional—were more likely to verbally teach and direct their sons than their daughters. In addition, they were more likely to use action verbs, numbers, and explicit language with their sons (Weitzman, Birns, and Friend, 1985).

Clearly, the earliest exposure to information about what it means to be male or female usually comes from parents, siblings, and other significant people in the child's immediate environment (Witt, 1997). Often, these individuals serve as observational models with whom the child can identify and ultimately imitate.

Parents also gender-socialize their children through the things they routinely provide for them. Clothes, for example, not only inform others about the sex of an individual, they also send messages about how that child ought to be treated and direct behavior along traditional gender lines (Shakin, Shakin, & Sternglanz, 1985). Frilly dresses do not lend themselves easily to rough and dirty play. Clothes for boys rarely restrict physical movement in this way and are made to withstand vigorous activity.

Toys and games that parents provide for their children are another influential source of gender information. A quick glance at Saturday morning television commercials or a toy manufacturer's catalog or web site reveals that toys and games remain solidly segregated along gender lines. Decades of research indicate that "girls' toys" still revolve around themes of domesticity, fashion, and motherhood and "boys' toys" emphasize action and adventure (Renzetti & Curran, 2003). In one study, there was significant agreement among adults as to what were the most "male" toys (guns, toy soldiers, boxing gloves, G.I. Joe, and football gear) and the most "female" toys (makeup kit, Barbie, jewelry box, bracelet, doll clothes) (Campenni, 1999).

Parents and other family members can also provide their children with explicit instructions on proper gender behavior, such as "Big boys don't cry" or "Act like a young lady." For instance, one recent study found that mothers expect more risky behavior from their sons and tend to focus more on disciplinary issues with them than with daughters. Conversely, mothers tend to be more concerned about injuries and safety issues with their daughters than with sons (Morrongiello & Hogg, 2004).

And it's not just mothers, by the way. One day, when my older son was about 11 months old and just beginning to walk, he crawled into the kitchen, opened several drawers, and hoisted himself up. Then he let go and for a brief instant proudly stood on his own. His moment of glory lasted less than a second, though, for as he turned to show us what he could do, he lost his balance and fell face-first into one of the open drawers. Through his hysterical crying, I could see that his lower lip was cut, swollen, and bleeding. He was clearly in pain and obviously wanted and expected some parental comfort. But as he approached us, blood dripping on the carpet, I blurted out, "This is great!! He just got his first fat lip!!" Somewhere in the deep recesses of my brain, I saw this event as a male rite of passage. After all, boys are supposed to fall down and sometimes get hurt. Instead of consoling him, I celebrated his injury. I've never lived this incident down, by the way.

As a consequence of differential treatment, both boys and girls learn to adopt gender as an organizing principle for themselves and the social world in which they live (Howard & Hollander, 1997). By the age of two or three or so, most children can accurately answer the question "Are you a boy or a girl?" (see, for example, Kohlberg, 1966) and begin to attribute more positive characteristics to their own sex than to the other. But to a young child, being a boy or a girl means no more than being named Douglas instead of Debra. It is simply another characteristic, like having brown eyes or curly hair. The child at this age lacks the full understanding that gender is a category into which every human can be placed (Kessler & McKenna, 1978). By the age of five or so, most children have developed a fairly extensive repertoire of gender stereotypes (often incorrect) that they then apply to themselves (Martin & Ruble, 2004). They also use these stereotypes to form impressions of others and to guide their own perceptions and activities. A boy, for instance, may avoid approaching a new girl who has just moved into the neighborhood because he assumes that she will be interested in "girl" things. Acting on this assumption reinforces the original belief that boys and girls are different. Indeed, gender, to children at this age, is typically seen as a characteristic that is fixed and permanent. Statements like "Doctors are men" and "Nurses are women" are uttered as inflexible, objective "truths." A few years later, though, their attitudes toward gender are likely to become considerably more flexible, although such flexibility may not be reflected in their actual behaviors (Martin & Ruble, 2004).

It's important to note that the process by which children learn their own gender identity is not a passive one in which they simply absorb the information that bombards them. As part of the process of finding meaning in their social worlds, children actively construct gender as a social category. From an early age, they are like "gender detectives," searching for cues about gender, such as who should and shouldn't engage in certain activities, who can play with whom, and why girls and boys differ (Martin & Ruble, 2004, p. 67).

Intersections
The Influence of Race on Gender Socialization

Most of the research on the role that parents play in the gender socialization of their children is based on samples of white, middle-class, two-parent families. Hence, the broad conclusions one draws about family influence on gender development must be made with caution. Some researchers have been trying to draw out the nuances of gender socialization among different ethnoracial groups to give us a better understanding. For instance, Marcella Raffaelli and Lenno Ontai (2004) have identified a set of unique cultural ideals that are relevant to gender socialization among many Latino/a groups:

- *Familismo*—cultural emphasis on family relations and childbearing as an integral part of femininity.
- *Respeto*—cultural emphasis on respect and hierarchy in social relations.
- Strong gender role divisions that contain expectations that women be submissive, chaste, and dependent and men be dominant, virile, and independent.

Often, these values are reflected in the different ways that Latino/a parents attempt to regulate the sexual activity of their children. For example, they place much more importance on virginity until marriage for daughters than for sons. More generally, parents place stricter rules and more limits on girls than on boys in such matters as involvement in afterschool activities and the age at which they allow their children to get jobs or drivers' licenses. In addition, Latina mothers tend to be more involved in the gender socialization of daughters and fathers more involved in the gender socialization of sons (Raffaelli & Ontai, 2004).

In a study that compared African American and white parents, the researchers found that white parents are significantly more likely to place a high value on their children's happiness and to see teaching as their most important parenting role. Black parents were more likely to value doing well and being obedient in school and to see being a disciplinarian and a provider as their most important parenting roles (Hill & Sprague, 1999).

The sex of the child can further influence these tendencies. For example, white parents are more likely than black parents to emphasize obedience for sons more than for daughters. Withdrawing privileges is more commonly used to discipline boys rather than girls in black families (Hill & Sprague, 1999).

Although the socialization of young African American males and females is not entirely the same, parents tend to emphasize the importance of hard work, independence, and self-reliance equally among sons and daughters (Hale-Benson, 1986). The emphasis on gender equality seems to be more common in African American families than in other types of American families. Several historical trends—the high proportion of African American women in the paid labor force, the presence of female-centered households, and a history of racial discrimination and exclusion—can't help but influence notions of gender and the way African American parents teach it to their children. Some have gone so far as to say that age and competency—and not gender—are the chief determinants of children's roles in African American families (Peters, 1988).

Some sociologists have argued that apparent race differences in gender socialization may actually be an artifact of the way race and class intersect in this society. Among working-class white parents, traditional gender socialization is more common than among working-class black parents. Indeed, low-income African American parents often have higher expectations for their daughters than for their sons (Hill & Sprague, 1999). However, upper-middle-class black parents are more likely to socialize their sons and daughters into traditional gender roles than upper-middle-class white parents are (Hill, 1999).

Androgyny To diminish the heavy societal emphasis on gender distinctions, some parents and child development experts advocate **androgynous socialization**—bringing up children to have both male and female traits and behaviors (Bem, 1974). Advocates for androgynous socialization see no biological reason, except for a few anatomical and reproductive differences, to distinguish between what males and females can do.

Modern parents are probably more likely than their predecessors to attempt to overcome gender stereotypes in the raising of their children. Yet, as you recall from the story at the beginning of this chapter, parents' ability to carry out androgynous socialization may be somewhat limited. Four- and five-year-old children often engage in strongly gender-stereotypical play, regardless of the attitudes and beliefs expressed by their parents (O'Brien & Huston, 1985). Findings like these have led some researchers to argue that the effects of androgynous socialization are more likely to show up later in life rather than in childhood, after individuals have developed the cognitive maturity and the confidence to incorporate nontraditional gender attitudes and beliefs into their everyday lives (Sedney, 1987). But some sociologists are much more pessimistic. They question whether parents or anyone else ever has the ability to change such deeply ingrained lessons as gender roles (Lorber, 1994). Gender structures every organization and shapes every interaction in society, often in ways we're not consciously aware of. Individual parents may have little hope of seriously altering their children's understanding of gender. Androgynous socialization is difficult because it always involves, at least to some degree, the violation of widely held gender norms. Unfortunately, children whose behavior doesn't conform to generally accepted standards of gender risk ridicule or worse.

The social costs of violating gender norms are not felt evenly by girls and boys, or by women and men, however. Consider the different connotations and implications of the words *sissy* and *tomboy*. The *tomboy* may fight, curse, play sports, and climb trees, but her entire sexual identity is not called into question by the label. In fact, in some situations, she is just as likely to be included by other children as shunned, as when, say, she is asked to play in informal games of football or basketball with neighborhood boys. Girls, in general, are given license to do "boy things" (Kimmel, 2004). Indeed, tomboy-ness, if considered negative at all, is typically seen as transitory, a stage that a girl will eventually grow out of. How many TV shows or movies have you seen in which a precocious tomboy reaches puberty, sprouts breasts, discovers boys, discards her rough-and-tumble ways, puts on makeup and a dress for the first time, and unveils to stunned friends and family her true feminine beauty?

For boys, life on the other side of the gender fence is much more precarious. The chances to play girl games without ridicule are rare and the risks for doing so are steep. The *sissy* is not simply a boy who enjoys female pursuits. He is suspiciously soft and effeminate. His sissy-ness is likely to be seen as reflective of his sexual essence, a sign of his impending homosexuality.

Several years ago, there was a television commercial for men's cologne that opens with a woman lying by herself on an unmade bed. She has a smile on her face as if recalling a recent satisfying sexual encounter. She gets up, goes to the closet, removes a man's dress shirt from a hanger, and puts it on. She puts on a tie and then grabs a man's hat off of a chair and dons it. Finally, she picks up a bottle of the cologne, looks at it for a second, and dabs some on her neck. At that moment, the phone rings. She answers it and coyly says, "Hi, honey. I was just thinking about you." The ad works, of course, because putting on her partner's clothes and cologne is taken as a sexy way for her to feel close to him. But imagine if an ad for women's perfume used a similar approach: The scene opens with a man alone in a bedroom putting on his lover's lacy sundress. He spritzes some of her perfume on his neck and wrists. When the phone rings, he picks up the receiver and in a deep, husky voice says to the woman on the other end, "Hi, honey. I was just thinking about you." Would you consider this ad sexy? Doubtful.

Part of the reason for this asymmetrical response to gender-crossing behavior is the connection between the gender differences and gender inequalities that exists in society. Simply put, in a society structured around and for the interests of men, stereotypically masculine traits (strength, assertiveness, confidence, and so on) are likely to be valued culturally and interpersonally. Hence, many women conclude that their own success requires such traits. Even young children learn that these traits are valued more highly than stereotypically feminine traits:

> Boys and girls both understand the inequality between women and men, and understand, too, that their less-than-equal status gives girls a bit more latitude in the types of cross-sex (gender-inappropriate) behavior they may exhibit. Girls think they'd be better off as boys, and many of them declare that they would rather be boys than girls. By contrast, boys tend to see being girls as a fate worse than death. . . . [A little boy comes] to understand that his status in the world depends upon his ability to distance himself from femininity. By exaggerating gender difference, he both assures and reassures himself of his higher status. (Kimmel, 2004, pp. 132–133)

LEARNING RACIAL IDENTITIES

According to some child development experts, racial identity doesn't fully emerge until adolescence. But some research shows that children as young as three—no matter what their racial background—recognize skin color differences and hold a wide array of racial attitudes, assumptions, and behaviors (Van Ausdale & Feagin, 2001).

Although everyone has a racial identity, different groups assign different degrees of importance to the role of race in their lives. For some, racial identity organizes virtually every aspect of their daily lives; for others, it is for all intents and purposes irrelevant. Whether racial identity is all-encompassing or minimal depends on the group's historical position in the racial stratification system. The more advantaged a group's position, the less important racial identity is for the effective socialization of children within that group.

It's not surprising, then, that few sociologists have attempted to explain how white children come to understand and see themselves as white people, even though whiteness, like any other racial identity, must be learned, developed, and performed (Van Ausdale & Feagin, 2001). Those who do study the development of white racial identity typically focus on how white children move through various stages of prejudice—from early phases in which they acquire common racial stereotypes and beliefs in white superiority to later stages where a nonracist identity and a commitment to racial equality emerge (Helms, 1993). White parents may attempt to instill pride in their children's religious identity or hyphenated ethnicity (for instance, Greek-Americans, Italian-Americans, Irish-Americans), but they rarely have to teach their children about the conflicts and dilemmas that their race will create for them. Instead, learning to be white is less about defining one's race as it is about learning how to handle privileges and behaviors associated with whiteness in society (Van Ausdale & Feagin, 2001). Chances are good that schools and religious organizations will reinforce the socialization messages expressed to white children in their families—for example, that "hard work will pay off in the long run" or "you can be anything you want as long as you work hard." Because the messages that white children receive about race are likely to focus on the race of others, not their own race, the assumption that race is an insignificant component of their identity is perpetuated.

For children of color, however, racial socialization occurs within a different and much more complex social environment (Hughes & Chen, 1997). These children must live simultaneously in two different worlds: their ethnoracial community, which values them, and the "mainstream" (that is, white) society, which may not. Hence, they're likely to be exposed to three different types of socialization experiences while growing up: that which includes information about the mainstream culture, that which focuses on their minority status in society, and that which focuses on the history and cultural heritage of their ethnoracial group (Scott, 2003; Thornton, 1997). In ethnoracial groups that have been able to overcome discrimination and achieve at high levels—such as some Asian American groups—ethnic socialization can focus simply on the values of their culture of origin. But among groups that, by and large, remain disadvantaged, such as African Americans, Native Americans, and Latino/as, parents' discussion of race and ethnicity is more likely to focus on preparing their children for prejudice, hatred, and mistreatment in a society set up to ignore or actively exclude them (McLoyd, Cauce, Takeuchi, & Wilson, 2000; Staples, 1992). For instance, these children may be taught that "hard work" alone might not be enough to get ahead in this society. Even children of color from affluent homes in racially integrated neighborhoods need reassurances about the racial conflicts they will inevitably encounter (Comer & Poussaint, 1992).

But even within a particular group, there can be tremendous variation in the content of racial socialization. For some parents of color, race is one of the central concerns in raising their children. They may believe that they are not simply raising an "American" but an American with a particular ethnoracial background. Parents who anticipate that their children will face a hostile environment teach them to be comfortable with and proud of their own ethnicity. For other minority parents, however, race may play only a minor role in the socialization process. They may feel reluctant to discuss race or racism because they fear that such a discussion might make their children bitter, resentful, and prejudiced against others (Thornton, Chatters, Taylor, & Allen, 1990). Some critics argue that such parents cannot instill a positive racial identity in their children.

Ethnoracial socialization can be especially problematic when racial identity itself is complicated. Take, for instance, adopted children who are members of a different ethnoracial group than their parents. Since passage of the Multiethnic Placement Act of 1994, federally funded agencies have been prohibited from considering race, culture, and ethnicity in their placement decisions, making it easier for couples to adopt children of different racial backgrounds. According to the U.S. Department of Health and Human Services (1994), about 14% of all adoptions involve parents and children of different races. Most of these adoptions take place between white parents and a minority child—African American, Latino/a, or Asian.

Today, approximately 59% of American children awaiting adoption are members of ethnoracial minorities (cited in Vidal de Haymes & Simon, 2003). Many adoption agencies take the position that a permanent home is more important than racial matching of parents and children. Advocates of transracial adoption also argue that the child, who likely comes from a financially depressed and deprived background, will have better opportunities in a more "advantaged" environment. In addition, they point out that transracial adoption has the potential to transform a racially divided society into a racially integrated one by creating such integration within individual families.

Transracial adoption has not been without its critics, however. In 1972, the National Association of Black Social Workers (NABSW) passed a resolution, still in effect today, against the adoption of black children by white parents. The group argued that transracial adoptions are harmful to black heritage and that to maintain the integrity of their culture, Blacks must be loyal to its uniqueness. They pointed out that a black child growing up in a white family will never learn about his or her own culture and will therefore never develop a positive racial identity. White parents can never provide a black child with sufficient information about what it is like to be black in a predominantly white society.

Considering the larger historical and political context, we can understand why some groups fear that transracial adoption weakens their racial identity and culture. In the 1960s and 1970s, for example, nearly 30% of all Native American children were removed from their families and put up for adoption in non–Native American homes. Social workers at the time deemed thousands of Native American parents unfit because of poverty, alcoholism, and other problems. So devastating to tribal cultures was the removal of these children that the Indian Child Welfare Act was passed in 1978, giving tribes special preference in adopting children of Native American heritage (Egan, 1993). However, this law has come under attack after reports of tribes contesting the adoption by white parents of children with only a minute trace of Indian ancestry.

In terms of their general adjustment, children of color placed in white homes do just as well as other adopted children. However, when it comes to issues of self-esteem, ethnoracial identity, and strategies for living in a racist society, children who are adopted by parents of the same race or ethnicity tend to do better. Furthermore, the vast majority of white families that adopt children of color live in predominantly white neighborhoods and send their children to predominantly white schools. Although these parents are aware of the importance of exposing their children to other people of color, they tend to minimize the importance of race in their children's lives and downplay incidents that involve racial slurs or acts of discrimination (Vidal de Haymes & Simon, 2003).

Intersections
The Effects of Gender and Class on Racial Identities

The intersection of race, class, and gender is especially apparent during adolescence, when concerns about identity and self-definition may be central features of everyday life (Dion & Dion, 2004). Being a girl or boy, poor or non-poor, and white, black, or Latino/a have varying implications for well-being depending on how these factors are combined. Poor children from an oppressed racial or ethnic group are especially vulnerable to an accumulation of disadvantage that can influence their psychological well-being over time (McLeod & Owens, 2004).

Consider the findings of sociologist Mary Pattillo-McCoy (1999), who spent three-and-a-half years in a middle-class black Chicago neighborhood she called "Groveland," interviewing residents of all ages. In many respects, the Groveland families were just like families in any other middle-class neighborhood. Parents saw their children's development into self-sufficient adults as their primary goal. And most of them had the wherewithal to pay for private schools, sports equipment, dance lessons, and so on. The black children in

Groveland had access to computers and other resources that black children in poor neighborhoods did not.

But the black middle-class families in Groveland had to deal with markedly different problems than their white counterparts. For example, 79% of Blacks in Chicago are likely to live within a few blocks of a neighborhood where at least one-third of the residents are poor; only 36% of white, middle-class Chicago dwellers live so close to a poor neighborhood (cited in Pattillo-McCoy, 1999). Thus, Groveland parents had to spend a lot of time trying to protect their children from the negative influences found in the neighboring poor, inner-city areas. In doing so, they faced some challenges other middle-class parents were unlikely to face:

> Groveland parents . . . set limits on where their children can travel. They choose activities—church youth groups, magnet schools or accelerated programs in the local school, and the Boy Scouts and Girl Scouts—to increase the likelihood that their children will learn positive values and associate with youth from similar families. . . . On their way to the grocery store or to school or to music lessons, Groveland's youth pass other young people whose parents are not as strict, who stay outside later, who have joined the local gang, or who earn enough money being a lookout at a drug house to buy new gym shoes. They also meet these peers in school and at the park. . . . For some teenagers, the fast life looks much more exciting than what their parents have to offer them, and they are drawn to it. The simple fact of living in a neighborhood where not all families have sufficient resources to direct their children away from deviance makes it difficult for parents to ensure positive outcomes for their children and their neighborhood. (pp. 211–212)

Another sociologist, Mary Romero (2004), has been studying the intersections of race, class, and gender in her research on the lives of Latina and African American domestic workers. In one article, she provides a lengthy life history of "Teresa," the daughter of a Latina live-in maid working in a predominantly white, upper-class neighborhood in Los Angeles. Teresa's entire childhood is spent in somebody else's house. At times, she is treated by her mother's employer and the employer's family as an ethnoracial outsider, a poor Latina whose appearance, language, and demeanor mark her, even to children her own age, as subordinate. At other times though—and often with little warning—she is treated as "one of the family," as when, for example, she is spontaneously invited to eat Thanksgiving dinner with the employer's family. The problem for Teresa is that such inclusive treatment is largely arbitrary and unpredictable. So she must learn to be sensitive to "signs" in order to determine her position in each social setting and ultimately select the appropriate actions. Teresa's racial identity is complicated by the different socioeconomic environments she straddles:

> Teresa and her mother maintained another life—one that was guarded and protected against any employer intrusion. Their other life was Mexican, not white, was Spanish speaking, not English speaking, was female dominated rather than male dominated, and was poor and working class, not upper middle-class. (p. 109)

It's easy to see how the development of Teresa's ethnoracial identity is inseparable from her socioeconomic standing. Imagine how different Teresa's sense of being "Latina" would have been if her parents had been wealthy Latino/a professionals. For that matter, consider how different her socialization experiences might have been if she had been the son of a maid rather than the daughter or had been white rather than Latina.

LEARNING SEXUALITIES

We're preoccupied with sexuality in this society. It's seemingly everywhere: in our magazines, our novels, our television shows, our movies, our music videos, our video games, our advertisements, our web sites, and our politics. The impact of all this sexual imagery is not trivial. A recent study of American teens, for instance, found that frequent exposure to sexually-oriented television shows like soap operas and music videos is associated with casual attitudes toward sex, higher expectations about the prevalence of sexual activity, and sometimes greater levels of actual sexual experience (Ward, 2003).

For all our cultural obsessions with sex, we really don't talk frankly about it all that much. Communities across the country have fought against things like contraceptive ads on television and sex education in schools. Although most parents can be quite proactive when it comes to teaching their children how to ride a bike, how to read, or how to use the stove, they can be rather tight-lipped when it comes to teaching their children how to be sexual. They are more likely to act as inadvertent models for their children or to articulate proscriptions (that is, what children shouldn't do) rather than positive lessons. Straightforward, direct sexual socialization is relatively uncommon.

Consequently, the information that children do receive tends to be largely informal, piecemeal, and peer-driven. When older siblings are present, they, and not parents, are typically the ones who provide information on intercourse and contraceptive use (Kornreich, Hearn, Rodriguez, & O'Sullivan, 2003). Moreover, given the heteronormative nature of our society, it's a good bet that early sexual lessons young people receive from others are heterosexual. Hence, sexual socialization can be especially difficult for people developing non-heterosexual identities.

Was I Just Born This Way? "Becoming" heterosexual in this culture is neither problematic nor abnormal. When parents say things to their young children like, "When you get married and have kids of your own someday, you'll see how hard it is to be a parent!" they are implicitly reinforcing the "normality" of a heterosexual identity. So not surprisingly, media and scientific attention has largely been devoted to discovering the origins of homosexuality, not heterosexuality.

Interpretations of the origins of homosexuality have changed considerably. In the late 19th century, psychiatrists and other medical professionals developed a view of homosexuality as a form of mental illness—a disease that could somehow be cured through medical means. In fact, as recently as 1973, the *Diagnostic and Statistical Manual* of the American Psychiatric Association listed homosexuality as a mental illness associated with psychopathic personality disorders.

In the 1950s and 1960s, most experts believed that homosexuality was a choice, a preference, which is influenced by interpersonal experiences and not by a person's biological inheritance. Psychological and sociological theories of the time focused on such factors as domineering mothers, submissive fathers, early childhood trauma, "failure" at heterosexuality, and a variety of emotional disturbances as the reasons why an individual would become homosexual. If homosexuality was learned, the thinking went, it could perhaps be unlearned. So psychiatrists at the time wrote extensively about how, with the appropriate therapy, homosexuals could "learn" to be heterosexual.

However, a growing body of literature is providing some evidence that sexual orientation is not chosen but is biologically determined. Attention has been paid to such factors as brain structure, genes, hormones, pheromones, and the prenatal uterine environment. In 1995, two scientists at the National Institutes of Health transplanted a single gene into the bodies of male fruit flies that caused them to display "courtship" behaviors with other male fruit flies (Zhang & Odenwald, 1995). Granted, the notion that a fruit fly could be "homosexual" in the same sense that a human could be is an overstatement, because sexual orientation is a human construction that includes not only physical desires but also psychological imagery and self-identity. Nevertheless, this research added to the mounting body of evidence that sexual orientation is rooted in biology.

In 1991, a California neuroscientist performed autopsies on the brains of men and women of known sexual orientation (LeVay, 1991). He found that the hypothalamus region in the center of the brain was substantially smaller among the gay men he examined than among the heterosexual men. Despite the researcher's plea for caution in drawing quick conclusions from his limited findings, this study became a catalyst for scholarly and not-so-scholarly debate on the origins of human sexual orientation (Ordover, 1996).

Another study found that the male relatives of known gay men were substantially more likely to also be homosexual (13.5%) than was the entire sample studied (2%). Indeed, the researcher discovered more gay relatives on the maternal side, fueling the contention that homosexuality is passed from generation to generation through women (Hamer & Coupland, 1994). Some researchers even contend that studies like this one point toward a "gay gene."

As compelling as these findings may be, we must interpret them with caution. The "high" rate (13.5%) of homosexuality among relatives of gay men, for example, means that in over 86% of the cases these relatives were not gay. In addition, a single gene is unlikely to be responsible for any complex human trait. We know, for instance, that genes are responsible for the development of our lungs, larynx, mouth, and the areas of the brain associated with speech. But such complexity can't be collapsed into a single "talking" gene. Similarly, genes determine the development of our penises, vaginas, and brains. But that's a far step from the contention that a single gene determines sexual desires, feelings of attraction, fantasies, and patterns of arousal.

Moreover, these studies really aren't examining the origins of sexual orientation. They're examining the origins of one type of sexual orientation: homosexuality. None of these researchers seems interested in explaining the origins of heterosexuality or bisexuality. For instance, if a certain structure in the brain is small in homosexual men and large in heterosexual men, is it somewhere in between among bisexual men?

Although the debate over the origins of sexual orientation is far from settled, let's suppose for the moment that sexual orientation is, in fact, biologically determined. What would be the social implications of such a contention? Some people argue that understanding sexual orientation as an innate characteristic beyond personal control, like hair or eye color, will make people more open minded about equality and more protective of the civil rights of gay and lesbian individuals. The long-standing concern that homosexuals shouldn't work in occupations involving children (Boy Scout leader, elementary school teacher, child care worker, and so on) because of their potentially corrupting influence would disappear, because environmental influence would no longer be considered a factor in the development of a child's sexual orientation.

On the other hand, information about the genetic origins of sexual orientation might be used to perpetuate the belief that homosexuality is a "defect" that needs to be fixed, thereby further stigmatizing gays and lesbians. Ideas about biological determinism inevitably carry the threat of encouraging us to try manipulating genes, the brain, hormones, or whatever the purported biological cause in order to adapt to prevailing social norms. For instance, some scientists have argued that exposure to certain levels of testosterone at certain times in fetal development is a crucial factor in the development of "sex centers" in the brain. If so, prenatal tests like amniocentesis could, perhaps, "predict" homosexuality. And if this "condition" can be predicted, "prevention" is but a short step away.

Intersections
The Effect of Gender on Learning Sexualities

Because of general differences in the ways that girls and boys are socialized in this society, the paths to sexual orientation are different (Levine & Evans, 2003). For instance, gay men tend to become aware of same-sex attractions, act on those attractions, and identify themselves as gay earlier than lesbians. On the other hand, lesbians tend to create ongoing love relationships with members of the same sex earlier than gay men. Furthermore, they're more likely to commit to a lesbian identity in the context of an emotional relationship; men tend to commit to a gay identity within the context of their sexual experiences. In other words, as with women in general, lesbians tend to associate their sexual identity with relationships and not so much with erotic activity.

Some researchers also argue that lesbians are more likely to view the acknowledgment of their sexual identity as a choice, whereas men tend to see it as a discovery (cited in Levine & Evans, 2003). In part, this difference may derive from the fact that the declaration of a lesbian identity is sometimes more of a political/philosophical statement than a statement about one's physical desires. In fact, one early study suggested that there are actually three types of lesbians: "ideological lesbians" (women for whom a lesbian identity is highly political), "personal lesbians" (women who want to establish an independent identity and see lesbianism as supportive of this goal), and "interpersonal lesbians" (women who find themselves involved with another woman and who experience this involvement as a discovery and not a purposeful choice) (Henderson, 1979).

Sociologist Valerie Jenness (2002) has argued that for women who fall into this latter category, becoming a lesbian involves a redefinition of the term *lesbian* so that it becomes less stigmatizing. Often, a lesbian identity develops long after women begin engaging in erotic activity with other women. Initially, their understanding of the social category "lesbian" is vague and derives not from personal experiences but typically from the media. Because these initial ideas about lesbians are likely to be negative or at best neutral, women at this stage see their own identities as incongruous with a lesbian identity. This woman lived with another woman for five years, and even felt that they were "married," but still didn't define herself as a lesbian:

> We considered ourselves married, although of course it was unofficial: we were both women. Never did I attach the label "lesbian" to either of us. I rarely thought of the term, and when I did I simply assumed that lesbians were women "out there" who were probably sick or deranged and at any rate were trying to be men. (quoted in Jenness, 2002, p. 138)

Before such a woman can define herself as lesbian, the meaning of the word to her has to change. As the connotations become more positive, the imagery associated with what it means to be a lesbian is likely to be seen as congruent with the individual's lived experiences, thereby making it easier to categorize herself as lesbian. Jenness warns, however, that the redefinition of what it means to be a lesbian is necessary, but not sufficient, for a woman to adopt a lesbian identity. Women can take a variety of different paths to defining themselves as lesbian.

Bisexualities In a society built around dichotomies in which people are likely to be categorized as either heterosexual or homosexual, developing a bisexual identity can be difficult. Sociologist Martin Weinberg and his associates (Weinberg, Williams, & Pryor, 2003) note that people who claim a bisexual identity face significantly more hostility than even homosexuals because their identity involves the rejection of two recognized categories of sexual identity:

> While the heterosexual world was said to be completely intolerant of any degree of homosexuality, the reaction of the homosexual world mattered more. Many bisexuals referred to the persistent

pressures they experienced to relabel themselves "gay" or "lesbian" and to engage in sexual activity exclusively with the same sex. It was asserted that no one was *really* bisexual, and that calling oneself "bisexual" was a politically incorrect and unauthentic identity. (Weinberg, Williams, & Pryor, 2003, p. 230)

Weinberg et al. found that settling into a bisexual identity often occurs many years after one experiences strong sexual attraction toward both men and women. Self-proclaimed bisexuals initially face a period of confusion and doubt as they struggle with an identity that doesn't fit into preexisting categories. This period can span years. Eventually, though, they come to see bisexuality as a plausible option and begin to apply the label to themselves.

What makes bisexuality especially interesting is its lack of social ratification. Homosexuals and heterosexuals alike often consider bisexuality to be a transitional stage. Indeed, the desire to form a permanent, monogamous relationship with someone requires that an individual "choose one or the other." Some Internet dating sites even prevent a person from retrieving information about both men and women. Hence, bisexuality continues to be a fluid identity long after its first application. Although most of Weinberg, Williams, and Pryor's subjects indicated that they didn't think they were in transition from homosexual to heterosexual (or vice versa), they did acknowledge that it was possible that some time in the future they might identify themselves as either homosexual or heterosexual. These expectations may simply reflect the power of a cultural ideology that defines sexual orientation in either/or terms.

LEARNING SOCIAL CLASSES

Conflict and functionalist sociologists alike tend to conceive of social class as more of a structural position than a component of personal identity. But just as we must learn to understand the intersections of our race, ethnicity, gender, and sexuality—and the values, tastes, styles, and behaviors that derive from those identities—so too must we learn to self-consciously place ourselves within the broader social stratification system. Aside from those in the upper class, though, who receive rather specific lessons about their roles in society, the class identity lessons we learn are usually subtler and more indirect than the lessons we receive for other social identities. Nevertheless, class identity provides us with an important lens through which we see the world and our relative position in it.

The relationship between social class and socialization might appear obvious. Some families have greater access than others to the economic resources that are associated with a comfortable childhood: lots of toys and athletic equipment, a nice house, access to a good school, parental support for "appropriate" activities. Children raised in such an environment are likely to reap the benefits that these material advantages create. But access to material resources does not, in and of itself, ensure a smooth childhood. In contrast, children who live in unstable or substandard housing or in unsafe neighborhoods and whose parents work long hours but still can't afford the amenities of a healthy life face special burdens—not only in terms of their physical needs but in terms of the identities they develop. Wealthy and middle-class children come to understand their "place" in society in far different ways than poor children do.

Consider the plight of children who spend some of their early years in homeless shelters. The expectations most of us take for granted—that we'll have enough food to eat, a place to sleep, and appropriate clothing—are unpredictable for them. The lack of a permanent home robs these children of a comforting daily routine and the opportunity to acquire a strong sense of self-worth (Arrighi, 2002). The sight of a mother or father losing control over the basic needs of life can damage the child's sense of trust and stability. Furthermore, children in homeless shelters don't have the luxury of learning about abstract concepts and ideas—something they're expected to know by the schools they sporadically attend.

Less obvious is the way that class can influence broader cultural ideologies about the socialization of children. Since the beginning of the 20th century, millions of anxious new parents have turned to child-rearing books—and later, web sites—for guidance and reassurance. Parents who use these sources of information have always tended to be at least middle class (Hulbert, 2004). So when so-called child-rearing experts change their advice—from, say, bottle-feeding to breast-feeding or from disciplinary spanking to time-outs—middle-class parents are more likely than poor or working-class parents to shift their practices accordingly. Middle-class parents also have the cultural and economic resources, as well as the time, to talk with their children, develop their educational interests, and play an active role in their schooling. The outcome is that middle-class parenting styles are more likely to coincide with professional philosophies about appropriate child care and that the parenting approaches available to poor and working-class parents will inevitably be seen as inadequate.

Perhaps the most important way that class influences socialization is through its effects on the values held by parents, who pass these values along to their children. Sociologist Melvin Kohn (1979) interviewed 200 American working-class and 200 middle-class couples who had at least one child of fifth-grade age. He found that working-class parents want their children to be neat and clean and to follow the rules, habits that will help them succeed in blue-collar jobs later on. Conversely, middle-class parents are more likely to promote such values as self-direction, independence, and curiosity. A more recent study found that middle-class parents are more likely than working-class parents to foster their children's talents through organized leisure activities and logical reasoning (Lareau, 2003). Other researchers have found this tendency especially strong among middle-class mothers (Xiao, 2000).

Obviously, not all middle-class parents or all working-class parents raise their children the same way, and many factors other than social class influence parental values and child-rearing approaches. Nevertheless, these general tendencies have been found regardless of the sex of the child, the size and composition of the family (Kohn, 1979), or the parents' race (Lareau, 2003). Moreover, others have found that despite cultural differences, this relationship between social class standing and socialization of values exists in Western European societies, namely Germany (Williamson, 1984), non-Western societies, like Japan, and formerly non-capitalist countries, namely, Poland (Schooler, 1996).

Class differences in socialization have important implications for children's futures. Working-class parents tend to believe that eventual occupational success, even survival, depends on their children's ability to conform to and obey authority (Kohn, 1979). Middle-class parents believe their children's future success will result from assertiveness and initiative. Hence, middle-class children's feelings of control over their own destiny are likely to be much stronger than those of working-class children. In a study of African American women, those from middle-class backgrounds reported that their parents had had higher expectations for them and were more involved in their education than women from working-class backgrounds reported (Hill, 1997).

Different parenting values and approaches to child rearing transmit different cultural advantages to children (Lareau, 2003). Take, for instance, how children learn to interact with others. Sociologist Annette Lareau (2003) conducted intensive interviews with 12 families of different racial and class backgrounds. She and her associates visited each family about

20 times over the span of a month. She found subtle, but important, class differences:

> There was quite a bit more talking in middle-class homes than in working-class and poor homes, leading to the development of greater verbal agility, larger vocabularies, more comfort with authority figures, and more familiarity with abstract concepts. Importantly, children also developed skill differences in interacting with authority figures in institutions and at home. Middle-class children . . . learn, as young boys, to shake the hands of adults and look them in the eye. . . . Researchers stress the importance of eye contact, firm handshakes, and displaying comfort with bosses during [job interviews]. In poor families . . . however, family members usually do not look each other in the eye when conversing. . . . They [may] live in neighborhoods where it can be dangerous to look people in the eye too long (p. 5).

As families climb the class ladder, children's sense of entitlement based on their class identity tends to increase as well. Middle-class children take for granted the right to be involved in activities like organized sports and music lessons, to attend summer school, and to go on class trips. Many of these activities replicate key aspects of the workplace, like meeting new people and learning to work effectively with them. Their travel experiences give them a level of comfort when called on to take a trip for business or interact with people from different regions (Lareau, 2003). All of these experiences and the skills that are developed in them will provide a smooth fit with the behaviors and expectations of other social institutions these children will encounter when they become adults.

Among the upper class, an even greater sense of entitlement is likely to be transmitted from parents to children. Parents always "endow" their children with varying amounts of cultural capital (family pedigree, reputations, skills, knowledge, social networks and connections, and so on). Even when not lavished with money and other financial resources, children of affluent parents may inherit other useful resources, such as a recognized family name and respect, privilege, and personal contacts that go along with it. Upper-class children are often taught to value their position and understand the responsibilities that come with it. Other children come to understand the responsibilities of their class position too, but they often absorb messages about their place in society that limit their aspirations.

Intersections
Class, Race, and Motherwork

According to sociologist Patricia Hill Collins (2001), socioeconomic status has long worked in tandem with a history of racial domination and gender inequality to shape the socialization of children. The relative economic security enjoyed by white middle-class mothers means they can devote much of their "motherwork" to tending to the emotional needs of their children. For poor mothers of color, however, child rearing revolves around three different themes:

- *Physical Survival.* Statistically, poor children of color face heightened rates of infant mortality and poverty (if they survive to childhood). In addition, they're more likely than advantaged children to live in environments where drugs, crime, industrial pollutants, and violence pose daily risks to their survival. Thus, for poor mothers of color, much of child rearing involves making sacrifices—of time, of their own physical well-being, of self-esteem—simply to ensure that their children are relatively safe and have enough to eat. Ironically, the concern with physical survival may actually mean spending less time with children because of the long hours of work that are necessary.

- *Power.* Poor mothers of color often feel powerless to control their own lives. They face the burden of overcoming the disillusionment and hopelessness that are likely to accumulate over years of interacting with dominant cultural, economic, educational, and political institutions. Furthermore, these institutions place poor mothers of color in positions that make them appear less powerful to their children. For instance, the current welfare system frequently forces poor mothers to choose between working for a wage and spending time with their children. For some groups—namely, African American and Native American women—the struggle for maternal empowerment is made more difficult by their ethnoracial histories of conquest.

- *Identity.* Maintaining a sense of self-worth in their children is a constant struggle for poor mothers of color. They fight to foster a meaningful racial identity for their children within a society that tends to malign people of color and to teach their children to survive in systems that are not structured to provide them with long-term advantages. This dimension of motherhood is unnecessary among white, middle-class mothers whose children face no such identity challenges. White children may be taught by their parents to fight against racial oppression, but the intactness of their own identity doesn't depend on the outcome of that battle.

The messages children receive about their class standing are, of course, most painful for those at the lower economic rungs of society. When combined with racial and gender disadvantage, class stratification creates special pressures for some parents that other parents are able to avoid.

IDENTITY SOCIALIZATION IN SCHOOLS

In contemporary industrial societies, the most powerful institutional agent of socialization after the family is the educational system. Indeed, the primary reason schools exist is to socialize young people. Children enter the system at about age 5 (or sooner if you count preschool), and most will spend at least the next 13 years of their lives in it. No other institution has such prolonged contact with the bodies and minds of individuals as the educational system.

Schools, of course, don't simply teach students basic educational skills like reading, writing, arithmetic, and science. More subtly, they teach them who they are and what they can expect from themselves in the future. In this way, schools can often solidify the gender, racial, class, and sexual identities that children initially developed within their families. Although teachers are the most visible agent of socialization associated with schools, influential identity lessons come from other sources as well, most notably peers.

PEER INFLUENCE

In everyday interactions, peers—close friends, acquaintances, neighbors, classmates—provide us with extensive information about our social identities. This influence is especially powerful among young people. As much as adults would like to think otherwise, peers have more access to children's everyday lives than just about anyone else does. Parents don't usually see their kids at school. Teachers don't usually see their students at home. But peers see each other everywhere: in school, at home, on the street, at malls, on sports teams, and in a variety of other locations. It's not surprising, then, that as children reach adolescence and struggle to establish an identity distinct from their families, they turn more and more to school peers as both a source of information about who they are and a reference point against which they measure themselves.

In many ways, peer groups reinforce the lessons about social identity learned at home, in part because neighborhoods and schools tend to be relatively uniform in social class and ethnoracial makeup. However, peer groups also help young people actively resist the efforts of families and schools to socialize them (Adler & Adler, 1998). For instance, feminist sociologists have found that even children raised in households where they are taught by their parents to believe that men and women are equal and that no activity needs to be sex-linked act in ways that are quite gender stereotypical when they're away from home with their friends and schoolmates (Risman & Myers, 1997).

Similarly, parental influence with regard to sexual behavior is often weak or nonexistent. The development of sexuality is almost exclusively peer-driven. Pressure on teens to become sexually active—and therefore to announce one's sexual identity—is sometimes direct and specific, as when one individual tries to persuade another to have sex. But more commonly, the pressure resides in a heightened sexual atmosphere that pervades teen life: fashion, language, music, computer games, and daily conversation. This sort of environment has enormous influence over adolescent sexual decision making (Rubin, 1990)—from prepubescent chasing and teasing to teenage sexual contact, dating, and romance. Moreover, this atmosphere is almost exclusively heterosexual. The identity costs of veering from heterosexuality can be especially steep in the teen subculture. Homosexual slurs and insults on the schoolyard are quite common. They effectively convey the message that non-heterosexual identities are unacceptable and impose heteronormative behavioral expectations and demands.

Though school performance is closely tied to future educational and economic outcomes, peer group concerns dominate life for school-age children and especially adolescents. Peer groups have the power to simultaneously unite and divide. On the one hand, conformity—in terms of appearances, beliefs, and behaviors—is the preeminent characteristic of peer groups. Young people quickly learn the culturally acceptable guidelines and the consequences for violating them (Adler & Adler, 1998). In so doing, they gain a sense of belonging and come to see the commonality between themselves and fellow members who claim similar identities.

On the other hand, peer relations are relentlessly critical and cruelly stratified, pitting individuals against each other. Attractiveness, prestige, and desirability are meticulously assessed and severely judged. Groups create elaborate criteria for inclusion and exclusion. Sometimes, these criteria reflect those that divide groups in the larger society, chiefly, gender, race, ethnicity, social class, and sexual orientation. Other times, the criteria are vague, arbitrary, and fluid—the right logo to wear on clothing, for example, which can change in an instant. Although the standards of popularity may vary from neighborhood to neighborhood or even from clique to clique, all peer groups have ways of determining who's in and who's not. Acceptance leads to power and status. But rejection is a sort of social death sentence, especially in adolescence, and has been linked to poor school performance, depression, physical illness, disruptive behavior, and impaired adult relationships (Sunwolf & Leets, 2004).

GENDERED LESSONS

In addition to families and peers, educational institutions—from pre-schools to universities—are key locations for learning and doing gender. In societies where girls and women are either segregated or formally excluded from educational institutions—such as many fundamentalist Muslim countries—the gender lessons students receive are stark. In U.S. society, female students are no longer prevented or discouraged from receiving an education. Indeed, more women than men are now enrolled in American colleges (U.S. Bureau of the Census, 2004). Yet research evidence suggests that the ways in which girls and women are treated in schools are still different from the treatment of boys and men.

Schools contain an abundance of subtle and not-so-subtle informal "lessons" about what is considered appropriate and inappropriate behavior for female and male members of our society. Teachers sometimes draw on sex as a basis for sorting students and organizing their activities or casually pit girls against boys for spelling or math competitions (Thorne, 1995). But the differential treatment needn't be so purposeful. As sociologists Myra and David Sadker (2002) point out, "Sitting in the same classroom, reading the same textbook, listening to the same teacher, boys and girls receive very different educations" (p. 583). Research over the past several decades has revealed patterns of differential treatment that create, for girls, a powerfully disabling educational climate:

- Girls receive less teacher attention and less useful feedback than boys.
- Girls talk significantly less in class than boys, and when they do speak up, they are more likely than boys to be reminded to raise their hands.
- Girls rarely see mention of the contributions of women in their textbooks, which continue to emphasize male accomplishments.
- Girls are more likely than boys to be the focus of unwanted sexual attention in school. (Sadker, Sadker, Fox, & Salata, 2004)

Girls and women have made progress over the past few decades, and teachers, school administrators, even textbook writers have become much more sensitive to these kinds of issues. Nevertheless, boys and girls still face differential treatment at the hands of those who control their books and classrooms. The consequences of such socialization experiences are neither harmless nor trivial. Even though they outperform boys on almost every standard measure of academic achievement in the early grades, by the time they finish high school, girls often fall behind. For instance, although the gap has closed, boys still outscore girls on the SAT and other aptitude tests, especially in math (U.S. Bureau of the Census, 2004). In addition, in college, males are more likely than females to take rigorous courses geared for math and science majors and achieve higher grades in those courses (College Board, 1998).

Segregating the Sexes Because boys and girls continue to have different school experiences, many educators have come to the conclusion that mixing them together in school settings may work to the disadvantage of students, especially girls, by reinforcing rather than reducing gender stereotypes. They argue for the establishment of single-sex schools and the inclusion of single-sex classrooms in public schools. They point out that girls who go to single-sex schools are more assertive, more confident, and more likely to take classes in math, computer science, and physics than girls in coeducational schools. Boys in single-sex environments are less likely to get into trouble and more likely to pursue interests in art, music, and drama than their coeducational counterparts (National Association for Single-Sex Public Education, 2004). Furthermore, graduates of single-sex schools—both girls and boys—are more likely to go to prestigious colleges and more likely to attend graduate or professional school than graduates of coeducational high schools (Lee & Marks, 1990).

Same-sex educational environments have become popular over the last decade. Today there are about three dozen same-sex public schools in the country, almost all established after 1996. Another 72 coeducational schools now offer single-sex classes (cited in Mendez, 2004). Some private schools are now opting for a blend of mixed-sex and single-sex education, with boys and girls learning together in elementary school and high school but being taught separately during the turbulent middle-school years. As one prominent educator puts it, "Girls who are 'confident at 11 and confused at 16' will more likely be creative thinkers and risk-takers as adults if educated apart from boys in middle school" (quoted in Gross, 2004, p. A16).

The gendered identity lessons that people receive in school don't only come from teachers and administrators, though. Many of these lessons are self-taught. For instance, boys and girls often segregate themselves on the playground, in the cafeteria, and in the classroom. Such separation becomes more complete as children get older (Thorne, 1995). When they do interact with one another, the nature of such interaction can reinforce rather than diminish the sex boundaries. Sociologist Barrie Thorne (1995) observed a variety of school settings. She found that cross-sex interactions often consisted of chasing, invasions, and rituals of pollution in which one group considers contact with the other group as contaminating. However, rather than attribute these tendencies simply to essential sex differences between boys and girls, she argues that they are contingent on group size, the nature of the activity, and the risk of being teased.

Certainly, self-segregation along sex lines is the rule in the school years. Even very young children can be quite diligent about conveying their attitudes toward gender appropriateness and sanctioning other children who don't conform or who cross their self-imposed boundaries. But this sort of sex segregation is by no means inevitable.

Intersections
Gender, Race, and Bullying

As you can see, schools can be hostile places, especially in the teen years, when kids are at their mean-spirited best and gender identities are fragile. When we think of the torment and harassment that take place within American schools, what tends to come to mind are boys intimidating other boys or harassing girls. Aggression continues to be the hallmark of masculinity, from childhood to adulthood.

On the other hand, parents and teachers tend to discourage direct physical aggression in girls (Fagot & Hagan, 1985). So it might be surprising to learn that a subculture of girls' aggression and bullying not only exists but, according to one author, is pervasive from elementary school to high school and may be just as harmful as boys' aggression.

Rachel Simmons (2002) interviewed girls between the ages of 10 and 14 in 10 different schools over the span of a year. Some schools were private; others public. Some were predominantly white; others had a majority of black or Latino/a students. Some were coeducational; others were all-girls schools. She talked to students, parents, teachers, and staff in group meetings, one-on-one interviews, over the phone, and by e-mail. She found across all settings that female bullying is commonplace. But it is not the sort of direct physical intimidation that characterizes male bullying. Female bullying frequently focuses on relationships (such as excluding someone socially for revenge, ignoring a person as a form of punishment, sabotaging a friendship, spreading rumors, and so on). The object is not to inflict physical pain but to humiliate the victim socially, destroying the person's reputation, and undermining her self-esteem. As Simmons describes it:

> Girls use backbiting, exclusion, rumors, name-calling, and manipulation to inflict psychological pain on targeted victims. Unlike boys, who tend to bully acquaintances or strangers, girls frequently attack within tightly knit networks of friends, making aggression harder to identify and intensifying the damage to the victims. . . . Girls fight with body language and relationships instead of fists and knives. . . . In this world, friendship is a weapon, and the sting of a shout pales in comparison to a day of someone's silence. There is no gesture more devastating than the back turning away. (Simmons, 2002, p. 3)

Simmons attributes the use of these alternative forms of aggression to the pervasive social norms of feminine restraint. However, the power of these norms is not felt uniformly by girls from all races and classes. She points out, for instance, that among African Americans, Latinas, and working-class white girls, there is a tradition of direct conflict and outspoken "truth telling." Many of the African American and Latina girls she interviewed indicated that they were socialized by their parents to use independence, confidence, and assertiveness to resist the discrimination that they would inevitably face. These girls—from both working-class and middle-class backgrounds—made clear distinctions between committed "friends," whom they trusted, and "associates" or acquaintances, whom they didn't trust. The reason given for not trusting them was often that they were "two-faced," meaning that these girls had a tendency to talk behind their backs. But whereas white girls might just accept the behind-the-back whispering that goes on, African American and Latina girls saw such talk as grounds for confrontation. As one African American first-year high school student put it, "You've got to learn how to stick up for yourself. You can't let people push you down." Another said that when she hears that someone is talking about her, she says to that person "If you have something to say, say it to my face" (quoted on p. 187).

Simmons is quick to point out that such general racial tendencies do not apply universally. Not all girls of color were willing to be confrontational when they were harassed or belittled; not all white girls responded passively. One middle-class white student, for instance, recounted an incident in which she and her two sisters were confronted by two other girls: "We did not tolerate any crap, we knocked the shit out of these girls. Don't get me wrong, though, I never looked for, or wanted to fight" (quoted on pp. 179–180).

> The intersections of race and class can make girls' responses to bullying particularly difficult. The middle-class African American girls Simmons interviewed uniformly reported frustration over the fact that their assertive attempts at bringing out the truth were often rebuffed or punished. The very characteristics they had been taught were signs of strength were likely to be interpreted as "mean" or "bitchy" by others. Although they felt it was important to stand up for themselves, they also felt some reluctance to risk raising the ire of other middle-class students who might then stereotype them as "loud" and "disruptive."

Coaching Masculinities The vast majority of research on the institutional context of gender socialization (schools, media, and so forth) tends to focus primarily on girls and the structural and interpersonal disadvantages they face growing up in a relatively sexist society. Only recently has academic attention turned to understanding the process by which boys develop gender identities in this society. Although schools provide powerful gender lessons to both boys and girls, masculinity among boys is equally likely to develop within the context of organized sports.

Sociologist Michael Messner (2002) conducted extensive interviews with 30 male former athletes from different ethnoracial and class groups. Even though some boys don't like sports and choose not to participate, it is still the case that most boys, to a greater or lesser degree, are judged according to their ability or lack of ability in competitive sports. For most of the men Messner interviewed, becoming involved in sports when they were young was not much of a decision. They said they did it simply because "it's just what everybody did." They recounted their earliest experiences with sports as an exclusively male world of fathers, older brothers, uncles, classmates, and coaches who served as athletic role models. Even fathers who were otherwise absent or emotionally distant tended to be involved in their sons' athletic lives.

The sports world is a logical place for the development of traditionally masculine identities because of the heavy emphasis on competition and conquest. It is a hierarchical world where, despite the "it's not whether you win or lose but how you play the game" rhetoric, importance is placed on winning. Just being out there and participating is certainly presented to boys as a good thing, but being better than others is the key to acceptance and approval.

It's especially important to consider the role of race and social class in the relationship between sports and masculinity. For boys from all class levels, early indicators that they have "some skills" when it comes to athletics are responded to by their families and their peers as a good thing. However, males from ethnoracial minorities or from lower-status backgrounds are more likely than white middle- and upper-class males to see athletic success as a survival strategy—a way to improve their economic lot in life. In a middle-class or upper-class environment, boys have more options. By the time they reach high school and beyond, many decide to shift their focus away from sports toward the development of their careers. For them, organized sports are just one of several ways in which they can establish a positive and masculine identity. For lower-status boys, though, the broader social context—education, economy, the community— narrows rather than expands their options later in life. They come to perceive sports as their only option. Sports are *the* place, rather than *a* place, within which to construct their masculine identities.

The irony of this emphasis on athletic success in the development of masculinity is that almost all boys who participate in competitive sports will fail at some point in their lives. Only a tiny fraction of athletes ever "make it" to the top levels of their sports. Messner cites statistics showing that the odds of attaining professional status in a sport are 4 in 100,000 for white men, 2 in 100,000 for black men, and 3 in 1 million for Latino men. Disadvantage, despair, and threats to masculinity can multiply in communities where athletic success is presented as the only way to "make it" but so few actually do.

CLASS AND RACE LESSONS

Schools play an important role in class socialization. In public schools, for instance, working-class and poor kids are subtly taught their place through authority relationships with teachers and principals so that they will be prepared for the subordinate work positions they will probably occupy in the future (Bowles & Gintis, 1976). In such environments, students are likely to be closely monitored for behavioral conformity and expected to follow a laundry list of formal and detailed rules. Discipline and compliance with teachers' and administrators' directions are primary goals (Brint, 1998). More advantaged students not only have more resources at their disposal, they are likely to speak, dress, and comport themselves in ways that teachers associate with "good students" (Brint, 1998). Consequently, they may receive preferential treatment even from teachers who could be described as fair and open-minded.

Socialization experiences in school are particularly important in the formation of identities for students who come from the highest reaches of the upper class. They frequently spend their childhood in private schools, their adolescence in boarding schools, and their college years in heavily endowed private universities (Domhoff, 1998). A study of more than 60 elite boarding schools in the United States and Great Britain showed how the philosophies, programs, and lifestyles of boarding schools help transmit power and privilege (Cookson & Persell, 1985). In addition to the standard curriculum, these schools teach things not likely to be found in public schools, such as conversational etiquette, styles of dress, aesthetic tastes, values, and manners. Required attendance at school functions; participation in esoteric sports such as lacrosse, squash, and crew; the wearing of school blazers or ties; and other "character-building" activities are designed to teach young people the expected lifestyle of the ruling class into which they were born.

This school experience forms an everlasting social, political, and economic bond among all graduates, and the schools act as gatekeepers into prestigious universities. After they leave these universities, graduates connect with one another at the highest levels in the worlds of business, finance, and government. In this way, the privileged social status that is produced and maintained through the elite educational system practically guarantees that the people who occupy key political and economic positions will form a like-minded, cohesive group with little resemblance to the majority whose lives depend on their decisions.

Race is also an integral part of the school experience. In 1954, the U.S. Supreme Court ruled, in Brown v. Board of Education of Topeka, that racially segregated schools were unconstitutional because they were inherently unequal. School districts around the country were placed under court order to desegregate. But 50 years later, the outcome of that crucial court decision is murky at best. Millions of students of color today attend schools that are just as segregated as they were in 1954. Sixty-six percent of all African American public school students and 70% of Latino/a students attend predominantly minority schools, defined as those schools with more than 50% of their enrollment made up of either African American or Latino/a students. And about a third of black students attend schools in which at least 90% of the students are not white (Orfield & Yun, 1999). At the same time, most white public school students go to schools that are nearly all white, even in cities that have large minority populations.

Not everyone thinks this situation is a bad thing. For many families of color, the benefits of forced integration have not been worth the burden their children must bear. Indeed, some African American parents today question the utility of integration and have even gone to court to prevent it. As one mother put it, "Integration? What was it good for? They were just setting up our babies to fail" (quoted in Winter, 2004, p. 27).

Nonetheless, when African American and Latino/a students are segregated into schools where the majority of students are not white, they are likely to find themselves in schools where poverty is concentrated. This is not the case with segregated white students, whose majority-white schools almost always enroll high proportions of middle-class students (Orfield & Yun, 1999).

This combination of class and race creates vastly different educational opportunities. Jonathan Kozol (1991), a teacher turned social critic, wrote a stinging exposé of how class and race influence education in a book titled *Savage Inequalities*. Kozol argues that disparities between wealth and poverty—which have become more extreme since he wrote the book—have created a two-tiered public educational system that solidifies broader social inequalities. He compares a variety of different public and private school systems. Two public high schools in particular—a poor, predominantly African American school in East St. Louis, Illinois, and an upper-middle-class, predominantly white school in Rye, New York—serve to illustrate the extremes of educational stratification in this society.

At the time Kozol wrote his book, East St. Louis was one of the poorest cities in the country. There were no obstetric services for pregnant women, no regular system of trash collection, and few jobs. Because of pollution emitted by nearby chemical plants, it had one of the highest rates of childhood asthma and lead poisoning in the country. It was not uncommon for raw sewage to back up into people's homes. Childhood malnutrition was rampant. The destitution of the city inevitably spilled over into the public schools. Teacher layoffs were commonplace, the facilities were decrepit and dangerous, and textbooks were tattered and outdated. The athletic facilities were so bad that visiting football teams wanted to play without a halftime break so they could get out quicker. The chairperson of the Illinois State Board of Education said that East St. Louis "is simply the worst possible place I can imagine to have a child brought up" (quoted in Kozol, 1991, p. 25). Not surprisingly, only a very tiny percentage of the students enrolled in the public schools in East St. Louis are able to overcome the obstacles to learning that these conditions create. Only a little over half ever graduate from high school. The socializing messages these children receive about their identities and their futures are bleak. It's easy to see how their disadvantages might be difficult if not impossible to overcome.

In Rye, New York, the conditions couldn't be more different. Rye is a middle- to upper-middle-class suburb about 40 minutes from New York City. The high school campus is well-manicured, and the gray stone building gives it the appearance of a New England prep school. The students have access to a relaxing carpeted lounge where they can "stretch out and be comfortable while reading" (quoted on p. 125). The library is wood-paneled, the auditorium is newly renovated, and banks of computers are available for student use. The teachers are well-paid and highly motivated. Only 1% to 2% of the students are Latino/a or African American. The students have several advanced placement courses they can take. Rarely does a graduate not go on to college.

While the disparities in educational opportunities between these two schools are dramatic and obvious, the subtle differences that get communicated to the students are also worth noting. School is not just about learning a particular curriculum; it is about learning who one is and how one fits into the broader social structure. The children in Rye are learning that the society in general and the educational system in particular are there to serve their interests. They come to believe that their futures are bright, that all that holds them back is lack of effort on their part. The sky indeed is the limit. In East St. Louis, however, the students learn a very different message about their "place" in society. Success and comfort are goals well beyond their grasp. Certainly, there are students who do "get out" and make something of themselves. But they are clearly the exceptions that prove the rule. Their disheartening surroundings only serve to reinforce the disillusionment that they learn in their homes.

These discrepancies are not limited to a few isolated districts. In 2004, a poll of over 3,000 teachers in California, New York, and Wisconsin found a two-tiered educational system in which teachers and students in poor, minority schools spend their days in broken-down, insect-infested buildings. These schools have higher turnover rates among teachers, more unfilled vacancies, lower levels of parental involvement, and fewer textbooks and other educational materials than more affluent schools do (cited in Jacobson, 2004). Compared to wealthier schools, poor schools offer fewer advanced courses, hire fewer teachers with credentials in the subjects they're teaching, and have less stable enrollments, higher dropout rates, and more students with untreated health problems. Furthermore, poor school districts face increasing financial pressures because of recent reductions in federal assistance programs.

The mix of race and class has important implications for students' futures. Concentrated poverty tends to be linked to lower educational achievement. And regardless of the quality of the school at the elementary and secondary level, the rising cost of higher education reduces the number of minority students who are able to attend college. Consequently, Blacks and Latino/as continue to have lower levels of educational attainment than Whites and Asian Americans, a trend that has economic consequences down the road (see Chapter 8).

CONCLUSION

One of the things that I hope you take from this chapter is the knowledge that the very essence of who we are—our gender, our racial and class identity, our sexuality—is not private property. All of us in one way or another are a reflection of larger cultural values, historical processes, and the attitudes and expectations of other people in our lives. This realization can be humbling and frightening. It would be more comforting to think that who we become is solely a product of our own doing—either in the form of our genetic predispositions or as a result of our personal hopes, dreams, and desires. If this were the case, we would have a great deal of control over what and who we become.

But social life is never that simple. Broader values surrounding gender, sexuality, race, and class will always determine how we incorporate those features of our identity into our own self-concept. If we're lucky enough to occupy the most advantaged locations on all these dimensions, chances are our lives will be comfortable, our self-concepts will be positive, and our prospects for a successful future will be bright. However, if we happen to occupy a devalued category, we face an uphill struggle. We can—and hopefully would—take pride in our gender, our ethnicity, our sexuality and extract from these components a strong sense of self-esteem. But if that esteem is undermined at the cultural and institutional levels, our pride will not automatically translate into greater social, economic, educational, and political opportunities.

[**INVESTIGATING IDENTITIES AND INEQUALITIES**
Go to your room: Race, gender, and childhood discipline]

You've seen in this chapter that early versions of ethnoracial, gender, sexual, and class identities are usually formed in families. Children receive implicit and explicit instruction from parents and other relatives in meeting the cultural expectations associated with these features of their identity.

This exercise involves brief interviews with fellow students. Try to interview at least five to eight people. Select a variety of individuals so that you have a mix of genders, races, and ethnicities. Ask them a series of questions about their experiences growing up. The following questions are some examples. You needn't use all of them, and you can alter the wording to fit the circumstances of particular respondents. You may also add other questions that you think would work better.

- From the time you were born to the time you entered college, in which of the following living arrangements did you spend most of your childhood?

  - living with both biological parents
  - living with one biological parent and a stepparent
  - living with one parent
  - living with another adult caretaker (for instance, grandparents)

- How many siblings do you have? How many lived with you while growing up (that is, until you entered college)?
- Can you recall your parent(s) or adult caretaker(s) ever talking to you about your race or your ethnicity? What is your earliest memory of such a conversation? What did it entail?
- Can you recall your parent(s) or adult caretaker(s) ever talking to you about being female (or male)? Can you recall them ever providing explicit instructions on how to act as a girl (or boy)? Describe.
- Can you recall your parent(s) or adult caretaker(s) ever talking to you about sexuality? If so, what assumptions do you recall them making about the sexual orientation of future partners?
- In general, how would you describe your relationship with your parent(s) or adult caretaker(s)?

  - very warm and close
  - warm and close
  - somewhat distant
  - very distant

- All children get into trouble from time to time. How did your parent(s) or adult caretaker(s) discipline you when you engaged in behavior they didn't like?

You can either tape-record or write down responses you get. Another option would be to have respondents send their answers to you via e-mail.

Once you've gathered your answers, look for patterns in people's responses. Are there any systematic differences in the way that men and women answered the questions? Were women more likely than men to receive "traditional" gender socialization messages or was it the other way around? What about racial/ethnic differences? Were certain ethnoracial groups more or less likely to be subjected to harsh physical discipline? What about the "race messages" they received? Can you determine if your respondents' sense of inferiority or superiority (based on either race or gender) was cultivated by their parents or caretakers? You should always be cautious about drawing general conclusions from information provided by a small group of people. But based on the responses to your questions, see if you can gain some insight into the role that families play in young people's racial and gender socialization.

Note: Most colleges and universities require that any student research project involving human subjects—even if it just entails asking people questions— be approved by a campus or departmental review committee. For instance, you will probably be required to show that your interviewees have consented to participate and that you've guaranteed that their identities will not be divulged. Make sure you talk to your instructor before proceeding with this exercise to see what steps you have to take in order to have it approved by the appropriate committee.

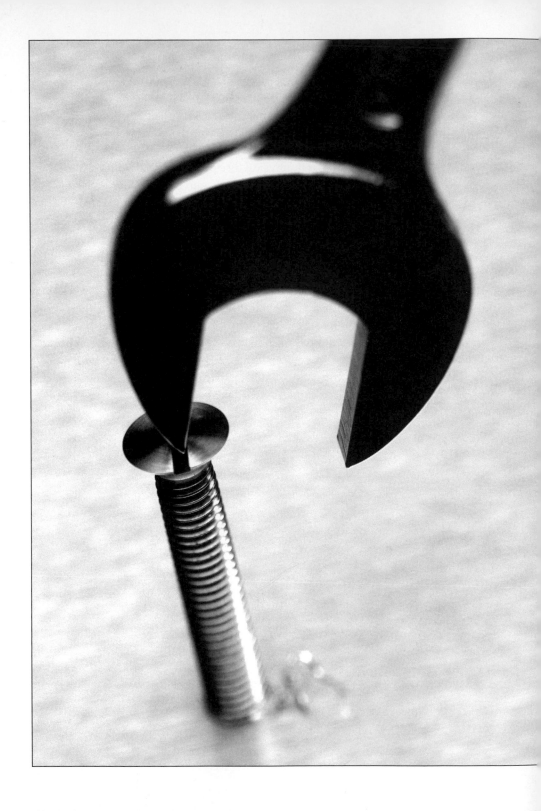

Inequalities

Race, class, gender, and sexuality are more than just noteworthy features of our social identities. If that's all they were, differences between groups would be nothing more than...well...differences between groups. But social identities are always related to unequal access to life chances.

Part 2 examines how the intersections of race, class, gender, and sexuality contribute to advantages and disadvantages in our dealings with others and in our institutional opportunities for a healthy life, legal protection, and economic well-being. ∎

CHAPTER 5

Expressing Inequalities
Prejudice and Discrimination in Everyday Life

When I was nine years old, my family moved from a suburb just outside of New York City to a suburb just outside of Los Angeles. The move represented many changes for us. My father's company had gone out of business and he was going to start a new job in California, managing a dry-cleaning store that one of his brothers owned. We went from living in a nice house on a small pond in a middle-class subdivision to living in a small, cramped, nondescript apartment right next to a freeway.

On the first day of school (I was just starting fourth grade), I immediately realized that I was different from the other kids. In New York, everyone I knew—my relatives, my friends, my schoolmates, my neighbors—was like me, racially and religiously. My family is Jewish, though not particularly religious. In the New York community where I had lived, public schools closed on the Jewish holidays in October. Back there, I didn't know anyone close to me who wasn't Jewish.

In California, I was an outsider. I'd never gone to school with kids who wore crosses or St. Christopher medals around their necks. Many of my fellow students were Latino/a. They had names that sounded different from any I'd heard before. They spoke with an unusual accent. Going to a new school is always a somewhat traumatic experience. But I felt like I was in a different world. The first few days, I ate lunch by myself. I was sad, but I figured sooner or later it'd get better.

When the 3:00 bell rang that first Friday, I was gleeful. The first week was mercifully over, and a weekend of rest and relaxation awaited. My escape was thwarted, however, by another fourth-grader who stopped me as I approached the schoolyard gate. Aside from brief sports-related encounters during recess, I hadn't ever spoken to him. He was much bigger than me, which was not all that surprising since at that time I was pretty little for my age.

He asked me what my name was and I told him. "Hey, you're a *new . . . man* around here! Get it?" He laughed at his own joke, apparently convinced that combining my last name with my status in the school was hilarious.

"Yeah, I am," I replied.

"So what *are* you?" he asked.

At first, I didn't know what he was getting at. "What do you mean?"

"You know, what church does your family go to?"

I paused. "I don't think we go to a church." In retrospect, that was kind of a stupid response, I know. Either you go or you don't go.

"Everybody goes to church!" he shouted in disbelief. At this point, some other kids had begun to mill around. "So which one do you go to?" For some reason, he figured pressing me with the same question, only louder, would produce the response he was looking for.

"I told you, we don't go to church," I said with all the sternness I could muster.

He looked at me as if I'd just spoken in tongues and pivoted away, no doubt puzzled by what to him was an incomprehensible response. I thought he was going to leave and that'd be that. But after a few steps, he spun around with a "Hey-wait-a-minute!" kind of look on his face. "You're not a Jew, are you?!"

In retrospect, I probably should have said something a movie tough guy would say, like "Yeah. What's it to you!?! You wanna make something of it!?!" Instead, I just nodded feebly, trying not to call attention to what I was fast coming to realize was a seriously stigmatizing identity.

He paused, as if to weigh the magnitude of this new information. Then he punched me in the face and walked away.

It's been nearly 40 years since this incident occurred, and it still makes my stomach flip to think about it. I've wondered a lot about why exactly it happened and what I could have done about it. The physical sting of his blow (which harmlessly landed on my cheekbone) wasn't nearly as painful as the humiliation I felt. Why was being Jewish such a punishable offense? How could he work up such hostility without knowing anything about me, other than my religion? As far as I could tell, there were hardly any Jews in this area. Maybe his parents had taught him to hate people of different religions or something. I convinced myself that I got punched in the face by someone who probably had no clue as to why he was punching me.

While his motivation has always remained a mystery to me, what was clear was that I had been tagged as an outcast. Like most kids that age, I just wanted to fit in. Being the new kid was bad enough. Being a new kid who was different from everyone else was childhood hell.

As fate would have it, a few days later, I was standing in line at an ice cream truck after school. A girl standing in front of me turned around and asked, "What religion are you?" I had learned my lesson. Without hesitation, I told her I was Catholic.

Perhaps the most insidious aspect of being targeted on the basis of some aspect of social identity—be it race, ethnicity, gender, sexuality, or religion—is the effect it has on one's self-concept. From that day on—through the rest of elementary school and well into junior high school—I tried to hide my ethnic/religious identity as best I could. I became ashamed of who I was. Of course, my close friends knew and accepted me (though I was annoyed by their constant attempts to set me up with the one Jewish girl in high school). But for everyone else, I denied and I concealed. I became quite adept at anticipating the trajectory of conversations, and if I sensed that talk was veering toward religion or some other topic that might reveal my identity, I'd deftly shift it to something safer. It was a stressful existence, to be sure. Although what happened to me in fourth grade may not match the intensity of the deep personal hatred and institutional disadvantage felt by racial, ethnic, gender, and sexual minorities, it did show me the external hostility and internal self-loathing that can arise from day-to-day dealings with difference and inequality.

In this chapter, I will examine the personal experience of prejudice and discrimination. It will serve as an introduction to the remaining chapters of this part of the book, which look in more detail at inequalities that exist in a variety of institutional areas of human life, including health and illness, law and justice, and economics and work. With all due respect to the crafters of the Declaration of Independence, opportunities to achieve life and liberty and to pursue happiness have never been distributed equally in this country. Although some groups have been able to transcend the status of "despised minority," others continue to suffer. The disadvantages some groups must cope with exist on several levels, ranging from the very personal level of individual perceptions, feelings, and face-to-face interactions to their contacts with the long-standing institutional structure of society itself.

STEREOTYPES: THE BUILDING BLOCKS OF BIGOTRY

The early 20th-century political commentator Walter Lippmann (1922) defined a **stereotype** as an oversimplified picture of the world, one that satisfies our need to see our social environment as a more understandable and manageable place than it really is. It is the overgeneralized belief that a certain trait, behavior, or attitude characterizes all members of some identifiable group. Stereotypes usually take the form "All _____ are _____."

While ethnoracial, religious, gender, and sexual stereotypes are the most familiar, other social groups can easily be the object of cultural stereotyping. Take, for instance, the blue-collar and service workers who occupy the "undignified," low-paying jobs that keep society going. Often referred to as "unskilled" workers, these individuals are consistently marginalized either by more affluent people who treat them as if they are invisible or by widely held cultural stereotypes that they are unintelligent and unrefined. Because there's a perception that the work itself is mindless, there's a belief that those who do it aren't that bright. Asked why the public is so disdainful of the working-class women who are hired to clean other people's homes, two maids replied, "They think we're stupid. They think we have nothing better to do with our time. We're nothing to these people. We're just maids" (quoted in Ehrenreich, 2001).

Although there may be a kernel of truth to stereotypes, they are never completely accurate. For instance, low-wage occupations often require an enormous amount of knowledge, judgment, and skill (Rose, 2004).

Hairstylists, for example, must show an astounding amount of aesthetic and mental agility when they turn vague requests ("I want something light and summery") into an actual hairstyle pleasing to the client. They must also have command of a remarkable range of knowledge—nutrition, hair growth patterns, the biology of skin, chemicals, and popular culture images of beauty—in order to provide their clients not only with a look they want but with advice on how to maintain a stylish appearance.

Casual observations easily refute the accuracy of even the most common stereotypes. Not all African Americans are poor and on welfare. Not all Italians belong to the Mafia. Not all Asian Americans are excellent math students. Not all Muslims are terrorists. Not all men are good at fixing things. Not all gay men like Broadway musicals. Not all wealthy people exploit those who are less advantaged. Overgeneralizations such as these can never be true for every member of that group.

THE NORMALITY OF STEREOTYPES

Our brains have a tendency to divide the world into distinct categories: good and bad, strong and weak, them and us (Rothenberg, 1992). Thus, we could say that stereotyping is a universal feature of human thought (Hamilton, 1981). By allowing us to focus on traits people have in common and to group them into easily identifiable categories, stereotypes make the processing of information and the formation of impressions more efficient. We can (and frequently do) construct stereotypes for every conceivable group into which we can place people. We stereotype people on the basis of the region of the country they come from, the type of car they drive, their clothing, or their hair color/style. As a college student, you have no doubt learned an entire repertoire of stereotypes that refer to different segments of your campus population: students who major in certain subjects, participate in certain sports or clubs, or live in certain dorms or Greek houses. Likewise, you've probably identified the appearances and behaviors that characterize "professors." You might even make fine character distinctions, say, between sociology professors and English literature professors.

Stereotypes are often quite resistant to change. They set expectations even in the absence of any confirmatory evidence and persist even in the face of contradictory evidence. If you believe that all professors are dull, egghead intellectuals who wear unfashionable clothing and are out of touch with modern youth culture, then you'll probably be reluctant to seek out a professor for advice on problems you're having in your personal life. Knowing one professor who is "with it" and insightful about such matters is probably not going to be enough to abandon the more general stereotype entirely, and that person will likely be dismissed as "an exception to the rule."

While such occupational stereotypes may influence—and even impede—interactions between individuals, they lack the broader societal significance of ethnic, religious, racial, gender, or sexual stereotypes. We learn these stereotypes at young ages, from our families, from the media, and from peers. Consequently, they have become fixtures on the social landscape, working their way into our thoughts and conversations, cultural imagery, and the everyday workings of larger organizations and institutions in society.

THE NEGATIVITY OF POSITIVE STEREOTYPES

Although the stereotyping of others is not the sole province of dominant groups, it always reflects power positions. Ironically, even apparently positive stereotypes can work to a group's disadvantage. Take, for instance, the characterization of Asian Americans as a "model" minority and the belief that women are naturally better parents than men. On the surface, these stereotypes seem complimentary. But a closer look shows how they can create damaging expectations and limit people's freedom to be unique individuals.

A "Model" Minority When it comes to the depiction of ethnoracial minorities in the United States, Asian Americans are often perceived as the "model" minority (a group whose success should be a lesson to other ethnoracial minorities). But such a label can be just as confining and oppressive as more negative labels. For one thing, it negates or trivializes some of the discrimination problems that Asian Americans actually face. It also allows white Americans to congratulate themselves on having overcome a legacy of prejudice and discrimination when in fact they haven't and to therefore avoid continued efforts to root it out (ModelMinority.com, 2003).

Positive stereotypes can quickly become negative. Asian American stereotypes are part of a broad continuum of no-win attitudes toward people of color in this society:

> When Blacks don't make it, it's because . . . their culture doesn't teach respect for family; because they're hedonistic, lazy, stupid,

and/or criminally inclined. But when Asians demonstrate their ability to overcome the obstacles of an alien language and culture, when the Asian family seems to be the repository of our most highly regarded traditional values, white hostility doesn't disappear. . . . [Instead,] the accomplishments of Asians . . . [are] credited . . . to the fact that they're "single minded," "untrustworthy," "clannish drones," "narrow people" who raise children who are insufficiently "well rounded." (Rubin, 1994, p. 188)

Furthermore, the well-publicized economic and academic achievements of Chinese-, Japanese-, and Korean-Americans mask high rates of failure and disadvantage among other Asian groups. For instance, schools often bundle Asian students from various ethnic subgroups into one category, thereby glossing over substantial differences in upbringing and education (Steinberg, 2003b). Laotian and Vietnamese teenagers often struggle in school, and in some areas their drop-out rates are higher than those of their white schoolmates. Half of Hmong families live below the poverty line, and children from these families tend to fall behind academically as well. In Minnesota and Alaska, at least 50% of Asian elementary school students are below basic reading levels (Lepkowska, 2004).

Asian Americans are often featured in news stories about successful high-tech companies, but they continue to face widespread bias in the workplace. Consider, for instance, the 2000 U.S. Department of Energy investigation of Wen Ho Lee, a Taiwan-born scientist at a nuclear weapons lab who was dismissed for security violations and suspected espionage. With little factual or legal evidence to support the charge that Lee was a spy, he was indicted on 59 counts and held in detention for nine months as a national security threat. The government emphasized his Chinese ethnicity, promoting the perception that he had "divided loyalties" that prevented him from being a "real" American (Gee, 2004). Asian American employees at other nuclear labs nationwide faced systematic harassment and denial of advancement because they too were suspected of spying. During interrogations, Lee was threatened with the destruction of his career, his reputation, and even the lives of his family. After four years and millions of dollars spent on the investigation, Lee was ultimately found innocent. But the damage had been done.

The Good Mother When it comes to positive stereotypes, few have more collective support than the belief that women are anatomically and hormonally predisposed to be better parents than men are. Although this stereotype only rose to prominence in the late 19th and early 20th centuries (Gillis, 1996), most people today simply take for granted that women are built to be mothers and that they possess some kind of "maternal instinct" that is an unalterable and universal fact of nature. As such, women tend to be guided and judged by a different set of parenting expectations than men.

Given the lofty status that family and parenthood enjoy in this society, the belief that women make better parents than men should translate into elevated cultural approval for mothers. But the belief that women are naturally inclined to be parents means that some people see a woman bearing and raising a child as rather unremarkable. While people still may marvel at the sight of a father pushing a stroller in a park or changing a diaper in a shopping mall bathroom, mothers engaging in such activities rarely elicit such a response. Their actions are far from praiseworthy; they're simply what mothers are supposed to do.

Not surprisingly, the women who are most culturally noticeable in this society are those who don't become mothers in the first place— whether by choice or not—or who are less-than-perfect parents when they do have children. These women are especially likely to be pitied, maligned, or looked on with suspicion (Hays, 1996). The criminal prosecution of women who drink alcohol or take other drugs while pregnant, the desire on the part of some lawmakers to limit women's access to legal abortion, and public concern over the negative consequences on children of mothers working outside the home illustrate the power and the paradox of stereotypical expectations regarding women and motherhood.

Ironically, at the same time women are expected or at least encouraged to become mothers, they often suffer financially from parenthood (Crittenden, 2001). Research consistently shows that mothers earn lower wages than women without children do. One study that charted the work experiences of over 5,000 women over a ten-year period found that on average mothers see their wages reduced by 7% per child (Budig & England, 2001). The penalties are actually larger for married mothers than for unmarried mothers. The researchers concluded that only about one-third of this penalty is attributable to deficiencies in past work experience or lack of seniority. They suggest that the bulk of the reduction in wages results either from the long-term effects of motherhood on productivity or from employer discrimination. Hence, we can see that what appear on the surface to be positive stereotypes about women and motherhood are actually linked to the broader gender inequalities that exist in society.

PREJUDICE: PERCEIVING INEQUALITY

Stereotypes, in and of themselves, are merely cognitive mechanisms we all use to find commonalities among groups and to simplify our perceptual worlds. Hence, they can be positive or negative or even neutral. When they become the basis for a set of rigidly held, unfavorable judgments, beliefs, and feelings about members of another ethnoracial, gender, class, or sexual group, however, they constitute **prejudice** (Allport, 1954). They are attitudes with an emotional, evaluative bias.

Prejudice tends to ebb and flow as social conditions change. When people's self-interest, their sense of cultural integrity, or their economic livelihood are threatened—by either the real or the perceived infiltration of others—prejudicial attitudes tend to become more open and hostile. For instance, widespread anti-Catholic sentiment became especially virulent in the late 19th and early 20th centuries as waves of Catholic immigrants entered the country looking for a better life. Native Protestants characterized Catholics—especially those from Ireland and Italy—as drunken, lower-class louts who were going to destroy the sanctity of the country. The passage in 1919 of the 18th Amendment prohibiting the use of alcohol marked, in part, a cultural victory of traditional, rural, middle-class Protestants over urban, lower-class Catholics (Gusfield, 1963). Financial stress can exacerbate such prejudices. As one out-of-work white auto mechanic put it, it's bad enough to have to compete with a white man for a job. "But a black guy? It would mean you lost a job to someone that everybody knows is lower than you" (quoted in Feagin & Vera, 2000).

Specific historical events can also shape prejudices. The equation of Muslims with violent terrorism has been a common attitude for decades, dating back to the murder of 11 Israeli athletes during the 1972 Summer Olympics in Munich. But the September 11, 2001, attacks served to bolster anti-Muslim prejudice. In one study of teachers' attitudes, relatively few of the respondents knew much about Islam. Nonetheless, one-third of them associated the word *Islam* with terms like *terrorists, enemy, trouble,* and *war* (Mastrilli & Sardo-Brown, 2002). Another study found that a high level of anti-Islamic imagery in the media supported the negative portrayal of Muslims and helped to fuel the belief that all Muslims are terrorists (Khalema & Wannas-Jones, 2003). These attitudes, of course, are not trivial. In the five months following the attacks, more than 1,700 incidents of violence against Muslims were reported (Montieth & Winters, 2002). A similar anti-Muslim backlash occured in England following the 2005 subway bombings in London.

On the other hand, some forms of prejudice are remarkably persistent over time. Over the years, research has found that women have been consistently perceived as more passive, emotional, easily influenced, and dependent than men (Broverman, Vogel, Broverman, Clarkson, & Rosenkrantz, 1972; Deaux & Kite, 1987; Tavris & Offir, 1984). Gender prejudice continues to be expressed in U.S. society, both overtly and subtly: physical domination, condescending comments, sabotage, and exploitation (Benokraitis & Feagin, 1991). One study found that although some forms of gender prejudice are motivated by hostility, others are motivated by benevolence, as when men assume women are helpless and thus feel compelled to offer help (Glick & Fiske, 1996). Such attitudes and behaviors not only place women in a lower-status position compared to men but also channel them into less advantageous social opportunities.

What often seems to be universal prejudice against certain devalued groups is usually more nuanced. Consider anti-homosexual prejudice (known variably as **heterosexism** or **sexual prejudice**). For many decades, gays and lesbians have been rejected, ridiculed, and condemned on moral, religious, criminal, or even psychiatric grounds. Attitudes have become somewhat more favorable in recent years. For instance, in the 1970s and 1980s, two-thirds of respondents to an annual nationwide survey considered homosexual behavior to be "always wrong." By the late 1990s, that figure had dropped to 56% (Yang, 1997). But what is perhaps more interesting from a sociological perspective is that anti-gay prejudice is not uniform throughout society. For instance, it is highest among individuals who know no gays and lesbians personally and are older, less educated, and living in rural parts of the U.S. South or Midwest (Finlay & Walther, 2003; Herek, 2000a). Despite the existence of pro–gay rights churches, most religions condemn or at least oppose homosexuality. Indeed, many churches, especially conservative and evangelical Protestant denominations, have added anti-homosexual statements to their official policies (Finlay & Walther, 2003).

Sexual prejudice seems to vary along gender lines as well. According to one study (Herek, 2000b), women tend to express fewer anti-gay attitudes, beliefs, and behaviors than men. But the object of attitudes is also gender specific. Heterosexual men tend to have more negative attitudes toward and feel more discomfort around gay men than they feel toward lesbians. Heterosexual women, in contrast, hold similar attitudes toward gay men and lesbians. Demonstrating one's heterosexuality and one's conformity to traditional gender roles seems to be of greater concern to men than women, which may explain the heightened male hostility toward gay men.

PREJUDICE, PRIVILEGE, AND IDEOLOGIES OF INFERIORITY

One of the unfortunate by-products of living in a multiracial, multiethnic, multireligious society is that we have perhaps as many types of prejudice as there are types of groups. The forms that American prejudice can take are infinite: anti-Semitic, anti-Black, anti-gay, anti-female, anti-male, anti-rich, anti-Republican, anti-Latino/a, anti-White, anti-Catholic, anti-Asian, and so on. If there's a group of people that is distinctive and identifiable, it's inevitable that someone will find these people unfit, unapproachable, or undesirable. When it comes to intolerance and hatred, we are truly an equal opportunity society.

But although "anybody" can hold stereotypes of others, judge them negatively, and disparage them as a result, it's important to remember that not all prejudice is created equally. To say, for instance, that a lesbian who hates heterosexuals is "just as prejudiced" as a straight person who hates homosexuals ignores the historical and cultural underpinnings of prejudice, the differences in power and privilege between these groups, and the different consequences that occur depending on who is expressing prejudice toward whom.

Furthermore, calling someone a racist or a bigot—no matter what group they happen to belong to—individualizes the behavior and obscures the group-level prejudice that is culturally, economically, legally, and socially supported (Wildman & Davis, 2002). It places the blame for unequal treatment on the individual and not on the broad systematic forces that are required for large-scale inequality to take hold and become a common feature of society.

For decades, sociologists have been examining how prejudice makes the jump from an individual attitude to a structural phenomenon. It appears that several factors are involved. Two of these factors are feelings of innate differences—"those people aren't like me"—and feelings of superiority—"those people are not as good as me." In this sense, prejudice exists not just in a set of feelings that individuals in one group have toward individuals in another group but in a perception of relative group position. The combination of feeling distinctive and feeling superior can easily give rise to expressions of hostility and social exclusion. The bully who punched me in the face in fourth grade clearly zeroed in on what he thought were my inherent (and inferior) differences from him and those like him.

Feeling different and feeling superior aren't in themselves sufficient to create group-level prejudice, however, because they could conceivably apply to the feelings one individual harbors toward another individual, regardless of group membership. Sociologist Herbert Blumer (1958/2004) introduced two other beliefs—entitlement and suspicion—that can transform individual-level prejudice into group-level prejudice. First consider entitlement, the belief that one's group has a rightful claim to certain privileges and advantages. Historically, this feeling has translated into exclusive claims to resources such as upscale residential neighborhoods; prestigious occupations or professions; positions of control and authority in the government; membership in privileged schools, churches, and recreational facilities; positions of social prestige and the symbols of these positions; and certain areas of intimacy and privacy.

Arguably, this feeling of entitlement can exist in the absence of prejudice. In a feudal system, for example, a lord may feel his position of entitlement is simply a reflection of the natural order of things; in a tribal culture, a chief may feel the same way toward commoners. If these claims are accepted by everyone as legitimate, they wouldn't constitute prejudice.

But when feelings of entitlement combine with a suspicion that the subordinate group covets the privileges of the dominant group, prejudice results. In other words, the subordinate group is perceived to be threatening or is feared to threaten the advantaged position of the dominant group. Acts that are suspected to be attacks on the "natural" superiority of the dominant group or intrusions into their sphere of privilege—as when women enter traditionally male occupations or organizations—are crucial in arousing group prejudice.

What's important about all these feelings—difference, superiority, entitlement, and suspicion—is that they combine to reflect the hierarchical positioning of groups in society. Feelings of superiority by definition place others below one's own group, and feelings of differentness place them beyond it. And the feeling of entitlement excludes others from the privileges of group position. Consequently, prejudice can rise and fall in response to the threat of changes in one group's social position relative to another group's.

Ideologies of inferiority and perceptions of entitlement and threat have long been used to explain why certain groups lag behind others in such areas as educational achievement, financial success, and even morality. They often provide "scientific" justification and a seemingly intellectual climate for the perpetuation of prejudice and inequality. Usually, such ideologies revolve around the notion of biological predisposition and "natural" differences between groups.

Race and Biological Weakness In the 18th and 19th centuries, few white people doubted the "truth" of natural racial rankings: Indians below Whites, and Blacks below everyone else. Even idols of Western culture and advocates for human liberty—George Washington, Thomas Jefferson, Abraham Lincoln, Charles Darwin—believed in the "natural inferiority" of some races, beliefs that were commonly accepted knowledge at the time but would be considered bigoted or at the very least racially insensitive today.

The acceptance of these conventional racial rankings—from the scientific community to the public at large—arose not from objective data and careful research but from a shared worldview and a cultural belief that racial stratification was natural, inevitable, and proper (Gould, 1981). Such beliefs easily morphed into independent support when framed in the language of science. Scientists, like everybody else, have attitudes and values that shape what they see. Such thinking need not be the result of outright dishonesty or hypocrisy; rather, it is the combination of the way human minds work and the generally accepted knowledge of the day.

Despite historical and contemporary efforts to find a link between "inferior" race-based genes and intelligence, creativity, or other valued abilities, none has been found (Hacker, 1992). For one thing, comparing racial groups on, say, intelligence overlooks the range of differences within and between groups. Many African Americans are more intelligent than the average White; many Whites are less intelligent than the average Native American. Variations such as these are difficult to explain in terms of the genetic superiority of one race over another. Moreover, such comparisons ignore a problem I described in Chapter 2: that race itself is a meaningless biological category. How can we attribute racial differences in intelligence to genetic differences when there is no single gene associated with race?

Despite the lack of scientific support, beliefs about racial inferiority— be they genetic, anatomical, or cultural—always serve to privilege dominant groups. When these beliefs become part of the cultural stock of knowledge, they discourage subordinate groups from attempting to question their disadvantaged status. In addition, they provide moral justification for maintaining a society in which some groups are routinely deprived of their rights and privileges. Whites could justify the enslavement of Blacks or the conquest of Native Americans, and Nazis could justify the extermination of Jews and other "undesirables," by promoting the belief that those groups were inherently subhuman.

In its less extreme forms, the idea that racial inferiority is innate remains appealing to those alleged to be superior. If observable physical differences among races are inherited, why not differences in social behavior, moral character, occupational placement, leadership ability, and so on? The belief in innate racial inferiority places the blame for suffering and economic failure on the individual rather than on the society in which that individual lives.

Gender and Biological Inevitability Like racial prejudice, the supporting ideology for gender prejudice is biologically based. The belief that men and women are biologically, naturally different has historically served not necessarily to generate hatred against women but to maintain their subordinate status in society.

For the field of medicine in the 19th and early 20th centuries, few claims had wider acceptance and appeal than the contention that women were the products and prisoners of their reproductive anatomy (Scull & Favreau, 1986). Everything supposedly known about women that made them different from men—their subordinate place in society, the predominance of the emotional over the rational, their capacity for affection, their love of children and aptitude for child rearing, their "preference" for domestic work, and so on—could be explained by the existence and functioning of their uteruses and ovaries (Ehrenreich & English, 1979; Scull & Favreau, 1986). Scholars and physicians at the time warned that young women who studied too much were fighting against nature, would badly damage their reproductive organs, and would perhaps even go insane in the process (Astbury, 1996; Fausto-Sterling, 1985). So the official exclusion of women from colleges and universities was not only justifiable but necessary for health reasons and for the long-term good of society.

Some functionalist sociologists have also cited biological differences between men and women as an explanation for the persistence of gender inequality in society (e.g., Parsons & Bales, 1955). They often cite sex-linked behaviors in nonhuman animals as evidence of the biological underpinnings of male-female behavioral differences among humans

(Sperling, 1991). They argue that the "objective" fact that males tend to be physically stronger and that females bear and nurse offspring has created many recognized and necessary sex-segregated roles. Among humans, this specialization of roles at work and in the family is purported to be the most effective way to maintain societal stability. By giving birth to new members, by socializing very young children, and by providing affection and nurturing, women make invaluable contributions to the reproduction of society. The common occupations that women have traditionally had outside the home—teacher, nurse, day care provider, maid, social worker, and so on—tend simply to be extensions of their "natural" tendencies (for more on gender inequality in the labor force, see Chapter 8). Similarly, men's physical characteristics have been presumed to better suit them for the roles of economic provider and protector of the family. If it's true that men are "naturally endowed" with such traits as strength, assertiveness, competitiveness, and rationality, then they are best qualified to enter the serious and competitive world of work and politics (Kokopeli & Lakey, 1992). Such beliefs remain entrenched. In 2005, the president of Harvard University created a stir when he stated publicly that innate sex differences explain why more men than women succeed in science and math careers (Dillon, 2005).

At the cultural level, the qualities we consider naturally feminine are often degraded and seen as less socially valuable than those considered masculine. As you will recall from Chapter 4, girls do suffer sometimes when their behavior is considered "boylike." But when a boy is accused of acting like a girl, it implies weakness, frailty, and lack of ability. Even today, many men consider accusations of femininity the ultimate insult. In 2004, the governor of California, Arnold Schwarzenegger, made headlines for calling his political opponents "girlie men." During the presidential campaign that year, Vice President Dick Cheney openly questioned the manhood of Democratic candidate John Kerry: "He talks about leading a 'more sensitive war on terror,' as though al Qaeda will be impressed with our softer side" (quoted in Lakoff, 2004, p. 3).

The problem with depicting masculinity and femininity as natural, biological phenomena is that it confuses sex with gender (see Chapter 2). But things besides genes, hormones, and other biological factors always shape social behavior. Even the sex-linked activities of nonhuman animals, from rodents to baboons, are not inevitable and can be influenced by environmental conditions (Sperling, 1991). Furthermore, the ideology of biological inevitability overlooks extensive similarities between the sexes and extensive variation within each sex. For instance, men as a group do tend to be more aggressive than women as a group. Yet some women are much more aggressive than the average man, and some men are much less aggressive than the average woman. Indeed, social circumstances may have a greater impact on aggression than any innate, biological traits. Some studies show that when women are rewarded for behaving aggressively, they can be just as violent as men (Hyde, 1984).

THE HIDDEN PRIVILEGE OF SOCIAL DOMINANCE

People who are members of dominant racial, sexual, or gender groups often have trouble appreciating the humiliating effects of everyday encounters with prejudice that other groups experience. They misinterpret the withdrawal of disadvantaged groups and their desire to stick with others like themselves as "separatism" rather than as a reasonable response to consistent expressions of prejudice. This dynamic is clearest with regard to race and ethnicity. Whenever discussions of race relations arise at my university for example, white students inevitably identify the tendency of students of color to socialize only with other students of color as the reason for interracial difficulties. "If they want to be fully integrated into campus life, they should eat lunch with white students or join predominantly white fraternities and sororities. But they don't make the effort." What these white students fail to realize is that such voluntary isolation is often a reaction to a long chain of interpersonal experiences that can make students of color feel like outsiders. Predictably, many Whites in the United States think people of color are obsessed with race and ethnicity and find it difficult to understand the emotional and intellectual energy that minorities devote to the subject (Haney López, 1996).

In a society in which they are the statistical and cultural majority, U.S. Whites rarely have to define their identity in terms of race. As I mentioned in Chapter 1, whiteness is unremarkable and unexamined. It is so obvious and normative that white people's racial identity is, for all intents and purposes, invisible. Whites enjoy the luxury of **racial transparency** or "having no color" (Haney López, 1996). Many Whites become conscious of their racial identity only when they find themselves in the company of large numbers of people of a different race. Even among academics, whiteness had gone largely unstudied until the past decade or so.

The invisibility of whiteness as a racial position doesn't mean that white people are never discussed. On the contrary, they're spoken about all the time. You can't turn on the television or pick up a newspaper without seeing white people. But when white people talk about other white people, the discussion is couched in terms of, simply, "people." Whites need not be bigots nor feel racially superior or more deserving than others to enjoy the privileges that their lack of skin color brings. The power of whiteness reproduces itself regardless of people's intentions, because it is seen not as whiteness but as normal (Dyer, 2002).

If whiteness is "normal" and "invisible," then what are the stereotypes used to describe—and perhaps even stigmatize—it? Sociologist Ruth Frankenberg (2002) interviewed 30 white women of various nationalities, sexualities, and political orientations to determine how they perceived "whiteness." To many of these women, being white meant being cultureless. Whiteness was difficult if not impossible to describe, especially when not modified by specific ethnicities, regions, or classes. Many of them shared the habit of turning to elements of white culture as an unspoken norm, such as when comparing Latin music to "regular" music (when regular meant "white"). When these subjects did describe whiteness, they depicted it as "bland" or "blah." White culture, they seemed to suggest, lacked the vibrancy and "color" that other ethnicities seemed to have. But again, such a seemingly negative portrayal paradoxically conveys power. Other cultures are more interesting than white culture only because their elements fall outside the mainstream, outside the "normal." In addition, whiteness is often signified by commodities and brand names—Wonder bread, Kleenex, mayonnaise, and so on—thereby linking it to the broader economy in ways that other ethnicities aren't.

The curious combination of invisibility and ubiquity is also apparent in white people's sense of their own ethnicity. Sociologist Charles Gallagher (1997) asked white college students to describe themselves in ethnic or racial terms. Few chose to consider their ethnicity at all. The majority labeled themselves simply as "white" or "Caucasian," ignoring hyphenated ethnicities such as "Italian-American" or "Irish-American." So complete was their extraction from any ethnic identity that some called themselves "plain old American," "mutt," or "nothing." Even the handful of students who did acknowledge their ethnicity acknowledged that it was in name only, implying that the label bore little importance for how they lived their lives on a daily basis. They couldn't speak the language of their European ancestors and didn't feel compelled to date or marry someone from within their ethnic group. So although whiteness remains largely indescribable, it has also become a proxy for ethnicity among young Whites.

In fact, academics are not immune to lumping all Whites into a single category, regardless of ethnicity. In the mid-1990s, a book called *The*

Bell Curve (1994) evoked enormous controversy. Its authors, Richard Herrnstein and Charles Murray, argued that white people are genetically predisposed to score better on standardized intelligence tests than other racial groups, especially African Americans. But treating the over 200 million "white" people they refer to as a single, monolithic group is problematic at best and misleading at worst. It can't account for the wide variation in academic achievement among Whites of different national backgrounds. For instance, at the time the book was written, 21% of white Americans of Irish descent completed college, whereas 22% of Italian-Americans, 33% of Scottish-Americans, and 51% of Russian-Americans did so (Hacker, 1994).

The connections between the invisibility of whiteness and broader social inequalities cannot be ignored:

> Each thing with which "they" have to contend as they navigate the waters of American life is one less thing Whites have to sweat: and that makes everything easier, from finding jobs, to getting loans, to attending college. . . . The virtual invisibility that whiteness affords those of us who have it is like psychological money in the bank, the proceeds of which we cash in every day while others are in a perpetual state of overdraft. (Wise, 2002, pp. 107–108)

One white author (McIntosh, 2001) cataloged all the everyday privileges she enjoyed (and often didn't notice) simply because she was white. They included such advantages as the ability to shop alone in a department store without being followed by suspicious salespeople, to buy greeting cards or children's picture books featuring people of her race, and to find bandages that match her skin color. The privilege of not having to think about race provides advantages to Whites whether or not they approve of the way they have acquired those advantages.

Intersections
Wealthy White Men and Perceptions of Race

One of the great ironies of inequality in American society is that perceptions of those who are the most powerful and influential are often the least understood. For instance, the views and perspectives of wealthy white men with regard to race have received virtually no academic attention. To overcome this deficiency, sociologists Joe Feagin and Eileen O'Brien (2003) interviewed about 100 affluent white male executives, managers, administrators, and professionals about a range of racial issues. Understanding the perceptions of these men is important because many of them have the ability to influence local and national views on race matters. They have the power to shape policies, laws, and actions involving ethnoracial minorities and majorities.

Because of their socioeconomic status, these men lived most of their lives in segregated well-to-do neighborhoods. As children and teenagers, most of them attended schools that had few, if any, ethnoracial minorities. Only a handful of the interviewees reported long-term friendships with people of other races.

Hence their initial and sometimes most significant encounters with ethnoracial minorities were often with domestic and other service workers, usually female maids or male servants:

> Although I don't remember my first experience of meeting a black person, I would assume it was . . . my grandfather's chauffeur when I was five years old. So to me, Blacks at that point were people that waited on you.

> My very first contact with a black person was with a black maid who essentially raised my sister and [me].

> Honestly, the first black person I ever met was probably a household employee at my parents' house a long time ago. (all quoted in Feagin & O'Brien, 2003, pp. 34–35)

Recollections of these initial contacts tended to be fond. Many men spoke lovingly of these household servants because these people played a significant role in raising them (some respondents referred to their black maids and nannies as "second mothers"). However, they also were taught, early on, that there was a social distance between their families and "the help" that had to be maintained. Furthermore, it's clear that the men didn't see these individuals as real people with real lives. For instance, most were unaware of the impact that being a domestic servant had on these individuals' relationships with their own families.

Feagin and O'Brien found that in many ways these men are not that different from "ordinary" white Americans when it comes to racial attitudes. They often share the same negative images of Americans of color. Furthermore, they often indicate a desire to maintain many white privileges in society as well as their control over major social institutions. But since they are generally highly educated, they are well aware that they should not be too explicit in expressing their racial attitudes.

Interestingly, while most white people in this society don't think much about their race and profess "not to see" race, these men seemed quite aware of the fact that as society becomes increasingly more multiracial, whiteness—

and more specifically, white maleness—may no longer be the certain boost for success that it once was. Their understanding of "whiteness" included both the knowledge that it works in their favor and the perception that they are now "victims" in a multiracial society that is slowly taking away their advantage:

> I feel that I am definitely becoming discriminated against because I am white. . . . [It's] harder for me to get a job in a governmental agency than for a Latino or an African American or any other ethnic. It's harder for me than any other group. . . . If you just watch the news . . . , just look at the news anchors themselves. They always try to have a woman, a black, a Latino, Asians. They never have white males. (quoted in Feagin & O'Brien, 2003, p. 85)

Not all the men interviewed by Feagin and O'Brien felt this way. A minority of them expressed positive attitudes toward race relations. These individuals often voiced dismay over racial and class inequality and spoke of the need for a significant shift in the balance of economic and political power in the United States. The factor that seemed to separate these men from the others who held more traditional (and negative) attitudes toward race is the nature of the relationships they've had with Americans of color. Those who had long-term friendships or extended regular contact with members of other races were the ones who showed a willingness to consider dismantling the structures that perpetuate racial inequality.

WITHIN-GROUP PREJUDICE

When most people think of prejudice and bigotry, they think of negative feelings that cross broad racial, ethnic, religious, gender, or sexual lines, especially in the direction of most powerful toward least powerful groups. However, because definitions of race are social constructions, people often make finer, within-group distinctions between fellow members that are largely invisible or irrelevant to outsiders but nonetheless constitute an additional layer of prejudice. Take, for example, the skin color prejudice that exists among African Americans.

Skin color prejudice (also known as **colorism**) originated during the period of slavery when whiteness was equated with all things refined and beautiful and blackness represented the sinister and the ugly (Hill, 2002). In such an environment, skin color (along with other race-related physical features like hair texture, nose shape, and lip prominence) became the paramount indicator of social status. Both Whites and light-skinned black slaves came to consider darker-skinned slaves to be less civilized and intellectually inferior (Graham, 1999). Light-skinned slaves were often allowed to work in the main house; dark-skinned slaves were usually relegated to the fields.

During the early to mid-20th century, many African American churches, social clubs, fraternities, and other organizations still used lightness tests to determine the suitability of candidates for membership. The so-called brown bag test restricted membership to those whose skin was lighter than the color of a brown paper bag. Here's how one author describes growing up in such an environment:

> I recall summertime visits from my maternal great-grandmother, a well-educated, light complexioned, straight-haired black southern woman who discouraged me and my brother from associating with darker-skinned children or from standing or playing for long periods in the July sunlight, which threatened to blacken our already too-dark skin. . . . At age six, I already understood the importance of achieving a better shade of black. (Graham, 1999, pp. 1, 4)

Even the "black power" movement of the 1960s and 1970s (in which young African Americans celebrated their blackness) didn't do much to dent the widespread preference for light skin tone.

Such a preference exists today among African Americans of all ages—especially children and college students from affluent families:

> It is hard to find an upper-class black American family that has been well-to-do since before the 1950s that has not endured family conversations on the virtues of "good hair, sharp features, and a nice complexion." These code words for having less Negroid features have been exchanged over time for more politically correct ones, but it is a fact that the black upper class thinks about these things more than most. This is not to say that affluent Blacks want to be white, but it certainly suggests that they have seen the benefits accorded to lighter-skinned Blacks with "whiter features"—who are hired more often, given better jobs, and perceived as less threatening. (Graham, 1999, p. 377)

Studies have indeed found that lighter-skinned Blacks have higher educational attainment, more prestigious occupations, and higher annual incomes than darker-skinned Blacks, regardless of their parents' socioeconomic status, sex, region of residence, age, or marital status (Hill, 2002; Keith & Herring, 1991).

Skin-tone distinctions within an ethnoracial group reflect the broader racial values of the culture at large. Many scholars argue that this sort of stratification comes from a deeply embedded racial ideology that equates character, prestige, and merit with skin tone. Hence, in the United States, individuals and institutions distribute rewards to those who most closely approximate white, European standards.

Intersections
Race, Gender, and Colorism

A fair amount of research suggests that skin-color distinctions are more important for African American women than for African American men. For African American women, dark skin has long been associated with unfeminine physical strength and the unflattering "Mammy" image. One African American woman recalls the pain of being told frequently, "You're pretty attractive for someone so dark" (Graham, 1999, p. 37). In the interests of being perceived by others as attractive, black women are often compelled to imitate whiteness through the use of skin bleaches and hair dyes and straighteners. Indeed, most beauty products marketed toward black women are designed to make them look more like white women.

Not surprisingly, evidence suggests that African American men find lighter-skinned women more sexually desirable. And African American celebrities who are considered "sex symbols" (Halle Berry, Beyoncé, Vanessa Williams) typically approximate white beauty standards. Using data from the National Survey of Black Americans, sociologist Mark Hill (2002) found a strong preference for women with lighter skin. Interestingly, female respondents were just as likely as male respondents to express a preference for lighter-skinned women.

Using the same survey data, sociologists Maxine Thompson and Verna Keith (2004) examined how African American men and women internalize these cultural messages. They were particularly interested in how people felt about themselves (self-esteem) and their perceived ability to master situations, control their own lives, and achieve success (efficacy). They found that light skin color was associated with higher levels of efficacy for black men, but not for black women. Traditional notions of masculinity demand that men achieve outside the home and exhibit competence. The researchers found that dark-skinned men often feel powerless, whereas light-skinned men often feel better able to improve their socioeconomic status. Conversely, color is closely associated with self-esteem for black women, but not for black men. Light-skinned African American women showed the highest feelings of self-worth and confidence. These findings reflect the wider cultural tendency for women, of all races and ethnicities, to be judged on the basis of their physical appearance and not necessarily their social achievements.

Colorism is not limited to African Americans. For instance, the degree of "Indian-ness," or the darkness of one's skin, has long determined a person's status in Mexican society. After controlling for all other relevant factors, dark-skinned Mexican Americans who have a Native American physical appearance have fewer years of education than light-skinned Mexican Americans who appear more European (Murguia & Telles, 1996); they are more likely to live in segregated, low-income neighborhoods (Relethford, Stern, Caskill, & Hazuda, 1983); and they consistently earn lower wages (Telles & Murguia, 1990). In Mexico, most people are of mixed lineage, so that nearly all of them could be considered at least part Indian. Nevertheless, Mexicans who are considered Indians are the object of severe discrimination. More than 80% of Mexico's Indian communities suffer high levels of poverty. Nearly half of all Mexican Indians are illiterate, and only 14% complete sixth grade. Many Mexicans today, especially in the larger cities, use hair dyes, skin lighteners, and blue or green contact lenses to appear more European (DePalma, 1995).

Cultural background may also be the basis for within-group prejudice. Many black immigrants from the West Indies, for example, refuse to call themselves "black" when they come to this country. West Indian immigrants generally make substantially more money than U.S.-born Blacks and live in better neighborhoods (Gladwell, 1996). They often try to distance themselves as much as possible from U.S.-born Blacks, whom they feel are socially, culturally, and financially inferior. The effect, according to one observer, is to reinforce, even legitimate, prejudice against other Blacks:

> The success of West Indians is not proof that discrimination against American Blacks does not exist. Rather, it is the means by which discrimination against American Blacks is given one last, vicious twist: I am not so shallow as to despise you for the color of your skin, because I have found people your color that I like. Now I can despise you for who you are. (Gladwell, 1996, p. 79)

Not having experienced the debilitating effects of discrimination, West Indian immigrants often have difficulty, as do some Whites, understanding why American Blacks have such a tough time "making it" in U.S. society.

Some African immigrants and their children also seek to distinguish themselves from downtrodden black Americans by calling themselves "African" or using some form of hyphenation that incorporates their country of origin, like "Nigerian-American" or "Ethiopian-American." At the same time, though, there is some debate over whether foreign-born

black citizens who want to call themselves "African American" can legit-
imately claim the label. Some black Americans argue that the term
"African American" should refer only to the descendants of slaves
brought to this country centuries ago and not to new immigrants from
Africa who do not have a heritage of bondage, segregation, and discrimination. Many fear that immigrants and their children will co-opt the
hard-won opportunities acquired as a result of the civil rights movement.
Says one man who traces his ancestry back to slavery:

> We've suffered so much that we're a bit weary and immigration seems
> like one more hurdle we will have to climb. . . . These are very aggres-
> sive people who are coming here. I don't berate immigrants for that;
> they have given up a lot to get here. But we're going to be in com-
> petition with them. We have to be honest about it. That is one of the
> dividing lines." (quoted in Swarns, 2004a, p. A14)

Indeed, there is some evidence that black immigrants and their children
have more education and higher median incomes than native-born Blacks
(cited in Swarns, 2004a).

DISCRIMINATION: INEQUALITY IN ACTION

Stereotypes and prejudice in and of themselves would be of little significance if they didn't sometimes motivate people to act against others.
Discrimination refers to the unfair treatment of people based on some
identifiable social characteristic such as race, ethnicity, gender, sexuality,
or class. From forced enslavement and immigration restrictions to segregation and interpersonal violence, discrimination has historically been one
of the defining characteristics of American society. In the past few decades,
however, some historically disadvantaged groups have made tremendous
progress, largely because of the 1964 Civil Rights Act, which prohibits
discrimination or segregation on the grounds of sex, race, color, religion,
and national origin. Nevertheless, discrimination still exists.

Discrimination operates at several levels. Sometimes, it resides in the
actions of individuals. At other times, however, it is embedded in the
everyday workings of larger systems and institutions.

PERSONAL DISCRIMINATION

When we think of racism, sexism, classism, heterosexism, or any other
"ism," what usually comes to mind are examples of **personal discrimination,**

unfair treatment of certain groups by individual people. This type of discrimination includes the use of derogatory names, biased treatment during face-to-face encounters, avoidance, exclusion, and threats or acts of violence. It's personal discrimination that receives the most media attention, especially when it is violent and brutal, such as racially or sexually motivated hate crimes or gender violence. Consider personal discrimination directed at sexual minorities. People with homosexual or bisexual orientations—as well as people assumed to be or accused of being gay—routinely experience violence, discrimination, and interpersonal rejection (Herek, 2000a). In a survey of Massachusetts high school students, for instance, 22% of gay respondents said they'd skipped school in the past month because they felt unsafe, and another 31% said they'd been threatened or injured in the past year (cited in Brooke, 1998). In a nationwide study of gay, lesbian, and bisexual college students, 32% had experienced some form of harassment, ranging from derogatory remarks to outright violence, and close to 20% feared for their physical safety because of their sexual orientation (Rankin, 2003). More results of the college study are shown in Exhibit 5.1.

Even though personal discrimination is expressed and felt at the individual level, it may be linked to widespread cultural ideologies and societal systems of privilege and may have institutional implications. The judicial system offers many examples. For instance, in 2003, a white state district court judge in Louisiana attended a Halloween party in blackface, an Afro wig, handcuffs, and a prison jumpsuit. One might reasonably question the judge's ability to represent the judicial system in an unbiased way in a black defendant's case. Another example is the victimization of imprisoned gay men. Upon entry into the prison, they may be taken hostage by gangs, given women's names, and rented out to other inmates for a variety of sex acts. One inmate reported that he was forced into oral and anal sex every day for 18 months (Liptak, 2004b). The claims and complaints of these prisoners are usually ignored by prison officials, thereby allowing the violence to continue.

Personal discrimination may influence the political system as well. In an attempt to keep black voters from the Milwaukee polls in the 2004 presidential election, someone distributed fliers in predominantly black neighborhoods a few weeks before election day falsely stating that anyone convicted of any offense—however minor—and people with family members who'd been convicted of any offense were disqualified from voting and could get 10 years in prison and lose custody of their children if they tried to vote (Schultze, 2004).

Exhibit 5.1: Anti-Gay Harassment

Percentage of gay, lesbian, bisexual or transgender college students (n = 1,669) who within the past year . . .

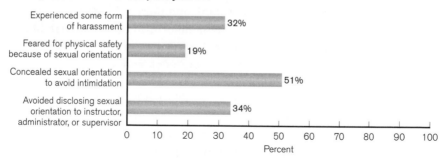

Percentage of gay, lesbian, bisexual or transgender students who experienced . . .

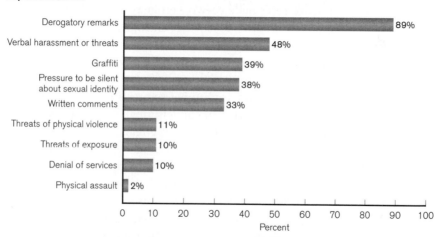

Percentage of gay, lesbian, bisexual or transgender students who experienced some form of harassment . . .

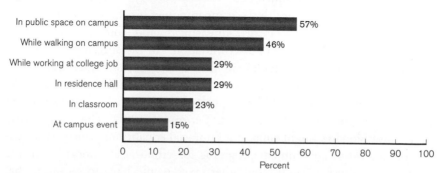

(Source: Rankin, 2003)

Quiet Bias Some forms of personal discrimination can be subtler and more difficult to detect than the overt acts most often brought to our attention. Where blatant discrimination can be "hot, close, and direct," subtle discrimination can be "cool, distant, and indirect" (Meertens & Pettigrew, 1997, p. 54). "Quiet bias" might take forms that, at first blush, don't appear discriminatory at all. Take, for instance, the high school guidance counselor who sympathetically steers poor and working-class students away from "hard" subjects and toward vocational courses. Similarly, in the workplace, women are sometimes subjected to superficially courteous or chivalrous behavior that is meant to be protective but ends up reinforcing women's subordinate position. Whether the motivation is malevolent or benevolent, such actions reinforce inequality. Poor and working-class students steered toward less demanding classes are prevented from acquiring the background they'll need to succeed. Women treated as non-adults by their male co-workers may find it hard convincing others that they have what it takes to be in high-paying positions of authority. Such quiet bias is far more common than more noticeable acts of personal discrimination and can, over time, be just as harmful.

You may recall from Chapter 3 that community and legal pressures have had a significant impact on traditional expressions of bigotry. For instance, some people may subscribe to conventional stereotypes of other groups and feel hostility toward them but not engage in acts of discrimination because of laws or customs that discourage open discrimination. These individuals may interact with members of the despised group on a regular basis but suppress the expression of their underlying negative feelings. In short, the only reason such a person—what one sociologist calls the "timid bigot"—doesn't openly discriminate is because she or he is not allowed to do so (Merton, 1949). What's troublesome about such individuals is that if such restrictions are ever lifted, discriminatory activity would likely be unleashed.

The underlying feelings that accompany quiet bias don't need to be hate or hostility. Instead, discomfort, uneasiness, and sometimes fear, can motivate a less obvious type of discrimination. For instance, a person might disagree strongly with a statement like "Mexicans have jobs that white people should have" but at the same time agree with a statement like "Mexicans living here should not push themselves where they are not wanted" (adapted from Meertens & Pettigrew, 1997). The person who subtly discriminates might support ethnoracial equality in principle but justify opposition to government programs for ethnoracial minorities on the seemingly nonprejudiced grounds that taxes would have to go up or that one's rewards should be based exclusively on personal achievements and not race.

Quiet bias has several features that distinguish it from the blatantly discriminatory ideologies (Ansell, 2000):

- Sanitized, coded language that adheres to nondiscriminatory values but is nonetheless prejudicial in its effect. For example, words like "welfare" and "crime" often tap into racial anxieties.
- Avid disavowals of discriminatory intent. The benign-sounding language provides only superficial evidence that the person is unbiased, however.
- Co-opting of classical anti-discrimination arguments. For example, a popular slogan from the civil rights movement—"Judge people not by the color of their skin but by the content of their character"—is adopted by those who argue that affirmative action is largely to blame for the continued oppression of people of color. Anti-racist "bureaucrats" rather than discriminators become the new villains.
- Shift from explaining inequality as an innate, biological matter to explaining it as a matter of cultural differences and national identity. For example, discussions of the so-called culture of poverty avoid attributing a group's failures to their genes—as is the argument of more traditional forms of racial prejudice—but attribute them instead to the group members' antisocial behavior, pathological family structures, and immoral value systems.

The shift in the manner in which underlying prejudice is expressed and communicated has serious societal consequences. When bias remains camouflaged, people are tempted to assume that discrimination has disappeared, making it unnecessary to help groups that have traditionally been the objects of discrimination (Bonilla-Silva, 2003). It is easier in some ways to confront overt bigotry and hatred based on assumptions that differences between groups of people arise from their essential nature.

The Enduring Importance of Race Some social observers have noticed the decline of overt racial discrimination and concluded that it is dead. In fact, some sociologists have been among those arguing that racial discrimination is actually based on differences in social class rather than race. If this belief were accurate, however, the lives of middle- and upper-class women and members of ethnoracial minorities, both part of the hypothetically privileged social class, should be relatively free of discrimination. Yet they are not. For instance, many highly successful professionals of color report that even they experience a lack of respect, an inability to fit in, low expectations, the presumption of failure, pigeon-holing, exclusion, and even outright harassment. An African American woman who happens to be a Georgetown University law professor recounts an interaction with a colleague, a middle-aged white man, who explained to her that she should not be offended at being called a "jungle bunny" because "you are cute and so are bunnies" (quoted in Cose, 1993, p. 23). Another colleague told her she reminded him of his family's former maid.

The result of such treatment is often utter frustration and despair:

> I have done everything I was supposed to do. I have stayed out of trouble with the law, gone to the right schools, and worked myself nearly to death. *What more do they want?* Why in God's name won't they accept me as a full human being? Why am I pigeonholed in a "black job"? Why am I constantly treated as if I were a drug addict, a thief, or a thug? Why am I still not allowed to aspire to the same things every white person in America takes as a birthright? Why, when I most want to be seen, am I suddenly invisible? (Cose, 1993, p. 1)

Sociologist Joe R. Feagin (1991) conducted in-depth interviews with 37 middle-class, college-educated U.S. Blacks all across the country and asked them to describe the barriers they'd encountered in employment, education, and housing. These people reported being the objects of discriminatory incidents in such public places as hotels, jewelry stores, and restaurants. The incidents that occurred in places of business consisted of avoidance, rejection, poor service, and closer scrutiny. When they occurred on the street, they consisted of verbal epithets, "hate stares," and even police threats and harassment. These events disturbed the subjects not only because of the prejudiced attitudes that lay behind them but also because the subjects had come to believe that their upward social mobility protected them from such treatment. A successful New York lawyer once said that when he walks into a store, the staff doesn't see his Ivy League university degrees or his status as an associate in his law firm. They see him only as a black man, thereby stripping him of his credentials and achievements (Williams, 1991). This everyday discrimination demonstrates that ethnoracial minorities, no matter what their class standing, are still being stereotyped and discriminated against on the basis of their race or ethnicity.

Less obviously, the belief on the part of these individuals that their class status ought to shield them from discriminatory treatment is yet another way of drawing us-them distinctions. Their rage and frustration imply that socioeconomic achievement and advantage should have enabled them to transcend the ethnoracial prejudice and discrimination that more understandably adheres to people of lesser means. Notice what this black, female college professor's description of her experiences implies about the "other" Blacks she seeks to distance herself from:

> Because I'm a large black woman, and I don't wear whatever class status I have, or whatever professional status [I have] in my appearance when I'm in the grocery store, I'm part of the mass of large black women shopping. For most Whites, and even for some Blacks, that translates into negative status. That means that they are free to treat me the way they treat most poor black people, because they can't tell by looking at me that I differ from that. (quoted in Feagin, 1991, p. 109)

Such an attitude is also reflected in the tendency for middle-class people of color to "use" the display of their middle-class standing as a resource when necessary. For instance, some of Feagin's respondents indicated that when making transactions over the phone, they use a "white voice" to ensure that they get fair treatment. The heartbreak of such a strategy is twofold. First, it acknowledges that race is so important in this society that knowledge of one's race would inevitably prompt unfair treatment. Second, it shows that poorer members of ethnoracial minorities who lack the signifiers of class stature are doomed to a life of discrimination.

Intersections
Race, Class, Gender, and Everyday Social Encounters

Although encounters with personal discrimination can be disheartening for middle- and upper-class members of ethnoracial minorities, poor or working-class men are perhaps most susceptible to the preconceptions and prejudices of others in social interactions. Sociologist Elijah Anderson (1990) observed everyday public encounters in a racially, ethnically, and economically diverse area of Philadelphia. This community was home to two neighborhoods: one black and poor, the other middle- to upper-income and predominantly white. Anderson was particularly interested in how young black men—the overwhelming majority of whom were civil and law-abiding—dealt with the biased assumption of residents that they are dangerous criminals.

What Anderson discovered was that residents of both neighborhoods were incapable of making distinctions between law-abiding young black men and criminally involved young black men. So they relied on broad stereotypes: Whites are middle-class, law-abiding, and trustworthy; young black men are poor, crime-prone, and dangerous. Black residents, as well as white residents, were likely to defer to and avoid contact with unknown black men on the street. Women—particularly white women—clutched their purses and edged up closer to their companions as they walked down the street. Many pedestrians crossed the street or averted their eyes from young black men whom they perceived as unpredictable and menacing.

In response, some of these men developed strategies to overcome the immediate assumption that they were dangerous. For instance, in hopes of deflecting any negative prejudgments, some conspicuously carried props with them in public that they felt both symbolized higher class status and represented law-abiding behavior (for instance, a briefcase, a shirt and tie, a college identification card). In addition, they often used friendly or courteous greetings as a kind of preemptive peace offering, designed to signal to others their civil intentions. Or they went to great lengths to behave in ways contrary to what they presumed were others' stereotypes of them:

> I find myself being extra nice to Whites. A lot of times I be walking down the streets . . . and I see somebody white. . . . I know they are afraid of me. They don't know me, but they intimidated. . . . So I might smile, just to reassure them. . . . At other times I find myself opening doors, you know. Holding the elevator. Putting myself in a certain light, you know, to change whatever doubts they may have. (Anderson, 1990, pp. 185–186)

Such interactional strategies require an enormous amount of effort and place responsibility for ensuring social order on these men. They feel compelled to put strangers at ease so they can go about their own business. Such actions indicate an understanding that their mere presence makes others nervous and uncomfortable. They understand that they must work hard to be perceived as trustworthy in public interactions.

Global Ethnic Violence Given the focus on U.S. society so far, it would be tempting to conclude that the sorts of prejudice and discrimination I've described are uniquely American phenomena. But around the world, discrimination—especially violent ethnoracial discrimination—is the rule, not the exception. For instance, in Eastern European countries such as Bulgaria, Romania, Hungary, and the Czech Republic, personal discrimination against the Roma—or Gypsies—is the norm. They have been despised for centuries and characterized as thieving subhumans with no respect for the law. They are stereotyped as loud, dirty, indecent, and sloppy. In 1998, city officials in a village in the Czech Republic proposed that a 15-foot wall be built to separate the Romas who live there from the rest of the townspeople. According to a poll of Czech attitudes, 39% of the population feel that "only force is effective" in dealing with Romas (cited in Erlanger, 2000). As a result of such attitudes, Romas suffer disproportionately from poverty, interethnic violence, discrimination, illiteracy, and disease. Unemployment among European Romas is about 70% (cited in Perlez, 1998). In Sofia, the capital of Bulgaria, the unemployment rate among Romas is 94%. In some Roma neighborhoods, 80% of residents have only an elementary school education (Wood, 2005).

At a time when people from every corner of the globe are linked technologically, economically, and ecologically and when mass migrations mix people from different races, religions, and cultures in unprecedented numbers, racial and ethnic hostilities are at an all-time high. Pick up the newspaper and you'll see stories of conflict and violence between Jews and Palestinians in Israel, Chechens and Russians in the former Soviet Union, Macedonians and Albanians in the Republic of Macedonia, Janjaweed and Darfurians in Sudan, Hindus and Muslims in India, Lendus and Hemas in Congo, Georgians and Ossetians in the Georgian Republic, Tajiks and Pashtun in Afghanistan, Kurds and Arabs in northern Iraq, or the Ijaw and Itsekiri in Nigeria. Racial and ethnic hatred costs the lives of millions of people around the world each year.

Such ethnic conflict often has little to do with material or economic interests. It tends to center on less tangible resources such as power, security, respect, or social status. Ethnic groups fight about such abstractions as identity and cultural recognition. Conflicts usually arise from distorted images between groups, which create deep emotions, extreme opinions, and ultimately explosions of violence (Forbes, 1997).

Although ethnic hatred is so widespread and persistent that it may sometimes seem to be an inescapable element of the human condition, human beings have also demonstrated a commitment to living in harmony. In an effort to overcome the ethnic hatred that led to years of bloodshed and the ethnically inspired massacre of close to a million people, the Rwandan government has embarked on a national program to purge people of their ethnicity. By decree, distinctions between ethnic Hutu and Tutsi have been wiped out. References to ethnicity have been ripped out of schoolbooks and erased from government identification cards. The government insists that if awareness of ethnic differences can be learned, so can the idea that ethnicity doesn't exist. Hutus and Tutsis go to reeducation camps where they learn to identify themselves simply as "Rwandan." Those who speak too provocatively about ethnicity or claim that a particular ethnic group has too much power can be put in jail for the crime of "divisionism" (Lacey, 2004).

INSTITUTIONAL DISCRIMINATION

Personal discrimination can be practiced by anyone against any other group. Even members of the least powerful, most disadvantaged segments of society can harbor personal animosity toward others. With regard to gender, for instance, men aren't the only ones who can be personally discriminatory. Certainly some women dislike men, judge them on the basis of stereotypes, hold prejudiced attitudes toward them, consider them inferior, and even discriminate against them socially or professionally. And sometimes, those in dominant positions can feel the effects of societal disadvantage. For instance, some people have argued that men are disadvantaged by the long history of social and legal pressures on them to fight in war, thereby risking their lives and their bodily and psychological health. Others have highlighted judges' alleged preference for maternal child custody after a divorce as another example of men being victimized by discrimination (Benatar, 2003).

We must keep in mind, though, that the historical balance of power in most societies has allowed men as a group to subordinate women socially and sometimes legally in order to protect male interests and privileges. Because men tend to dominate major social institutions, their discriminatory actions have more cultural legitimacy and more serious consequences than women's discrimination.

Indeed, when groups lack societal power, their discrimination is of little significance within the larger social structure. In a television commercial for Diet Coke some years back, a group of bug-eyed women stare out of an office window during their work break at a muscular construction worker who has just taken off his shirt. As the sweaty worker downs his Diet Coke, the ogling women fantasize all sorts of things. The commercial grabbed attention by reversing the more common situation in which men sexually objectify women. But the two types of sexual objectification don't carry the same meaning. Such sexual attention may be an enjoyable experience for men because it doesn't have the weight of a long tradition of subordination or the threat of violence behind it. A man who is being ogled isn't being socially or economically reduced to his physical attractiveness. For women, who continue to fight to be taken seriously in their social and professional lives, sexual objectification is a reminder that their value in this society is judged primarily, or even exclusively, on their looks. Therefore, such treatment serves to reinforce, rather than reduce, gender inequalities.

Institutional discrimination—established laws, customs, policies, and practices that systematically reflect and produce inequalities in society, whether or not the individuals maintaining these practices have discriminatory intentions—can only work to the advantage of those who already wield power and control major social institutions. Because women, poor people, African Americans, Latino/as, Asian Americans, Native Americans, sexual minorities, and other groups have historically been excluded from key positions of authority in dominant social institutions, they often find themselves victimized by the routine workings of such structures. Chapters 6, 7, and 8 will examine in more detail the broader institutional causes and consequences of this sort of discrimination.

On occasion, institutional discrimination is obvious and codified into the law. Until the early 1990s, for example, South Africa operated under an official system of *apartheid* whereby non-white groups were legally segregated and subjected to sanctioned forms of political and economic discrimination. In the United States, the forceful relocation of Native Americans in the 19th century, repressive Jim Crow laws in the 20th-century South, and the internment of Japanese Americans during World War II are all examples of legislated policies that purposely worked to the disadvantage of already disadvantaged groups.

But most of the time, institutional discrimination is even less easily recognized than the quiet, subtle forms of personal discrimination I described earlier and therefore is more difficult to address. Because institutional discrimination is a built-in feature of social arrangements, it is often masked by business policy and other institutional concerns. Imagine, for example, that a company has decided to build a manufacturing facility in a middle-class, predominantly white suburb instead of a racially mixed, central-city community because taxes are cheaper, highways are more accessible, and neighborhoods are "safer." On the surface, such a decision has nothing to do with race or the desire to prevent people of color from working there. It was done because it made good financial sense to the company. However, the distant location of the factory prevents qualified people of color—whose residences are likely to be concentrated in the city and who may lack affordable transportation—from ever working there. The outcome, therefore, disadvantages members of particular racial groups even though the motivation isn't purposely discriminatory.

Sometimes, institutional discrimination is cloaked in claims that seem quite reasonable on their face, as when taxi companies or home delivery businesses protect the safety of their drivers by enacting policies that prohibit service to what they consider to be dangerous neighborhoods. Although such practices may be considered "good" business policy and are not intentionally discriminatory, their consequences very well may be. High-risk neighborhoods tend to be inhabited primarily by people of color. A few years ago, Domino's Pizza got into a public controversy when it was revealed that the company was distributing software to its outlets to let them mark addresses on computers as green (deliver), yellow (curbside delivery only), or red (no delivery). The "red" and "yellow" addresses were considered "risky" but also happened to be highly concentrated in minority neighborhoods. The delivery policy was subsequently changed.

Attitudes toward particular groups can become entrenched in the culture of particular industries. Take, for instance, the real estate industry. The National Fair Housing Alliance (2004) estimates that 3,702,000 incidents of housing discrimination based on race or ethnicity alone occurred in 2003. This figure doesn't even include unfair housing practices based on religion, gender, family status, or disability. On occasion, such housing discrimination is personal, the result of individuals' blatant "we don't want you people here" attitudes. More commonly, though, it is institutional, politely and subtly driven by company policy (Pearce, 1979). Discriminatory policies include reduced availability of houses or rental units for minorities, reduced access to financial assistance, steering of minority buyers toward particular neighborhoods, and, within minority communities, reluctance to inspect property for sale, low asking prices, lack of encouragement of prospective buyers, and higher commissions and other selling costs.

While some minority families are being steered into less desirable neighborhoods, others are being steered out of the housing market entirely. In 1999, a research organization in Washington, D.C., sent pairs of Whites and ethnoracial minority group members to seek mortgages from lenders throughout the nation. Members of each pair had the same assumed income, assets, job, and credit history. The minorities were less likely to receive information about loan products, received less time from loan officers, and were quoted higher interest rates. A similar study found that African Americans were twice as likely as Whites, and Latino/as one-and-a-half times as likely as Whites, to be denied a conventional 30-year home loan (cited in Kilborn, 1999). When they do receive home loans, African Americans and Latino/as pay higher interest rates than Whites; the discrepancy is particularly noticeable for members of minority groups with above-average incomes (cited in Leonhardt, 2002). Concern over such discrepancies led the National Association of Realtors and the U.S. Department of Housing and Urban Development to enact a cultural awareness program for real estate agents, to make them more aware of "racial steering" and help to increase minority opportunities in housing (Tahan, 1997). Despite these efforts, however, housing discrimination continues today.

Discrimination also exists in the home mortgage or home improvement loan business. Many banks use zip codes to mark off the neighborhoods they consider high risk—that is, where property values are low and liable to drop even further. These practices make it much more difficult or even impossible for individuals in such areas to borrow money to buy or improve a home. Unfortunately, these are often the areas where working-class members of ethnoracial minorities are most likely to find affordable housing. Thus, although individual bank officers are not expressly denying loans to minority group members—they are merely following their employers' policy on loan risk—the resulting practice works to the disadvantage of those minorities.

As a consequence of these institutional practices, residential segregation based on class and race pervades the American landscape. For instance, over 83% of Detroit-area Blacks live in the central city (Russell Sage Foundation, 2000). Such segregation is highly resistant to change despite laws designed to prevent housing discrimination that have existed since the 1970s. Though segregation rates have gone down slightly over the past two decades, African Americans are more residentially segregated than Latino/as, Asian Americans, and Native Americans. But members of all of these groups are still more likely than not to live in racial or ethnic enclaves, especially in metropolitan areas (Iceland, Weinberg, & Steinmetz, 2002; Massey & Fischer, 1999).

Residential segregation is not just about the frustration of being limited in where you can live. Research indicates that it is associated with a variety of negative effects, such as a reduced likelihood of running successful businesses (Fischer & Massey, 2000) and an increased likelihood of contracting certain deadly diseases (Collins & Williams, 1999). Like most forms of discrimination, the effects are far-reaching and harmful.

In sum, the distinction between personal and institutional discrimination is crucial. Privileged groups can protect or even enhance their advantaged positions through organizational practices and policies that often appear to have little, if anything, to do with race, ethnicity, class, sexuality, or gender. Indeed, what distinguishes personal from institutional discrimination is often the ability to pinpoint blame for the resulting disadvantage. If someone refuses to admit me to a club or serve me in a restaurant because she or he despises people of my race, the blameworthy party is fairly obvious. But who's responsible for nationwide residential segregation? Who's responsible for the low SAT scores of inner-city high school students? Who's responsible for relatively high rates of unemployment, low rates of health insurance coverage, and low rates of personal computer ownership among ethnoracial minorities? If all personal hatred, prejudice, and discrimination were to end today, entrenched systematic arrangements that benefit some at the expense of others—be they in hospitals, retail businesses, workplaces, courthouses, schools, or any other institutional location—would continue.

CONCLUSION

In his novel *The Painted Bird* (1965), Jerzy Kosinski tells the tale of an unnamed boy in an unnamed Eastern European country caught in the confusion of the beginnings of World War II. When he is six, his middle-class parents, like thousands of others, send him to the countryside in the hope that he will be spared the brunt of the war. He is entrusted to the care of a peasant woman who dies shortly after he arrives. He has no way of contacting his parents and so must fend for himself. His problems are multiplied because he has dark hair, dark eyes, and speaks an educated dialect while those amongst whom he lives are blond, blue-eyed, and speak a peasant dialect. Because he is dark and different, he is assumed to be either "a Gypsy or a Jewish stray," neither of which is a good thing to be, considering that the Germans at the time are rounding up both to be sent to the death camps. Hence, it is very dangerous for the peasants in the area to protect him, and he is treated with suspicion, cruelty, and almost constant violence.

For a while, the boy lives under the protection of Lekh, a huge man who makes a living as a bird catcher. When Lekh would become angry, which happened frequently, he would mollify his rage by torturing one of his captured birds:

> After prolonged scrutiny, he would choose the strongest bird. . . .
> Lekh would turn the bird over and paint its wings, head, and

breast in rainbow hues until it became more dappled and vivid than a bouquet of wildflowers. . . . When a sufficient number of birds gathered above our heads, Lekh would give me a sign to release the prisoner. It would soar, happy and free, a spot of rainbow against the backdrop of clouds, and then plunge into the waiting brown flock. For an instant the birds were confounded. The painted bird circled from one end of the flock to the other, vainly trying to convince its kin that it was one of them. . . . But dazzled by its brilliant colors, they flew around it unconvinced. . . . We saw soon . . . how one bird after another would peel off in a fierce attack. Shortly the many-hued shape lost its place in the sky and dropped to the ground. (Kosinsky, 1965, pp. 43–44)

In this scene, we can see the key theme of this chapter—the interface between social difference and unequal treatment. What is especially poignant about this story is that the differences that serve as the basis for such treatment needn't be "real"—in the sense of being biological and inevitable. We, ourselves, create the boundaries that separate groups and then respond to "outsiders" as if their outside status is "natural." Just as Lekh knew, such a process is a set-up because rarely do individuals embrace those who appear different, whether it's a painted bird, a sexual or ethnoracial minority, or a nine-year-old kid coming to grips with his differentness in a new school.

I would have preferred to end this chapter on a positive note, claiming that prejudice and discrimination are relics of the past and that differences based on skin color, ethnicity, religion, gender, and sexuality have become irrelevant, carrying as much social significance as, say, differences based on eye color or hair color. But I can't. Blatant prejudice and discrimination still exist, though not as obviously as they did half a century ago. But even when prejudice and discrimination seemingly disappear, it is often because they have given way to quiet, almost imperceptible forms that reside not in hatred, bloodshed, and legal exclusion but in quiet distrust, polite avoidance, and the impersonal day-to-day workings of our major social institutions.

In the story of the painted bird, however, there is some hope. You see, if we are the ones who create the differences that result in harmful, discriminatory treatment, then we have the power to change them. The people of any society decide which differences are irrelevant and which differences are legitimate for making crucial social and legal distinctions between groups of people. We can change perceptions, alter behaviors, and even modify social institutions if we decide it's worth our while to do so.

[INVESTIGATING IDENTITIES AND INEQUALITIES]
Race and retail: Personal and institutional
discrimination in everyday life

Often, social inequality is felt most forcefully in the interpersonal indignities that people of particular ethnoracial, gender, class, or sexual groups must contend with in their day-to-day lives. To the outside observer who has never had to deal with the humiliation, these experiences might seem trivial and insignificant, mere annoyances rather than crises. However, to those who face this sort of treatment, the cumulative effect can be demoralizing and have long-term consequences for their self-esteem, state of mind, and even physical health.

This exercise requires that you enlist the assistance of three close friends: a person who is of the same race as you but of a different sex, and a man and a woman who are both of a race different from yours. If you have trouble finding people to help you, consider working with students who are in your sociology class. Once you've selected your accomplices, identify at least two retail businesses—perhaps in a nearby shopping mall—in which salespeople typically approach customers as they enter the store to ask if they need assistance. Examples of such businesses include clothing stores, jewelry stores, electronics stores, and so forth. One of the stores you choose should sell expensive items, like jewelry, computers, or upscale clothing. The other should sell moderately priced products, such as sporting goods or bath and body products. Avoid stores where it is likely that the salespeople will recognize you or your accomplices.

At different times, each of you individually will go to each store acting as if you were a customer interested in buying a gift for someone. It's important that you and your accomplices decide ahead of time what sort of product you will be "shopping" for and the price range you have in mind so that each of you is looking for the same thing. Try to dress in casual clothing, neither sloppy nor formal. Although you won't actually end up buying anything, try to appear as if you are a serious shopper. Be as polite as you can be. Try to ask relevant questions about the products in question.

While in the store, pay close attention so you can answer the following questions (or variations on them or even additional questions that you devise on your own):

- Was the store busy or quiet? About how many other customers were in the store when you arrived? About how many people were working?
- How long did it take for a salesperson to approach you? What was this person's race? His or her approximate age?
- Did she or he ask you any questions that seemed designed to determine your ability to pay (such as "will this be cash or charge?" or "what were you thinking in terms of price?")? Did the salesperson seem to steer you in the direction of particular products?
- Did she or he ask friendly sorts of questions that seemed to have nothing to do with the products being sold there, such as where you were from, if you were a student or not, and so forth? Did she or he make any comments about your appearance?
- Did the salesperson stay with you the entire time you were in the store, or did she or he shift attention to other customers or co-workers?
- Did you feel pressured to buy something?
- How would you characterize the salesperson's assistance? Helpful? Courteous? Uninterested? Rude? Provide specific evidence from the encounter to support your characterization.

When you've completed your shopping excursions, immediately record your observations. The longer you wait, the harder it will be to remember specific details.

Compile the experiences of each person in your group. Use the material on personal and institutional discrimination in this chapter to interpret your findings. Although one should be cautious when generalizing from such a small number of experiences, try to identify any noticeable differences in the way "customers" of different races or sexes were treated. If there were differences, describe them in detail. Who seemed to be treated more favorably? Did the salespeople seem to be making assumptions about your socioeconomic status? Did the differences seem more pronounced in the expensive store or in the moderately priced store? Do you think the differential treatment was a result of the personal proclivities of the salesperson or a result of company policy? Why do you think so? If you noticed no differences along racial or sex lines, how do you account for that experience? Try to draw some general conclusions about the effects of race and sex on public encounters.

CHAPTER 6

Inequalities in Health and Illness

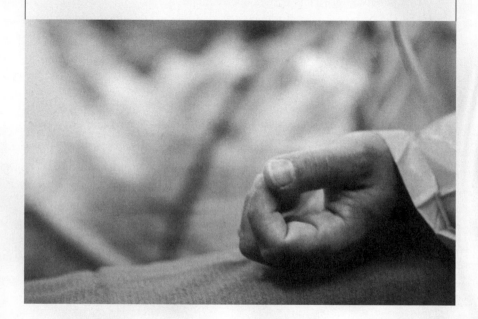

In the summer of 2001, my family and I took a month-long vacation to China and Thailand. About five days into the trip, in the city of Xian in central China, I seriously injured a disc in my lower back. The pain was absolutely unbearable. We spent several more agonizing days sightseeing in China and then flew to Bangkok, where my wife's sister, her husband, and their teenage son lived. Noticing the misery etched on my face as we got off the plane, they decided to take me to a hospital near their apartment. I was told not to worry because it was a private "Western" hospital, meaning that the style of medicine and the approach to treatment was like what you'd find in the United States and in most developed countries.

Had the circumstances been different (that is, if I weren't in agony), I might have been a little disappointed rather than comforted by this information. I've always had an interest in Eastern medicine and tend to be rather critical of Western medicine's quick reliance on drugs and more intrusive sorts of treatments. So it would have been sociologically interesting to experience an unfamiliar brand of medical care. But I was in no position to be curious or to hang on to my principles. I needed help for the pain, some kind of prescription, and I needed it fast.

When we arrived at the hospital, I was immediately startled by the conditions. Even though it was touted as one of the best hospitals in the area, by U.S. standards it was run-down, dingy, and noisy. Every available space seemed to be occupied by some sick or injured person patiently waiting to see a doctor. They were crammed into little waiting areas or lined up in hallways. No one complained. No one looked aggravated. Many had staked out their little patch of floor, setting up blankets for themselves and their children. By the looks of it, I surmised that most of them had come to the hospital assuming they'd be there for the long haul.

For one brief moment, I considered bolting for the door. But I wasn't going to get very far in my condition. My sister-in-law helped me register, and the receptionist curtly told me in broken English to "have a seat and wait until your name is called." So I found a chair and tried to settle in and make the best of it. After about five minutes, a young woman in a starched white dress and one of those old-fashioned nurses' hats ventured into the sea of waiting patients, thumbing through the papers on her clipboard. I didn't pay too much attention to her because by my estimate at least 50 people were ahead of me. Suddenly, she yelled out my name. "Huh? That can't be me," I thought to myself. She waited about 10 seconds and shouted my name again. It was me! I gleefully hoisted up my aching body and followed her out of the waiting area.

Now, if you've ever been to an American hospital, you know that at this point you'd probably be sent to another room to wait some more. But immediately, someone took my vital signs. Then two extremely friendly people escorted me to the x-ray room. From there, a different person took me to a therapy room, where I was placed on a bed with some kind of heating device pressed against my back. An alarm rang after about 30 minutes, and another person instantly came in and walked me to a doctor's private office. The doctor soon entered and, in English better than mine, proceeded to describe to me in great detail the nature of my injury. Her presentation included visual aids—a bright color poster of the human spine and a life-size plastic skeleton. She gave me three prescriptions—pain pills, pills for stomach problems caused by the pain pills, and vitamin B complex. In addition, she xeroxed several pages of a book she had on reha-bilitation exercises that she said would help in my recovery and gave me a back brace that looked like a girdle. Finally, as I got up to leave, she gave me a business card with her office phone number on it. "Call me directly if you have any questions, ok?"

My back didn't get much better, but all in all, it was a remarkably pleas-ant experience. I was amazed at the care I received, which was far friendlier and more attentive than any you'd see in the United States. But something kept bugging me. Why didn't I have to wait like all those other people? And why did the doctor, who had scores of patients lined up to see her, spend so much time casually chatting with me? Surely a hospital with that volume of patients couldn't possibly treat everyone the way I was treated.

As we left, I asked my sister-in-law why I had received what I con-sidered to be preferential treatment. Her response was quick and short. "Well, they knew you were an American, and they knew you'd be able to pay on the spot." Indeed, though I'm not wealthy by any stretch of the imagination, I was able to pay in cash because all the services and prescriptions I received were very inexpensive. Some time later, I read a couple of stories about Thai people who died on their way to government hospitals after being turned down at private hospitals like the one I went to because they didn't have money. And I've since learned that it's com-mon practice in some Thai hospitals to make sure patients pay up front, before they receive any treatment. I felt lucky and guilty at the same time.

Even if you've never been to Thailand, or any other foreign country for that matter, my story must certainly sound a little familiar. This theme, "the more money you have, the better the health care you receive," is just as true in this country as it is in Thailand. As medical costs—insurance premiums, prescription drugs, hospital care, and so on— soar beyond the reach of more and more Americans, effective health care is fast becoming a luxury, not an inalienable right.

Working-class and poor people receive less preventive health care than wealthy people and often must endure inadequate treatment in crowded public clinics. According to the U.S. Census Bureau (DeNavas-Walt, Proctor, & Mills, 2004), about 45 million Americans (and over 8 million chil-dren) currently have no health insurance. Because of rapidly escalating health care costs and job losses, this number is increasing. Uninsured par-ents face decisions that more affluent parents never do, such as choosing between buying a child a birthday gift and paying to have the child's cav-ity filled. Without this safety net, one sickness or one accident can destroy a family financially.

At the same time, those at the top can afford the best, most personal care available. For instance, for an annual fee of upwards of $20,000, wealthy individuals can buy "boutique," "premium," "deluxe," or "platinum" medical services: special access to the physician via 24/7 cell phone, fax, and e-mail; same-day appointments with a guaranteed waiting time of no more than 15 minutes; nutrition and exercise physiology exams at the patients' homes; doctors or nurses to accompany them when they go to see specialists; and routine physicals that are so thorough they can last up to three days (Belluck, 2002; Garfinkel, 2003). One physician provided a common justification for the growing disparity: "Is it health care for the rich? I guess so. But when you come to my clinic, I'm not concerned about the national health care picture. I'm concerned about you" (quoted in Tyre, 2005, p. 53).

This chapter will explore the relationship between our physical well-being and our racial, class, gender, and sexual identity. This relationship is a complex one that exists at several levels. First, how do social identities influence the social construction of health and illness? How do social inequalities affect our bodies, especially with regard to physical appearance and food-related conditions like hunger and obesity? Finally, how do race, class, gender, and sexuality—individually and in combination—influence susceptibility to illness and access to health care?

THE SOCIAL CONSTRUCTION OF HEALTH AND ILLNESS

Before examining the relationship between social identities and health-related inequalities, we must first look at the socially constructed nature of illness. "Healthy" and "sick" are not simply objective, physical standards found universally but are social creations that often vary dramatically between groups and within the same group over time. Conditions that are considered problematic or life-threatening in one culture might be considered quite normal in another. Diseases that are common in one society may not even exist in others. For instance, in Malaysia, a man may be diagnosed with *koro*, a sudden intense anxiety that his sexual organs will recede into his body, causing death. In some Latin American countries, a person can suffer from *susto*, an illness tied to a frightening event that makes the soul leave the body, causing unhappiness and sickness (American Psychiatric Association, 2000). Neither of these conditions exists as a medical diagnosis in other parts of the world. But they are not simply anthropological curiosities. They show that notions of health and illness are always shaped by culture.

Even cultures that are quite similar in other ways can have very different conceptions of health and illness. In the United States, people tend to see their bodies as machines that require basic upkeep and annual checkups for routine maintenance. In addition, diseases are considered enemies that need to be conquered. Not surprisingly, American doctors are much more likely than European doctors to take an aggressive approach to the treatment of illnesses, frequently prescribing drugs and resorting to surgery (Payer, 1988). U.S. women have more radical mastectomies, deliveries by cesarean section, and routine hysterectomies while still in their 40s than women in Europe. To be a "good" doctor in the United States typically means doing something proactive and forceful, even when there is some doubt as to what the best course of action is.

In contrast, doctors in Great Britain tend not to recommend routine examinations, seldom prescribe drugs, and order about half as many x-rays as U.S. doctors do (Payer, 1988). British patients are also much less likely to have surgery. For British doctors, the operating principle seems to be "when in doubt, do nothing." These attitudes also influence the perceptions of patients. People who are quiet and withdrawn—which U.S. doctors might consider symptoms of clinical depression in need of immediate attention—tend to be seen by British psychiatrists as perfectly normal.

Definitions of health can change over time even within the same culture. Consider these examples of how ideas about health fluctuate, all of which occurred in 2004:

- An international study of heart disease patients found that what is generally accepted as "normal" blood pressure may still be too high, exposing people to serious health risks that could be prevented if they lowered their blood pressure even further (Kolata, 2004b).
- Federal health officials in the United States lowered the threshold level for harmful cholesterol (Kolata, 2004a). Millions of people who went to bed one night thinking that their cholesterol was in the "healthy" range woke up the next day with cholesterol levels that are now considered "unhealthy" and "risky."
- In 2005, the U.S. Department of Agriculture released a new "Food Guide Pyramid"—a revised version of the icon it developed in 1992 to help Americans eat more healthfully. The consequence of these new guidelines will, no doubt, change our ideas about an optimal healthful diet.
- The Centers for Medicare and Medicaid Services, which runs the federal health program for the elderly and disabled, announced that it now defines obesity as a disease. Prior to this announcement,

obesity was considered a behavioral choice, meaning that the agency routinely denied coverage for weight-loss therapies, such as stomach surgery, diet programs, and counseling (Stein & Connolly, 2004).

In addition to determining the nature of illness, cultural and historical attitudes also influence what it means to be a sick person. Every society has a **sick role,** a widely understood set of expectations regarding how people are supposed to behave when sick (Parsons, 1951). The sick role entails certain obligations (things sick people are expected to do) as well as certain privileges (things sick people are entitled to):

- Because we tend to think of most illnesses as things that happen *to* a person, the individual may be exempted from responsibility for the condition itself. Nevertheless, she or he also has a moral obligation to recognize the condition as undesirable, as something that should be overcome as soon as possible.

- The individual who is allowed to occupy the sick role is excused from ordinary daily duties and expectations (Newman, 2004). National legislation, namely the Family & Medical Leave Act, and private workplace sick leave policies are the institutional manifestation of these expectations. Sick people are also entitled to ask for and receive care and sympathy from others and, depending on the magnitude of the malady, may even be given relief from the ordinary norms of etiquette and propriety. Think of the nasty moods, actions, or insults you're able to "get away with" when you're sick that people wouldn't tolerate from you if you were well.

- The person in the sick role is required to take the culturally prescribed actions that will aid in the process of recovery, including, if the condition is serious enough, seeking help from a culturally appropriate health care professional (Parsons, 1951). Sometimes, to obtain the privilege of exemption from normal social obligations, you must be documented as officially ill (Lorber, 2000). Without a "doctor's note" to validate an illness, your boss might not give you the day off or your instructor might not allow you to take a makeup exam. In the United States, such documentation is usually considered valid only if it comes from traditional medical doctors, not from holistic healers, chiropractors, homeopaths, osteopaths, or any other alternative practitioner outside the mainstream. In addition, being legally "disabled," securing insurance reimbursement, even being officially born or dead all require physician's documentation. These legal requirements keep people under the control of the medical system (Lorber, 2000).

Failure on the part of sick people either to exercise their rights or to fulfill the obligations of the sick role may elicit sanctions from the group (Coe, 1978). For instance, those who do not appear to want to recover or who seem to enjoy being sick quickly lose certain privileges, such as sympathy. A person may also give up legal rights by not seeking or following expert advice. In some cases, parents who are members of religious groups that eschew medical intervention have been arrested and charged with child endangerment for not acquiring culturally approved medical assistance for their sick children (Newman, 2004).

While different cultures define the sick role differently, it can also vary considerably along social class and gender lines within the same culture (Freund & McGuire, 1991). In the 19th century, for example, the sick role was considered appropriate for middle- and upper-class women because it was thought to reflect their refinement and delicacy. It was expected, even stylish, for affluent women to faint frequently or spend days in bed for "nerves," "sick headaches," "neurasthenia," or "female troubles." Lower-class women, by contrast, were considered stronger and heartier. Their purported physical strength simultaneously made them better able to withstand illness but less socially refined. In reality, because they depended on the wages they earned working, they simply couldn't afford to take days or weeks off from work and lie in bed. Hence, they weren't able to claim sick role privileges and exemptions from their ordinary responsibilities. Even giving birth did not relieve working-class mothers from their job duties.

Similar class differences in the sick role exist today. Someone might have a debilitating disease, but without health insurance she or he may not have the wherewithal to seek the care of health professionals (and receive an official diagnosis) or may not be able to take time off of work for fear of losing her or his job. In short, socioeconomic factors may preclude such people from claiming sick role status.

THE EMBODIMENT OF INEQUALITY

Social inequalities leave their mark on our bodies even before we enter a formally recognized sick role. Some time ago, a colleague returned from a trip to Hungary, where economic and environmental devastation has made adults look 20 or 30 years older than they are. Hungarians consistently estimated his age to be in the mid-20s (he was actually in his mid-40s at the time). One person said to him, "You Americans wear your affluence on your faces."

People's physical appearance often reflects their level of economic comfort. Listen to how one sociologist describes how poverty marked her as a child:

> What I recall most vividly about being a child in a profoundly poor family was that we were constantly hurt and ill, and because we could not afford medical care, small illnesses and accidents spiraled into more dangerous illnesses and complications that became both a part of who we were and written proof that we were of no value in the world. . . . At an early age my brothers and sister and I were stooped, bore scars that never healed properly, and limped with feet mangled by ill-fitting, used Salvation Army shoes. When my sister's forehead was split open by a door slammed in frustration, my mother "pasted" the angry wound together on her own, leaving a mark of our inability to afford medical attention . . . on her forehead. (Adair, 2004, p. 195)

The cycle of poverty-generated physical handicaps is a vicious one for the working poor. Consider this description of a woman who has been turned down time and again for jobs and promotions:

> The people who received promotions tended to have something that Caroline did not. They had teeth. Caroline's teeth had succumbed to poverty, to the years when she could not afford a dentist. . . . Where showing teeth was an unwritten part of the job description, she did not excel. . . . If she were not poor, she would not have lost her teeth, and if she had not lost her teeth, perhaps she would not have remained poor. (Shipler, 2004, pp. 52–53)

The marks left on our bodies by social inequalities may come from the day-to-day physical toll of economic insecurity, from not eating enough, or from eating too much unhealthful food. Some people have the economic wherewithal to correct bodily flaws they find undesirable; others must bear the stigma of their socioeconomic status as if it is a "brand of infamy" (Adair, 2004).

TO EAT OR NOT TO EAT

Food plays a large part in our lives. And I don't just mean that it keeps us alive. It is a key component of some of our most important events—the first time a baby eats "solid" food or uses utensils properly, family-affirming holiday traditions like Thanksgiving and Christmas, and even personally important moments like wedding receptions and wakes.

But some of our greatest collective anxieties revolve around food as well. For those who don't have enough to eat, each day brings a life-and-death struggle to secure the next meal. For those who have too much to eat, life is a daily battle to avoid weight gain. As we'll see, these ends of the anxiety continuum are correlated quite closely with economic security, socioeconomic standing, race, and gender.

Hunger For the vast majority of Americans, who are concerned with weighing too much, the reality of not having enough to eat is a distant one. But "in a world where the rich spend millions on ways to avoid carbohydrates and the United Nations declares obesity a global health threat, the cruel reality is that far more people struggle each day just to get enough calories" (McNeil, 2004, p. 4:1).

When most Americans hear the word *hunger,* they are likely to conjure images of famine-ravaged countries in sub-Saharan Africa or destitute villages in Latin America or Southeast Asia, where naked, dusty children, stomachs bloated with the telltale signs of malnutrition, plead for scraps of food. Indeed, in some countries, starving people resort to eating the leather off furniture or strapping flat stones to their stomachs to lessen the hunger pangs. In the slums of Haiti, people eat sunbaked biscuits made of butter, salt, water, and dirt (McNeil, 2004). According to the United Nations, hunger plagues an estimated 852 million people around the world and kills 5 million children each year (cited in Becker, 2004). In addition, about one out of four children worldwide is dangerously underweight (de Onis, Blössner, Borghi, Frongillo, & Morris, 2004).

A common misconception about hunger is that food supplies are inadequate to feed all the people in the world because of natural factors such as droughts and soil erosion. But abundance, not scarcity, best describes the world's food supply. Even the "hungriest" countries have enough food to feed all their people (Food First, 1998). Shortages of food are human, not natural, phenomena. Food is always available to those who can afford it. Social institutions and human policies determine who eats and who doesn't. For instance, women's education and status are associated with the quality of their children's nutrition; where women are deeply discriminated against, more children go hungry. Diseases such as HIV/AIDS and malaria can contribute to hunger by shortening the lives of breadwinners in poor countries and by preventing adults from passing down farming skills to future generations. Inadequate transportation can make it difficult for food to reach the people who need it most.

Politics and economics play a role as well. Many developing countries, like India and Brazil, export huge amounts of food while millions of their people are starving or malnourished. In an attempt to modernize, they often spend a disproportionate amount of money on building cities and industrializing their economies. As a result, farmers in rural areas aren't provided the incentives to grow as much food as they could. In other societies, civil wars and border disputes also take up a significant proportion of revenue that might otherwise go to domestic food production. Corrupt governments and warring factions may also disrupt food production and distribution and prevent food supplies from reaching the neediest people.

Whatever hunger's cause, as long as it seems a faraway problem, Americans can continue to convince themselves that it can comfortably be addressed with benefit concerts and high-profile charity events. But sooner or later, we will be forced to acknowledge the magnitude of the problem in our own country. Approximately 11% of American households are "food insecure"—meaning that some members don't have enough to eat or the family uses strategies like eating less varied diets, participating in food assistance programs, or getting emergency food from community food pantries (Zeller, 2004). That means that about 35 million poor Americans—including almost 13 million children—now live in households that experience hunger or the risk of hunger, an increase of 1.3 million since 2001 (Nord, Andrews, & Carlson, 2003).

Obesity At present, the problem of American hunger and malnutrition continues to go largely unnoticed. Instead, food-related bodily concerns in the United States are more likely to focus on the opposite end of the scale: people who eat—and perhaps weigh—"too much." About one-fifth of all Americans today and at least one-fourth of children are obese (meaning that they're at least 20% over their "desirable" weight). Both the former U.S. Surgeon General and the director of nutrition at the Centers for Disease Control have called American obesity an "epidemic." One expert on the matter stated that if overeating were left unchecked, all Americans would be obese within the span of a few generations (all cited in Critser, 2000).

Obesity is associated with several critical health problems, including heart disease, atherosclerosis, and diabetes. But the interpersonal and economic consequences of being overweight can be just as devastating as its health effects. In U.S. society, and in most industrialized societies, people are likely to judge an overweight person as lacking in willpower and as being self-indulgent, personally offensive, and even morally and socially unfit (Millman, 1980). A study of mental health caseworkers found that these individuals, despite their training, were more likely to assign negative attributes (for example, being too emotional or agitated, being unhygienic, engaging in inappropriate behavior) to obese patients than to thin patients (Young & Powell, 1985). Research has found significant discrimination against obese people at every stage of the employment cycle as well, including hiring, placement, compensation, promotion, discipline, and discharge (Roehling, 1999). In high-visibility occupations such as public relations and sales, overweight people might be regarded as unemployable because it was feared that they would project a negative image of the company they are working for.

The devaluation of overweight people is not universal. In Mexico, for instance, people are significantly less concerned about their own weight and are more accepting of overweight people than individuals in the United States are (Crandall & Martinez, 1996). In Niger, being overweight is considered an essential part of female beauty, so women sometimes take steroids to gain bulk or even ingest feed and vitamins that are meant to be consumed by livestock (Onishi, 2001). Among the Calabari people of southeastern Nigeria, soon-to-be brides are sent to farms where caretakers feed them huge amounts of food to fatten them up for the wedding day (Onishi, 2002).

Because of advances in global communication technology, however, images of American thinness have infiltrated places that once had different ideals of female beauty (Croteau & Hoynes, 2000). For instance, the 2001 Miss World was a Nigerian woman named Agbani Darego, an extremely tall and thin woman who conformed to American rather than Nigerian weight ideals. Older Nigerians considered her sickly thin. But younger Nigerians, who are more likely to be exposed to Western images, felt otherwise (Onishi, 2002). As recently as 10 years ago, the ideal body in Fiji was robust, and "going thin" was a cause for concern. But in the mid-1990s, satellite television began beaming U.S. television shows like *Melrose Place* and *Beverly Hills, 90210* (with their thin young actresses) to remote parts of the South Pacific. Soon after, Fijian girls not only began adopting the clothing and hairstyles of the women in these shows, they began showing serious symptoms of eating disorders that had been nonexistent on the island up to that point. By 1998, 69% of Fijian girls said they had been on a diet at some point in their lives and 15% had induced vomiting to control their weight. Fijian girls who said they watched television three or more hours a night were 50% more likely than girls who watched less television to describe themselves as "too big or fat" (cited in "Fat-phobia in the Fijis," 1999).

In earlier eras in U.S. society, being stout was considered a sign of good health, not surprising since most of the illnesses that concerned people at the time were wasting diseases like tuberculosis. Being fat was also associated with good, cheerful character (Gilman, 2004). In addition, up until the 20th century, plumpness was associated with prosperity, because only people who had the financial means could afford to eat enough food to make them overweight. In studying excavations in New York City, anthropologist Nan Rothschild (1990) found that wealthy areas in the 18th century could be identified by the remains of heavy meat bones; poorer neighborhoods were indicated by cheaper vegetables and fish. By the 1980s, however, that pattern had completely reversed.

Today, the lighter the food one eats, the higher one's status. Because of poor grocery distribution in low-income neighborhoods, fresh fruits and vegetables typically are more expensive than in suburban stores. Furthermore, diet, weight loss, exercise, and health are more likely to be concerns among wealthy rather than among poor Americans. In fact, one of the clearest indicators of the economic status of a community is the presence of health food supermarkets and private health clubs.

Conversely, obesity in the United States today tends to be equated with poverty (Gilman, 2004). The link between obesity and poverty disproportionately affects the young and ethnoracial minorities, particularly Latino/as and African Americans. For example, Starr County, Texas, is one of the poorest counties in the nation and is 98% Mexican American. By age four, 24% of children in this county are overweight or obese. By the time they enter elementary school, 50% of boys and 35% of girls are overweight or obese. In addition, over half of the adults have Type 2 diabetes, an affliction closely associated with obesity (Weil, 2005). Exhibit 6.1 presents the overweight statistics for the American population by age, race, and gender.

Weight problems are compounded in these communities by the fact that some key determinants of physical health—safe playgrounds, access to high-quality, low-cost food, and transportation to play areas—are either inadequate or nonexistent. In addition, high-calorie, high-fat fast food is

Exhibit 6.1: Overweight by Age, Gender, Race/Ethnicity

Percentage of population who are considered overweight

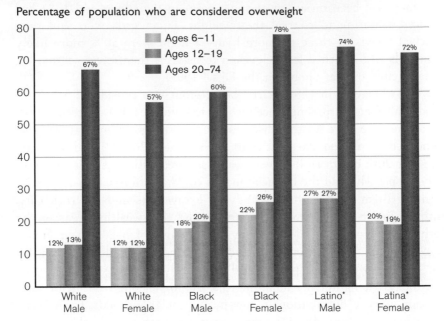

*For this table, Latino/as consist only of Mexican Americans

(Source: National Center for Health Statistics, 2003, Tables 68 & 69)

cheaper and more abundant than healthful food. Not surprisingly, fast-food companies have grown more aggressive in targeting poor, minority communities. One out of every four McDonald's hamburgers sold today is purchased by consumers in inner cities (Critser, 2000).

Obesity—along with related maladies like diabetes and hypertension—may also account for the rise in delivery-room deaths among poor mothers of color. According to the Centers for Disease Control (1999), almost 20 African American mothers die giving birth out of 100,000 live births each year; among white mothers, the figure is 5.3 per 100,000. Socioeconomic factors—and the food-related experiences they create—may be the most important factor in understanding race gaps in maternal mortality (Critser, 2000).

The association between obesity, class, and race is often tinged with prejudice. The stigma of fat tends to combine with the stigma of poverty and of non-whiteness. Many cases have been reported of fat children being removed from their homes because their obesity is taken as a sign of abuse and neglect. These cases almost always involve people of color and the poor or working class. Their blameworthiness, as perceived by the state, stems from a combination of unacceptable cultural traditions and their own alleged ignorance (LeBesco, 2004).

Intersections
Race, Class, Gender, and Weight

Although the American distaste for obesity applies to both sexes, it is felt particularly strongly by women, who are more likely than men to evaluate their self-worth in terms of their physical appearance. Not surprisingly, they're also more likely than men to be dissatisfied with their bodies, a dissatisfaction that is frequently framed in terms of weight (Renzetti & Curran, 2003).

Weight concern is deeply ingrained in American women. The behavioral consequences of distress over weight are widespread. According to statistics compiled by the National Eating Disorders Association (2004):

- Forty-two percent of 1st–3rd-grade girls want to be thinner, 51% of 9–10-year-old girls feel better about themselves when they're on a diet, and 81% of 10-year-olds are afraid of being fat.
- Ninety percent of college women attempt to control their weight through dieting.
- On any given day, about half of American women are on a diet, even though within 1–5 years, 95% of them will likely regain the weight they've lost.
- About 90% of Americans diagnosed with eating disorders (anorexia, bulimia, binge eating) are girls or women.

Weight concerns are not shared equally by all U.S. women. As you can see if you refer back to Exhibit 6.1, about 78% of African American women and 72% of Latina women are overweight, compared to 57% of white women (National Center for Health Statistics, 2003). Yet white women are significantly more likely than women of ethnoracial minorities to be concerned about their weight and to exhibit disordered eating behaviors (Abrams, Allen, & Gray, 1993). In one study, 90% of white junior high and high school girls voiced dissatisfaction with their bodies compared to 30% of black teens (Parker, Nichter, Nichter, Vuckovic, Sims, & Ritenbaugh, 1995). Indeed, black adolescents tend to perceive themselves as thinner than they actually are, whereas white adolescents tend to perceive themselves as heavier than they actually are.

African American women, especially poor and working-class African American women, worry less than women of other races about dieting or about being thin (Molloy & Herzberger, 1998). When African American women do diet, their efforts to lose weight are more realistic and less extreme than white women's attempts. More affluent African American women, though, are likely to be exposed to dominant white preferences, attitudes, and ideals about beauty and weight. Indeed, the risk of disordered eating increases for African American women who have a strong desire to assimilate into the dominant white culture (Abrams, Allen, & Gray, 1993). But in general, black women are less dissatisfied than white women with their body weight and therefore have higher self-esteem, have a more positive body image, and suffer from fewer eating disorders.

The relationship between race, class, and weight is complicated. On the one hand, the life circumstances of poor people and people from ethnoracial minorities increase the risk of obesity. But dissatisfaction with body size is lower in these groups than among middle-class Whites. One study found that although African American women are more likely than white women to weigh more than 120% of their recommended body weight, they are significantly less likely to perceive themselves as overweight or to suffer blows to their self-esteem as a result (Averett & Korenman, 1999). To some observers, women who don't see their weight as problematic and therefore aren't motivated to improve the healthiness of their lifestyle face serious health risks. On the other hand, excessive concern with weight and body image creates other potentially serious problems, like disordered eating habits, which can be equally dangerous.

IT'S NOT HOW YOU FEEL, IT'S HOW YOU LOOK

Concerns with bodily appearance go beyond weight anxiety. For centuries, people around the world have caused themselves serious pain and injury in their attempts to conform their bodies to cultural definitions of attractiveness. In traditional China, for example, young girls had their feet tightly bound to prevent them from growing and to thus produce the tiny feet that were considered attractive. Today, hundreds of Chinese women each year, convinced that being taller will improve their job and marriage prospects, subject themselves to a procedure in which their leg bones are broken, separated, and stretched. Metal pins and screws pull the bones apart a little less than a millimeter a day, sometimes for close to two years. Many women undergoing this treatment have lost the ability to walk; others have suffered permanent, disfiguring bone damage (Smith, 2002).

In U.S. society, women used to wear tight, suffocating corsets to achieve a desirable "hourglass" figure. Today, American women rip out their facial and body hair through tweezing or waxing, wear spine-altering high heels, and limit their daily caloric intake to dangerously low levels all for the purpose of reaching a particular beauty ideal. American women spend about $6 billion on fragrance, $6 billion on makeup products, and $8 billion on hair and skin care products each year (cited in C. Newman, 2000). Women who want full, plump lips can now use a lip gloss called "Lip Venom," a product that combines cinnamon, wintergreen, ginger, and jojoba to irritate and swell the lips. The creators say it delivers "shiny, fuller, bee-stung lips." One user described the experience: "With every passing minute, the burning intensified until my eyes were almost watering" (quoted in Walker, 2004, p. 22).

Some people take even more extreme measures to alter their appearance. According to the American Society for Aesthetic Plastic Surgery (2004), an estimated 8.3 million Americans had cosmetic surgeries (for instance, liposuction, rhinoplasty, breast augmentation or reduction, facelifts) and nonsurgical cosmetic procedures (such as Botox injections, laser hair removal, microdermabrasion) in 2003, an increase of 20% over 2002. Women accounted for 87% of the total. A growing number of affluent women are pursuing a contemporary version of foot binding, undergoing potentially dangerous cosmetic foot surgery to reduce the size of their toes so that they can fit into narrow high-heeled shoes (Harris, 2003). Cosmetic surgery is big business; in 2003, Americans spent over $9 billion on these procedures.

It's tempting to see concerns with physical appearance and the desire to cosmetically alter one's face or body as exclusively the province of white, wealthy women. But that's not entirely the case. Ethnoracial minorities account for about 20% of all cosmetic procedures (American Society for Aesthetic Plastic Surgery, 2004). For instance, the number of African American men and women seeking facial or reconstructive surgery more than tripled between 1997 and 2002. For years, the African American community has frowned upon cosmetic surgery and supported larger body types, wider noses, and not-so-perfect features. Some still see cosmetic surgery as an insult to "one's ancestors and to the culture" (Samuels, 2004, p. 48). But some social observers say that this increase in plastic surgery is simply an extension of other social trends, including concern with appearance and the growing affluence of African Americans. African Americans have become the biggest consumers of beauty products in the United States.

Asian American women are more likely than any other ethnoracial group to pursue cosmetic surgery (Kaw, 2002). But the specific procedures they seek are different from those preferred by other groups. White women might opt for liposuction or breast augmentation and African American women for lip or nasal reduction surgeries, but Asian American women are more likely to undergo surgeries to make their eyes appear wider and "less Asian." Their desire to have such a procedure reflects the fact that they've internalized the larger society's negative appraisal and stereotyping of "Asian" features. A 21-year-old Chinese American woman who had the surgery said, "When I look at other Asians who have no folds and their eyes are slanted and closed, I think of how they would look . . . more awake [if they had eye surgery]." Another said she had the surgery so she could "avoid the stereotype of the 'oriental bookworm' who is dull and doesn't know how to have fun" (both quoted in Kaw, 2002, p. 358).

Although the vast majority of people who are concerned about their appearance are women, men are not entirely immune to concerns over body image. Cultural constructions of masculinity are changing. Men are paying more attention to their looks. Male grooming products now account for a significant piece of the cosmetics market. Indeed, men are now being encouraged to see the relationship between their physical appearance and economic advantage. As one cosmetic surgeon put it, "A youthful look gives the appearance of a more dynamic, charging individual who will go out and get the business" (quoted in Bordo, 1999, pp. 195–196). Between 2002 and 2003, the number of men who had surgical and nonsurgical cosmetic procedures increased by 31% (American Society for Aesthetic Plastic Surgery, 2004). And more American men than ever are dieting or are having weight reduction surgeries, such as liposuction, apronectomies (tummy tucks), and gastric stapling (Gilman, 2004).

We can see in these trends that the cultural value placed on appearance is so strong in this society that it has begun to overcome traditional gender, ethnoracial, and class differences in how people view their bodies and the extent to which they'll go to alter them.

UNEQUAL AND UNWELL: THE STRATIFICATION OF HEALTH AND HEALTH CARE

To people whose lives are a daily struggle for survival, weight-loss programs and expensive elective surgeries to alter physical appearance are luxuries they will never enjoy. But they, like everyone else, will almost certainly get sick at some point in their lives and will eventually die. Unfortunately, the chances of getting sick and getting well are not equally distributed. Imbalances in susceptibility to illness and access to effective health care are unquestionably one of the hallmarks of human civilization worldwide. In the United States, health and health care are also stratified along class, ethnoracial, gender, and sexual lines.

GLOBAL INEQUALITIES

According to the World Health Organization (1995), poverty is the single greatest cause of ill health in the world today:

> Poverty is the main reason why babies are not vaccinated, why clean water and sanitation are not provided, why . . . drugs and other treatments are unavailable and why mothers die in childbirth. It is the underlying cause of reduced life expectancy, handicap, disability, stress, suicide, family disintegration, and substance abuse. (p. 1)

For the over one billion people worldwide who live on less than one U.S. dollar per day, basic health services and medicines are nonexistent. People living in extreme poverty lack every conceivable correlate of good health: safe drinking water, decent housing, adequate sanitation, sufficient food, health education, professional health care, transportation, and secure employment.

At the level of global economics, poor and middle-income countries are home to more than 80% of the world's population and carry 90% of the world's disease burden but only account for 11% of worldwide health care spending (Carr, 2004). As a result, poor countries lag behind wealthier countries on almost every social indicator of health: infant and child mortality, stunted growth, malnutrition, childhood vaccinations, prenatal and postnatal care, and life expectancy (Population Reference Bureau, 2004a). Millions of people die prematurely each year from diseases that, in more prosperous countries, are preventable, curable, or nonexistent. In Africa, for instance, infectious and parasitic diseases accounted for more than half of all deaths in 2001; in Europe, such diseases accounted for only 2% of all deaths (Carr, 2004). Exhibit 6.2 illustrates the relationship between health spending and life expectancy.

HIV/AIDS presents the most troubling global imbalances. The vast majority of HIV-infected people around the world are poor and don't have access to the effective, but extremely expensive, drug treatments that are readily available in the West. Consequently, though the number of AIDS cases and AIDS deaths is dropping in Western industrialized countries, it continues to increase in less developed countries (UNAIDS, 2004). Impoverished countries in sub-Saharan Africa alone account for 62% of the world's

Exhibit 6.2: Global Imbalances in Health

Total annual spending on health per person (in U.S. dollars)

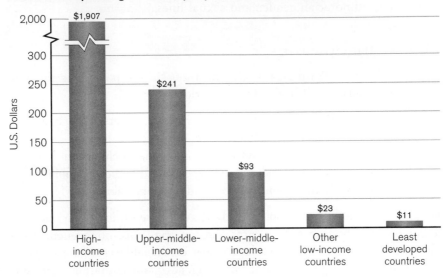

Life expectancy at birth 1995–2000

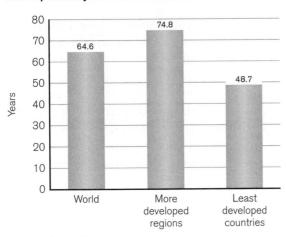

(Source: Carr, 2004)

victims of HIV/AIDS between the ages of 15 and 24, though not all countries in the region have the same rate of infection. Close to 9% of the adult population in these countries is infected with the disease (UNAIDS, 2004). In 2003 alone, 2.2 million Africans died of AIDS. In Durban, South Africa, for example, the magnitude of AIDS deaths is so sweeping that the city has run out of space to bury AIDS victims, and gravediggers are forced to re-open existing graves and inter fresh bodies on top of old ones (Wines, 2004a). By contrast, the number of AIDS deaths in all high-income countries *com-bined* (the United States, Western Europe, Australia, New Zealand, and Japan) in 2003 was around 20,000 (UNAIDS, 2004).

The effect that this disease has had on overall life expectancy is stag-gering. In the developed regions of North America and Europe, people born this year can expect to live into their mid-70s. In the poorest, least developed countries in the world, life expectancy is well below 50. In African countries with high rates of HIV infection (Zimbabwe, Swaziland, Lesotho, Zambia, Malawi, Central African Republic, and Mozambique), life expectancy has now dropped below 40 (Dugger, 2004). Such startling figures will have severe long-term consequences as millions of the world's poorest children become orphaned and face a lifetime of despair.

To make matters worse, HIV/AIDS is fast becoming a "feminized" epidemic, with more and more women becoming infected at earlier ages. Nearly 50% of adults living with HIV are women, up from 35% in 1985. In sub-Saharan Africa, girls and young women make up 75% of those between 15 and 24 who are HIV-positive (Lalasz, 2004). To experts, one of the most important reasons for the increase of AIDS cases in women is that in many poor countries, particularly those in sub-Saharan Africa, men make all sexual decisions, including the use of contraceptives. Fur-thermore, poverty can force a woman to engage in what is sometimes called "transactional sex," risky clandestine relationships with four or five men who help her out financially in exchange for sex (Wines, 2004b).

Poor women around the world face persistent and pervasive health risks beyond HIV/AIDS. Because they occupy subordinate statuses in most societies and face extra economic and social burdens as a result of childbearing and child rearing, global health inequalities hit them and their children particularly hard (Ashford, 2005). Wealthier women are four times as likely as poorer women to have access to modern contra-ception and five times more likely to give birth in the presence of a medically trained assistant. Children of poor mothers are three times more likely to be stunted in their growth and twice as likely to die as children of wealthy mothers (Population Reference Bureau, 2004a). Mal-nutrition among poor women and girls around the world wreaks havoc on their health as well as the health of their children in numerous ways, such as low birth weight, impaired physical and mental development, and increased risk of maternal mortality and chronic disease in adulthood (Ransom & Elder, 2003).

It's important to note that the serious health problems faced by people in poor countries don't emerge solely from harmful living conditions or cultural subordination. They are frequently influenced by global economics and politics. It's estimated that 165,000 people worldwide, mostly children, die each month from malaria and over a thousand women a day die in childbirth. One in four people do not have access to clean drinking water (cited in Hamilton, 2005). Wealthy countries could easily afford to provide regular vaccines, mosquito nets, soil nutrients, sufficient food, or clean water supplies to poor countries to address these treatable problems. In fact, in 2005, the United Nations declared that ending world hunger and disease was "utterly affordable" and would require only that wealthy countries commit one-half of 1% of their total incomes to aid poor countries. However, many of these nations have been notoriously reluctant to provide such assistance. The United States, for example, currently provides less than one-fifth of 1% of its total income, the smallest percentage among major donor countries (Dugger, 2005). Expenditures for health care in poor countries tend to be politically unpopular in wealthy countries.

The exception is the generous response by citizens of wealthy countries when some dramatic natural disaster occurs. For instance, in the aftermath of the catastrophic 2004 tsunami, which killed over 200,000 people in South Asia and Eastern Africa, tens of billions of dollars were raised worldwide for relief efforts. The U.S. government pledged $950 million. Celebrity musicians held benefit concerts. Actors and actresses answered phones during telethons. Some professional basketball players donated $1,000 for every point they scored in a game. Close to 30% of Americans donated money to the cause, and another 37% indicated that they intended to do so (Lester, 2005). Two weeks after the disaster, the charitable organization "Save the Children" had received more than $10 million in donations over the Internet alone. In a typical month, the organization receives between $30,000 and $50,000 (Strom, 2005). As well-intentioned as these efforts were, it's unlikely that such generosity could be mobilized to create healthier living conditions in poor countries or to fight the lower-profile, chronic diseases that plague people around the world on a daily basis.

WEALTH AND HEALTH IN THE UNITED STATES

Socioeconomic inequalities in health and health care exist *within* countries as well. Even in relatively healthy countries like Netherlands, Finland, the United States, and Great Britain, poor people die five to ten years sooner, on average, than wealthy people (Carr, 2004). Diseases, nutritional deficiencies, birth complications, injuries, substance abuse, and violence tend to be concentrated among the poorest people in any society. Such discrepancies are by no means new. As far back as the 16th and 17th centuries, records show a relationship between socioeconomic inequalities and health. In 17th-century Geneva, for instance, average life expectancy was 18 for the lowest socioeconomic group and 36 for the highest group (cited in Rogmans, 2001).

In the United States today, the overwhelming empirical evidence indicates that rates of illness increase and life expectancy decreases as one climbs down the socioeconomic ladder (Marmot, 2004). The poorer you are, the greater your risk of headaches, varicose veins, respiratory infection, childhood asthma, hypertension, emotional distress, low-birth-weight babies, and heart disease (Perez-Peña, 2003; Shweder, 1997). Poor people's living and work conditions are more likely to be unhealthy. They are exposed to more environmental toxins and have access to less effective medical care than more affluent Americans. Consider these other findings:

- Poor children in both urban and rural regions of the country have lead levels in their blood that far exceed national health standards. About 12% of children living in poor families have dangerous blood lead levels compared to about 2% of children in high-income families. In every income group, African American children are more likely than children of other ethnoracial groups to have elevated blood lead levels (Northridge, Stover, Rosenthal, & Sherard, 2003).
- Tobacco use is highest among people who have working-class jobs, have achieved a low level of education, and earn a low income (Barbeau, Krieger, & Soobader, 2004). These trends exist in most, but not all, ethnoracial and gender groups.
- Large agribusinesses expose their poor, itinerant, and largely minority employees and their employees' children to untold health risks by spraying deadly pesticides and herbicides in the wind, sending workers into the fields too soon after the chemicals have been applied, and failing to provide sinks, showers, and laundries so the workers can wash off the harmful substances. The most obvious health effects are vomiting, nausea, dizziness, headaches, skin rashes, bronchitis, and asthma. Less immediate but more serious effects include childhood brain tumors, leukemia, non-Hodgkin's lymphoma, and sarcoma. The incidence of birth defects is 3 to 14 times

higher among farmworkers than among the general U.S. population (Shipler, 2004).

As in underdeveloped countries, illness and poverty interact in ways that are especially dangerous to children. Low-income families typically have problems paying rent, buying food, obtaining access to health services, providing transportation, and providing a safe physical environment for their children. Poor mothers, and especially mothers of color, are more likely than wealthier mothers to give birth to underweight babies. Children born with below-normal birth weight get lower average IQ and achievement test scores, have more frequent learning disabilities and attention disorders, are more likely to have health problems like asthma that lead to greater absences, and are less likely to graduate from high school (Rothstein, 2002).

It might be tempting to attribute such class disparities in health to the lifestyles of people on the bottom socioeconomic rungs of society. However, it is impossible to ignore the institutional activities that aggravate the problem. In 2001, for instance, because of cuts in welfare benefits, poor infants and toddlers were 40% less likely to be "food secure"—that is, to have access to nutritionally adequate and safe food—than they were two years earlier. They also had a 90% higher risk of being hospitalized during an emergency room visit (Children's Sentinel Nutrition Assessment Program, 2002).

Not only do people without sufficient economic means face greater health risks than others, they may also lack the ability to get effective treatment once they do get sick. According to the U.S. Census Bureau (2004), 30% of people who fall below the poverty line are not covered by any health insurance. Without health insurance, a catastrophic illness or a long-term medical condition can destroy an already struggling family. To make matters worse, many states are cutting back on subsidies for health care, further increasing the number of people with no coverage. In Texas, for example, more than a half million children enrolled in state- and federally-subsidized insurance programs lost their dental, vision, and most mental care coverage in 2003 due to budget cuts (Strom, 2003).

THE COLOR OF HEALTH

As with other forms of inequality, it's difficult if not impossible to separate the effects of race from the effects of class. Nevertheless, a substantial body of research points to the fact that people of color have historically received poorer health care than Whites in this society and are less likely than Whites to have access to health insurance. Almost 33% of Latino/as (especially those from Mexico and Central America) and 19.4% of African Americans lack any kind of health insurance, compared to 11% of non-Hispanic Whites (DeNavas-Walt, Proctor, & Mills, 2004).

As a consequence, members of ethnoracial minorities continue to face long-term disadvantages in health and health care. For instance, African Americans make up about 12% of the female population in this country but account for 64% of female HIV infections (cited in Cowley & Murr, 2004). According to the U.S. Bureau of the Census (2004), the overall five-year cancer survival rate for African Americans is 55.2%; the survival rate for white cancer patients is 65.5%. Exhibit 6.3 shows other discrepancies in the relationship between race/ethnicity and the cause of death. For most causes, death rates for Blacks are far above those of any other ethnoracial group, largely because of inequalities in income, education, and occupation—all of which are related to increased risk of mortality (Population Reference Bureau, 2002). The exceptions are suicide and cirrhosis of the liver, for which Native Americans rank at or near the top. Here, too, institutional factors are likely responsible. The hopelessness of life on destitute reservations, where economic and educational opportunities are virtually nonexistent, can create a level of despair so great that it may only be lessened through alcohol or suicide.

Exhibit 6.3: Age-Adjusted Death Rates for Selected Causes by Gender, Race, and Ethnicity (Deaths per 100,000)

Cause of death	Male	Female	Non-Hispanic White	Black	American Indian	Asian	Latino/a
All causes	1,029	722	843	1,101	687	492	659
Heart disease	305	204	246	317	160	138	192
Cancers	244	165	197	243	131	119	132
Stroke	59	56	56	79	41	51	45
Injuries	50	22	6	38	51	17	31
Suicide	18	4	12	5	10	5	6
Cirrhosis of the liver	13	6	9	9	23	3	16
Homicide	11	3	4	21	7	4	8
HIV infection	7	2	2	23	3	1	6

(Source: National Center for Health Statistics, 2003, Table 29)

Even when insurance coverage, incomes, and severity of illness are the same, members of ethnoracial minorities in the United States do not receive the same quality of health care as do white Americans (Institute of Medicine, 2003). People of color are less likely than Whites to be given appropriate medication for heart ailments or to undergo bypass surgery. They're less likely to receive kidney dialysis, kidney transplants, or the most effective treatment for HIV infections. Other studies have found that African American cancer patients receive fewer effective surgeries and get less adequate pain medication than white patients with similar characteristics (cited in Mayberry, Mili, & Ofili, 2000). On the other hand, patients of color are more likely than Whites to receive "less sophisticated" treatments like arm and leg amputations. One study found that African American patients with circulatory problems were more than twice as likely as comparable Whites to have a leg amputated. In addition, African Americans with prostate cancer were far more likely than other men to have their testicles removed (cited in Feagin & McKinney, 2003).

Whether these differences are a result of conscious individual bigotry or something more systemic is a matter of some debate. It seems unlikely that doctors would purposely give patients of particular ethnoracial groups substandard care. What's more likely—and in some ways more insidious—is that subtle stereotypes influence the way doctors perceive their patients. For instance, one study found that doctors view white patients as more intelligent and more likely to abide by medical instructions than patients of color (cited in Feagin & McKinney, 2003). In another study, several hundred physicians were shown videotapes of "patients" (actually actors) with heart disease. Even when these patients reported similar symptoms, test results, class standing, and occupations, the physicians were more likely to recommend high-tech cardiac procedures for white than for black patients.

The differential treatment of certain groups is often motivated by financial concerns. Consider, for instance, racial differences in organ transplants. According to the Organ Procurement and Transplant Network (2004), in 2003 the national kidney transplant waiting list consisted of 39% Whites and 35% African Americans. (This figure in and of itself is telling: African Americans make up only about 12% of the population yet account for over one-third of people in need of kidney transplants.) However, that same year, Whites received 57% of all kidney transplants while African Americans received only 23%. This discrepancy may be linked to the "green screen," a term used to describe transplant policies in some hospitals. In addition to clinical information, financial information is sometimes used to decide which patients should be excluded from their lists of eligible candidates. A new liver, for example, can cost over $250,000, so most hospitals want evidence of insurance coverage up front. Because ethnoracial minorities are less likely than Whites to have medical insurance, they are also less likely to receive a referral for transplant surgery (Stolberg, 1998).

Environmental Discrimination Health disparities along ethnoracial lines are sometimes not so obvious. For instance, people in neighborhoods where hazardous waste treatment facilities or other sources of industrial pollution exist are disproportionately exposed to the unhealthful effects of air pollution, water pollution, and pesticides. In the interests of economic expansion, companies—often with the support of local governments and labor groups—decide on the location of such facilities based on factors that, on the surface, have nothing to do with the ethnoracial configuration of communities: the cost of land, population density, and geological conditions. But because the more desirable industrial areas tend to be the areas where existing houses can be bought up and demolished cheaply, industrial facilities are disproportionately likely to be built in areas populated by poor members of ethnoracial minorities.

Furthermore, if a community is poor and inhabited largely by people of color, there's a good chance that environmental protections help it less than a community that is affluent or white (Bullard, 2001). For instance, because Native American reservations have less stringent environmental regulations than other areas, they have been targeted by the U.S. military for the location of stockpiles of nuclear, chemical, and biological weapons and by private companies seeking to build solid waste landfills, hazardous waste incinerators, and nuclear waste storage facilities (Hooks & Smith, 2004). In addition, when it comes to the federal government cleaning up polluted areas, predominantly white communities see faster action, better results, and stiffer penalties for polluters than communities where ethnoracial minorities predominate (Bullard, 2001).

Poor African American communities are often the hardest hit. Seven oil refineries and several hundred heavy industrial plants are situated along a stretch of the Mississippi River between Baton Rouge and New Orleans known as "cancer alley" (Koeppel, 1999). A study of toxic emissions in this area by the Environmental Protection Agency showed that 9 of the 10 major sources of industrial pollution are in predominantly black neighborhoods (Cushman, 1993). Overall, the greater the proportion of black residents in a community, the more likely it is that there will be industrial sources of air pollution within a two-mile radius of people's homes (Perlin, Sexton, & Wong, 1999).

The phenomenon of environmental discrimination is complicated. Often, a destitute community welcomes a hazardous facility as a much-needed source of employment. For instance, in 1998 the Louisiana chapter of the National Association for the Advancement of Colored People (NAACP) supported the construction of a $700 million plastics plant in St. James Parish that it knew could pose dangerous health risks to the neighborhoods nearby. African Americans made up 81% of the residents within four miles of the proposed site (Hines, 2001). At the time, the region suffered an unemployment rate of 12% and a poverty rate of 44%. The average income among its black residents was less than $5,000 a year. So the possibility of a steady source of employment, no matter how dangerous, was quite attractive. Nobody wants a garbage dump, landfill, incinerator, or polluting factory in their backyard. But if these are the only ventures that will provide steady employment for residents, poor communities are left with little choice but to support them. The president of the NAACP said, "Poverty has been the No. 1 crippler of poor people, not chemical plants" (quoted in Cooper, 1998, p. 532).

Health Care Suspicions The undeniable fact about the American health care system is that the poorer you are and the darker your skin, the worse the health care you'll receive. So it's not all that surprising that Whites, the wealthy, and the well-educated report that they are more trusting of the health care system than their darker, poorer, and less educated counterparts are (Schnittker, 2004). Suspicions of the system received graphic support several months after the September 11, 2001, attacks. Two anthrax-laden letters passed through a Washington, D.C., post office where 1,700 mostly working-class people of color were employed. When the letters arrived on Capitol Hill, public health officials immediately evacuated congressional buildings, tested all the people who worked in those buildings, and provided workers with antibiotics. But the post office was not closed right away and workers there were left untested and untreated until two of them died (Shipler, 2004).

Mistrust is especially pervasive among African Americans. Much of their anxiety is sharpened by memories of the federal government's infamous Tuskegee experiment. In 1932, the U.S. Public Health Service began a study in Tuskegee, Alabama, to learn about the natural course of untreated syphilis. In exchange for their participation, 400 black men—all poor and most illiterate—received free meals, free medical exams, and burial insurance. The researchers and health care workers never told the men that they had syphilis. Instead, they were told that they had "bad blood," for which they would receive treatment. In reality, they received no treatment. Even when penicillin—the most effective treatment for syphilis—became available in the early 1950s, the men were not treated. In fact, the Public Health Service went to great lengths to prevent the men from receiving treatment. Even as they began to die or to go blind or insane, penicillin was withheld. When the experiment was made public in 1972—four decades after its inception—it was finally stopped. Since then, the federal government has paid out more than $9 million in damages to victims and their families and heirs.

The legacy of the Tuskegee study has been a pervasive distrust of medical research among many African Americans today. Indeed, even well before this study, African Americans were routinely used as subjects, sometimes nonconsensual subjects, for new medical treatments, experimental procedures, and medical demonstrations. Today, many African Americans—as well as Latino/as and Native Americans—avoid participating in medical research because of their fear of being used as guinea pigs and suspicions of malicious attempts to intentionally cause illness (cited in Alvidrez & Areán, 2002). Furthermore, members of ethnoracial minorities are often skeptical that their participation in clinical studies would be a benefit either to them personally or to their communities. One survey of African Americans about their attitudes toward research on cancer treatments found that only 43% felt medical research in the United States is conducted ethically (cited in Alvidrez & Areán, 2002). It's no surprise, therefore, that ethnoracial minorities are underrepresented in medical research across all health fields.

Mistrust has also been cited as one of the reasons why African American and other patients of color have been slow to seek medical care and testing for diseases like HIV/AIDS (Richardson, 1997), are less inclined to submit to breast cancer screenings (Thompson, Valdimarsdottir, Winkel, Jandorf, & Redd, 2004), and are less likely than Whites to get surgery for early stages of deadly diseases like lung cancer (Bach, Cramer, Warren, & Begg, 1999). Because of their mistrust, members of ethnoracial minorities may obtain health care only when their problems become severe or even beyond help, leading to the perception that the treatments themselves may be not only ineffective but perhaps even harmful.

Whether these deeply ingrained suspicions are warranted or not is in some sense irrelevant. Medical mistrust needn't derive from specific historical events or even be based on factual data in order for it to have significant effects on people's lives. There only needs to be a cultural ideology of mistrust for it to perpetuate itself among the members of any group (Cort, 2004).

GENDERED HEALTH

Because of different anatomies, women and men face many different health-related issues. Men don't get ovarian cysts; women don't get prostate cancer. But beyond these differences, the reasons behind gender differences in health and illness are less anatomically inevitable. For instance, men tend to occupy more physically demanding jobs and engage in riskier physical activity than women. Hence they've historically been at greater risk for various bodily injuries and stress-related ailments. According to figures from the U.S. Bureau of the Census (2004), men have higher rates of cancer (excluding breast, cervical, and ovarian types) and lower overall life expectancy than women. However, women are far more likely than men to undergo surgical and diagnostic procedures. Indeed, the three most common short-stay surgical procedures for women—repair of lacerations during childbirth, cesarean section, and hysterectomy—all deal with exclusively female anatomy and physiology. The three most common short-stay procedures for men—cardiac catheterization, removal of coronary obstruction, and coronary bypass—are not sex-specific.

Women may be healthier, in general, than men. But, historically, women have been more susceptible than men to being labeled "ill" or "sick" by the medical establishment (Rothman, 1984). Normal biological events in women's lives—menstruation, pregnancy, childbirth, and menopause—have long been "**medicalized**" or "**pathologized**," meaning that they were considered problematic conditions in need of medical attention. The social message was clear: Women, biologically frail and emotionally erratic because of their anatomy and physiology, cannot be allowed to work too hard or be trusted in positions of authority (Fausto-Sterling, 1985).

According to anthropologist Sherry Ortner (1996), the pathologization of women's normal functioning is due, in part, to the fact that many areas and processes of women's bodies serve a procreative function but no apparent function for the health or stability of the individual. As these body parts perform their specific reproductive functions, they can be the source of discomfort, pain, even danger. Breasts, for example, serve no organic purpose for the woman and can be removed at any time in her life if they become diseased. Ovarian secretions function for the benefit of the egg, promoting its maturation, but they can cause disequilibrium in the woman. Menstruation can be painful and is stigmatized in many cultures. When she is pregnant, a woman's intake of vitamins and minerals is channeled into nourishing the fetus, thereby depleting her strength and energy. And, of course, childbirth itself is a painful and potentially hazardous experience. In short, compared with a man, more of a woman's body space and more of her lifetime are taken up with natural processes involved in reproducing the species, sometimes at great risk to personal health.

Premenstrual Syndrome Perhaps the female body process that has received the most medical attention is premenstrual syndrome (PMS). A woman recently wrote in to *Shape* magazine concerned about the fact that her emotions fluctuate. The columnist advised her that although mild "mood swings" can be normal, it would be wise for her to first rule out premenstrual syndrome as the possible cause (Paul, 2004). The fact that PMS is automatically assumed to be the culprit attests to the level of acceptance the diagnosis has reached in this society. People inside and outside the medical profession so readily believe in the essential reality of PMS that it has become the default explanation for any emotional inconsistencies women may have. Yet, despite the current popularity of PMS as a catchall diagnosis, it's not altogether clear exactly what it is. Some women experience premenstrual bodily changes; others report emotional changes; and some have a combination of both. Over 100 symptoms have been identified as characteristic of PMS, including (but not limited to):

- physical complaints (muscle stiffness, headache, cramps, backache, fatigue, insomnia, chest pains, ringing in the ears, fuzzy vision, numbness)
- impairments of concentration (confusion, distractibility, lowered judgment)
- dizziness (faintness, cold sweats, nausea, hot flashes)
- water retention (weight gain, skin disorders, painful breasts)
- emotional problems (crying, anxiety, anger, irritability, mood swings, depression, tension) (Fausto-Sterling, 1985)

Premenstrual syndrome as a diagnosable condition is a relatively recent social construction. It first began to receive widespread public notoriety in the 1980s. A criminal case in Great Britain had a lot to do with popularizing PMS. A woman who ran over her boyfriend with her car was convicted of manslaughter, not murder, after her attorney successfully argued that she was suffering from PMS at the time of the crime, a condition that made her irrational and uncontrollably violent. As a condition of her probation, the woman was required to receive monthly hormone injections to control her symptoms (Renzetti & Curran, 2003).

The value of identifying PMS as "real" malady is disputable. Some feminists in the 1970s and 1980s pressed for research money and scientific attention to be given to bodily processes, such as premenstrual syndrome, that only women experience. But the focus on PMS masks the fact that menstrual processes do not affect healthy women's ability to function, that some women actually experience positive changes prior to their periods, or that men experience periodic hormonal fluctuations that affect their mood, as much as women do, if not more (Tavris, 1992). The pervasiveness of PMS as a diagnosable condition also means that women who may experience normal mood changes during their menstrual cycles are encouraged, indeed expected, to consider them abnormal. As one author puts it, "Biomedical researchers have taken a set of bodily changes that are normal to women over the menstrual cycle, packaged them into a 'Premenstrual Syndrome,' and sold them back to women as a disorder, a problem that needs treatment and attention" (Tavris, 1992, p. 133). PMS has thus become a financial boon for medical researchers and drug companies.

Debate continues among psychiatrists as to whether or not PMS (or as it is called in official diagnostic manuals, *Premenstrual Dysphoric Disorder*) is a mental illness. Certainly, women around the world experience varying degrees of grumpiness, irritability, and other symptoms related to hormone cycles. In many areas, these experiences are perceived as normal and expectable. The issue, then, is whether these "symptoms" ought to be labeled as a medical problem. To do so reinforces the belief that women's bodies are highly susceptible to disorders and are therefore always in need of medical attention.

From a sociological perspective, it seems highly likely that women's experiences with the "symptoms" surrounding menstruation are related to the place that menstruation occupies in the larger culture. We live in a culture that, by and large, has tried either to ignore menstruation or to present it as shameful. Only relatively recently—as evidenced by the glut of commercials and advertisements for "feminine hygiene" products—has it come out of the closet. But, of course, the attention we as a culture devote to menstruation continues to be almost exclusively negative, focusing on overcoming bothersome premenstrual symptoms or camouflaging the unsightly or otherwise unappealing by-products of menstruation itself.

The Medicalization of Childbirth Another area in which women's normal functioning has been medicalized is childbirth. Until the 19th century, doctors were almost completely absent from the birthing process. Female midwives and other women in the family or in the community commonly attended women during and after childbirth (Howell-White, 1999). Birth was considered a woman's affair. Every effort was made to keep men as far away as possible. Only in extremely wealthy families or when the mother's life was in danger was a male doctor consulted (Ulrich, 1990).

By the middle of the 20th century, the hospitalized birth became the delivery method of choice for middle- and upper-class white women, although poor, minority pregnant women still found hospitals largely out of their reach. In 1900, only 5% of American births took place in hospitals; by 1939, over 50% of all births and 75% of urban births occurred there. The overwhelming consideration for hospitalized expectant mothers was the minimization of pain (Mitford, 1993). Obviously, pain has always been an element of childbirth. But with advances in medical technology, affluent women were beginning to believe that they had a right to avoid pain if at all possible. Initially, expectant mothers were put to sleep with chloroform or ether throughout labor and delivery. Eventually, localized anesthetics—drugs that alleviated pain but allowed women to remain conscious throughout the delivery—became popular.

The medicalization and hospitalization of childbirth increased women's dependence on the predominantly male medical profession. During typical deliveries, relatively little attention was paid to the mother's comfort, well-being, or self-esteem. Typically, she was placed in a position with her legs widespread in the air and her genitals totally exposed. Once labor began, doctors commonly resorted to invasive procedures such as the use of forceps and suction. Episiotomies—incisions that increase the size of the vaginal opening to give the baby more room to emerge—became a common part of the birthing process. Clearly, a medicalized childbirth meant that the doctor, not the mother, delivered the baby.

But by the 1950s, concern began to grow over the possibility that babies might be harmed in some way by the use of drugs and other common invasive procedures during delivery. And some women were starting to publicly voice their concerns about the dehumanizing conditions of hospital delivery wards. As one mother of three in the 1950s wrote:

> Women are herded like sheep through the obstetrical assembly line, are drugged and strapped on tables while their babies are forceps-delivered. Obstetricians today are businessmen who run baby factories. Modern painkillers and methods are used for the convenience of the doctor, not to spare the mother. (quoted in Gillis, 1996, p. 173)

As a result of such criticisms, "natural" childbirth—deliveries without the aid of anesthetics, suction, or forceps—became popular in the 1960s and

1970s. It restored women to a more central role in the birth process. The popularity of "natural" childbirth—less medical intervention, more maternal contact with the newborn right after birth, and so on—was accompanied by a nostalgic desire to return to a simpler, less technological childbirth experience. Expectant mothers, and their sometimes reluctant husbands, were encouraged to attend childbirth classes to learn special breathing techniques that could ease the delivery without resorting to drugs. Today, many hospitals have turned their cold and sterile "delivery" rooms into homelike, reassuring "birthing" suites. The goal is to re-create the benefits of the cozy home birth of the 19th century, but to do so within a safe hospital setting.

Although more expectant couples are choosing to give birth at home these days, with the aid of a trained nurse-midwife and with relatives, friends, and other children in attendance, the vast majority of births today are still medical procedures that occur in hospitals. Furthermore, episiotomies are used in 90% of all American births even though recent research has shown that these procedures have no benefits and actually cause more complications for women who receive them (Hartmann, Viswanathan, Palmieri, Gartlehner, Thorp, & Lohr, 2005). Cesarean sections are performed in almost 25% of births, and most mothers use some sort of pharmaceutical pain control (Davis-Floyd, 1996; Gillis, 1996).

The Gendering of Medical Practice and Research Because of the tendency in the medical profession to see the normal functioning of women's bodies as problems in need of control, doctors can specialize in women's health care—but not in men's. Obstetricians and gynecologists deal exclusively with the reproductive and sexual matters of female patients. There are no comparable specialties of medicine devoted to men's reproductive health.

Given the special attention women's health problems receive, it's ironic that research on women's general health needs has been rather limited. Twenty years ago, the United States Public Health Service reported that a lack of medical research on women limited our understanding of their health concerns (Rothman & Caschetta, 1999). The reason often given for their exclusion from medical studies was that their menstrual cycles complicated the interpretation of research findings. This way of thinking has been so pervasive that even female rats are commonly excluded from basic medical research. In addition, medical researchers have historically been reluctant to perform research on women of childbearing age because of fears that exposing them to experimental manipulations might harm their reproductive capabilities. In fact, in the 1970s and 1980s, federal policies and guidelines actually called for the blanket exclusion of women with childbearing potential from certain types of drug research. That meant that any woman capable of becoming pregnant, regardless of her own desires to do or not to do so, could be excluded. Concerns were less with threats to women's health than with the possibility of liability if reproductive damage due to exposure to the experimental drug occurred (Hamilton, 1996).

To alleviate the problem, Congress in 1993 passed a law stipulating that women must be included in clinical trials in numbers sufficient to provide evidence of the different ways men and women respond to drugs, surgical treatments, and changes in diet or behavior. Nevertheless, a 2000 study found that many researchers were not complying with the law, perpetuating a lack of understanding of how men and women respond (cited in Pear, 2000). In 2003, the Agency for Healthcare Research and Quality reported that recent research on coronary heart disease (CHD) still either excludes women entirely or includes them only in limited numbers. Consequently, the therapies used to treat women with CHD—a disease that kills 250,000 women a year—are based on studies conducted primarily on middle-aged men (cited in "Research findings affirm," 2003).

Men's Health Another irony about the relationship of gender and health is that while "women's problems" have long been the focus of medical attention and intervention, men are actually less healthy. Men are more likely than women to suffer from diseases of the heart, cancer, accidents, liver disease, cerebrovascular disease, suicide, and homicide. Infant mortality rates are higher among males than females, and women can expect to live longer than men (Sabo, 2003). Of course, the health experiences of all men are not alike. For instance, African American, Native American, and Latino men are more likely than white men to be poor, work in low-paying and dangerous jobs, live in polluted environments, face the threat and reality of crime, and worry about meeting their basic needs. Hence, men's health always varies along racial and class lines.

The one area in which men's health has received medical attention comparable to the focus on women's health is not heart disease or accidents but rather the far less serious area of sexual performance. It's a good bet that in an evening of television viewing, you'll see a commercial for a drug that treats impotence or erectile dysfunction, or that "naturally enhances" penis size. Impotence can best be characterized as an embarrassment or an inconvenience but certainly not a grave, life-threatening illness. Still, a significant proportion of medical research today is devoted to developing more of these "lifestyle" drugs—those that improve the social lives of generally healthy men. Drugs to treat erectile dysfunction are a $2 billion a year industry (Elliott, 2004). About 6 million American men have taken Viagra, the most popular of such drugs, since its introduction in 1998, and about a million more have taken either of its prime competitors, Cialis and Levitra (Tuller, 2004).

As with the development of many drugs, Viagra's discovery as a treatment for erectile problems was accidental. Its generic form—sildenafil citrate—was initially designed in the late 1990s as a treatment for heart ailments. But the detection of the unanticipated side effect of creating erections led to a flurry of clinical trials and ultimately massive public demand. Originally, physicians recommended Viagra only to men who had lost sexual function as a result of injury or illness. However, it has quickly come to be viewed as an appropriate aid for otherwise healthy men who are not satisfied with their sexual performance. The official definition of erectile dysfunction is no longer the "inability to get an erection" but is now the inability to get an erection that is adequate for "satisfactory sexual performance" (Bordo, 2003; Potts, Grace, Gavey, & Vares, 2004). Some healthy men actually go so far as to equip themselves with a Viagra pill before a night on the town as a form of sexual "insurance" to guard against potential performance problems (Kirby, 2004).

In a culture where everyday life is framed as a series of competitions, it's not surprising that impotence and erectile dysfunction would be presented as one of the most horrible conditions than can befall a man. According to promotional material from Viagra's manufacturer, Pfizer, erectile dysfunction inevitably affects confidence, self-esteem, health, and happiness. Hence, a deficiency in performance is not seen merely as a "failure" isolated in one region of the body; it implicates the whole man and is inseparable from his total personality (Bordo, 2003). It represents the very loss of manhood (Loe, 2001).

Furthermore, similar to the way in which PMS has become medicalized, so too has erectile dysfunction. Before drugs like Viagra, erectile changes were seen as a normal part of the aging process. As one man put it:

> I think you've got to recognize that . . . as you get older you've got less physical ability, you can't walk as far, as vigorously . . . and the same with sex, you've got to accept it. . . . I don't treat it as negative because I think . . . I just accept it as a fact. I think your drive diminishes as well, the need to have sex as frequently. (quoted in Potts et al., 2004, p. 492)

However, the publicity surrounding erectile dysfunction may produce a societal expectation that a "healthy and normal" life for older men requires the continuation of a "youthful" focus exclusively on penetrative intercourse (Potts et al., 2004).

In a more general sense, drugs like Viagra support the view that "normal" and "healthy" sexual functioning requires penile-vaginal sex with orgasms, particularly male orgasms. Ironically, the availability of these drugs highlights the fact that much of the sexual difficulty men experience is not necessarily physiological in origin but may be grounded in anxiety and insecurity brought about by the cultural emphasis on successful performance:

> The hype surrounding [erectile dysfunction drugs] encourages rather than deconstructs the expectation that men perform like power tools with only one switch—on or off. Until this expectation is replaced by a conception of manhood that permits men and their penises a full range of human feeling, we will not yet have the kind of "cure" we really need. (Bordo, 2003, p. 152)

In short, Viagra has been as much a cultural event as a biotechnological one (Marshall, 2002). The drug has reshaped our views of gender and sexuality under the guise of technological progress (Loe, 2001) and has altered our sense of sexual normality as well as men's sense of personal efficacy. The availability of Viagra means that every man who experiences erectile problems is encouraged, even expected, to seek a pharmaceutical solution.

HOMOSEXUALITY AND HEALTH

Erectile dysfunction is presented in the media and in the culture at large as an exclusively heterosexual condition. It can affect any man, however, including homosexual men. For the most part, sexual minorities face the same health issues that heterosexuals face. But the way gay men, lesbians, and bisexuals are treated within the health care system can be quite different than the way heterosexuals are treated.

As we saw in Chapter 5, perceptions of homosexuals as sinful or sick have a long history. Since the late 19th century, some doctors have attempted to "cure" individuals of their desire for same-sex intimacy. Over the years, "curative treatments" have included castration, ovary removal, hypnosis, aversion therapy, radiation, psychoanalysis, and even lobotomy, (Romesburg, 1997). Today some psychologists and psychiatrists still prescribe so-called conversion and reparative therapies in an attempt to restore gay and lesbian patients to "healthy" heterosexuality.

Social rejection, stigmatization, and discrimination can impact the physical health of lesbians, gay men, and bisexuals by increasing their levels of self-hatred and anxiety (Meyer, 1995). Living in a hostile social—and sometimes family—environment puts these individuals at high risk of drug abuse, depression, and stress-related ailments. A disproportionate number of suicides among young people in the United States each year (some estimate as much as 30%) are attributable to the emotional turmoil over sexual orientation issues and the cultural stigma surrounding same-sex relationships (Hillier & Harrison, 2004).

The heteronormativity and the presumption of heterosexuality that underlie most health care situations also create problems for patients who are members of a sexual minority. For instance, medical examinations that involve health care personnel and patients of a different sex almost always presuppose sexual tension. Efforts to desexualize these encounters (say, for example, by having a chaperone present when a male gynecologist gives a pelvic examination) may actually reinforce stereotypical expectations (Giuffre & Williams, 2000). But heteronormative presumptions in medical interactions don't just create interpersonal awkwardness. They can actually impede access to adequate health care. Consider this scenario:

> You are a 37-year-old lesbian who hasn't been to a gynecologist in 10 years. . . . You have what you think is a garden-variety infection. . . . The first thing you are asked to do is complete the patient history form. . . . For marital status you are only given four choices: married, single, widowed, or divorced. Since you have lived with the same woman for the past 12 years, you hardly qualify as single but there is no other option allowed that fits. . . . Next question: "Are you sexually active?" "Yes." . . . Next question: "What type of birth control do you use?" . . . Answering "none" means that you will have to explain why a sexually active single woman would not use some form of birth control. . . . Or you could tell the truth. . . . The choice to "come out" in vulnerable situations is never an easy one, and when the intake form does not include your reality that decision is even more stressful. (Fields & Scout, 2001, p. 182)

Put in such situations, many people decide that the stress is too much and avoid seeing physicians altogether.

In addition, health professionals sometimes bring negative feelings to bear on their treatment of gay, lesbian, and bisexual patients (Saulnier, 2002). In the mid-1980s for instance, as the AIDS epidemic took hold and people's fears were unleashed, many doctors and nurses around the country refused to treat gay male patients. Homophobia persists in some settings and has, in fact, been institutionalized, becoming part of broad-based policies. For example, in 2004, the state of Michigan passed a law that allows health care providers to refuse to treat patients because of their sexual orientation if their objection is a matter of conscience based on ethical, moral, or religious grounds. Although incidents of outright medical discrimination may no longer be as common as they once were, developments like these, and the climate they foster, create additional burdens in the health care experiences of sexual minorities who already face difficult circumstances in their everyday lives.

CONCLUSION

In the summer of 1995, a weeklong heat wave killed over 700 people in Chicago, more than twice the number of people who died in that city's famous fire of 1871. Thousands of others were stricken by heat-related illnesses. Severe weather patterns alone could not fully account for the calamity. It was not as much a disaster of nature—like a hurricane or earthquake—as it was a disaster of inequality. The overwhelming majority of victims in Chicago were poor and elderly people who couldn't afford air-conditioning or fans and who ended up suffocating in their sealed, stifling homes (Klinenberg, 2002). Some of them lived in dangerous neighborhoods and were afraid they'd be burglarized if they left their windows and doors open at night. Furthermore, insufficient government funding left poor, isolated seniors in stigmatized minority neighborhoods and housing projects, on the periphery of formal assistance networks that could have provided them with some heat relief.

A similar but even more devastating tragedy occurred in Paris in August 2003 when over 11,000 people died during a record-breaking heat wave. Like the heat wave in Chicago, the majority of victims in Paris were elderly people—80% of those who died were over 75 (Crabbe, 2003)—who were left to cope with the heat on their own. By and large, these were not well-to-do people living out their golden years in comfort. August is holiday month in Paris. As a colleague of mine who was there at the tail end of the heat wave recounted to me, the population of Paris during August is overwhelmingly made up of poor, working-class people or immigrants. People with the economic means leave the city in droves that month to vacation in country homes, mountain villas, or beach resorts. When socio-economic disadvantage was coupled with isolation—most of the elderly victims either lived alone or were left behind by families that went on vacation—catastrophe ensued. Government officials were apparently reluctant to cut short their own vacations to deal with the crisis. They waited until the temperatures began to fall to launch an emergency response, such as opening up hospitals that had closed for the August vacation season.

These heat wave catastrophes serve as metaphors for the main theme of this chapter: Our personal health and well-being cannot be understood without taking into consideration inequalities based on race, class, gender, and sexuality. That is not to say that particular races or classes or genders or sexual groups are genetically or biologically predisposed to be more or less healthy than other groups. Nor are race, class, gender, and sexual differences simply a matter of diverse lifestyles, cultures, and tastes. Instead, broader conceptions of difference—and the imbalances that derive from those conceptions—have very real consequences for the quality, comfort, and length of people's lives.

[**INVESTIGATING IDENTITIES AND INEQUALITIES**]
Hospital stays: The unequal contours
of American health care

This chapter has highlighted imbalances in access to health care based on class, gender, race/ethnicity, and sexuality. One of the keys to a sociological understanding of such inequalities is that they are usually institutional, existing at a level above that of individuals who work in the system. In other words, differential treatment is not simply due to biased doctors, nurses, and other staff. Sometimes, the inequalities reside in the structure of health care facilities themselves.

For this exercise, locate several types of health care facilities in your area. It would be especially effective to visit some in both poor communities and more affluent communities. Try to visit a private hospital and a public/community hospital. If you have time, you can also go to a veterans' hospital, an outpatient facility, or a community free clinic.

Your task is to describe the physical characteristics of each facility in as much detail as possible. Limit your observations to the areas that are publicly accessible. It would be inappropriate to go into patients' rooms, examination rooms, intensive care units, and other "off-limits" space. Pay particular attention to the following characteristics:

- *Physical layout of the building.* Does it appear to be relatively new, or does it show signs of wear? Can you tell if there have been any recent renovations or additions to the building? How much attention is devoted to the decor of the facility? Is there any artwork (wall paintings, sculpture, and so on)? How would you describe its quality? Is there any music playing? Are the directional and department signs legible and easy to follow? Are they in languages other than English? Are the outside grounds landscaped attractively? Are the furnishings in the various waiting rooms comfortable? Are entertainment media available to people who are waiting (such as televisions, magazines, and so on)? In general, would you characterize the environment as comforting or sterile?

- *Amenities.* What sorts of nonmedical services are available to visitors? Cafeteria? Gift shop? Chapel? How would you describe the quality of these services?
- *Social identity of the patients, visitors, and staff.* Do the patients and visitors seem to be of a particular ethnic or racial group? Can you discern their socioeconomic status? Is there any ethnoracial diversity among the staff?
- *The way clients (patients and visitors) are treated.* Try to spend some time in the various public waiting areas of the facility (outpatient surgery, emergency room, and so on). Does the staff (nurses, orderlies, physicians, clerical administrators) treat clients in waiting areas with kindness and respect? Do they interact much with family members or friends of patients? Are some people treated differently than others? Does it seem that people are forced to wait for a long time before they get to see medical staff?

(*Note*: To save time, you may be able to gather some of this information on the hospital's or the clinic's web site. In addition, www.hospital-data.com is a web site that provides profiles of thousands of hospitals and medical clinics around the country.)

Once you've compiled information for a few different health care facilities, compare them to see if there are any obvious imbalances in the quality of care that patients receive and the settings within which they receive them. Provide detailed evidence from your observations to support the existence of the imbalances you identify. Use your conclusions as a starting point to discuss the current state of the American health care system. Assess whether different levels of care are available to different segments of the population.

CHAPTER 7

Inequalities in Law and Justice

The other night, my son and I watched a show on television that presented the 100 scariest movie moments of all time. The scenes—taken from the classic horror films of the 1920s to the high-tech, multimillion-dollar blockbusters of today—ranged from creepily suspenseful to graphically gruesome. Although many of the clips were truly terrifying or disgusting, we went to bed comfortable in the knowledge that everything we saw was phony. These movies were meant to entertain. The evil villains, monsters, space aliens, and demons were actors, animatronic beasts, or computer-generated images. The blood and gore were merely makeup tricks. The frightening surprises were simply the products of skillful moviemaking. Had these films been documentaries about *real* evil, we would have had trouble sleeping that night.

Even the most ingenious Hollywood effects seem amateurish, though, compared with the actual tales of human cruelty that litter the historical record. The Torture Museum in San Gimignano, Italy, houses one of the world's most extensive collections of ghastly devices invented for inflicting agony on and ultimately destroying people. Among them are the Inquisition Chairs, upholstered with flesh-piercing metal spikes that were common instruments of torture in Europe until the 1800s. Some models had a cutaway hole in the seat so the victim's bottom could be burned by hot coals. Another device, the "Wooden Horse," consists of a wooden saddle in an upside-down V-shape. The victim would be forced to straddle the saddle. Weights would then be placed on his or her feet one by one. The mounting pressure would eventually split the body in half ("Crime and too much punishment," 1997). It seems as if we're at our creative best when thinking up ways to hurt each other.

Such devices may be things of the past, but we're no less vicious nowadays than we were 500 years ago. What is particularly troubling is that the violence and aggression we inflict on one another today is rarely as random and arbitrary as it is in movies. When it comes to violence, some types of people have a greater chance of being victimized than others. Sometimes, people are mistreated or brutalized simply because of who they are or what they look like. Consider this brief sampling of events that have occurred over the past few years:

- A gay college student in Wyoming is pistol-whipped, tied to a fence, and left to die. At his funeral, protesters from a church in Topeka, Kansas, hold up signs reading "God Hates Fags!" The church's web site has a picture of the man depicted burning in hell. The same web site has a similar photo of a lesbian who was mauled to death by two dogs several years ago. Above her picture, it reads "God used literal dogs to kill a figurative dog."
- A young Nebraska woman who lived her life as a man is discovered, raped, and shot to death. In California a few years later, a 17-year-old boy who lived as a woman is beaten and strangled to death.
- A black man in Texas is chained to the back of a truck driven by two white men and dragged along country roads until his body is torn apart. In the ensuing years, his grave is desecrated twice with racial slurs carved into the headstone.
- A man in Westchester County, New York, makes more than 1,500 calls to teenage girls and women in the county, threatening to kill or injure them.

- A popular video available on the Internet, called *Bumfights*, shows homeless men pummeling each other, setting their hair on fire, pulling out their own teeth with pliers, and running headfirst into walls. The homeless men and women are offered cash, food, liquor, clothing, and motel rooms in exchange for performing any kind of vicious brawl or painful stunt the filmmakers ask.
- A Sikh man is punched and kicked into unconsciousness by several men who ridicule him for wearing a turban they refer to as "dirty curtains."
- Three white Long Island, New York, teenagers use a Fourth of July rocket to set fire to the house of a sleeping Mexican family.

According to the FBI (2003), in 2002, there were close to 6,000 racially or ethnically motivated offenses (mostly against African Americans), over 1,500 religiously motivated crimes (mostly against Jews), and about 1,500 sexually motivated crimes (mostly against gay men and lesbians). According to the Council on American-Islamic Relations, incidents of harassment, violence, and discriminatory treatment against Muslims increased 70% between 2002 and 2003 ("Anti-Muslim incidents increase," 2004). Over the past decade, 43 states plus the District of Columbia have found it necessary to amend their criminal codes to deal with bias-motivated or hate crime. In each case, the law carries either additional or heightened penalties for these crimes.

Not only do different groups face different likelihoods of being assaulted, they have vastly different experiences with the people, agencies, and institutions that supposedly exist to protect us from wrongdoing. Some people can "get away with" more when they cause harm to others. And those in positions of authority seem to respond to some people more harshly than to others when acts of violence—or any crime, for that matter—occur.

In this chapter, I will look at the complex relationship between law, justice, crime, and social inequality. Just how fair is our justice system? For instance, whose interests are represented in the ways that laws are written? Who suffers? How do race, class, gender, and sexuality affect the likelihood of criminal victimization? How are people's interactions with police, courts, and prisons influenced by personal and institutional discrimination?

THE SOCIAL CONSTRUCTION OF LAWS

It's often said that we live in a society of laws. Laws dictate the actions of companies that produce the innumerable goods and services we use in our daily lives. Laws direct the government and other social institutions.

Virtually everything we do—driving cars, paying taxes, ingesting particular substances, solving disagreements with others—occurs under some set of legal rights and restrictions. We may disagree with some laws from time to time or complain when we feel they impose too many restrictions on our activities, but it's hard to imagine living in a society without laws. Most of us come to trust that the people in our legal institutions who define and uphold these laws—lawmakers, judges, police, and so on—will always act to protect the common good. In short, laws presumably protect good people from the actions of bad people.

POWER, POLITICS, AND LEGAL DEFINITIONS

It seems obvious that certain acts are defined as crimes because they threaten or offend a majority of people in society. But according to some conflict sociologists (for example, Quinney, 1970), the law is actually a political instrument used by specific groups to further their own interests, often at the expense of others. The law, they argue, is created by economic elites who control the production and distribution of major resources in society. For instance, tobacco kills an estimated 400,000 people annually; one out of every five American deaths is smoking-related (Centers for Disease Control, 2003b). More people die from tobacco use than from the use of all illegal drugs combined. Aside from toxic poisons, it is probably the single most lethal substance we can ingest. Yet it remains legal, with only age restrictions on its purchase and usage. The tobacco industry is powerful, both economically and politically. It has one of the most influential lobbies in Washington. The economies of several states depend on tobacco. With such powerful friends, it's highly unlikely that the use of tobacco would ever be criminalized.

Laws, of course, are determined by the actions of elected legislators—who often bear little resemblance to the constituents they serve. Politicians may represent themselves as "just regular folks" or claim to be able to "feel our pain," but in truth lawmakers tend to come from lives of privilege. Close to half of the first-term members of Congress elected in 2002 had a net worth of over $1 million (Salant, 2002). In contrast, the median net worth of all U.S. households is about $86,000 (U.S. Bureau of the Census, 2004). The four primary presidential and vice-presidential candidates for the 2004 election were all white, male, and multimillionaires. Three of them went to Yale (Bush, Kerry, Cheney) and two (Kerry, Bush) are descendents of old, aristocratic New England families. Only one (Edwards) made rather than inherited his fortune (Toner, 2004).

Today, running for public office, especially at the national level, takes millions of dollars. Even if they don't have that kind of money themselves, successful candidates are often bankrolled by wealthy donors and patrons who pump money into campaigns because they see a particular candidate as the one most likely to support their economic interests (Knott, 2004). Legislators, of course, can also be greatly influenced by powerful segments of society through lobbying groups, political action committees, individual campaign contributions, and so on. As a consequence, the higher a group's political and economic position in society, the greater the likelihood that its values and interests will be reflected in and protected by the law.

Through the mass media, dominant groups also influence the public to look at crime in ways that are favorable to them. When politicians talk about fighting crime, or when news shows report fluctuations in crime rates, they are usually referring to street crimes (illegal drug use, robbery, burglary, murder, assault, and so on) rather than corporate crimes, governmental crimes, or crimes more likely to be committed by people in influential positions. This bias creates a way of perceiving crime that becomes social reality. We easily accept the "fact" that the people and crimes highlighted in the media are the most serious threat to our personal well-being and the well-being of the entire society.

Once we come to believe that our own interests are in danger, we become willing to tolerate the violation of others' civil rights in the interests of controlling crime. In the months following the attacks of September 11, 2001, the federal government eased restrictions on the surveillance, apprehension, interrogation, and detention of suspected terrorists. To many people, this is the price we must pay in order to control "the crime problem" or to ensure public safety.

It's not surprising, then, that the actions seen to be characteristic of relatively powerless segments of society are more likely to be criminalized and are punished more severely than the actions of the most powerful segments. Consider, for instance, the legal punishments for the possession of crack cocaine versus powdered cocaine. The average length of a prison sentence for selling less than 25 grams of crack cocaine is 65 months; for powdered cocaine, it is 14 months (Coyle, 2003). Some law enforcement officials argue that crack cocaine is more closely associated with violence than powdered cocaine is, it is more dangerous to the user, and it is more likely to cause birth defects in babies whose mothers use it while pregnant. However, studies of the two forms of cocaine indicate that their effects are in fact quite similar. In addition, the effects of maternal crack use on fetuses are no different from those of tobacco or alcohol use (cited in Coyle, 2003). Some sociologists have concluded that crack laws have as much to do with race, poverty, unemployment, and homelessness as with the properties of the drugs themselves (Duster, 1997). The common perception is that the typical user of powdered cocaine is a white suburbanite and that the typical crack user is young, urban, and a member of an ethnoracial minority. Official crime statistics support this perception, although the discrepancy has grown smaller in the past decade. In 2000, 93% of those convicted of crack possession were black and Latino/a; only 6% were white. By contrast, 30.3% of those convicted of powdered cocaine possession were black, 18% were white, and 51% were Latino/a (though most of these individuals are white) (Coyle, 2003).

THE LAWS OF INTIMACY

Criminal law is not the only reflection of the influence of social inequality in the legal system. Laws that control our private, intimate choices also serve the interests of some at the expense of others. Take, for instance, the formation of romantic relationships. No one tells us with whom to fall in love. We don't live in a society in which our relationships are arranged for us by our families. But our intimate experiences are always subject to societal, and sometimes state, control. Marriages, for example, are legal contracts. Each state determines the lawful age at which people can marry as well as health requirements, inheritance rules, property division in case of divorce, and so on. Laws also prohibit being married to more than one person at a time and marrying certain blood relatives.

In some societies, the violation of legal restrictions on intimacy can be lethal. In several rural areas of India, for example, it is considered incest if two people from the same village fall in love. In 2003, two young lovers from a small town in the state of Uttar Pradesh were beaten to death by members of their own families for breaching this taboo (Waldman, 2003).

But even in this country, where we assume that the formation of relationships is based solely on the desires and attractions of the people involved, the law has historically restricted certain types of intimate contact. Sometimes, as in the case of race, legal prohibitions applied to intimacy that crossed an identity boundary; other times, as with same-sex marriage, the prohibitions apply to intimacy that *doesn't* cross such a boundary.

Miscegenation   Fear and condemnation of interracial relationships have been a part of American culture, politics, and law since the first European settlers arrived here close to 400 years ago. The first law against miscegenation—sexual contact and marriage between people of different races—was enacted in Maryland in 1661, prohibiting Whites from marrying Native Americans or African slaves. According to this law, a white woman who married a black slave became a slave herself (Bardaglio, 1999). Over the next 300 years or so, 38 more states put miscegenation laws on the books, expanding their coverage to include Chinese, Japanese, Koreans, Indians, and Filipino Americans. These laws were enacted to prevent a mixing of the races (referred to as "mongrelization") that would destroy the racial purity (and assumed superiority) of Whites (Lemire, 2002).

Because of the "one-drop rule" for determining who was black that was in effect at the time (a single drop of "Negro blood" in one's ancestry made a person a "Negro"), white men were largely exempt from anti-miscegenation laws. This conception of race meant that a white woman could give birth to a black child, but a black woman could never give birth to a white child. So white men could "roam sexually among women of any color without threatening the color line" (Bardaglio, 1999, p. 115).

For black women, interracial sexual contact was more likely to be a punishment in itself rather than the reason for punishment. Sexual access of white men to black women was the cornerstone of male power from the beginning of the country, much of it through rape and other forms of coercive sexuality (Hall, 1995). Any assertion of a woman's will could be met with sexual violence. In early America, enslaved women were especially vulnerable since their rape could lead to pregnancy and thus could increase a slave owner's "holdings." White men had a powerful economic incentive to engage in interracial sex. The incentive became even stronger in the early 19th century when the importation but not the reproduction of slaves was outlawed in the United States. In addition, lighter-skinned, mixed-race slaves typically fetched a higher price at market. The ability to afford light-skinned slaves symbolized the owner's social status (Nagel, 2003).

The fact that white men could force themselves on black women with virtual impunity didn't end with slavery. In 2004, an elderly black woman named Essie Mae Washington revealed that she was the late Senator Strom Thurmond's daughter. Thurmond was a powerful white senator from South Carolina who advocated racial segregation in the mid-20th century. Not only did Thurmond contradict his virulent segregationist leanings back in 1925 when he impregnated his family's teenage black maid, he also violated the law against statutory rape and miscegenation. Yet he received no punishment (Crenshaw, 2004b).

Black men have not experienced the same level of tolerance regarding interracial sexual relations. Whites worried that the same strength and virility they exploited in black male slaves for economic gain could be wielded as a weapon of vengeance through the sexual assault of white women. After slavery was abolished, fears of black male sexuality—combined with the fear that freed Blacks would penetrate the economic and cultural worlds of Whites—served to justify Jim Crow laws. In 1896, the U.S. Supreme Court ruled that racial segregation was constitutional, and it continued to be legal until the middle of the 20th century.

Fears of black male sexuality spawned much violence against black men, especially in the South. Well into the 20th century, lynching and the threat of lynching were effective tools of vigilante justice, typically justified in terms of the "protection of white womanhood." The Ku Klux Klan's original charter was to "protect women's chastity" after the emancipation of slaves (Baldauf, 2000). Unlike official justice agencies, like the police, a lynch mob could operate with no limits and sometimes without an actual crime. In fact, less than a quarter of lynch victims were actually accused of rape or attempted rape (Hall, 1995). Lynching was, most of all, a tool of psychological intimidation, "an instrument of coercion intended to impress not only the immediate victim but all who saw or heard about the event" (Hall, 1995, p. 436).

Violent disapproval of interracial sexual contact continued well into the 20th century. It reached a highly publicized turning point in the summer of 1955. That year, a 14-year-old African American boy from Chicago named Emmett Till traveled by train to visit his relatives in Mississippi. He boasted to his cousins there that, in Chicago, he had many friendships with white girls. On a dare from one of his cousins, Emmett went into a candy store and talked to the white woman who worked there, Carolyn Bryant. Ms. Bryant interpreted the conversation as a flirtation. Not long after that, two white men—one of them Carolyn's husband, Roy—showed up at Emmett's uncle's house, took Emmett, and drove off. A few days later, Emmett's body was found floating in the Tallahatchie River, with a bullet hole in his head, a 75-pound fan tied around his neck, and a horribly battered face. Mr. Bryant and another man were arrested and charged with his murder. At the trial, the defendants testified that they didn't mean to kill Emmett but wanted to teach him a lesson. It took the all-white jury 75 minutes to find the defendants not guilty.

A legal response to anti-miscegenation sentiment came over a decade later. It began in 1958 when a Virginia couple, Richard and Mildred Loving, were awakened in the middle of the night by the local sheriff and two assistants and immediately arrested for violating Virginia's law prohibiting interracial marriage. Richard was white and Mildred was "colored." The Lovings were sentenced to one year in jail but then learned that the judge would suspend the sentence if they left the state and promised not to return for 25 years. In the 1950s, the majority of states, including California, Oregon, Indiana, all the mountain states, and every state in the South, legally prohibited interracial marriage (Liptak, 2004a). But the Lovings found a home in Washington, D.C., and had three children. While there, they embarked on an appeal of their conviction. In 1967, the Supreme Court ruled in favor of the Lovings, concluding that using racial classifications to restrict freedom to marry was unconstitutional.

Since the Loving case, public opinion about interracial marriage has shifted. The year after the decision, Americans still disapproved of interracial marriage by a margin of three to one. Over thirty years later, two-thirds of Americans approved of it (Rosenbaum, 2003). It's important to note, though, that such sentiment varies along ethnoracial lines. A nationwide survey conducted by the Henry J. Kaiser Family Foundation found that 77% of Blacks, 68% of Latino/as, 67% of Asians, but only 53% of Whites said it makes no difference whether a person marries someone of the same race or of a different race (Fears & Deane, 2001).

In light of such changes in attitudes, it is not surprising that behaviors have changed as well. The number of interracial marriages has grown exponentially, from 300,000 in 1970 to 3.1 million today (Lee & Edmonston, 2005). These numbers don't include the 1.9 million marriages between Latino/as and non-Latino/as. Today, about 6% of American marriages involve people of different races.

Yet this change is not equally distributed across all racial combinations. About 30% of married native-born Asians and Latino/as have a spouse of a different race, mostly white, and the rates are even higher among people in their 20s and 30s. In contrast, only 10% of young Blacks marry someone of a different race (Lee & Bean, 2004). Indeed, many Americans in black-white relationships still experience disapproval. About half of the black-white couples in the Kaiser study felt that biracial marriage makes things harder for them, and about two-thirds reported that their parents had a problem with the relationship, at least initially (Fears & Deane, 2001). And the legal system can also be less than accommodating. Even today, rural judges can sometimes make it difficult for interracial couples to marry (Staples, 1999).

Same-Sex Marriage The issue of legal restrictions on intimacy has become especially volatile recently with the controversy over legalization of same-sex marriage. In some countries, gays and lesbians can have their relationships legally ratified. Belgium, Spain, and the Netherlands allow gay couples to legally marry. Likewise, gay Canadian couples are currently allowed to marry in the provinces of Ontario, British Columbia, Quebec, and Manitoba. France, Denmark, Spain, Portugal, and Germany allow same-sex couples to enter "civil unions" or "registered partnerships," which grant them some of the benefits and responsibilities of heterosexual marriage (Lyall, 2004).

In the United States, however, the issue is anything but settled. As a result of a 2004 State Supreme Court ruling, Massachusetts became the only state to allow gay marriage, though that decision was immediately challenged. That same year, a Superior Court judge in Washington State ruled that laws barring same-sex marriages violate the constitutional rights of gay couples. Vermont had legalized civil unions (but not marriage) for gay couples a few years earlier. But most states—42 at last count—have moved in the opposite direction, making their refusal to recognize such marriages explicit by enacting "Defense of Marriage" acts that officially define marriage as a union of a man and a woman.

The federal "Defense of Marriage Act" of 1996 is another barrier to nationalizing the Massachusetts ruling. Nevertheless, in 2004, a spirited debate began over an amendment to the U.S. Constitution that would definitively ban gay marriage. In that year, the U.S. House of Representatives also proposed the "Marriage Protection Act." Essentially, this law would prevent federal courts from hearing complaints from gay couples who might argue that their are being deprived of their constitutional rights if states don't recognize same-sex marriages that were allowed elsewhere. According to civil rights organizations, this bill would set a dangerous precedent. Congress would be able to override federal courts' responsibility for guarding constitutional freedoms of all kinds, for all sorts of minority groups ("A radical assault," 2004).

State and federal legislation usually reflects public opinion, and public opinion on legalizing same-sex marriage is indeed mixed at this point. While acceptance of gays and lesbians in the military, in the workplace, as elementary school teachers, and as politicians has grown over the past several decades, support for laws allowing gay marriage is tepid at best. A nationwide survey found that the majority of Americans (about 61%) were opposed to a law that would allow homosexuals to marry (Grossman, 2003). During the 2004 election, voters in 11 states approved amendments to their state constitutions banning same-sex marriage. The average margin of victory in those votes was over 40%. Even people who consider themselves supportive of gay rights in general are ambivalent about legalizing gay marriage (Seelye & Elder, 2003).

Although the vast majority of gays and lesbians fervently desire the right to legally marry, not all do. Those most interested in legal marriage want children or face pressing concerns about health and mortality (Belluck, 2003). Younger couples are inclined to see legal obstacles to marriage as a clear sign of their second-class status. However, some older couples who came of age in the 1960s and 1970s see marriage as a heterosexual institution that symbolizes an oppressive system they don't want to be a part of. Something is lost, they feel, in the struggle to "assimilate" and be just like heterosexual married couples. Some long-term couples even consider the offer of marriage a bit insulting, considering how long their relationship has already lasted without "official" recognition.

In addition, there is some concern that if the movement to legalize same-sex marriage is effective, it will reinforce the idea that the only legitimate intimate relationship is marriage and therefore may actually limit the diversity of "acceptable" relationships rather than expand it. In 2003, a court in Ontario, Canada, turned down a request by a lesbian couple to simultaneously recognize them (the biological mother and her partner), as well as the biological father, as the legal parents of a young boy. If it's true, as some people claim, that two parents are better than one, then having three legal parents would seem to be even better. However, such an arrangement violates the traditional assumption that the monogamous pairing of two adults is the essential component of any stable, and culturally valuable, relationship.

Another fear is that if legal marriage is available, all gay couples will be expected to want it. Those who don't could find themselves marginalized and stigmatized. Some legislators in the state of Massachusetts wanted to get rid of domestic partnership benefits for same-sex cohabiting couples should marriage become a permanent legal option for them. The logic is that if marriage is available, domestic partnerships will become irrelevant. Marriage would be formally privileged above any other type of relationship, and discrimination based on sexual orientation would be supplanted by discrimination based on marital status.

The merits of these debates notwithstanding, legalizing same-sex marriage has practical significance. Marriage conveys protected legal status. Legally married couples are eligible for over a thousand benefits, such as inheritance rights, pension and Social Security benefits, insurance coverage on a spouse's policy, eligibility to live in certain apartment complexes, savings from joint tax returns, the ability to make medical decisions for a partner in an emergency, and visitation rights in prisons and hospital intensive care units. People in other types of relationships are not legally entitled to such benefits. For instance, homosexual partners of victims of the September 11th attack on the Pentagon were not eligible for the same survivor benefits offered to heterosexual spouses in the state of Virginia that heterosexual spouses were entitled to (Farmer, 2002).

Furthermore, state and federal amendments that seek to prevent same-sex marriage could disproportionately affect gay couples of color, who already face racial and anti-gay bias. According to the 2000 U.S. Census, there are approximately 85,000 black same-sex couples in the United States. Their households are about twice as likely as white same-sex households to include children. But they also report lower median household incomes and lower home ownership than both black heterosexual couples and white same-sex couples. Hence, their inability to gain access to the legal and financial benefits of marriage creates additional disadvantage by hurting their ability to provide for children, buy houses, and prepare for retirement (Dang & Frazer, 2004).

If Canada is an indication of what occurs when same-sex marriage is legalized, the issue may actually be more symbolic than practical, however. After legalization, Canadian gays and lesbians did not run in droves to the courthouses to marry. There's no official tally of how many gay couples have wed there, but gay rights groups put the number at only about 3,000 nationally in the first year. Of those, they estimate 1,000 were Americans who returned to the United States after getting married (Mulkern, 2004). Even in Vermont, fewer couples than expected have taken advantage of the state law allowing them to register their "civil unions" (Belluck, 2003).

RACE, CLASS, AND JUSTICE

"There can be no equal justice where the kind of trial a [person] gets depends on the amount of money he [or she] has." (Justice Hugo Black quoted in Cole, 1999, p. 3)

The relationship between social inequalities and the law is nowhere more apparent than in the way people are processed through the massive criminal justice system once they allegedly break the law. And perhaps no other criminal case in history brought the matter of legal inequalities to the forefront of American consciousness as much as the O. J. Simpson trial in 1995. As you may recall, Simpson—an African American, former star football player, and international celebrity—was tried for and acquitted of the murder of his white wife, Nicole, and her white companion, Ron Goldman. Before, during, and after the trial, about three-quarters of African Americans maintained that Simpson was not guilty; at the same time, about three-quarters of white Americans thought he was guilty (Cole, 1999).

Many Blacks considered Simpson's acquittal a reversal of centuries of injustice in which the mere accusation that a black man had murdered two Whites would have been sufficient to see him lynched. They pointed to the suspicious actions of police officers who handled the evidence in this case and the racist remarks of one of the prosecution's key witnesses. To them, the verdict showed that perhaps the system wasn't always set up to disadvantage people of color. They felt they had every reason to cheer (Cole, 1999).

To many Whites, though, the case was a bewildering travesty of justice. The evidence against Simpson, they believed, was overwhelming. His blood was found at the scene of the murder; the victims' blood was in his car and on his clothes; one of Simpson's gloves had hair from the two victims, fibers from their clothes, and their blood on it. To many Whites, it seemed like the predominantly black jury in the case had blatantly ignored the evidence and voted for one of their own.

The Simpson case is important, however, precisely because of what these polarized reactions overlooked: It wasn't just about race. Simpson wasn't like any other black murder defendant. He had a predominantly black jury, substantial financial resources, and celebrity status. Most black defendants can't afford private attorneys let alone a high-powered, high-profile "dream team" of lawyers. Ironically, the features of the case that worked to Simpson's advantage, and that led to such outrage among Whites, are the same features that have historically benefited Whites in court—the ability to buy a good defense, a face not stereotypically associated with crime, a jury composed of members of one's own race. It's safe to say that had Simpson been unknown and destitute—as many defendants of color are—the case would have turned out quite differently.

No matter what your opinion of the verdict in this famous case, one thing that it illustrates is clear: Justice is not now, nor has it ever been, blind. In theory, under the Constitution, every American is entitled to the same legal protections. In practice, however—from the way laws are written to the way people are treated by police, processed through the courts, and punished—equal protection and equal treatment are an illusion.

RACIAL PROFILING

A quick glance at statistical information on the relationship between race and crime reveals that the system is dramatically imbalanced. For instance, African Americans make up about 13% of the population, but they account for 38% of all arrests for violent crime, 31% of property crimes, and 35% of drug violations. Convictions are even more skewed: African Americans account for 44% of convictions for violent crimes, 39% of property crimes, and 53% of drug crimes (U.S. Bureau of Justice Statistics, 2002).

These sorts of official statistics paint a grim picture of the relationship between crime and race, but they may mislead us into thinking that Blacks are simply more criminally inclined than members of other ethnoracial groups. In the 2000 National Crime Victimization Survey, 24% of crime victims reported that their assailants were black. That same year, however, close to 40% of individuals arrested for these crimes were black, indicating that police are especially likely to use race as one of the factors in making an arrest (Reiman, 2004).

Oversimplified images of criminals always fall short of applying to all individuals. The vast majority of African Americans do not commit crimes, just as the vast majority of Muslims are not terrorists, and the vast majority of Italians are not involved in organized crime. Nevertheless, the degree to which such images are assumed to characterize an entire group is important because it can influence the reactions of individuals and the criminal justice system itself. For instance, after the attacks of September 11, 2001, federal, state, and local governments faced the difficult dilemma of trying to balance security concerns with individual freedom. The use of race—in particular, "looking Middle Eastern"— as a factor in stopping "suspected terrorists" became a widely accepted law enforcement practice. Not only has the profiling of Arabs and Muslims been tolerated to a large degree, but some citizens and even some legislators have actually demanded it on the grounds that these individuals are statistically more likely to be terrorists (Beinart, 2003). However, virtually none of the thousands of people who have been detained and questioned on this basis have been publicly charged with terrorism (American Civil Liberties Union, 2004).

Less extreme but more common has been the use of racial profiling in traffic and drug enforcement. In Texas, for example, police are more than twice as likely to search black and Latino/a motorists as Whites during traffic stops (cited in Yardley, 2000). One nationwide study found that after controlling for other relevant factors, such as type of vehicle, vehicle defect, severity of the driving offense, and so on, the odds of citation, search, arrest, and use of force are significantly higher for African American and Latino/a drivers than for white drivers. The odds are even higher for young men in these ethnoracial groups (Engel & Calnon, 2004). Tape recordings of individual encounters reinforce these statistics:

> In one, a bewildered black man explained to the state troopers that this was the seventh time he'd been stopped; in another, a black man shakes his head because it's the second time in minutes that he's been stopped. In one of the relatively rare stops of a white driver, [the trooper] asks the motorist how he is doing. When the man answers, "Not very good," [the trooper] replies, "Could be worse—could be black." (Cole, 1999, p. 37)

Such bias extends to air travel as well: In a study of an airport in Memphis, about 75% of the air travelers stopped by Drug Enforcement Administration agents were black, yet only 4% of the flying public is black (cited in Duke, 1994).

Police often argue that, like it or not, race in some cases constitutes "reasonable suspicion," something the U.S. Supreme Court has ruled is justifiable grounds for investigatory stops. Police further defend their use of race in deciding which drivers or pedestrians to stop by pointing to the statistics showing that African Americans and Latino/as are more likely than Whites to be arrested and convicted of the most common street crimes. According to the police chief of Los Angeles, who happens to be African American, "In my mind it is not a great revelation that if officers are looking for criminal activity, they're going to look at the kind of people who are listed on crime reports" (quoted in J. Goldberg, 1999, pp. 53–54). This line of thinking is pervasive among civilians as well. Reverend Jesse Jackson once said, "There is nothing more painful to me at this stage in my life than to walk down the street and hear footsteps and start thinking about robbery—then look around and see somebody white and feel relieved" (quoted in Cole, 1999, p. 41).

Is racial profiling as a crime control tactic effective? When law enforcement agents stop and interrogate people of color, are those individuals more likely than Whites to be carrying illegal drugs, weapons, or other forms of contraband? A study of over 1 million cases found that close to 17% of white drivers who were searched were actually carrying drugs or weapons, compared to 9% of Latino/a drivers, 7% of black drivers, and 0% of drivers of other races/ethnicities (Engel & Calnon, 2004).

In light of these sorts of statistics, local, state, and federal law enforcement agencies around the country have come under attack in recent years for their racial profiling policies. Increasingly, targets of the practice are filing and winning discrimination suits. In 1998, a civil rights group and 11 black motorists filed a lawsuit charging that the Maryland State Police used a "race-based profile" in stopping drivers along a stretch of interstate highway and searching their cars and belongings for drugs and weapons (Janofsky, 1998). The state of Maryland agreed to stop the practice, although recent evidence shows that a disproportionate number of motorists stopped on state highways in Maryland—more than two-thirds—continue to be people of color (Jost, 2000). In a 1999 settlement, New Jersey officials acknowledged in court that state troopers had unfairly singled out black and Latino/a motorists in traffic stops. Several former troopers testified that they would park alongside the turnpike and shine their headlights into passing cars, looking for black drivers to pull over (Hosenball, 1999).

In 2003, President Bush ordered a ban on racial profiling among federal law enforcement agencies—although the ban does not apply to cases that are deemed to have national security implications (Lichtblau, 2003). To date, a least 6 states (including New Jersey) have passed laws banning racial profiling and 15 others are considering doing so. At the time of this writing, the U.S. Congress is debating a bill called the "End Racial Profiling Act," which would track and provide steps to eliminate profiling based on race, ethnicity, religion, or national origin (American Civil Liberties Union, 2004).

CLASS AND CRIME

Many people in the United States take for granted that poor, minority street criminals are a dangerous and costly threat (Reiman, 2004). But ordinary lower-class street crime is actually less of a constant and imminent physical danger than unsafe work conditions; dangerous chemicals in the air, water, and food; faulty consumer products; unnecessary surgery; and shoddy emergency medical services. Approximately 16,000 Americans were murdered in 2002 (U.S. Bureau of the Census, 2004). Yet, on average, 56,000 Americans die each year on the job or from occupational diseases such as black lung disease and asbestosis. Tens of thousands more die from pollution, contaminated foods, hazardous consumer products, and hospital malpractice (Mokhiber, 1999). Corporate crime also poses greater economic threats to Americans than street crime does. The FBI estimates that burglary and robbery cost the United States $3.8 billion a year. In contrast, the cost of "white-collar" crimes like corporate fraud, bribery, embezzlement, insurance fraud, securities fraud, and so on amounts to over $400 billion a year (Reiman, 2004).

If you've been paying attention to the news over the past few years, you might think that corporate crime is being energetically prosecuted. The early 2000s brought a virtual parade of corporate executives facing federal charges. Maybe you remember seeing them on televised "perp walks," wearing handcuffs and designer suits. Chief executives at some of the biggest American companies, including Adelphia Communications, Enron Corporation, AOL-Time Warner, ImClone Systems, Tyco International, and WorldCom, Inc., were accused of engaging in a host of illegal activities, such as bank fraud, wire fraud, stock fraud, money laundering, and deceptive accounting schemes. Even the venerable Martha Stewart was convicted on charges of securities fraud, perjury, and obstruction of justice. The activities of these individuals led to the misappropriation of tens of billions of dollars. In the case of Enron, tens of thousands of employees lost their pensions. In addition, investor confidence plummeted along with stock prices, contributing more problems to an already weak economy.

At first, politicians were quick to jump on the anti–corporate crime bandwagon, passing legislation that increased penalties for some of these crimes. In 2002, President Bush appointed a Corporate Fraud Task Force that he said would operate like a "financial crimes SWAT team" (quoted in Johnston, 2002, p. 6). But the group had no direct authority to investigate or prosecute cases and no money or additional staffing for the effort. In general, although many executives faced serious criminal charges and some lost their jobs or had their assets frozen, to date only a few have been given lengthy prison sentences. Martha Stewart served a five-month sentence at a minimum-security, campus-like facility in the mountains of West Virginia and left prison more popular and in better financial shape than when she went in (Glater, 2005).

Corporate executives and white-collar criminals have always served much lighter punishments than perpetrators of other types of crimes. According to one study, the average person convicted in the savings-and-loan scandal of the early 1990s received 36.4 months in prison for stealing $100,000 or more. During the same period, someone committing burglary valued at $300 or less received an average sentence of 55.6 months. In the

1980s, well-known white-collar criminals Michael Milken and Ivan Boesky each served around two years in prison for their role in insider trading scandals that involved millions of dollars (cited in Valenti, 2002). Now imagine that you are a poor, young man who held up a bank and stole millions of dollars. It's unthinkable that you would receive such a mild sentence.

Why aren't these costly corporate acts considered as deviant or dangerous as face-to-face street crime? According to conflict sociologist Jeffrey Reiman (2004), the answer resides in the circumstances surrounding these acts. People typically perceive the injuries caused by corporate crime as unintentional, indirect, and a consequence of an endeavor defined in this culture as legitimate or socially productive: making a profit. In most people's minds, someone who tries to harm someone else is usually considered more evil than someone who harms without intending to. Moreover, being harmed by a street criminal is a more terrifying experience than being harmed indirectly by a white-collar criminal. Finally, harm that results from illegitimate activities is usually considered more serious than harm that is a by-product of standard business activities.

PRISONS

In this day and age, politicians at the local, state, and national levels can get elected only if they're perceived to be "tough" on crime. In some polls, over three-quarters of Americans felt that the justice system was not harsh enough in dealing with criminals (Gaubatz, 1995). Governments at the state and federal levels responded to these perceptions by implementing tougher policies—cracking down on drug users and dealers, scaling back parole eligibility, lengthening prison sentences, building more prisons, and most recently rescinding legal protections for people suspected of being linked to terrorism. By 1999, 15 states had abolished parole boards and early release programs, resulting in more prisoners serving their full sentences (Butterfield, 1999). Many states now have "three-strikes" laws that impose lengthy mandatory prison sentences for three-time offenders.

Not surprisingly, the inmate population has swelled. In 1970, there were fewer than 200,000 people in state and federal prisons; by 2002, that figure had grown to over 1.4 million, not including over 690,000 individuals held in local jails (Harrison & Karberg, 2004). At any given point in time, about 3.2% of the adult American population—or 1 in every 32 adults—is either on probation, on parole, in jail, or in prison (Glaze &

Palla, 2004). In 2003, the U.S. incarceration rate was 715 prisoners per 100,000 people (Harrison & Karberg, 2004). No other industrialized country comes close to this figure. For instance, the rate in Canada is 105 per 100,000; in Germany, it's 95 (cited in Uggen & Manza, 2002). State prisons in the United States are operating 17% above capacity, and federal prisons are operating 33% above capacity.

These statistics are distressing enough. What is even more disturbing is that the population of prisoners does not accurately reflect the general population (see Exhibit 7.1). For one thing, prisoners are overwhelmingly male. Although the female inmate population rose faster than the male population between 2002 and 2003, men still account for about 92% of all prisoners and are 15 times more likely than women to be incarcerated (Harrison & Karberg, 2004).

Ethnoracial identities of prisoners are also out of balance. Latinos and African Americans make up about 53% of the male population in state and federal prisons and local jails even though they comprise only about 27% of the general male population (U.S. Bureau of the Census, 2004). The Bureau of Justice Statistics estimates that 12% of black males, close

Exhibit 7.1: Race, Gender, and the American Inmate Population (State Prison, Federal Prison, or Local Jail), 2003

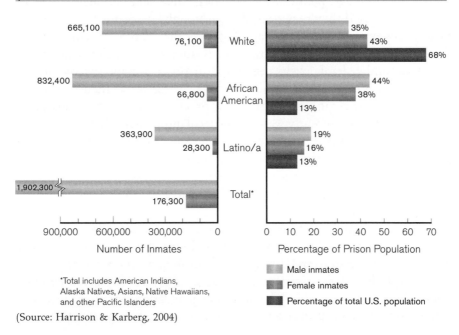

*Total includes American Indians, Alaska Natives, Asians, Native Hawaiians, and other Pacific Islanders

(Source: Harrison & Karberg, 2004)

to 4% of Latino males, but only 1.6% of white males in their 20s are currently in prison or jail (Harrison & Karberg, 2004). Race and ethnicity also affect the amount of time a convict spends behind bars. The average federal prison sentence for Blacks is about six years, compared to four years for Whites (United States Sentencing Commission, 2004).

Youthful offenders experience similar imbalances. A 2000 U.S. Department of Justice report found that at every step of the juvenile justice system, black and Latino/a youths are treated more severely than Whites charged with similar crimes. They are more likely to be arrested, held in jail, sent to juvenile or adult court for trial, convicted, and given longer prison sentences (cited in Butterfield, 2000). Some researchers argue that prison time has become a normal part of early adulthood for black men in poor neighborhoods. One recent study found that more young African American men today have spent time in prison than have served in the military or earned a college degree.

Furthermore, their risks of imprisonment rise steeply as level of education drops. For instance, close to 60% of black high school dropouts born between 1965 and 1969 had served time in state or federal prisons by their early 30s (Pettit & Western, 2004). Sadly, the inequalities that give rise to disproportionate incarceration in the first place may actually be deepened as a result of imprisonment. Early incarceration is associated with low wages, unemployment, family instability, further criminal activity and incarceration, and restrictions of political and social rights (Pettit & Western, 2004).

The highly publicized "War on Drugs" that began in the 1980s worsened racial disparities in incarceration. In 1970, 16% of federal prison inmates were there for drug offenses (U.S. Bureau of Justice Statistics, 2002). Today, that figure is 54% (Federal Bureau of Prisons, 2004). Curiously, while the rates of drug arrests and imprisonments were increasing, the number of people actually using drugs was decreasing. It seems that heightened media and political attention and increased budgets for law enforcement led to more police resources being used to target drug offenders. Many law enforcement agencies began targeting low-income, minority neighborhoods (Mauer, 1999). The number of African Americans arrested for drug offenses nearly tripled between 1980 and 1992. And for those youths charged with drug offenses, Blacks were 48 times more likely than Whites to be sentenced to prison (Butterfield, 2000).

The prison population is also skewed with regard to class. Jails and prisons have become the nation's poorhouses. In 2002, 69% of people in Atlanta who had been arrested on petty charges—shoplifting, trespassing, public drunkenness—and who were too poor to afford bail remained in jail for weeks and, in some cases, months, awaiting a lawyer and a court date, despite a law that requires anyone arrested for a misdemeanor to go before a judge or lawyer within 48 hours. All of them had spent more time behind bars than they would have had they been convicted of a crime (Rimer, 2002).

In and of itself, the statistical fact that the poor and ethnoracial minorities are overrepresented among those who spend time in prison for committing crimes needn't be evidence of discrimination or injustice. After all, if people from these groups commit more imprisonable crimes, then the fact that more of them ultimately wind up behind bars is simply an accurate reflection of reality (Tonry, 1995). Indeed, one of the most consistent findings in criminal research is the correlation between unemployment (a factor closely associated with economic disadvantage) and violent crime, property crime, and illegal drug use (Hagan, 2000). Furthermore, economic and educational disparities may also relate to differences in crime patterns and the way people are processed through the system. Certainly, those with little or no income and little schooling experience frustration at blocked opportunities and therefore may be pushed into criminal activities (Merton, 1957).

Nevertheless, other evidence shows that poor individuals from ethnoracial minorities are policed, prosecuted, and sentenced more punitively than wealthier Whites because law enforcement officials perceive them to be more threatening and dangerous (Reiman, 2004; Tittle, 1994). Even when they commit the same crime, poor Blacks and Latino/as are more likely than other offenders to be arrested, charged, and convicted and are typically sentenced to longer prison terms (Reiman, 2004).

The overrepresentation of the poor and ethnoracial minorities in prisons is not just a personal tragedy for individuals and families; it has implications at the societal level as well. For instance, many countries ban people in prison from voting, a consequence known as **disenfranchisement.** But the United States is the only country that permanently disenfranchises some felons who have served their sentences (Uggen & Manza, 2002): 33 states disenfranchise parolees, 29 disenfranchise offenders on probation, and 7 disenfranchise all felons and ex-felons, even after their sentences are complete (Goodnough, 2004). Only Maine and Vermont allow current and former prisoners to vote.

Widespread disenfranchisement may well have implications for national politics and policy. Sociologists Christopher Uggen and Jeff Manza (2002) reason that, because felons and ex-felons are disproportionately poor and members of ethnoracial minorities, most of them would have likely identified themselves as Democrats and voted for Democratic candidates. Had these individuals been allowed to vote, they would have likely reversed the outcomes of several close U.S. Senate elections over the past few decades and even the 2000 presidential election. That year, 4.7 million citizens—2.8% of the voting-age population—were disenfranchised because of felony convictions. In Florida, a state George Bush won by only 537 votes, tens of thousands of felons and ex-felons were removed from voter rolls. Uggen and Manza conclude that Bush's victory in this extremely close election clearly would have been reversed had felons and ex-felons been allowed to vote.

RACE, CLASS, AND DEATH

The most extreme state-supported punishment for crime is the death penalty. While debate over the deterrent effects of capital punishment continues to rage, another issue has garnered attention: bias in administering the death penalty. According to Amnesty International (2003), since the death penalty was reinstated in 1977, the evidence indicates clearly that Whites and people of color—especially African Americans—have been treated differently. Since that time, 40% of defendants who have been executed have been Latino/a or African American, and over 50% of the current death row population is Latino/a or African American. A 1998 study of capital cases in Philadelphia revealed that the odds of receiving a death sentence were four times higher for African Americans than for defendants of other races (cited in Dieter, 1998).

The race of the victim may actually have as much to do with the decision to pursue a death sentence as the race of the defendant. For instance, African Americans are six to seven times more likely than Whites to be murdered. Hence, Blacks and Whites are the victims of murder in about equal numbers. But the overwhelming majority of people put to death since 1976 (over 80%) were convicted of killing white victims. In contrast, 13% of those executed were convicted of killing Blacks, and 4% involved Latino/a victims (Amnesty International, 2003). To put it another way, since 1977, 12 death penalty cases have involved white defendants and black victims; in that same time, 189 cases involved black defendants and white victims (Death Penalty Information Center, 2004).

One of the hallmarks of the American criminal justice system is that defendants are entitled to be judged by a jury of their peers. In theory, such an arrangement overcomes the individual bias and arbitrariness of having a single person, namely the judge, render all verdicts. However, racial discrimination in jury selection is a persistent problem. Attorneys are entitled to "preemptory challenges," the ability to strike a potential juror from the jury without offering any explanation. In 1986, the U.S. Supreme Court ruled that race-based preemptory challenges were unconstitutional. But they still occur. In a study of 100 criminal trials in Dallas County, Texas, over a one-year period, prosecutors challenged 405 of 467 eligible black jurors, five times the number of potential white jurors who were dismissed (cited in Cole, 1999).

Racial bias can also influence juries' decisions. Even though jurors in capital cases face extraordinary responsibility, they are ordinary people. They inevitably come to the courtroom with their own set of prejudgments. For instance, black jurors may be more sympathetic than white jurors to mitigating evidence presented by a black defendant, whose background and experiences they may feel they understand. A study of capital cases in Philadelphia found that death sentences for black defendants are less likely when black jurors are more numerous (cited in Bowers, Steiner, & Sandys, 2001).

Sociologist Benjamin Fleury-Steiner (2002) examined transcripts of interviews with 66 black and white jurors who had served on capital murder cases involving black defendants. Some white jurors voiced overt racism and contempt for the defendant they had sentenced to death ("If [he'd] been white . . . , I would've had a different attitude"). But others painted a subtler picture of racial inferiority. Here's how one white interviewee recounted her impressions of a black defendant during the trial:

> I saw the defendant as a very typical product of the lower socioeconomic, black group who grew up with no values, no ideals, no authority, no morals, no leadership, and this has come down from generation to generation. . . . I just saw him as a loser from day one, as soon as he was born into that environment, and into that set of people who basically were into drugs, alcohol, illegitimacy, AIDS, the whole nine yards. This kid didn't have a chance. That's how I saw the defendant. And there are 10,000 others like him out there, which is very tragic. (quoted in Fleury-Steiner, 2002, p. 562)

You can see that even though she considers the defendant's life tragic, she nonetheless draws on some extensive stereotypes about his presumably inferior racial environment. His actions confirmed what she "already knew" about Blacks.

Among other interviewees, the "inferiority" was often couched in race-neutral terms like the defendant's "dark or menacing" appearance (one black defendant was described as a "chained gorilla"), governmental programs ("the welfare system makes these people"), or displeasure with a defendant's attempt to use his life of racial disadvantage as an excuse. The anger of some jurors stemmed from their feelings about not only the defendant's actions but also the circumstances represented by the defendant and his family.

On the other hand, many of the black jurors who were interviewed felt more hostility and alienation toward their fellow white jurors than they did toward the defendant:

> They wanted to fry those black boys. I'm serious, that's the feeling I got. I felt that they didn't give a shit one way or the other. . . . They felt like these two black boys took a white man's life: We're going to burn them. That's the impression I got. (quoted in Fleury-Steiner, 2002, p. 570)

Others became frustrated by their thwarted attempts to educate the white jurors who they felt were unfamiliar with poor Blacks' lifestyles and therefore were basing their death sentence decisions on unfair racial stereotypes.

Close to two decades ago, the U.S. Supreme Court acknowledged the danger that racial attitudes might influence jurors' sentencing decisions in capital cases, especially when the defendant is black and the victim is white. In the case of Turner vs. Murray, the court ruled that a capital defendant accused of an interracial crime is entitled to have prospective jurors informed of the race of the victim and questioned on the issue of racial bias (Bowers, Steiner, & Sandys, 2001).

However, even when race doesn't seem to be a factor, socioeconomic status is. For instance, a study commissioned by the state of Nebraska of 177 murders over two decades found no differences in the treatment of capital defendants based on race. But it did find that defendants whose victims had high socioeconomic status faced a higher risk of receiving a death sentence than those whose victims were poor (cited in Amnesty International, 2003). The quality of legal representation for defendants in capital cases is also severely slanted along socioeconomic lines. When wealthy individuals, like O. J. Simpson, are tried for capital crimes (an occurrence that, in and of itself, is rather rare), they are usually able to afford effective legal representation. In contrast, poor defendants in such cases are often represented by public defenders, who have fewer resources available for investigative work and who may have little, if any, experience in such matters. For instance, in an Alabama case, the public defender for a poor man facing the death penalty had never tried a capital case and had no money to hire an investigator before the case went to trial. The man was sentenced to death. Similarly, a poor man in Texas, sentenced to death in 1996, was appointed an attorney for his appeal who had never handled such cases and who had been sanctioned several times for neglecting his clients. The man's appeal was denied, and he was executed in 2002.

Although race and class biases still exist in death penalty cases, some steps have been taken to try to alleviate the problem:

- In 1998, Kentucky became the first state to pass a "Racial Justice Act," a law that allows defendants in capital cases to use statistical evidence of racial bias to show that their race influenced the decision to seek the death penalty.
- In 2001, the governor of Illinois called for a moratorium on executions in his state after 13 men on death row—most of whom were either Latino or African American and all of whom were poor and were represented in their trials by public defenders—were proven innocent. Two years later, he commuted all death sentences in the state to prison terms of life or less after declaring the system fundamentally flawed and unfair (Wilgoren, 2003).
- In 2002, the governor of Maryland imposed a moratorium on executions in his state because of concerns over racial bias. In Maryland, 81% of homicide victims are African American, yet 84% of death sentences were cases involving white victims. Two-thirds of the people on death row there are African American (Amnesty International, 2004).
- In 2001, the American Bar Association passed a resolution calling for a nationwide moratorium on executions (Fleischaker, 2004).

GENDERED JUSTICE

Although legal inequalities are especially vivid with regard to race, ethnicity, and class, they also exist along gender lines. Although some men may claim legal disadvantage these days in areas like post-divorce child custody decisions, women have struggled for years to achieve equal legal protection in all areas of life.

GENDER AND THE LAW

Throughout history, women have been denied many of the legal rights that men take for granted. For instance, in the 18th century, when women got married, they lost many of the rights they enjoyed as single women, such as legal title to their property and the right to execute contracts. A married woman's legal identity was submerged into that of her husband; she literally didn't exist as an independent citizen (Crittenden, 2001). Husbands were allowed by law to chastise their wives, force them to stay at home, and even force sex upon them without legal sanction.

To counteract a long history of legal inequality, the U.S. Congress has passed many important laws aimed at improving the situation of women:

- In addition to its central focus on eliminating racial segregation, the 1964 Civil Rights Act contained provisions forbidding sex discrimination in employment.

- The 1972 Educational Amendments Act included a section forbidding sex discrimination in all federally funded institutions of education. This law includes Title IX, which requires schools receiving federal money to fund male and female athletic programs equitably.

- The 1993 Family and Medical Leave Act guarantees some working mothers (as well as fathers) up to 12 weeks of unpaid sick leave per year to care for a new child or a sick relative.

Courts in the United States have also made several noteworthy decisions that address women's concerns. In 1993, the U.S. Supreme Court ruled that victims of workplace harassment could win lawsuits without having to prove that the offensive behavior left them psychologically damaged—which in the past meant either a documented nervous breakdown or psychiatric hospitalization—or unable to do their jobs. Now, workers need prove only that as a result of harassment, the workplace environment "would reasonably be perceived as hostile or abusive" (Greenhouse, 1993). In 1996, the Court ruled that all-male public colleges and universities have to admit women.

These laws and court rulings haven't been completely effective in rooting out sex discrimination. In the United States and elsewhere, occupations are still highly segregated along sex lines. Female workers still earn significantly less than what male workers earn (see Chapter 8). And a woman's right to control her own body through legal contraception and abortion continues to be challenged.

Even laws ostensibly designed to protect women's rights have created unforeseen disadvantages. Divorce laws in the United States, which were revised in the 1970s to make the termination of marriages less adversarial and more just, have actually increased the number of women who become poor after a divorce (Arendell, 1984). Divorced husbands typically experience an increase in their standard of living, but divorced wives—who usually maintain physical custody of children after the divorce—suffer a decrease (Peterson, 1996). In California, for instance, after no-fault divorce laws were enacted, only 13% of mothers with preschool children received spousal support (cited in Tavris, 1992).

SEXUAL HARASSMENT

More than a decade after the Supreme Court affirmed women's right to work in environments free of sexual hostility or abuse, sexual harassment remains a common experience for girls and women. In a variety of institutional settings—from schools to workplaces to military bases—women are routinely exposed to unwelcome leers, comments, requests for sexual favors, and unwanted physical contact. The U.S. Equal Employment Opportunity Commission resolved 14,000 or so cases of workplace sexual harassment in 2003, but these figures obviously don't include episodes that are never reported (EEOC, 2004). Some estimate that as many as 70% of women experience some kind of harassment in the workplace ("Sexual harassment statistics," 2004). And according to the American Association of University Women (2001), about 83% of girls have been sexually harassed in school, ranging from the spread of sexual rumors about them to coerced sexual activity.

Harassment and sexual misconduct have been particularly problematic in the military. Over the past few years, we've heard many stories about the threatening actions and sex discrimination that female cadets, soldiers, and pilots have had to endure:

- When a woman fought a legal battle in the mid-1990s to be admitted into The Citadel—at that point, an all-male military academy of over 1,900 students—she became a target of harassment and ridicule (Vojdik, 2002).
- In 2000, the only female three-star general in the army at the time filed a sexual harassment complaint against another general. She retired a few months later.
- In 2003, several dozen female cadets at the Air Force Academy accused officials there not only of failing to investigate their sexual assault complaints but of discouraging women from reporting these incidents and retaliating against the women when they did complain (Thomas & Healy, 2003).
- In February 2004, the Pentagon revealed that over the preceding 18 months, there had been 112 reports of serious sexual misconduct— mostly rape and sexual assault—committed by male American

military personnel against female American personnel in Iraq, Afghanistan, and Kuwait (Schmitt, 2004).

Misconduct against women has become pervasive in the entire military system. A survey conducted by the General Accounting Office found that 59% of female students at the Air Force Academy, 50% at the Naval Academy, and 76% at West Point reported experiencing one or more forms of sexual harassment (cited in Katz, 2003). The problem goes beyond individually violent military personnel. In 2004, a Pentagon report concluded that the root cause of the problem is a decade's worth of failure on the part of commanding officers to acknowledge its severity (cited in Shanker, 2004).

Most feminist sociologists interpret sexual harassment as an attempt to reinforce positions of power (Uggen & Blackstone, 2004). Because harassment is about power, men can also be victims. Although images of either an overbearing, sexually aggressive female boss or a gay superior coming on to a male subordinate may come to mind, cases of men being sexually harassed more commonly involve heterosexual men creating a hostile environment for other heterosexual men. According to the Equal Employment Opportunity Commission (2003), sexual harassment charges filed by men increased from 9.1% of all cases to 14.9% of all cases between 1992 and 2002. These claims often involve "bullying," "hazing," "goosing," a variety of sexual insults, and other boorish behaviors. In 1998, the U.S. Supreme Court ruled that in cases of men harassing other men, a plaintiff could win a suit if the alleged harasser was homosexual and therefore motivated by sexual desire, if the harasser was motivated by a general hostility toward all men, or if men were systematically treated differently than women in the workplace (Talbot, 2002). By the logic of this final criterion, an alleged harasser who demonstrated equal contempt for both men and women would be innocent. Indeed, this defense was used successfully in 2000 in a case involving a male supervisor who had punished a female employee for not sleeping with him and threw away a male employee's belongings when he didn't give in to the supervisor's advances.

GENDER AND VIOLENCE

Definitions of male power have traditionally encompassed sexual aggression and physical violence as their primary features. The statistics support this observation. Men account for 89% of robberies, 86% of aggravated assaults, 90% of homicides, and 96% of rapes and sexual assaults in the

Exhibit 7.2: Type of Homicide by Gender, 1976–2000

Victims		Type of Homicide		Offenders
24%	76%	All homicides	88%	12%
62%	38%	Intimate	64%	36%
45.5%	54.5%	Infanticide	61%	39%
81%	19%	Sex-related	93%	7%
10%	90%	Drug-related	96%	4%
22%	78%	Argument	85%	15%
18%	82%	Gun homicide	90%	10%
43.5%	56.5%	Arson	80%	20%
45.5%	54.5%	Poison	63%	37%

Victims axis: 100 80 60 40 20 0 — Percent

Offenders axis: 0 20 40 60 80 100 — Percent

Legend: Male / Female

(Source: Fox & Zawitz, 2002)

United States (Fox & Zawitz, 2002; U.S. Bureau of Justice Statistics, 2003). Men are also more likely than women to be victims of violence, including not only assaults, robberies, and homicides but suicides, deaths in military combat, and even accidental deaths from working in hazardous occupations and participating in other high-risk activities (Gilligan, 2004). A look at Exhibit 7.2, which presents some of the data on gender and homicides, confirms this imbalance; except for intimate and sex-related violence, men are predominant as both offenders and victims.

Intersections
Poverty, Gender, and Human Trafficking

Violent victimization often crosses national boundaries. One of the most pernicious international forms of such violence is human trafficking. According to the U.S. Department of State (2002), in 2001, at least 700,000 and maybe as many as 4 million people worldwide, mostly women, were bought, sold, transported, or kept against their will. They may be forced to labor in sweat shops or become domestic servants. They might also be sold into prostitution, sex tourism, or even forced marriage. In China, where males significantly out-number females, young women and girls may be kidnapped by or sold to poten-tial bridegrooms by their impoverished families. Between 1991 and 1996, Chinese police freed about 88,000 women and girls who had been kidnapped for this purpose (Goodwin, 2003). The growth of trafficking in humans has reached crisis proportions in the countries where the trade originates, through which the captives are transported, and where they end up (Clark, 2003).

Human trafficking is not simply a foreign problem. In 2002, police in Plain-field, New Jersey, raided a house expecting to find a brothel of illegal aliens. Instead, they found a group of teenage girls from Mexico who were being held captive as sex-slaves in squalid conditions (Landesman, 2004). The CIA esti-mates that as many as 50,000 women and children from Asia, Eastern Europe, and Latin America are brought to the United States each year and forced to work as prostitutes, laborers, or servants (Brinkley, 2000).

Traffickers find victims in several ways. Frequently, they take out ads in local newspapers offering good jobs at high pay in exciting cities. In politically unstable countries with high rates of poverty and unemployment, destitute women may see these offers as opportunities to help their families financially. Traffickers often use fraudulent modeling, matchmaking, or travel agencies to lure unsuspecting victims. They may even visit families in local villages, assuring them that their daughters will be taught a useful trade or skill or even prom-ising parents that they themselves will marry the daughters. Traffickers deftly target the weakest and most vulnerable populations to victimize. Seventy per-cent of the world's poor are girls and women. Their low cultural status in many countries makes their victimization all that much easier. And they are increas-ingly at risk in precisely those environments that are usually considered safe: their communities and their families (Clark, 2003).

Traffickers use threats, intimidation, and violence to force victims to engage in sex acts or to work as slaves for the traffickers' financial gain. The vulnerability of trafficking victims is reflected in this Mexican woman's account of her ordeal. She was hoping to go to the United States and earn enough money to support her daughter and parents in Mexico. She was told that there were plenty of good jobs available in restaurants:

> I was transported to Florida and there, one of the bosses told me I would be working in a brothel as a prostitute. I told him he was mis-taken and that I was going to be working in a restaurant, not a brothel. He said I owed him a smuggling debt and the sooner I paid it off the

sooner I could leave. I was eighteen years old and had never been far from home and had no money or way to return. I was constantly guarded and abused. If any of the girls refused to be with a customer, we were beaten. . . . We worked six days a week, 12 hours a day. Our bodies were sore and swollen. If anyone became pregnant we were forced to have abortions. The cost of the abortion was added to the smuggling debt. The bosses carried weapons. . . . I never knew where I was. We were transported every fifteen days to different cities. I knew if I tried to escape I would not get far because everything was unfamiliar. The bosses said that if we escaped they would get their money from our families. ("Survivor stories," 2001, p. 1)

As this woman's account suggests, by moving their victims away from their homes, often to other countries, traffickers isolate them and render them helpless. The victims may be unable to speak the language of the place where they are held or may be unfamiliar with the culture. They also lose contact with friends and family, making them even more vulnerable to the traffickers' threats.

INTIMATE VIOLENCE

Aside from trafficking, the areas in which women's rates of violent victimization outpace men's—incest, rape/sexual assault, and domestic assault—are closely related to their familial or sexual disadvantage. Because they tend to be tied to intimacy, such violent acts have often fallen outside the criminal justice system or have been treated less seriously.

These crimes have existed for as long as humans have lived in societies; they exist throughout the world, in the most democratic societies as well as in the most repressive. Globally, women remain disadvantaged by such violence. Consider these examples:

- In Bangladesh, some men—usually spurned suitors—throw acid on the faces of women. Those who survive the attacks are typically left hideously deformed. One woman was forced by her parents to marry her attacker because they felt no one else would want to marry her. Most attackers are never arrested, and most who are arrested are never tried in court (Bearak, 2000).
- In India, young brides, who by custom live with their new husbands' parents, are commonly subjected to severe abuse if promised money (known as "dowry") is not paid. Sometimes dowry harassment ends

in suicide or murder. In 1998, about 7,000 wives—an average of 19 a day—were killed by their husbands for not providing adequate dowries ("Bridal dowry in India," 2000).

■ In Spain, violence against women has become so severe and so common that in 2004 the new prime minister, upon taking office, made it his first order of business to stamp out what he called "criminal machismo." He proposed legislation that would criminalize violent threats against women, provide more money to protect battered women, and create work-training programs for victims (Sciolino, 2004).

Such violence against women continues despite—or perhaps because of—some economic, educational, and political advances for women.

Rape and Sexual Assault In the United States, rape is the most frequently committed but least reported violent crime (U.S. Department of Justice, 2001). According to the National Crime Victimization Survey (U.S. Bureau of Justice Statistics, 2003), more than 248,000 women over the age of 12 report being raped or sexually assaulted annually, close to three times the roughly 96,000 incidents of forcible rape that were officially reported to the police in 2002 (U.S. Bureau of the Census, 2004). The most common reason victims give for not reporting a rape or sexual assault is fear of reprisal from their attackers (U.S. Bureau of Justice Statistics, 2003).

Rape and sexual assault are two of the most personal violent crimes. In 63% of rapes, 70% of attempted rapes, and 65% of sexual assaults the victim knew the attacker (U.S. Bureau of Justice Statistics, 2003). On college campuses, where about 3% of college women experience a completed or attempted rape during a typical college year, 90% of the victims know their attackers (U.S. Bureau of Justice Statistics, 2001).

Rape is a reflection of broader patterns of gender inequality. Throughout history, women have been viewed socially and legally as the property of men, first their fathers and later their husbands. Thus, in the past—and in many more-traditional societies today—rape was considered a crime against men or, more accurately, against men's property (Siegel, 2004). Any interest a husband took in a rape or sexual assault on his wife probably reflected a concern with his own status, the loss of his male honor, and the devaluation of his sexual property. Indeed, worldwide, rape and sexual assault are time-tested wartime tactics of terror, revenge, and intimidation, not only against female victims but also against husbands, sons, and fathers whose idea of honor is connected to their ability to protect "their" women (Brownmiller, 1975; Enloe, 1993).

In a more immediate sense, feminist sociologists have argued that throughout history, men have used rape, the threat of rape, and the fear of rape to exert control over women (Brownmiller, 1975). Fear of crime in general—and rape in particular—is a dominant force in women's lives. The mere existence of rape limits women's freedom of social interaction, denies them the right of self-determination, makes them dependent on men, and ultimately subordinates them (Griffin, 1986). The fear of rape can also affect women economically. For instance, women may avoid some neighborhoods with affordable housing because of potential danger. If a woman has a job that requires night work, she may be forced to buy a car to avoid walking at night or using public transportation. The threat of sexual assault may also limit where and when she is able to work.

Many people are inclined to believe that men who rape are sex-crazed strangers bent on harming and humiliating women because of some deep-seated psychological or hormonal defect. All one has to do to avoid being raped, then, is to avoid strange guys. However, rapists as a group have not been shown to be any more disturbed or crazy than non-rapists (Griffin, 1986; Warshaw, 1988). In fact, most rapists are quite "normal" by usual societal standards. Thus, we must consider the sociocultural characteristics that encourage, condone, or at the very least heighten the likelihood of rape. From that perspective, rape is less an act of deviance and more an act of overconformity to cultural expectations; less an act of defective individuals and more an act of "normal" men taking cultural messages about power, dominance, and assertiveness to their violent extreme (Jackson, 1995).

Globally, cultural beliefs about gender, power, and sexuality strongly influence societal and legal responses to rape and rape victims. Consider these examples:

- In Peru and Columbia, a man who rapes a woman—whether he knows her or not—can be absolved of all charges if he offers to marry her (Morgan, 1996).
- In Morocco, rape is defined as a crime against family order and public morality, not against individual women. The punishment—five to ten years in prison—is doubled if the victim is a virgin (Morgan, 1996).
- In Senegal, single women who are rape victims may be killed by their families because as nonvirgins they can no longer command a high

dowry; a married woman who's been raped may be killed by her "dishonored" husband (Morgan, 1996).

- In Iran, because Islamic tradition forbids the execution of virgins, any woman condemned to die for a crime she's committed must first lose her virginity through forced temporary marriage or rape (Morgan, 1996).

- About 60% of Pakistani women who file rape charges—which require two witnesses for a conviction—are later criminally charged themselves for having sex outside of marriage (cited in Fisher, 2002).

The United States has a more sympathetic response to rape victims. But the legal system still tends to favor men's interests by focusing on women's complicity or blameworthiness. In rape cases, unlike any other crime, victims typically must prove their innocence rather than the state having to prove the guilt of the defendant. One reason for the widespread tendency to hold women culpable for their own victimization is that the common definition of rape is based on sexual intercourse rather than on the violent context within which the act takes place. Thus, information about the circumstances of the act and about the relationship between the people involved must be taken into consideration. One study of convicted rapists found that those who sexually assaulted strangers received longer prison sentences than assailants who were acquaintances or partners of their victims, regardless of the amount of force used or physical injury to the victim (McCormick, Maric, Seto, & Barbaree, 1998).

Race and class differences may also come into play when prosecutors weigh the wisdom of proceeding with a rape case:

> I had to think about what the jury would think. They are from other areas, they are white and wealthy. Most of the defendants and victims are black and Latino. . . . The jurors don't understand why she went out at midnight. That was probably when she got her kids down to sleep and finally had free time to go out and party. But the people in Mission Hills don't think that way. (quoted in Frohmann, 1997, p. 540)

Despite the massive amounts of attention that have been devoted to rape and sexual assault in recent years, public perceptions remain resistant to change. Many people are unsympathetic toward rape victims if they put themselves at risk—by hitchhiking, attending a wild party, acting seductively, drinking with strangers, wearing "provocative" clothing, and so forth. In one study, male and female high school students were given a list of statements and asked to indicate the extent to which they agreed with them (Kershner, 1996). Of the male and female subjects, 52% agreed that most women fantasize about being raped by a man, 46% felt that women encourage rape by the way they dress, and 53% said they felt that some women provoke men into raping them. Moreover, 31% agreed that many women falsely report rapes, and 35% felt that the victim should be required to prove her innocence during a rape trial. Research has linked such attitudes to the heightened risk of rape and sexual assault on college campuses (Ching & Burke, 1999).

The important sociological point in studies like these is that many men and even some women don't always define violent sexual assault as a form of victimization. They think it is what men are expected to do under certain circumstances. These views have become so entrenched that many women have internalized the message, blaming themselves to some degree when they are assaulted.

As a consequence, women receive the cultural message that they must bear much—if not all—of the responsibility for preventing rape: Don't hitchhike. Don't walk alone at night. Don't get drunk at parties where men are present, and if you do drink, know where your drink is at all times. Don't initiate sex play. Don't engage in foreplay if you have no intention of "going all the way." Don't miscommunicate your intentions. Don't wear provocative clothing. Don't accept invitations from strangers (Newman, 2004). These precautions are sensible. But notice how they all focus exclusively on things that women should avoid to prevent rape and say nothing about the things *men* can do to stop it. Such instructions speak volumes about the nature of rape and the place of women in society.

Spousal and Partner Violence Nationwide, the home is one of the most dangerous locations for women. Exact statistics about the prevalence of spousal or partner violence are difficult to collect, because it is usually concealed and private, occurring in seclusion, beyond the watchful eyes of relatives, neighbors, and strangers. Even with the more stringent rules for police reporting of domestic calls that have been instituted by police departments across the country in the past decade or two, most incidents are never reported; others are dismissed as accidents. To complicate matters, definitions of abuse and reporting practices vary from state to state.

The statistics on spouse and partner abuse that do exist indicate that it is a widespread problem, although it has declined somewhat in recent years. According to the U.S. Bureau of Justice Statistics (Rennison, 2003), there were close to 700,000 non-lethal assaults committed by current spouses, former spouses, boyfriends, or girlfriends in 2001 (the last year for which such figures are available). Women accounted for 85% of the victims of these incidents. Another 1,247 women were killed by an intimate partner that year, accounting for one-third of all female murders. Interestingly, although the number of non-lethal acts of intimate violence dropped by over 40% between 1993 and 2001, the number of homicides has remained fairly constant (Rennison, 2003).

Other studies place the prevalence rate for intimate partner violence even higher. For instance, the National Violence Against Women Survey of 16,000 women and men nationwide found that nearly 25% of surveyed women and 7.6% of men said they'd been raped or physically assaulted by a spouse, partner, or date at some point in their lifetimes (Tjaden & Thoennes, 2000). Within the previous 12 months, 1.5% of women and 0.9% of men reported being raped or physically assaulted. According to these estimates, that means about 1.5 million women and over 800,000 men are assaulted by an intimate partner annually in the United States. Given the shame and stigma associated with reporting such violence, we can probably assume that all these figures are underestimates of the actual incidence of violence between intimates. Some researchers estimate that only about half of the cases of non-lethal violence against women are reported to the police (Rennison & Welchans, 2000).

Power and perceived threats to dominance and authority are underlying issues in almost all acts of intimate partner violence (Gelles & Straus, 1988). In male-dominated households, husbands sometimes turn to violence to intimidate their wives. But it's also true that in an achievement-oriented society like ours, husbands who lack the financial, occupational, and educational resources necessary to establish household dominance may turn to violence or coercion (Yllo & Straus, 1990). The effect of men's employment on violence was demonstrated in a study of 12,000 Canadian women over the age of 18 (MacMillan and Gartner, 1999). The researchers found that wives' exposure to spousal violence had little to do with whether or not they were employed. But when their husbands were unemployed, employed wives' risk of victimization increased significantly.

Although we've long since abandoned the belief that abuse victims should stay with their violent partners to try to "work things out," getting out of abusive relationships can be difficult, if not impossible, for some women. Nevertheless, we now expect women not to "put up with" being abused.

Ironically, because of this expectation, there's often a perception that women who don't leave are passive and weak-willed, even though the available evidence seems to suggest otherwise. One study of 1,000 battered and formerly battered women nationwide found that the vast majority tried a number of active strategies to end the violence directed against them (Bowker, 1993). They attempted to talk men out of beating them, extracted promises that the men wouldn't batter them anymore, avoided their abusers physically or avoided certain volatile topics, hid or ran away, and even fought back physically. Many of these individual strategies had limited effectiveness, however, and so most of these battered women eventually turned to people outside the relationship for informal support, advice, and sheltering. From these informal sources, the women generally progressed to organizations in the community, such as police, social service and counseling agencies, women's groups, and battered women's shelters. Some of these women were able, eventually, to end the violence; others weren't.

Women often leave their partners on multiple occasions before completely severing ties. One study of battered women who were in a shelter in the Midwest found that close to 80% of them had temporarily left their partners at least once prior to the current attempt, and 19% had left at least 10 times (Sullivan, Tan, Basta, Rumptz, & Davidson, 1992). Many women who return cite the lack of opportunities and resources outside the relationship, such as overcrowded shelters and no one to care for the children while they search for jobs.

Escaping abuse is made more difficult by the fact that women may actually be in greater danger after they leave. Approximately 25% of women killed by male partners were divorced or separated from the men who killed them. And 70% of reported injuries due to domestic violence occur after the couple has separated (Fine & Weis, 2000).

Furthermore, not all victims have equal chances of escaping abuse and receiving help. For instance, within certain communities of color, there are prohibitions against publicizing or seeking protection against domestic violence out of fear that doing so would reinforce racial stereotypes of minority men as violent (Crenshaw, 2004a). Services designed to help these battered women, like shelters, are often unattractive because of language barriers or the lack of other women of color in leadership positions.

Battered gay men and lesbians have an especially difficult time escaping the violence and getting help because of the animosity directed toward homosexuals in the larger society and the gay community's failure to acknowledge domestic violence as a serious problem. As a result, battered homosexual partners are even less likely than battered heterosexual wives to tell anyone about the abuse and seek help, putting themselves at risk for more severe and more frequent violence (Letellier, 1996).

Poor women also face daunting obstacles in leaving abusive relationships. They often live in neighborhoods that have few resources for battered women. In poor rural areas with no public transportation, the shelters that do exist may be inaccessible to women who live miles away and don't own cars. To make matters worse, governmental programs that may have helped these women leave in the past have been dismantled in recent years. Prior to the highly publicized welfare reforms of the mid-1990s, as many as two-thirds of women who received welfare payments had abuse in their backgrounds, suggesting that welfare may have been a way out for many battered women with children (Gordon, 1997). Today, however, fewer poor women are on the welfare rolls, and the unpredictability of the system may force many of them to stay in abusive situations in order to survive financially.

CONCLUSION

When children pledge their allegiance to the American flag each morning in school, they conclude with the phrase, ". . . and justice for all." The concept behind "justice for all" seems fairly straightforward, even to little kids: Everyone should have the same opportunities for a safe life, should be entitled to the same legal protections, and should be treated the same when accused of breaking the law. But we've seen in this chapter that this rather clear, simple standard has not been reached. Inequalities based on race, ethnicity, gender, class, and sexuality are woven into the fabric of our entire legal system. The discrepancies that I've touched on in this chapter are even more troubling when we weigh them against the key values of equality and fairness upon which this country was founded.

If you look up the word *justice* in the dictionary, you'll come across terms like *fairness, impartiality, integrity,* and *even-handedness.* But when we assess the information presented here, it's hard to avoid the conclusion that, for some of us, justice is a somewhat foreign concept. For the fortunate ones among us, our race, our gender, our class standing, and our sexual orientation will serve as a shield against being unfairly treated. But for many others, those traits offer little protection when it comes to the legal standing of our actions, criminal victimization, and the justice process and, indeed, may encourage the kinds of imbalances we've explored here.

It's true that things are getting better, however. We have moved away from the days in which injustices and inequalities were actually codified in the law; when certain members of this society were not afforded the luxury of being treated like full citizens and some were even defined as less than full human beings. But the Pledge of Allegiance rings hollow to many of those children who have to recite its lines each day. Complete "justice for all" remains an unattained goal.

[INVESTIGATING IDENTITIES AND INEQUALITIES]
Safe havens: Race, class, and the fear of crime

Certainly there are police officers, attorneys, judges, and jury members who harbor dislike, resentment, or hatred for members of certain groups and bring those feelings with them when they make crucial decisions on whom to interrogate, whom to arrest, whom to charge, whom to find guilty, whom to sentence, and so on. And it's pretty clear that those people with the economic means can purchase better treatment within the system. But just how does this system look from the perspective of citizens that it is supposed to protect?

To answer that question, interview a variety of people about their experiences with and attitudes toward the criminal justice system. Try to select people from different ethnoracial groups, different class levels, and different genders. You may ask your respondents questions face-to-face, via a paper-and-pencil questionnaire, or through an e-mail survey. Here are some possible questions to ask (though you should feel free to design your own set of questions):

- Have you ever been the victim of a crime? If so, was it a violent crime? Property crime? Fraud? Identity theft? For each instance of victimization:

  - What was your initial response after the victimization? Whom did you contact first? Police? Friends or neighbors? Family?
  - If you contacted the police, how long did it take for them to respond? Were they helpful?
  - To your knowledge, was the perpetrator ever caught? If so, were charges brought against him or her? Was there a trial? How did that end?

- If you've never been a crime victim, describe other direct contacts that you have had with police or security personnel (such as in airport security, at the scene of an accident, or during a traffic stop). How would you characterize the treatment you received during these contacts?

- What kinds of precautions do you currently take to avoid being victimized? List as many as you can think of.
- Describe your feelings about your campus police or the local police in the town where you attend college.

  - Do you consider them fair? Trustworthy? Helpful? Protective? Do they make you feel safe? If you answer no to any of these questions, how would you characterize them?
  - On a scale of 1 to 10, with 1 being very biased and 10 being very fair, how would you rate the local/campus police?
  - Do you know of any specific instances (involving you or people you know) in which local/campus police acted unfairly?

- On a scale of 1 to 10, with 1 being very fearful and 10 being not at all fearful, how would you rank your fear of being a crime victim where you live right now?

Based on your results, analyze whether certain groups (ethnic, class, racial, gender) are significantly less confident than others in their local police. Are there differences in people's fear of crime? Use your findings to address the question of whether the criminal justice system is really "just."

(*Note:* If you are unable to interview people for this assignment, you can modify it by examining national racial, gender, and class trends in crime and criminal victimization with data from the Bureau of Justice Statistics [www.ojp.usdoj.gov/bjs/] or the Federal Bureau of Investigation [www.fbi.gov/ucr/ucr.htm]).

CHAPTER 8

Inequalities in Economics and Work

My older son turned 18 while I was writing this book. Within a few days of his birthday, he received a letter in the mail from the Selective Service System reminding him in chirpy, upbeat language that he was now eligible to register with the service. The letter pointed out that, for his convenience, he could register online and that within seconds he'd receive his selective service number! They made it sound like he would win something.

What he was winning, as I'm sure you know, was the "right" to be called into military service. The mission of the Selective Service System is to provide manpower (women don't yet have to register) for the armed forces should Congress and the president decide, in the event of a national emergency, that a return to a military draft is necessary. Eighteen-year-old men are required by law to register. Failure to do so is a serious crime, punishable by a fine of up to $250,000 and imprisonment for up to five years. In addition, registration with the service is a requirement for such things as student financial aid, job training, and government employment.

Despite repeated statements from the president, some cabinet members, and various senators and congressional representatives at the time of my son's birthday that there would be no draft, I was worried. Like many people, I was closely following the military situation in the Middle East. At the time of this writing, the United States was struggling to find enough enlisted personnel to confront the insurgency in Iraq and to police Afghanistan. The military had been forced to resort to drastic measures such as "stop loss"—which bars soldiers from retiring or resigning—and "stop move"—which compels troops to continue assignments after their tours end (Van Auken, 2004). These policies have the potential to force thousands of soldiers to remain in uniform for a year or more after their contracts expire. I wondered how long it would be until the military situation was defined as a "national emergency" and the draft was reinstated.

To calm myself, I decided to think about the situation from a more sociological (and less parental) perspective. It didn't help my mood. As it turns out, our armed services are not a particularly accurate reflection of the population at large. Since the military became voluntary in the early 1970s, those who come from the most disadvantaged reaches of society have been overrepresented, especially during times of high unemployment. To poor and working-class people with limited educational and occupational opportunities, military service holds out the promise of stable employment, comprehensive insurance coverage, a living wage, free schooling, and the development of marketable skills.

In Iraq, for instance, U.S. military personnel have been disproportionately ethnoracial minorities from working-class families. For instance, while African Americans make up about 13% of the same-age civilian population, they constitute 22% of enlisted personnel. The figures are even more disparate for women. More than 35% of enlisted women are African American. The proportion of new recruits who are members of ethnoracial minorities increased from 23% in 1970 to 37% in 2000. It is all but impossible to find U.S. soldiers from very wealthy families serving in the Middle East (Halbfinger & Holmes, 2003). As you might guess, American casualties in the Iraqi war have overwhelmingly been from working-class families (Golway, 2004).

Military service is also attractive to working-class immigrants, many of whom are not yet U.S. citizens. In 2004, the U.S. Congress enacted a law that shortens the waiting period for immigrants seeking citizenship if they volunteer to serve in the military. Many immigrants have enlisted—and dozens have died—simply because they need the opportunity to improve their lives. As one professor put it, "The bottom line, whatever the casualties, is that [immigrants] are going to continue to join because they have to. They want to live better" (quoted in Davey, 2004, p. A21).

Those in decision-making positions—in the White House and in Congress—are almost exclusively middle class and above and have the political and economic wherewithal to keep their children out of harm's way. The fierce political debates that we hear over whether or not our troops should continue to be in Iraq are carried out, for the most part, by people who have no personal stake whatsoever in the war. At the time of this writing, only one member of Congress had a child serving on the front lines in Iraq.

The controversy over forced versus voluntary military service in wartime represents, in microcosm, the economic inequalities that exist in society today. As we've seen already in previous chapters, access to life chances is not equally distributed across all groups in society. In this chapter, I will focus on economic inequalities, both globally and locally, paying close attention to the intersections of race, class, and gender in determining people's chances of living a comfortable life. Since most people must earn a living by working for a salary or a wage, I will also spend quite a bit of time exploring the confluence of race, class, gender, and sexuality in the workplace.

UNDERPRIVILEGE AND OVERPRIVILEGE: ECONOMIC IMBALANCES IN EVERYDAY LIFE

Economic institutions are the most fundamental source of inequality in society today. In the previous two chapters, we focused on imbalances in the health and justice systems. But we can't understand people's unequal access to healthy lives and legal protections without taking economic imbalances into account.

GLOBAL INEQUALITIES

Economic imbalance is the global rule, not the exception. The average per capita yearly income in Western Europe, the United States, Canada, and Japan is well over $29,000; in the less developed countries of the world, it is just over $3,000 (Population Reference Bureau, 2004b). More than 2.7 billion people in less developed countries live on the equivalent of less than $2 a day. Close to half of all people living in sub-Saharan Africa survive on $1 a day (World Bank, 2003). Consider these other statistics:

- The wealthy developed countries of the world constitute roughly 20% of the world's population but earn 65% of the world's income, consume 86% of the world's goods, and use 85% of its water (McMichael, 1996; Shah, 2004).
- The 48 poorest countries account for less than 0.4% of global exports (Shah, 2004).
- Europeans spend the equivalent of $50 billion on cigarettes and $105 billion on alcohol each year. It would take only $13 billion to provide basic health care and nutrition and $6 billion to provide basic education for everyone in the world (Shah, 2004).

Although there is some evidence that economic growth in the developing world is on the increase (World Bank, 2004), global imbalances will continue to exist. Wealthy nations seek to retain their favored positions while keeping other nations in their place. In a global economy, such dominance is accomplished not by force but through financial pressure—as when powerful industrialized countries set world prices on certain goods (Chase-Dunn & Rubinson, 1977). Because their economic base is weak, poor countries often have to borrow money or buy manufactured goods on credit from wealthy countries. The huge debt they build up locks them into a downward spiral of exploitation and poverty. As a result, they have difficulty developing independent economies of their own and thus remain dependent on wealthy nations for their very survival.

AMERICAN INEQUALITIES

Even if economic inequality between societies were to decline, inequalities within societies would probably persist (Firebaugh, 2003). It's ironic that a society like ours, which extols the virtues of "equality" and "justice," is also perhaps the most stratified in the industrialized world. In 2002, the average annual income for the highest 5% of American families was $164,323; the average annual income for the lowest 20% of families was $24,000 (U.S. Bureau of the Census, 2004). Between the

1940s and the 1970s, incomes for all American households, whether rich or poor, grew at fairly similar rates. But since then, things have changed dramatically (Phillips, 2002):

- In 1973, the wealthiest 20% of American households accounted for 44% of the total U.S. income; in 2002, their share jumped to 50%. During that same time period, the share for the bottom 20% dropped from 4.2% to 3.5% ("Income gap of poor, rich widens," 2004).
- In 1965, the average American chief executive officer earned about 24 times more than the average worker. By 2003, that gap increased to 185 times more. Between 1992 and 2003, median workers' hourly wages rose by 8.7%. During that same time, the average CEO received an 80.8% raise (Mishel, Bernstein, & Allegretto, 2004).
- In 1981, the 10 highest-earning American corporate executives were paid, on average, $3.5 million a year; in 2000, the 10 highest-paid executives made, on average, $154 million a year (in constant dollars), a 4,300% increase (Phillips, 2002).
- The average American corporate chief executive now makes more in a single day than the average American worker makes in a typical year (Leonhardt, 2000).

Exhibit 8.1 depicts the increasing income gap between wealthy and poor Americans. Notice how the gap grew between 1995 and 2000.

Tax cuts have increased the income gap further. According to the Congressional Budget Office, between 2001 and 2004, one-third of tax cuts went to people with the top 1% of income; two-thirds of tax cuts went to the top 20% (Andrews, 2004). The average tax savings from these cuts for the highest-earning 1% of the population was about $67,000 per household. For middle-income families, the cuts added up to just under $600. And for the bottom 20%, the average saving was about $61 a year (Mishel, Bernstein, & Allegretto, 2004). As if these disparities aren't bad enough, the working poor are far more likely to be audited by the Internal Revenue Service than wealthy people are (Johnston, 2002). That's not surprising, given the fact that the IRS looks for tax cheating by wage earners far more closely than it does for people whose money comes from their own businesses, investments, partnerships, and trusts.

Inequalities in income lead to even more striking inequalities in wealth. A lifetime of high earnings and inheritance from privileged parents creates an advantage in ownership of durable consumer goods such as cars, houses, and furniture and of financial assets such as stocks, bonds,

Exhibit 8.1: Growing Gap Between Rich and Poor Americans

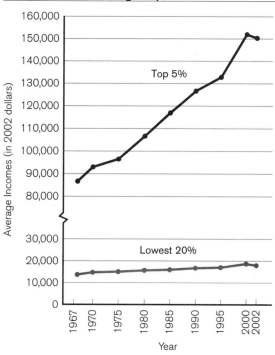

(Source: U.S. Bureau of the Census, 2003a, Table H-1)

savings, and life insurance. The most prosperous 20% of U.S. households owns over 80% of the nation's wealth (up from 76% in 1984). Households with annual incomes of over $100,000 control about 70% of all stock. And the wealthiest 1% of U.S. households, who enjoyed two-thirds of all increases in wealth over the past two decades, now owns close to 40% of the wealth. At the same time, the bottom 40% of households controls a mere 0.2% of the nation's wealth (Henwood, 2001; Keister & Moller, 2000; Mishel, Bernstein, & Allegretto, 2004).

Furthermore, because wealth accumulates over generations, historical ethnoracial discrimination in lending, housing, and employment hardens the wealth deficiencies for families of color. Twenty-six percent of Latino/a households, 32% of black households, but only 13% of white households had zero or negative net worth in 2002 (Kochhar, 2004). Even those whose income is comparable to that of Whites tend to have less wealth (Anderson, 2001). The recession of the early 2000s widened the wealth gap between black and Latino/a households and white households (see

Exhibit 8.2: Median Net Worth by Race and Ethnicity (in 2003 dollars)

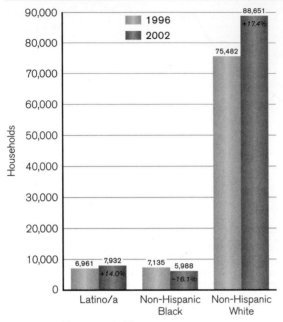

(Source: Kochhar, 2004, Table 1)

Exhibit 8.2), undermining the gains that ethnoracial minorities had made and reinforcing inequality.

We will never live in a society with a perfectly equal distribution of income and wealth. Some people will always earn more, have more, and maybe even deserve more than others. But the fact that the gap between rich and poor in the United States continues to grow challenges the notion that we live in a society where everyone is valued equally. As disparities in income and wealth expand, so too does the gap in quality of life and access to opportunity between those at the top of society and those at the bottom.

THE MIDDLE-CLASS SQUEEZE

The middle class—as an abstract ideal as much as a particular group of people—has historically occupied a lofty position in this society. Its moods, political leanings, values, habits, lifestyles, and tastes define U.S. culture. It's an identity to which many people aspire, and it's the standard against which other classes are measured and judged. It is also perhaps the most coveted constituency in politics. But if we look at the economic lives of people who are literally in the middle class—that is, whose income places them in the middle of the pack—we see some troubling recent trends.

In general, household incomes have risen steadily but slowly throughout the late 1990s and early 2000s. In 1980, the median household income (in current dollars) across all ethnoracial groups in the United States was $36,035. By 2003, it was $43,318 (DeNavas-Walt, Proctor, & Mills, 2004). The minimum wage has increased 90 cents an hour since 1996, helping to push up the earnings of the lowest-hourly-wage earners as well. And incomes of those households in the highest income brackets have, as always, surged skyward.

But the median wage actually dropped by about 2.2% between 2000 and 2002 (Mishel, Bernstein, & Allegretto, 2004). In 2004, the U.S. Bureau of Labor Statistics reported that the hourly earnings of non-management workers—ranging from nurses and teachers to assembly-line workers—showed the steepest decline since 1991. As you might expect, race and ethnicity are also a factor. As Exhibit 8.3 shows, the decreases are much less significant for Asian Americans and Whites than for other ethnoracial groups. Across the board, though, the average production worker took home about $525.84 a week in 2003, the lowest level of weekly pay since 2001 (cited in Porter, 2004). Many people haven't had raises in years but

Exhibit 8.3: Recent Trends in Median Income by Race

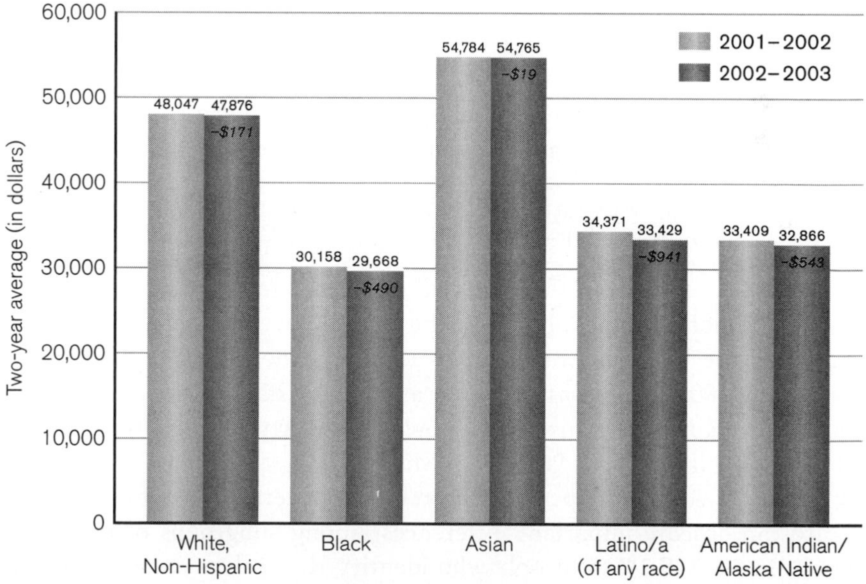

(Source: DeNavas-Walt, Proctor, & Mills, 2004, Table 2)

have seen the cost of living (in particular, food, energy, and health care costs) rise steadily.

Not only are jobs paying less than they used to, but there are fewer of them to go around. In 2004, between 5.5% and 6% of American adults (a little over 8 million people) were officially unemployed. Keep in mind that this number is artificially low: Another 1.6 million unemployed people were not counted because they hadn't actively been seeking employment in the past month (U.S. Bureau of Labor Statistics, 2004a). Indeed, the number of Americans with college degrees who were unemployed for over six months tripled between 2001 and 2004 (cited in Greenhouse, 2004). Because of corporate downsizing, a weak stock market, global instability, fear of terrorism, and a variety of other economic factors, 1.4 million jobs disappeared between March 2001 and June 2004. Despite an economic recovery at the end of 2003, 36 states had fewer jobs than they had three years earlier (Mishel, Bernstein, & Allegretto, 2004).

Some economists and politicians argue that unemployment is not a serious problem and that jobs in the future will be plentiful. However, the types of jobs that will be available may not be the sort that will strengthen people's middle-class status. According to the U.S. Bureau of Labor Statistics, 7 out of 10 occupations that are forecast to show the greatest growth between 2004 and 2012 are in low-wage service fields: retail sales, customer service, food service, cashier, janitor, waitperson, nursing aide, and hospital orderly (cited in Greenhouse, 2004). Most of these jobs pay less than $18,000 a year. By most accounts, high-paying jobs will continue to be in short supply, meaning that many college-educated people will be thwarted in their attempts to earn a comfortable living.

THE FACE OF AMERICAN POVERTY: IN THE SHADOW OF PLENTY

As you will recall from Chapter 2, the poverty rate—the percentage of residents whose income falls below the official poverty line—is one of the measures the U.S. government uses to assess the financial state of the country. In 2003 (the most recent year available), 12.5% of the population—or 35.9 million Americans—fell below the poverty line, up from 11.7% in 2001 (DeNavas-Walt, Proctor, & Mills, 2004).

When used to describe national trends in poverty, this overall poverty figure can obscure important differences among subgroups of the population. In 2003, 8.2% of people who identify themselves as non-Hispanic Whites and 11.8% of Asian Americans fell below the poverty line. That same year, 24.4% of Blacks and 22.5% of Latino/as (who could be of any race) were considered poor. The poverty rate in the South (14.1%) and West (12.6%) is higher than the rate in the Midwest (10.7%) and Northeast (11.3%). Finally, poverty is higher in rural areas (14.2%) than in metropolitan areas (12.1%), although it's highest in inner cities (17.5%) (DeNavas-Walt, Proctor, & Mills, 2004).

Although racial and ethnic minorities have consistently been rated among the poorest Americans, other groups have seen their status change over time. Before Social Security was instituted in 1935, many of the most destitute were those over 65. As recently as 1970, 25% of U.S. residents over the age of 65 fell below the poverty line. Today, only 10.2% of the people in this age group are poor (DeNavas-Walt, Proctor, & Mills, 2004).

Children's fortunes have gone in the reverse direction. About 13 million American children under the age of 18 (17.6%) live in households that are officially poor. This is a disproportionate share of the people in poverty. Children make up about 25.4% of the population yet account for 35.9% of all poor people in this country. As you would suspect, poverty figures for children vary dramatically along ethnoracial lines. About 34% of African American and 30% of Latino/a children under 18 live in poverty—compared to 9.3% of non-Hispanic white children.

Getting out of poverty is not simple, because it is a complicated condition with multiple causes and multiple consequences. A job alone may not be enough if a family also lacks health insurance. Good housing might not be enough if the house is far away from where the jobs are and the family lacks transportation. One incident can create a cycle of economic despair that lasts for years:

> A run-down apartment can exacerbate a child's asthma, which leads to a call for an ambulance, which generates a medical bill that cannot be paid, which ruins a credit record, which hikes the interest rate on an auto loan, which forces the purchase of an unreliable used car, which jeopardizes a mother's punctuality at work, which limits her promotions and earning capacity, which confines her to poor housing. (Shipler, 2004, p. 11)

Sleepless on the Street The most publicly visible consequence of economic instability is homelessness. Estimates of how many homeless people live in the United States range from 2.3 to 3.5 million (National Alliance to End Homelessness, 2005). According to a 2003 survey of 25 major American cities, 41% of homeless people are single men, 14% are single women, and 5% are children on their own. About half of the homeless population are African American, 35% are white, 13% are Latino/a, 2% are Native American, and 1% are Asian American. Seventeen percent of the homeless are employed, and less than a third are substance abusers (United States Conference of Mayors, 2003).

The fastest-growing segment of the homeless population is families with children. Between 2002 and 2003, requests for emergency shelter for families increased by 13%. In four out of five American cities, emergency shelters routinely have to turn away homeless families because they lack the space to provide adequate accommodations (United States Conference of Mayors, 2003).

Homeless people exist on the margins of society. In rural areas, they are invisible; in urban areas, they are faceless annoyances whom most people try to avoid or ignore. The general public tends to harshly stigmatize or be dismissive toward homeless people (Phelan, Link, Moore, & Stueve, 1997). They are walking evidence of economic failure and unfulfilled promise. Thus, community tolerance of homeless people wears thin in many places, leading some cities to impose restrictions on them in an attempt to reduce their visibility.

The homeless as a group tend to be so stigmatized that any racial or even gender disadvantage would not add that much to their already destitute state. It's hard to imagine homeless people being treated any worse than they already are just because they happen to be Latino/a or Asian or African American. However, race and ethnicity do appear to matter with regard to people's chances of becoming homeless. In Great Britain, for example, ethnic minorities compose about 8% of the population, yet they account for 22% of those considered homeless ("Probe into race link," 2002). In this society, Blacks are two to three times as likely as others to use homeless shelters (Culhane & Metraux, 1999).

No matter where it exists or whom it affects, homelessness in the United States has institutional causes: stagnant wages, changes in welfare programs, and, perhaps most important, the lack of affordable housing. As rising wealth at the top end of society drives up housing costs, the working poor are left unable to afford decent housing and have no federal or state programs to help (Shipler, 2004). In 2004, the Bush administration sought to cut the amount of rent subsidies in most large cities, forcing poor families to pay hundreds of extra dollars a month in rent (Chen, 2004).

According to the government, housing is considered "affordable" if it costs 30% of a household's income. The typical family hovering at or near the poverty line spends twice that—about 60% of its after-tax income—on housing. By comparison, the average middle-class homeowner spends only 23% of his or her after-tax income on house payments. In 2003, the nationwide median housing wage—the minimum amount of money a person would have to make to afford rental housing—was $15.21 an hour, close to three times the federal minimum wage and a 37% increase over the 1999 amount. At the state level, between 36% and 60% of renter households are unable to afford fair market rent for a two-bedroom apartment. Indeed, nowhere in the United States does a full-time, minimum-wage job provide enough income to afford adequate housing (National Low Income Housing Coalition, 2003).

Poverty's Border You will recall from Chapter 2 that the official poverty line for a family of four is an income of $19,157 a year. But because this figure is computed using outdated assumptions about people's spending patterns, it is likely set too low. Thus, it overestimates the number of families that earn an income high enough to be financially secure (thus rendering them ineligible for certain forms of governmental assistance) while underestimating the amount families actually need for economic stability and well-being.

Even if the method of computing the poverty line were revised to account for contemporary spending patterns, it would still be inadequate, because it is determined by current income alone. Economic factors that reflect a family's past, like assets and debts, are ignored. So, for example, a person who has racked up debt while unemployed or even in college but who has now found a job and is earning enough to rise out of poverty may discover that paying off past debts eats up so much income that he or she is actually worse off than before.

Thus, the official poverty statistics conceal the people who live on the fringe of poverty, often referred to as the "near poor" or the "working poor." According to the U.S. Bureau of the Census, 39 million people work full-time but earn such low income that they are struggling financially (Lalasz, 2005). These are the people who are employed but who face difficulties making ends meet. Their existence is fraught with irony. Because they fall above the poverty line, they escape academic attention and tend not to be the focal point of large-scale governmental assistance programs. At the same time, they are everywhere, doing the tasks with which others come into contact and on which they depend on a daily basis:

> They serve you Big Macs and help you find merchandise at Wal-Mart. They harvest your food, clean your offices, and sew your

clothes. In a California factory, they package lights for your kids' bikes. In a New Hampshire plant, they assemble books of wall-paper samples to help you redecorate. (Shipler, 2004, p. 3)

Beyond the financial difficulties and the relative invisibility, hovering on the margins of poverty has psychological consequences as well. For instance, the amount of food stamps one is allotted rises and falls as income changes. So every three months, people on food stamps must take time off of work and endure a humiliating meeting with their caseworkers to see if their food stamp allotment needs to be adjusted. The working poor who receive public assistance often find that they are treated with disdain when they come into contact with the various bureaucrats who act as gatekeepers to government programs (Gilliom, 2001). One woman on food stamps failed to include a utilities bill in the papers she provided to her caseworker. The caseworker punished her by withholding her food stamp benefits for two weeks. These types of interactions, coupled with the difficulties of managing relations with a boss, finding reliable day care, and coping with mountains of bills, can psy-chologically wither even the hardiest individual (Shipler, 2004).

The myth that surrounds economic disadvantage in this society is that people are poor or near-poor because they either don't work hard enough, don't care, or lack the skills and abilities to get ahead. Such an ideology works to justify social inequalities. If people suffer because of something they themselves have done (or have failed to do), then there's no reason to question the fairness of the economic system itself and therefore no motivation to rectify the situation at the structural level. The irony is that more than two-thirds of low-income people work (Lalasz, 2005). They frequently work long hours, sometimes in more than one job, often sac-rificing other aspects of their lives (such as family, education, and recre-ation) in the interests of economic survival. After years of disappointment and working hard just to barely get by, they either give up on the dream of economic comfort or slip back into poverty and government assistance.

THE ECONOMIES OF RACE

The economic outlook for ethnoracial minorities has shown some improve-ment over the last several decades. Asian Americans, in particular, continue to be better off financially than any other ethnoracial group, including non-Hispanic Whites. According to the U.S. Bureau of the Census (DeNavas-Walt, Proctor, & Mills, 2004), the median household income for people of Asian descent is $55,699 compared to $45,631 for Whites. In addition, 49.8% of Asian Americans attain a bachelor's or advanced degree compared to 27.6% of non-Hispanic Whites, 17.3% of African Americans, and 11.4% of Latino/as (U.S. Bureau of the Census, 2004). Nonetheless, the percentage of African American and Latino/a college graduates has risen steadily over the past 10 years, as has the proportion of ethnoracial minority families that could be considered middle or upper class. More black families are headed by married couples and more are living in homes they own than ever before ("Married households," 2003).

But this rosy economic picture has its share of thorns. African Americans, Latino/as, and Native Americans remain, on average, the poorest and most disadvantaged of all groups in the United States; their average annual income is still substantially below the national median. With the exception of Asian Americans, the rate of unemployment for people of color is almost twice as high as that of Whites (U.S. Bureau of the Census, 2004). Only about 57% of all Latino/a students complete high school (U.S. Bureau of the Census, 2004). And despite recent advances, workers from ethnoracial minorities tend to be concentrated in lower-paying jobs. Nineteen percent of American workers who earn minimum wage are African American and 17% are Latino/a (U.S. Department of Labor, 2004). African Americans make up 10.7% of the entire civilian U.S. workforce but only 3.6% of lawyers, 5.0% of physicians, and 4.4% of architects and engineers. Similarly, Latino/as make up 12.6% of the labor force but are underrepresented in the fields of law (4.0%), medicine (4.7%), and engineering (5.2%) (U.S. Bureau of the Census, 2004). At the same time, both groups are severely overrepresented in low-paying jobs (see Exhibit 8.4).

Exhibit 8.4: Ethnoracial Occupational Concentration, 2002

Occupations that are at least 25% African American	Occupations that are at least 25% Latino/a
• Taxi driver/chauffeur	• Private household cleaner/servant
• Postal clerk	• Maid/janitor
• Correctional officer/bailiff	• Gardener
• Security guard	• Sewing machine operator
• Nurses' aide/orderly/home health aide	• Construction laborer
• Barber	• Farmworker
	• Food preparation worker/dishwasher

(Source: U.S. Bureau of the Census, 2004)

Ethnoracial minorities are particularly vulnerable to economically motivated business changes, such as plant shutdowns, the automation of lower-level production jobs, and corporate relocations. For example, when a factory in a predominantly black or Latino section of a city moves to an all-white suburb, minority employees tend to face greater problems than white employees in securing housing in the new location or experience higher transportation costs in commuting to the job if they want to keep it.

The disappearance of blue-collar jobs has devastated many inner-city neighborhoods. As sociologist William Julius Wilson (2003) puts it:

> A neighborhood in which people are poor, but employed, is much different from a neighborhood in which people are poor and jobless. Many of today's problems in the inner-city . . . neighborhoods—crime, family dissolution, welfare, low levels of social organization, and so on—are fundamentally a consequence of the disappearance of work. (p. 301)

As populations drop and the proportion of nonworking adults rises, basic neighborhood institutions—stores, banks, restaurants, gas stations, and so on—become more difficult to maintain. Churches experience dwindling numbers and shrinking resources; clubs and community groups also suffer. As a consequence, formal and informal social controls in these neighborhoods become weaker. At such times, crime and violence are likely to increase, further deteriorating already troubled neighborhoods.

At the individual level, a person without a steady income falls into an irregular and incoherent life, lacking in specific expectations and goals. The effects are long-term, often crossing generations. As prospects for employment dwindle, the foundation of family relationships weakens. Children in households where adults are chronically unemployed or sporadically employed lack lessons in personal efficacy and the disciplined routines that come with steady employment. Furthermore, those who manage to become successful rarely stay in these communities, thereby depriving young people of contact with positive role models.

It's worth noting that the disappearance of work in inner-city ethnoracial enclaves is not just a matter of race, even though those most affected are members of ethnoracial minorities. It is a structural consequence of broad trends, namely deindustrialization and economic globalization, which lie largely above and beyond the control of the individuals who suffer the most. These trends are unlikely to change in the foreseeable future. Potential employers see deteriorating inner-city neighborhoods full of undesirable workers and decide that it is unwise to locate businesses or manufacturing facilities there. Even special federal tax credits that are provided as an economic incentive do little to draw new businesses to these areas. The concerns of these businesses are economic, not racial. But the result is that these neighborhoods have no opportunities for recovery, thereby compounding their destitution.

Intersections
Race, Class, and Immigration

Immigrants have always occupied a rather curious and ambivalent place in American society. In prosperous times, when labor is typically in short supply, they have been welcomed into this country as an essential contributor to the economy. In the early 20th century, their labor helped build roads and the U.S. rail system. They have historically filled unwanted jobs (such as landscaping suburban gardens, harvesting crops, laboring over a hot restaurant stove, or sewing clothes), opened businesses, and improved the lives of many U.S. residents.

But when times are lean or when political winds shift, they may become victims of exploitation, exclusion, hostility, and sometimes violence. Many individuals must tolerate insensitive treatment at the hands of supervisors. Some are denied promotions or fired without any explanation. More generally, they may be blamed for many of the country's economic and social woes. During these periods, people often describe the influx of immigrants as a "flood," subtly equating their arrival with disaster. In fact, in the wake of the September 11, 2001, attacks, immigration has become a national security issue. In 2003, the Immigration and Naturalization Service (now called the Bureau of Citizenship and Immigration Services) became part of the U.S. Department of Homeland Security, reflecting a major shift in the way immigration issues are defined.

The immigrants who bear the brunt of antagonism and resentment tend to be people of color from Latin America, Asia, or Africa. In the late 19th century, 90% of the immigrants who came to the United States were from northern and southern Europe. But in 2002, only 16.4% were from Europe. The bulk came from Asia (32%) and Latin America and the Caribbean (43%) (U.S. Bureau of the Census, 2004). In addition, 82% of undocumented immigrants come from Latin America; over two-thirds come from Mexico alone. This shifting configuration has changed the ethnoracial composition of the United States. In 1900, one out of every eight U.S. residents was of a race other than white; in 2005, the ratio is one in three; and by 2050, it is projected to be one in two (U.S. Bureau of the Census, 2004).

To the extent that expanded immigration means greater competition for unskilled jobs, working-class U.S. citizens of color are affected most. The issue of competition for jobs is especially volatile when it comes to illegal immigration. An estimated 5.3 million unauthorized workers are in the United States, including 700,000 restaurant workers, 250,000 household employees, and 620,000 construction workers. In addition, about half of all wage-earning farmworkers live here illegally (cited in Murphy, 2004). Despite the fiery rhetoric we hear frequently from politicians about closing the borders and cracking down on illegal immigrants, these workers play a vital role in the economy. Without them:

> Fruit and vegetables would rot in fields. Toddlers in Manhattan would be without nannies. Towels at hotels in states like Florida, Texas, and California would go unlaundered. Commuters at airports from Miami to Newark would be stranded as taxi cabs sat driverless. Home improvement projects across the Sun Belt would grind to a halt. And bedpans and lunch trays at nursing homes in Chicago, New York, Houston, and Los Angeles would go uncollected. (Murphy, 2004, p. 1)

Some economists argue that Social Security would go broke without payments from undocumented workers, many of whom—contrary to popular perceptions—pay income taxes (Murphy, 2004).

But others feel that these disadvantages would be short-lived if illegal immigration could be stopped. Employers would have to pay legal immigrants or citizens more to perform these (and other) tasks, but they'd get done. Prices for certain fruits and vegetables would spike initially, but farmers and agribusinesses would eventually find cheaper ways to harvest these crops. Some say that reducing our dependence on illegal labor (and cracking down on illegal immigration) would reduce stress on our social welfare system and relieve crowding in urban schools.

The issue remains unresolved. But one thing is certain: As long as American employers need cheap labor to maximize their profits, destitute foreigners see no occupational opportunities in their home countries, and U.S. immigration policy remains restrictive, people will continue to come here illegally in search of a better life.

THE ECONOMIES OF GENDER

In most countries around the world, women have much less earning power in the labor market than men (Cohen & Huffman, 2003). In the United States, the 1963 Equal Pay Act guaranteed equal pay for equal work and Title VII of the 1964 Civil Rights Act banned job discrimination on the basis of sex (as well as race, religion, and national origin). Yet a significant gender gap in earnings remains. According to the U.S. Bureau of the Census (2004), the median annual earnings for all U.S. men working full-time, year-round, is $39,429; the figure for women is $30,203. Thus, even among the fully employed, a woman still earns only about 76 cents for every dollar a man earns. The differences are even more pronounced for African American and Latina women, who tend to earn less than white women in general.

Why does the wage gap continue to exist? According to a recent report issued by the U.S. General Accounting Office (2003), work patterns account for the most variation in men's and women's earnings. Compared with men, women work fewer hours per year, are more likely to work part-time, and temporarily leave the labor force for longer periods than men.

Another reason is occupational segregation and the types of jobs women are most likely to have. One study of workers in major U.S. metropolitan areas found that women in female-dominated jobs earn the lowest wages (less than $6.95 per hour) while men in male-dominated jobs earn the highest wages ($11.60 per hour) (Cohen & Huffman, 2003). For the five "most female" jobs in the United States (that is, those more than 96% female)—preschool teacher, secretary, child care worker, dental assistant, and private housecleaner/servant—the average weekly salary is $407. For the five "most male" jobs (those less than 4% female)—airplane pilot, firefighter, aircraft engine mechanic, construction worker, and miner—the average weekly salary is $886 (U.S. Department of Labor, 2003; U.S. Bureau of the Census, 2004).

Some economists and politicians argue that the gender gap in wages is not an outcome of discrimination but is simply a by-product of the fact that men on the whole have more work experience, more training, and higher education than women. However, gender differences in education, labor force experience, and seniority—factors that might justify discrepancies in salary—account for less than 15% of the wage gap between men and women (National Committee on Pay Equity, 1999). For instance, the average income of full-time female workers in the United States is significantly lower than that of men with the same level of education or training. In fact, women with bachelor's degrees earn only a bit more than men with high school diplomas (median annual income of $30,788 versus $27,526). Similarly, women with a doctorate can expect to earn only slightly more than men with a bachelor's degree (median income of women with doctorates is $52,336 compared to $50,600 for men with bachelor's degrees) (U.S. Bureau of the Census, 2004). The logical conclusion is that wage disparities between men and women are not simply a consequence of different levels of education and training but instead reflect the pervasive institutional disadvantages that women of all races face in the labor market.

Intersections
Race, Gender, and the Poverty of Single Parenthood

As we've already seen, poverty is not equally distributed among different races or genders. But the combination of race and gender, especially when coupled with marital status, creates a recipe for financial disaster. The poor people who receive government assistance in this society are predominantly women (and their children), disproportionately non-white, and almost exclusively single parents. In this country, women are more likely than men to be the sole caregivers of children born out of wedlock and more likely to have custody of children after a divorce (Hays, 2003). As a result, one out of every four children in the United States lives with only their mother. And 52% of these children are poor (Fields, 2003; Fields & Casper, 2001). Twenty-eight percent of single-mother families are poor compared to 13.5% of single-father families (DeNavas-Walt, Proctor, & Mills, 2004).

The reason so many single mothers are poor is that they suffer from what some sociologists have called the "triple whammy." First, like all women, they are paid lower wages than men when they work. Second, like all mothers who work outside the home, they must juggle paid and unpaid work. Taking care of children when employed requires the time and flexibility that few low-paying or part-time jobs provide. Finally, unlike married mothers, single mothers must perform this feat without the help of another adult (Albelda & Tilly, 2001). Child-rearing responsibilities restrict single mothers' economic opportunities by limiting their work schedules and job locations, their availability to work overtime, and their ability to travel, attend conferences, take off-hour training workshops, and take advantage of other chances for advancement.

Race compounds the problem. People of color have consistently been less likely than Whites to have the economic resources to get them through tough times. Because of lower marriage rates, women of color are also more likely than their white (and male) counterparts to become single parents.

The current welfare system further complicates the situation for single mothers. In the interests of reducing the welfare rolls, the government enacted massive reforms in 1996. As a result, financial assistance to the poor is no longer a federal entitlement. Instead, each state receives a block grant and decides for itself how best to distribute the money to needy individuals. In addition, eligibility is limited, recipients are required to seek employment after two years of receiving benefits, and there is a five-year lifetime limit on benefits. The idea behind such restrictions is that mandatory work requirements will teach welfare recipients important work values and make poor single mothers models for their children. The irony is that the prototype of the "good mother" in this society has always been the devoted stay-at-home mother. Yet, for poor single women on public assistance, such a goal is not only unattainable but discouraged. Even though raising children can provide far more satisfaction for many poor women than the drudgery of a low-paying, dead-end job, they are forced to place their work roles above their parent roles. They must often work long hours, and because these jobs frequently lack sick leave or paid vacation, poor working mothers may have trouble taking time off to care for sick children.

The tragedy of such a trade-off is that even when poor single mothers work, the employment opportunities that are available to them are insufficient to provide any financial stability for their children. One study of 100,000 welfare recipients found that three years after leaving the welfare system and getting jobs, 70% of them still earned wages that placed them well below the poverty line (Economic Roundtable, 2000). Most women who leave the welfare rolls for work eventually return to public assistance because they aren't earning enough to make ends meet.

Even though single parenthood is so closely related to poverty, it doesn't necessarily follow that marriage is an easy escape. In 2004, the Bush administration proposed a $1.5 billion initiative that would promote marriage, especially among low-income couples, by training couples in the interpersonal skills needed to cooperate in maintaining a household. They cited evidence showing that children fare best, financially and emotionally, when raised in married, two-parent families (Pear & Kirkpatrick, 2004). This approach may have merit. But what it overlooks is that two-parent households are best for children only when the family is financially stable. Most women end up marrying men of their same social class, which in this case means either poor or working-class men. So the family is still subject to financial stress. Although married couples, on average, may be wealthier than single mothers, marriage in and of itself cannot lift single mothers out of poverty (Ehrenreich, 2004).

Many poor single mothers themselves don't see marriage as the solution to their economic problems. Sociologist Kathryn Edin (2003) interviewed 130 poor black, white, and Puerto Rican single mothers in Philadelphia. She found that most of them want to marry but only if they can marry men who represent upward mobility and who are not abusive. Such men, they point out, are in short supply in the neighborhoods in which they tend to live. Mothers whose boyfriends live with them often impose a "pay and stay" rule, kicking the men out if they aren't employed and are not contributing toward household expenses. As one Puerto Rican mother put it:

> I didn't want to be mean or anything, [but when he didn't work], I didn't let him eat my food. I would tell him, "If you can't put any food here, you can't eat here. These are your kids, and you should want to help your kids, so if you come here, you can't eat their food." Finally, I told him he couldn't stay here either. (quoted in Edin, 2003, p. 164)

These mothers are all too aware that any additional threat to their precarious financial situation, even when it involves someone they care deeply for, can be tragic for them and for their children.

Edin's research is important because it shows that very few women avoid marriage simply to maintain their welfare eligibility, as many critics claim. In fact, marriage is often a marker of respect in ethnoracial minority communities. They remain unmarried because they have come to the rational conclusion that marriage would actually make their lives more difficult. If they can't enjoy economic stability and respectability from marriage, they see little reason to expose themselves or their children to men's unreliability, economic dependence, and perhaps even violence.

ON THE JOB: RACE, CLASS, GENDER, AND SEXUALITY IN THE WORKPLACE

Work is a key component of the identity and the self-esteem of most American adults. Upon meeting someone, we typically ask, "So, what do you do?" This question is not so much about how you occupy your time but about who you are.

Unfortunately, we are not always free to choose any occupation that appeals to us. Large-scale economic trends, which may make certain jobs scarce or even obsolete, are only part of the picture. Race, class, gender, and to some degree sexuality can also influence the way people prepare for occupations, whether or not they get hired in the first place, how they're treated on the job, and their prospects for promotion. Consequently, discrimination can impact not only economic stability but how people ultimately define themselves and others.

PROFESSIONAL TRAINING

The influence of race, class, gender, and sexuality on people's work experiences begins early. For instance, a study of third-year medical school students reveals that although the proportions of women, people of color, and openly identified gay, lesbian, and bisexual students enrolled in North American medical schools have all increased over the past 40 years, subtle forms of bias still create a climate that can marginalize and alienate them (Beagan, 2001). Women report being mistaken for nurses, being called "girls," and being ignored by instructors. Students of color report high degrees of racial segregation in extracurricular activities. Students from poor and working-class families describe their struggle to construct the "right look," the professional appearance they feel is expected in medicine. Students from upper- and upper-middle-class backgrounds seem to have an easier time "fitting in." Such subtle inequities may appear normal, natural, and acceptable. However, they convey unmistakable information about who does and who doesn't belong.

In pursuit of a better understanding of identity-based inequities in professional training, sociologist Robert Granfield (2005) conducted in-depth interviews and surveys with students attending a prestigious East Coast law school. He was especially interested in the experiences of students who came from poor or working-class backgrounds. Initially, the working-class students saw their class background as a badge of honor, indicating how far they had come and what they were able to overcome. Many of them entered the legal profession in the first place because they wanted to help the downtrodden. But the students quickly came to see their working-class backgrounds as a burden. For instance, they became self-conscious of the way they spoke and noticed that their instructors assumed all students came from the same privileged class background. Their feelings of "differentness" added a layer of stress to the already stressful experience of being a law school student. They worried that, despite their solid academic records, they wouldn't make it.

Rather than simply dealing with their feelings of alienation, many working-class students actively tried to distance themselves from their background. They often tried to mimic the more privileged students in terms of dress, speech, and demeanor. Some students in Granfield's study reported that their ultimate success in the legal profession came from their ability to appear privileged.

But the costs of such success can be steep, and not just because the strategy may ultimately fail. Many working-class students of color were unable to shed the stigma of their class background or the suspicions of others about their credentials and continued to feel like outsiders. Furthermore, law school—like medical school and other professional and graduate schools—takes a tremendous amount of work. Success often comes to those who can invest enormous amounts of time and energy in their studies. Spending time perfecting the accoutrements of an upper-class lifestyle necessarily takes time away from one's coursework, putting these students at a competitive disadvantage in the classroom. Finally, many of these students ended up feeling deceptive and experienced the added burden of believing that they had "sold out" and let their group down.

THE CORPORATE CLOSET

The Civil Rights Act of 1964 says that a person cannot be denied a job or fired from existing employment simply because of his or her gender, race, religion, or ethnicity. Sexual orientation, however, doesn't currently enjoy such explicit federal protections. There are some safeguards against unfair treatment, however. Just prior to leaving office in 2000, President Clinton issued an executive order banning such discrimination for all civilian employees in the executive branch of the government. Numerous counties and municipalities—not to mention 14 states and the District of Columbia—also ban workplace discrimination based on sexual orientation (Leonard, 2003).

But the legal status of sexual minorities in the workplace remains complicated. Open homosexuality has traditionally been a sure ticket to the unemployment line. In many parts of the country, public school officials remain uncomfortable with the idea of having openly gay and lesbian teachers on their staffs.

Suspicions of homosexuality can sometimes be just as detrimental to people's careers as actual homosexuality. For example, the Ladies Professional Golf Association (LPGA) must constantly deal with what they call "the image problem"—the belief that many female professional golfers are hypermasculine lesbians. The viability of the association depends on its ability to address this perception. Thus, the LPGA public relations staff works hard to emphasize the femininity and heterosexuality of the golfers. For instance, they frequently publish articles on the dilemmas faced by wives and mothers on the tour (Crossette, 1997).

In many other workplaces as well, open homosexuality is still considered dangerous. Consider these examples:

- Currently, no active male professional baseball, basketball, hockey, or football player is openly gay. A few athletes in individual sports—most notably, tennis players Billie Jean King and Martina Navratilova, diver Greg Louganis, golfer Karrie Webb, and figure skater Brian Orser—have openly revealed that they are gay or lesbian. According to one web site, of all the athletes in any sport worldwide who have ever come out, only six (two major league baseball players and four professional football players) competed in a major American professional team sport. And all of these individuals made their revelations long after their playing days were over ("Out athletes," 2003). Some heterosexual athletes have publicly admitted that they would feel hostile toward a teammate who revealed that he was gay.

- In the 1980s, tens of thousands of men and women were discharged from military service for being homosexual, with white lesbians being the most common target. The open ban on homosexuality was replaced in 1993 by a "Don't Ask, Don't Tell" policy. According to this rule, military personnel are not asked about their sexual orientation and cannot be discharged simply for being gay. However, engaging in sexual conduct with a member of the same sex still constitutes grounds for discharge. Despite the prohibitions of the official policy, many gay and lesbian military personnel in Iraq are open about their sexuality or are known as homosexual to a majority of the troops in their units. There is no evidence that their presence undermines unit cohesion. Nevertheless, they report that the official policy impedes their ability to bond with their peers, to achieve maximum productivity, and to gain access to support services (Frank, 2004).

- In 2000, the United States Supreme Court ruled that the Boy Scouts of America could legally exclude gay men from employment in its organization, citing that it is a private, religiously based association and is free to choose its members however it wishes. The Boy Scouts claimed that gay troop leaders did not provide the sorts of role models they wanted young scouts exposed to.

Such open discrimination is becoming less common. In fact, corporate America appears to be at the forefront of a gay rights movement. Of the nation's top 500 companies—including such corporate giants as Apple Computer, IBM, Nike, Xerox, Levi Strauss, Eastman Kodak, Capital One, and Prudential—95% now officially forbid discrimination based on sexual orientation (Edwards & Hempel, 2003). Defense contractors such as Raytheon and Lockheed routinely sponsor gay support groups in their manufacturing facilities. American Express and Lehman Brothers promote their gay financial advisers in advertisements in gay, lesbian, bisexual, and transgender publications. More and more workers feel comfortable displaying a picture of a same-sex lover on their desks or bringing a partner to company gatherings.

All this is not to say, however, that gay and lesbian employees are free from corporate discrimination. Homosexuality is still legal grounds for firing an employee in 36 states. And in one survey, 41% of gay employees said they'd been harassed, pressured to quit, or denied promotion because of their sexual orientation (Edwards & Hempel, 2003). Indeed, some gay and lesbian workers believe that discrimination increases as they climb through the corporate hierarchy. There are only a handful of openly gay CEOs among the top companies in the country, and those who are gay are reluctant to discuss their sexuality publicly.

RACIAL DISCRIMINATION IN THE WORKPLACE

Members of ethnoracial minorities have historically faced enormous impediments in the business world, both as employees and as customers. In recent years, such top Wall Street companies as Prudential Securities, JP Morgan Chase, and Smith Barney have paid tens of millions of dollars to settle racial discrimination cases (Gasparino, 2004). In 1996, a former executive at Texaco revealed taped recordings of company officials using blatantly racist slurs and mocking symbols of Jewish and African American holidays. Black employees were sometimes called "porch monkeys" or "orangutans," asked to caddie golf games for their white bosses, or given birthday cakes decorated with rude caricatures and watermelon seeds. In addition to these personal indignities, they were also paid significantly less than white employees in the same positions (Solomon, 1996).

Evidence of less blatant institutional-level discrimination against customers can be seen in a variety of situations. For instance, loan companies usually demand a credit history, some form of collateral, and evidence of potential success before they will lend money to prospective businesses. These are standard business practices, but they perpetuate racial inequality because members of groups that have been exploited in the past tend to be poorer to begin with and thus have poor credit ratings and no collateral. Admittedly, poor people are greater credit risks than those with economic resources, and businesses in poorer communities must pay more for insurance because of the greater likelihood of theft or property damage. But of course, the higher costs of doing business in a poor community usually make small-business loans to minority group members even more indispensable.

Business concerns, not deep-seated racial hatred, are allegedly behind many other examples of racial discrimination by businesses:

- In 1999, a Miami restaurant was sued for its policy of adding an automatic 15% tip to the bills of black customers, a practice that was instituted because, according to the owner, "Blacks don't tip well" (Bragg, 1999).

- In 1999, the Adam's Mark Hotel in Daytona Beach, Florida, was charged with discriminating against African Americans who had gathered for the annual Black College Reunion. The lawsuit asserted that the hotel required black guests to wear orange wristbands to enter the hotel and pay a $100 damage deposit, a $25 deposit to have the room telephone turned on, and a $300 deposit for access to mini-bars. None of these policies applied to Whites staying in the hotel (Holmes, 1999).

- In the mid-1990s, a group of black customers sued the Denny's restaurant chain, claiming that the restaurant required Blacks to pay a cover charge or pay in advance for meals, refused to honor its free Birthday Meal offer to Blacks, subjected Blacks to racially derogatory remarks, threatened or forcibly removed black customers, and locked the doors so Blacks couldn't enter (Kohn, 1994, p. 44).

- In 2004, the Cracker Barrel restaurant chain agreed to overhaul its training and management practices after the U.S. Department of Justice accused it of widespread discrimination against African American diners in 50 locations. Black customers were routinely given tables apart from Whites, seated after white customers who had arrived later, and given inferior service. Rather than being isolated incidents committed by bigoted servers, the practices were a consequence of organizational policies to which managers directly contributed (Lichtblau, 2004).

In all these cases, senior executives, convinced that minority customers were costing their companies money, issued orders that were widely interpreted by employees to mean they had to discriminate on racial grounds (Kohn, 1994). The companies claimed that their actions were motivated by business concerns. Hence, they did not perceive them as racist but as a function of the competitive, profit-driven nature of the economic marketplace. Racial and ethnic discrimination in business settings is sometimes difficult to overcome precisely because it may occur for reasons other than overt racial or ethnic hatred. It is part of the taken-for-granted rules about doing business.

AFFIRMATIVE ACTION: OVERCOMING INSTITUTIONAL DISCRIMINATION

Although this sort of institutional discrimination may not be the result of conscious bigotry on the part of individual people, it is likely to be more harmful than personal discrimination in the long run and more difficult to stop. If tomorrow all people in the United States were to wake up completely free of any hatred, prejudice, and animosity toward other groups, institutional discrimination would still exist. As Chapter 5 explains, because it is a problem that often lies at the structural level, it requires a structural solution.

The most far-reaching structural attempt to solve the problem of institutional discrimination has been a loosely defined governmental policy developed in the 1960s referred to as **affirmative action.** Affirmative action is a program that seeks out or provides equal opportunities to members of ethnoracial minority groups and women for educational or occupational positions in which they had previously been underrepresented. The assumption is that past discrimination has left certain people ill equipped to compete as equals today. Another assumption is that organizations will not change discriminatory practices unless they are forced to do so.

The protections and remedies embedded in affirmative action policies have been used successfully in several areas of social life. Cities have bused children to schools outside their neighborhoods to reduce school segregation. Businesses, unions, universities, and local governments accused of discrimination in hiring or admission have been sued under the 1964 Civil Rights Act, fostering widespread attempts to increase diversity. In part because of such action, more than 40% of U.S. colleges and universities reported enrollment gains among African Americans and Latino/as during the mid-1990s (cited in Worsnop, 1996). People of color now hold a greater percentage of management, white-collar, and upper-level blue-collar jobs than ever before. Even young black men—historically the most economically disadvantaged and alienated group in the United States—are employed in record numbers (Nasar & Mitchell, 1999). Wages and salaries relative to those of Whites have also improved somewhat.

But today, affirmative action has also become a lightning rod for deeply held feelings about race, gender, and justice. Some politically liberal critics argue that the lives of people for whom affirmative action policies were originally designed—the poorest and most disadvantaged—remain largely unchanged. For instance, although top U.S. colleges are accepting more students of color, these students tend to come from middle-class or upper-class backgrounds. About 8% of Harvard's undergraduates are African American. But the vast majority of these students are West Indian or African immigrants, children of immigrants from these regions, or children of biracial couples. Only a few are from families in which all four grandparents were born in this country and were descendents of slaves

(Rimer & Arenson, 2004). It's these students who were supposed to be the beneficiaries of affirmative action. They are the ones most disadvantaged by decades of racial discrimination, poverty, and inferior educations.

In addition, universities are often more concerned with improving admission rates than with students' success once they're enrolled. Although the population of entering college students increasingly includes members of historically underrepresented ethnoracial groups, many schools don't provide enough support to ensure that these students actually graduate. The six-year graduation rate for Native American, Latino/a, and African American students is well below 50%, compared to 60% for white students and 65% for Asian students (Carey, 2005). Because a college degree is associated with success later in life (bachelor's degree holders earn about twice as much a year as those with high school diplomas), such educational disappointment can have far-reaching effects on the education system, the economy, and society at large.

Other critics consider affirmative action demeaning to the people it is supposed to help and unfair to everybody else. They say it undermines standards by favoring the unqualified. Conservative critics call it a form of "reverse discrimination." They argue that preferential treatment of any group, even one whose rights have been historically unrecognized, amounts to a form of discrimination, usually against those who have been historically advantaged, namely white males. They believe that enough has been done for minorities and that now the deck is stacked against Whites.

Contrary to popular belief, however, admissions officers and employers are not compelled to institute quotas or to compromise their standards to meet affirmative action goals. They are simply required to make sure historically underrepresented groups have access to application information, to gather all relevant information on all qualified applicants, and to offer both minority and majority candidates the same opportunities for interviews and the like (Cherry, 1989). Quotas have been only a last resort, reserved for situations in which organizations are not making good-faith efforts to seek out qualified minority candidates. For example, if a firm announces a job opening in newspapers that reach only the white community or uses discriminatory procedures to eliminate minorities from employment, the government can then impose quotas.

Ironically, those who are most likely to be treated preferentially when it comes to college admissions are largely white, affluent "legacies," or children of alumni. Playing favorites with alumni children is practiced at almost all private colleges and many public institutions as well. At some highly selective universities, legacies are twice as likely to be accepted as unconnected applicants with similar or better credentials (Larew, 2003). Some schools reserve a certain number of spaces for legacies. In one recent year at Harvard, marginally qualified legacies outnumbered all African American, Mexican American, Puerto Rican, and Native American students combined.

People in the United States strongly disagree about whether past discrimination entitles ethnoracial minorities to preferential treatment in education or hiring. When asked whether they favor affirmative action for "women and minorities," a majority of Americans (close to 60%) say they're in favor. But when asked about affirmative action for minorities only, the approval rate drops. And while black and white Americans may agree on the value of diversity, they disagree on such issues as whether affirmative action itself is discriminatory, whether people should be compensated for past discrimination, and whether black and white children have the same chance to get a good education ("Attitudes toward affirmative action," 2003).

Court proceedings reflect this ambivalence. In 1996, a federal court barred the University of Texas from using race as a factor in admissions. The Court implied that race-based affirmative action plans—even if used for the purpose of correcting racial imbalances—are discriminatory and therefore unconstitutional. Since this ruling, there has been a significant decrease in black and Latino/a admissions at the University of Texas. The number of white students admitted to the university has stayed the same, and the number of Asian American students has risen (Steinberg, 2003a). However, affirmative action was upheld in a landmark 2003 case involving admissions policies at the University of Michigan. The U.S. Supreme Court ruled that race may be considered in a limited capacity by universities in their admissions decisions. Immediately after this ruling, the University of Texas announced it would resume the practice of using race as a factor in admissions decisions (Winter, 2003). Though the Supreme Court decision addressed only policies in public, tax-supported institutions, it will no doubt have implications for private schools and businesses around the country.

Affirmative action remains a controversial solution to institutional racism. Even if economic opportunities have been equalized, it doesn't mean that the accumulated disadvantages of the past have been entirely erased. For a long time to come, members of certain ethnoracial minorities will continue to be underrepresented in traditionally white positions. Can U.S. citizens achieve complete equality without forcing those who have benefited historically to give up some of their advantages? The answer to this question is complex, controversial, and emotionally charged and will have a great impact on the nature of ethnoracial relations in the United States in the coming years.

GENDER AND WORK

Like members of ethnoracial and sexual minorities, women have a long history of discriminatory treatment in the workplace. Thus, before we talk about the relative positions of men and women in the paid labor force today, we have to trace a bit of history. As we'll see, the differential treatment of women in the workplace has, for centuries, been supported by a somewhat biologically based ideology that the different genders are naturally suited to different economic and occupational pursuits.

Separate Spheres Until the early to mid 19th century, the economies of most societies in the world were primarily agricultural. In the United States, people's lives centered around farms, where husbands and wives were interdependent partners in making a living; women provided for families along with men (Bernard, 1981). Although the relationship between husbands and wives on the farm was never entirely equal—wives still did most if not all of the housekeeping and family care—complete male dominance was offset by women's important contributions to the household economy (Vanek, 1980).

With industrialization, things began to change. New forms of technology and the promise of new financial opportunities and a good living drew people (mostly men) away from the farms and into cities and factories. For the first time in history, the family economy was based on money earned outside the household. Women no longer found themselves involved in the day-to-day supervision of the family's business as they had once been. Instead, they were consigned to the only domestic responsibilities that remained necessary in the growing industrial economy: the care and nurturing of children and the maintenance of the household.

The result was the development of a **separate spheres ideology,** beliefs that promoted the notion that women's natural place is in the home (the *private sphere*) and men's is in the work world outside the home (the *public sphere*). This ideal, in turn, fostered the belief that men and women are innately predisposed to different pursuits. Women were assumed to be inherently nurturing, demure, and sacrificial—a perfect fit for their restricted domestic roles. Their "natural" weakness and frailty were

assumed to make them ill suited to the dog-eat-dog life of the competitive labor force and to justify their limited job opportunities. The ideal for
men, on the other hand, was rugged self-reliance, power, and mastery of
job and family. Men were thought to be naturally aggressive, calculating,
rational, and bold—a perfect fit for the competitive demands of the marketplace. As long as men controlled the public sphere, they could wield
greater economic and political power within society and translate that
power into authority at home. The ideology of separate spheres was used
to justify restrictions on women's involvement in economic, political,
and educational activity and men's lack of involvement in family and
community.

In truth, the reality of American family life has never quite fit the
image painted by the ideology of separate spheres. Even in the late 19th
century, many women were in the industrial labor force. By 1900, one-
fifth of American women worked outside the home (Staggenborg, 1998).
But the experiences of working women varied along class and race lines.
For middle- and upper-class white women, few professions other than
teaching and nursing were available, and these jobs paid poorly. Most of
the women from these advantaged groups who did work entered and
exited the labor force in response to family demands or took up volunteer work to fill their free time. In contrast, poor women worked mostly
in unskilled jobs in clothing factories, canning plants, or other industries.
Working conditions were often dangerous and exploitative. The one thing
they shared with middle- and upper-class women was low pay compared
with men doing the same jobs.

The conditions for women of color were especially bad. Black domestic servants, for instance, frequently left their own families to live in their
employers' homes, where they were expected to work around the clock.
Throughout history, poor African American women have rarely had the
luxury of being stay-at-home spouses and parents. In 1880, 73% of black
single women and 35% of black married women reported holding paid
jobs. Only 23% of white single women and 7% of white married women
reported being in the paid labor force at that time (cited in Kessler-Harris,
1982). Ironically, the privileged, upper-class white women who could
afford to embrace the notion of separate spheres were able to do so only
because they depended upon other women—their servants—to do much
of the household labor (Boydston, 2001).

The years following World War II represented the heyday of the separate spheres ideology. Media messages emphasized women's obligations
to take their rightful position on the domestic front. Men pursued

advanced educational opportunities during this period, but few women entered college. Of those who did, two out of three dropped out before graduating. Most women left because they feared that a college education would hurt their marriage chances (Mintz & Kellogg, 1988) or because they had already married and chose to abandon their educational pursuits to turn their attention to raising their families (Weiss, 2000).

Since the 1950s, though, the boundary separating men's and women's spheres has steadily eroded. Exhibit 8.5 depicts these trends, in both higher education and labor force participation. In 1960, about a third of female high school graduates enrolled in college (compared to over 50% of male high school graduates). By 2001, 64% of women were enrolled in college, slightly higher than the percentage of men (60%) (U.S. Bureau of the Census, 2003b). In 1950, a little over 30% of adult women were in the paid labor force; today, around 60% of all women over 18 work in the paid labor force (U.S. Bureau of the Census, 2004). Furthermore, 69.2% of married mothers and 73.1% of single mothers are employed (U.S.

Exhibit 8.5: Historical Trends in Male and Female Preparation for and Involvement in the Economic Sphere

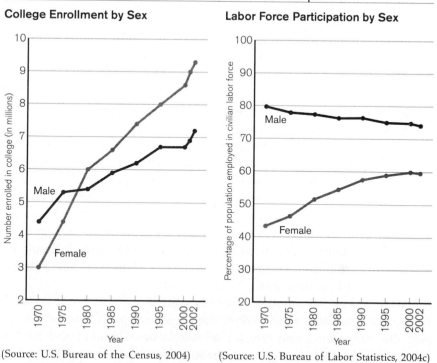

College Enrollment by Sex   Labor Force Participation by Sex

(Source: U.S. Bureau of the Census, 2004)   (Source: U.S. Bureau of Labor Statistics, 2004c)

Bureau of the Census, 2004). The increase in female labor force participation has been particularly dramatic in such traditionally male-
dominated fields as engineering, medicine, law, and administration. For
instance, in 1983, 15% of lawyers and 16% of physicians in the United
States were women; by 2003, those figures had nearly doubled (U.S.
Bureau of the Census, 2004).

Yet despite these trends, occupational segregation on the basis of sex
is still the rule and not the exception. According to the U.S. Bureau of
the Census (2004), in 2003, women constituted 96.6% of all secretaries,
92.1% of all registered nurses, 95.1% of all child care workers, 98.9% of
all dental hygienists, and 97.8% of preschool and kindergarten teachers.
Despite their increased presence in traditionally male occupations,
women are still underrepresented among dentists (23.7%), physicians
(29.9%), engineers and architects (14.1%), lawyers (27.6%), and law
enforcement officers (12.4%). Most of the changes that have taken place
in the sex distribution of different occupations come from women
entering male lines of work. Men have not noticeably increased their representation in female-dominated occupations. The number of male
nurses, kindergarten teachers, librarians, and secretaries has remained
low and virtually unchanged over the past two decades (U.S. Bureau of
the Census, 2004).

The separate spheres ideology persists in the home as well. On average, women who work full-time outside the home spend about 19 hours
per week on housework, while men spend only about 10 hours (cited in
Glazer, 2003). To be sure, the hours that women spend on housework are
down from an average of 32 hours in the mid-1960s and men have
increased their contribution from 4 hours per week, but still men contribute only half as much time as women do to the maintenance of the
household. According to a survey conducted by the U.S. Bureau of Labor
Statistics (2004b), only 19.5% of men report doing any housework and
35% report engaging in food preparation. By comparison, 55% of women
do housework and 66% prepare food. Even when a husband is unemployed, he does much less housework than a wife who puts in a 40-hour
week. Interestingly, husbands who say that all the housework should be
shared still spend significantly less time doing it than their wives (Institute for Policy Research, 2002).

What makes this situation especially troubling is that domestic work
is actually invaluable to the entire economic system. If a woman were
paid the minimum going rate for all her labor as mother and house-
keeper—child care, transportation, cleaning, laundry, cooking, bill paying,

grocery shopping, and so on—her yearly salary would be well over $35,000, more than the average salary of male full-time workers ("Mom's market value," 1998). But because societal and family power are a function of who brings home the cash, such work does not afford women the prestige it might if it were paid labor. As you can see, the persistence of gendered expectations regarding "proper" pursuits for men and women— even if they aren't a completely accurate portrayal of people's real lives—is important.

Gender Discrimination in the Workplace The standard assumptions that drive the typical workplace often subtly work against women. Think of the things a person generally has to do in order to be considered a valuable worker by a boss: work extra hours, travel to faraway business meetings, go to conferences, attend training programs, be willing to work unpopular shifts, entertain out-of-town clients. Notice how these activities assume that people will have the time and the freedom from familial obligations to do them. Because women, especially mothers, still tend to have the lion's share of responsibility at home, they have more difficulty making time for these activities than male employees do and therefore are less able to "prove" to their bosses and co-workers that they are committed, enthusiastic employees.

The deep-seated nature of assumptions about what one needs to do to get ahead is reflected in the experiences of men and women who cross traditional gender lines in their jobs. Women in traditionally male occupations (like law, medicine, and engineering) carry extra burdens as they try to adjust to the workplace expectations and overcome the prejudices of others. When college students were asked to evaluate two highly qualified candidates for a job in engineering—one had more education; the other had more work experience—they preferred the more educated candidate 75% of the time. But when the more educated candidate had a female name, she was picked only 48% of the time (cited in Angier & Chang, 2005).

In addition, women's wages don't measure up to men's in traditionally male occupations, and women are more likely than men to face subtle obstacles to promotion to a management position, a phenomenon sometimes called the **glass ceiling** (Padavic & Reskin, 2004). For instance, the median weekly income for male lawyers is $1,619, but female lawyers with the same seniority earn only $1,413 a week. Likewise, female physicians and surgeons make, on average, $688 a week less than male physicians and surgeons (U.S. Department of Labor, 2003).

Female lawyers report that they are often given low-status projects to work on, which are not only less interesting but also a professional dead end. Consequently, their rate of promotion is lower than that of their male counterparts, and they remain underrepresented in private practice, law firm partnerships, and in such high positions as judges on the federal courts, district courts, and circuit courts of appeals. In addition, women are more likely than men to enter the legal profession in relatively low-paying positions in the government or in public interest firms, hampering the trajectory of their careers (Hull & Nelson, 2000).

Similarly, although it is much easier for women to become physicians today than it once was, they still face pressures and problems that their male counterparts rarely face. Not only are they paid less relative to men at similar career stages; they also tend to be segregated into particular specialties that reflect common gender expectations. For instance, 70% of obstetrics/gynecology residents today are women (Lewin, 2001). In addition, female physicians who want to alter their work schedules to fulfill parental roles sometimes face unsympathetic male colleagues. Male doctors may feel that their female counterparts will not perform their fair share of unappealing tasks, such as being on-call around the clock (Lowes, 2002).

The relatively few men who cross gendered occupational boundaries tend to have entirely different experiences. Male nurses, librarians, or elementary school teachers may confront some prejudices and discrimination from people outside the profession, particularly assumptions regarding their sexuality. But with the exception of fashion modeling and prostitution, men in traditionally female occupations consistently outearn women (Williams, 2004). Male secretaries make about $40 a week more than female secretaries. And male nurses can expect to earn $119 more per week than female nurses (U.S. Department of Labor, 2003). In fact, men who want to be librarians or nurses or secretaries discover that there is actually a preference for hiring them. And the more women there are in an occupation, the greater men's—and especially white men's—chances of being promoted into supervisory positions (Maume, 1999). These men sometimes ride a **glass escalator**—invisible pressures to move up in their professions, often regardless of their desire to move up. For instance, a male nurse who just wants to take care of patients might be encouraged, even expected, to become a floor supervisor or pursue a position in hospital administration.

The problems women face in the workplace are not confined to nontraditional occupations. For instance, women who work as salesclerks in department stores are likely to be in the lower-paying departments (for example, clothing and housewares), whereas men are likely to be in the more lucrative departments (for example, furniture and large appliances). In 1997, Home Depot, the home improvement discount chain, paid $87.5 million to settle a lawsuit brought by female employees who claimed they were systematically relegated to cash register jobs rather than given higher-paying sales positions.

In 2004, a federal judge ruled that a class action, sex-discrimination lawsuit against Wal-Mart, the nation's largest employer, could proceed because of evidence that it had systematically paid female workers less than male workers and had given them fewer promotions. The suit could eventually include as many as 1.6 million current and former female employees. The pay disparities at Wal-Mart exist in every region of the country and in most job categories. And the salary gap widens over the span of workers' careers, even for men and women hired at the same time in the same job (Joyce, 2004). For instance, a female assistant store manager in one California store made $23,000 a year less than a male assistant manager with the same seniority. Although 65% of all Wal-Mart employees are women, only 33% of managers are women (Greenhouse & Hays, 2004).

Intersections
Gendered Racism in the Workplace

Sociologists Yannick St. Jean and Joe Feagin (1998) were interested in the double burden of gender and race on people's work-related identities. They conducted in-depth interviews with middle-class African American men and women to understand how the distinctive combinations of race and gender affect their everyday work lives.

The researchers conclude that discrimination against African American women is pervasive in workplaces. They may face stereotyping, excessive demands, and exclusion from friendship groups. Frequently, black women carry the stigma that comes with the assumption that they were hired because of their race and gender and not because of their qualifications for the job. Hence, the question of their ability is raised over and over. Sometimes, such questions are camouflaged, as when ordinary competence is seen as remarkable and worthy of praise. Here's how a school counselor described this experience:

> What I resent is, a lot of times that if I do something and do it well, it's like "Oh my God," like they are so surprised. "Oh, you write really

well. You speak really well." . . . They thought they were compliment-
ing me. But, actually, I was a little offended. . . . I got the feeling it was
like, ". . . You are black and I did not know you could really talk like
that." (quoted in St. Jean & Feagin, 1998, p. 42)

However, St. Jean and Feagin note that black women are often more
acceptable to white male managers, supervisors, and co-workers than black
men. From a white male manager's perspective, black women can be controlled
and managed more easily than men. As one white male accountant noted:

If there's a choice between a black woman and black man, all
things being equal, the black woman will be given the benefit of the
doubt. . . . I'm not saying that black women are necessarily less aggressive, or anything like that, but it's sometimes too intimidating. . . .
Corporate America would probably rather deal with a black woman
than a black man (quoted on p. 57).

There is a long tradition, dating back to Reconstruction, of black women
being the sole or primary breadwinners in their families. Today, black women
have actually seen their opportunities increase relative to black men's. According to the U.S. Bureau of the Census (2004), more black women than men go
to and graduate from college and more work as professionals. In 2000, over
1 million black women were enrolled in undergraduate and graduate programs
at American colleges and universities, compared to 635,000 black men.
Between 1977 and 1997, the number of bachelor's degrees awarded to black
men increased by 30%, while the number increased by 77% for black women
(cited in "Report on Black America," 2000). In addition, college-educated black
women generally hold better-paying jobs than black men.

You can see that combining race and gender reveals subtle nuances in the
way discrimination functions in employment situations. Hiring a black woman
may provide a company with "evidence" that it is "diversifying" its workforce.
However, the gendered nature of hiring practices obscures the underlying
biases that still exist.

CONCLUSION

I've spent a lot of time and space in this chapter assessing economic and
occupational inequalities based on race, ethnicity, gender, class, and sexuality. The progress that has been made in overcoming the blatant and massive inequalities of the past is real and commendable. But the progress is
incomplete. And even though things aren't as bad as they once were, the

dogged persistence of economic inequality—borne out by official statistics as well as people's everyday experiences—is troubling.

So as I conclude this chapter, I'm left with a perplexing sociological question. Given the undeniable economic inequality that exists both locally and globally today, why aren't we more bothered by it? Why aren't we distressed by the misery and hardships of others? Why aren't there massive demonstrations over the growing gap between the very rich and the very poor? Do we see poverty, unemployment, and homelessness simply as unfortunate side effects of an economic system that works the way it's supposed to? I think the answers lie less in the factual reality of economic inequality than in our own perceptions of it. Just because inequalities exist does not necessarily mean that people will perceive them as unfair.

Let me explain. *Equality* means that people get the same things and are treated the same way. *Fairness*, on the other hand, refers to a situation in which people's outcomes are proportional to their inputs. In other words, fairness means that everybody gets what they deserve. Imagine two people investing in a particular stock. Person A invests $1,000; Person B invests $100,000. If they both get the same rate of return on their investments, you'd expect that Person B's profit would be 100 times greater than Person A's, right? Their objective payoffs would be extremely unequal, but most people would consider them to be perfectly fair. Why? Because Person B invested more and therefore deserves more in return. By separating equality from fairness, we can see that a situation that appears unequal can still be considered fair.

In a situation where the investments and payoffs are obvious, the difference between equality and fairness is easy to see. But can we apply this kind of fiscal thinking to the sorts of inequalities discussed in this chapter? If we define an investment as anything that entitles a person to certain outcomes, then personal traits and even elements of one's social identity can count as an investment. If you believe, for example, that men have more to offer in the paid labor force than women (because you think they're stronger, more rational, more competitive, and so on), then you probably wouldn't think it's unfair to pay them more than women, even if they're in the same occupation. Similarly, if you believe, as some retail chains have argued, that white people in sales positions bring certain financial advantages into a situation (for instance, that customers feel more comfortable around them or that they're more trustworthy), then you might conclude that they "deserve" to be given more visible and more lucrative positions than members of ethnoracial minorities do. It's only when we can convince ourselves that people are getting what they deserve that we can ultimately accept, and maybe even justify, their suffering.

All social movements that attempt to overcome past injustices— the Civil Rights Movement, the Women's Movement, the Gay Rights Movement—are about the same thing: human investments and the calculation of fairness. All have tried to make the claim that the unequal distribution of rewards in society (access to higher education, good-paying jobs, political participation, legal protection, effective medical care, and so on) is unjust. Showing that inequalities exist is the easy part. Reams of statistical evidence can back up claims that some people aren't getting as much as others. We can show that men and women get different salaries for the same job or that members of ethnoracial minorities are confined to certain occupations or that openly gay employees lose their jobs more frequently than heterosexuals.

The hard part is to prove, argue, or maybe simply assert that these inequalities are unfair. If differences in race, gender, class, or sexual orientation are accepted as unequal investments, then there is no unfairness, no injustice. When people claim that gays and lesbians don't deserve equal protection under the law because their behavior is immoral, they are essentially making an argument that homosexuality is not as high an investment as heterosexuality and therefore doesn't necessitate the same treatment under the law. Only when inequality is seen as unfair—when it becomes impossible to justify the different outcomes for certain racial, gender, class, or sexual groups on the grounds that some are more deserving than others—can meaningful social change occur.

[**INVESTIGATING IDENTITIES AND INEQUALITIES**]
Living on the outskirts of poverty: A balanced budget

This chapter has provided a lot of information on the lives of people who are economically disadvantaged. But even people whose income is above the official poverty line can sometimes find it difficult to make ends meet.

Imagine a family of four living in your hometown: a mother, a father, and two children ages three and seven. Suppose that both parents work full-time outside the home. They each earn the federal minimum wage: $5.15 an hour. If they both worked 40 hours a week, 52 weeks a year, they'd each earn roughly $10,712 for a total pre-tax household income of $21,424. Using the 2004 tax rate schedule, they would pay about $2,500 in income taxes, making their annual take-home pay $18,924. The parents' pre-tax income is more than $2,000 above the official poverty line for a family of four, which is $19,157 *before taxes*, so they are not "officially" poor.

Make a list of all the goods and services this family needs to function at a minimum subsistence level—that is, at the poverty line. Be as complete as possible. Assume that the seven-year-old attends school all day and the three-year-old must be cared for by someone during the day. Consider food, clothing, rent for an unfurnished two-bedroom apartment, household amenities, utilities (gas, electricity, water, sewage, trash, if applicable), transportation, medical care, child care, entertainment, and so on.

Now estimate the minimum monthly cost of each item. If you currently live on your own and must pay these expenses yourself, use those figures as a starting point (but remember that you must estimate for a family of four). If you live in a dorm or at home, ask your parents (or anyone else who regularly pays bills) what their expenses are for household goods and services. Call a local day care center to see what it charges for child care. Call local utilities companies to see what the average gas, electric, and water bills are in your community. Go to the local supermarket and compute the family food budget. Don't forget, you have to feed four people three meals a day, every day. For those items that aren't purchased on a monthly basis (for example, clothing and household appliances), estimate the yearly cost and divide by 12.

Once you have estimated the total monthly expenses, multiply by 12 to get the annual subsistence budget for the family of four. If your estimate is higher than the family's take-home pay, what sorts of items could you reduce or cut out entirely to make ends meet? Justify your choices about what categories of expenses can be reduced or cut. Did you have to make any tough choices (for instance, between money for food and paying the electric or gas bill)?

Describe the quality of life of this hypothetical family. What sorts of things are they forced to do without that a more affluent family might simply take for granted (for example, annual vacations, pocket money, a second car, eating out once a week)? What would be the impact of poverty on the lives of the children? How will the family's difficulty in meeting its basic subsistence needs translate into access to opportunities (education, jobs, health care) for the children later in life?

CHAPTER 9

The Futures of Inequality

ike many young American kids, my early reading experiences included
piles of colorful books by Dr. Seuss. Of course, being six years old and
struggling with all those peculiar words and creatures, I didn't notice at
the time that there were deeper meanings—sometimes even controversial
sociopolitical messages—cleverly buried in these silly stories. I just liked
the pictures and the rhymes.

Let me tell you about a Seuss short story called *The Sneetches*. This
tale is about two types of bird-like creatures called Sneetches, who are
physically indistinguishable from each other except for one key characteristic. The Star-Belly Sneetches sport green stars on their bellies. The
Plain-Belly Sneetches have bare bellies. The green stars are small and
barely noticeable. Nonetheless, the Star-Belly Sneetches are elitist snobs
who interpret the stars as symbols of their lofty status. And they spend

most of their time figuring out ways to belittle, exclude, and discriminate against the Plain-Belly Sneetches. The Plain-Bellies are kept out of all sorts of social activities including picnics, parties, and children's games.

The Plain-Bellies develop a massive inferiority complex, reflected in their sad, mopey faces. They seem to spend all their time wallowing in envy, wishing they had stars on their bellies like their more advantaged counterparts.

Then one day, everything changes. A stranger arrives in town, promising that for $3 he can fix things for the Plain-Belly Sneetches. He has them walk into an odd-looking contraption, and miraculously they emerge from the other end with stars on their bellies. The formerly Plain-Belly Sneetches are ecstatic. They've successfully leveled the playing field, and they fully expect to be treated as equals from now on.

Though the original Star-Belly Sneetches are dismayed by the fact that it'll be hard for them to tell which Sneetch is which, they continue to believe in their own superiority. But they need some way to prove it. At that point, the stranger approaches the Star-Belly Sneetches and promises that he can easily return them to their place of privilege. He assures them that "Belly stars are no longer in style," and that for a mere $10 each, his machine can remove theirs. They gladly pay the money. Once they are all star-less, they parade around singing the virtues of their own dominance, this time based on their now plain appearance.

Things get messy at this point. The Plain-Belly Sneetches have smelled the sweet aroma of equality and don't want to return to their lowly status. As is always the case when powerful groups feel their position is being threatened, the historically advantaged Star-Belly Sneetches will do anything to maintain their privilege. So each group pays more and more money to the stranger to either add or remove belly stars depending on whether they want to look like or distinguish themselves from the other group. Pretty soon, both groups go broke, and the stranger skips town.

The story ends on a high note as the Sneetches suddenly realize that they're all alike and all equal, regardless of whether they have belly stars or not. It's not clear why they start thinking this way; after all, they've lost all their money. But it's the sort of "happily ever after" ending that little kids can live with.

We see illustrated in this children's storybook, unmistakably and importantly, the socially constructed nature of difference and inequality. As is the case in human societies, positions of dominance and subordination do not automatically rise from natural and inherent characteristics but from socially created and sometimes arbitrary ones. Dr. Seuss's story provides an appropriate introduction to this final chapter on the futures of social inequalities because it shows, albeit in a simplified and fanciful way, the malleability of social relations and the possibility of change.

What the story gets wrong, however (and, of course, we can't expect Dr. Seuss to touch all the sociological bases), is that although the differences that foster inequalities may be socially created, they're rarely, if ever, so interchangeable or capricious as they are in this story. Those groups with little power seldom have the wherewithal to create social equality, let alone turn the tables of stratification, by altering the perceptions of more dominant groups. And within a given society, ideologies of inequality based on race, gender, class, and sexuality become embedded in the culture and in important social institutions to the point that they're difficult to reverse.

The 19th-century British statesman William Gladstone once said, "You can't fight against the future" (quoted in Seldes, 1985, p. 161). Still, definitions of difference are not always permanent and universal. The criteria used to determine social inequalities can vary across time and from culture to culture. Thus, the future is not some inevitable destiny that looms around the temporal bend. Just like societies of the present, future societies are molded and shaped by human action. I've chosen to use the word "futures" rather than "future" in the title of this chapter to reinforce this idea that our experiences with inequality are not set in stone. We have the ability to determine the course of ethnoracial, class, gender, and sexual identities in the future. We can choose to live in a society that continues to be structured around unequal privilege, or we can transform society into one marked by authentic equal relationships and opportunities.

POSSIBILITIES: ALTERING INEQUALITIES

One of the inherent difficulties in promoting equality—and one that should be fairly obvious by now—is that even though inequalities are created and maintained by people in their interactions with others, they eventually make their way into impersonal social institutions, where they become embedded and somewhat impervious to individual action. Institutions, by their very nature, are quite resistant to social change. Often, what are needed to influence institutional change are organized, large-scale, collective actions known as **social movements.** The Civil Rights

Movement, the Women's Movement, the Labor Movement, the Living Wage Movement, the Gay Liberation Movement, and others have achieved some notable successes over the years but have never completely altered the institutional landscape. So, as we've seen in Chapters 5 through 8, institutional inequalities based on race, gender, class, and sexuality remain the rule rather than the exception in our day-to-day lives.

Consequently, the task of transforming entire systems of privilege and disadvantage or even resisting their influence on a personal level seems daunting. Students in sociology courses commonly leave at the end of a semester feeling as if there's nothing they can do to change structures that systematically work to the advantage of some at the expense of others. "What's the use?" "The problem's too big!" "You can't fight City Hall!" "I give up!" Maybe you're feeling that way right now. But many people underestimate their ability to impact social institutions.

Even though the structure of society seems massive and often detached from the desires of ordinary people, it ultimately depends on human actions for its very survival. People can and frequently do change things. Whether through acts of support or defiance, we create and re-create the very social institutions under whose powerful influence we live. Our history is filled with stories of individuals and groups of individuals who—for better or worse, depending on your position—have altered the course of society.

Some of the most influential individual acts may at first blush appear rather insignificant. One of my favorite examples concerns the activities in 1960 of four black students at North Carolina Agricultural & Technical State University in Greensboro. Ezell Blair, Franklin McCain, Joseph McNeil, and David Richmond spent a lot of time talking in their dormitory rooms about the state of the Civil Rights Movement. They knew about bus boycotts in Alabama and the desegregation of schools in Arkansas. But they didn't think that enough was being done in the still-segregated South. They decided it was time for them to contribute to the effort.

What they decided to do was to go to the lunch counter at the local Woolworth's department store and order coffee and doughnuts. That might not seem like such a big deal to people in the 2000s, but in the 1960s South, Blacks were forbidden by law to eat in facilities that weren't designated as being "for Blacks only." After buying some school supplies in another part of the store, they sat down at the lunch counter and placed their orders. As they expected, the stunned waitperson replied, "I'm sorry, we don't serve you here" (McCain, 1991, p. 115). They stayed there for 45 minutes, politely pointing out that they had been served in another part of the store without any difficulty. Angry white customers gathered around, shouting racial slurs at them and even trying to forcibly remove them. The four students never responded and never fought back. They simply sat there waiting to be served until the lunch counter closed for the day.

Unlike speeches and boycotts, the acts of these four young men openly and directly defied the entrenched system of everyday segregation. They attracted the attention of religious leaders, community activists, and students from other area colleges, both black and white. Despite the abuse they knew would await them, they returned a few days later, only this time with more demonstrators. At one point, they and their fellow protestors occupied 63 of the 65 seats available at the lunch counter. This was the first social movement covered by television, so word of their actions spread quickly. They received endorsements from religious organizations like the North Carolina Council of Churches. Within weeks, young African Americans and sympathetic Whites had engaged in similar acts in nine states and 54 cities in the South as well as several areas in the North, where stores were picketed. After several months of protests, Woolworth's integrated its lunch counter.

The "sit-ins," as they came to be called, eventually proved to be one of the most effective tactics of the Civil Rights Movement: "The students sat in. Went to jail, came out, sat in again. Marched. Picketed. Sat in again. And went to jail again. They simply would not stop" (Farmer, 2004, p. 1). Indeed, some sociologists have argued that many of the social movements for change that burst onto the scene in the 1960s—including the Women's Movement, the Antiwar Movement, and the Student Free Speech Movement—could trace their philosophical and tactical roots to the actions of these four students (Cluster, 1979). Today, college students have staged sit-ins to protest the working conditions in clothing and footwear factories overseas and to protest the war in Iraq. Admittedly, the participants in these movements might have developed the sit-in as a tactic on their own, even if those four Greensboro students had been served coffee and doughnuts at Woolworth's. The point is, though, that the widespread collective movements that arose from the actions of these individuals in 1960 had an enormous impact on the massive changes that occurred in the United States and beyond over the next 40 years.

But you'll also notice that these four young men alone couldn't change things on their own. It takes more than the actions of oppressed individuals for meaningful, long-term change to occur. The movements for social change that tend to be the most effective must successfully frame the unfairness of particular social phenomena to gain support from various segments of the population. They must also be well organized (often at the national or even international level), have a coherent set of beliefs, values, and ideas, and make use of current technologies to spread the word and mobilize resources. What's especially important is the formation of coalitions, the bringing together of different groups in different structural positions. Consider these examples of the power of coalitions:

- The Civil Rights Movement has been effective because participants have come from all racial groups and all geographic areas. Many of the individuals who fought successfully for Blacks' voting rights in Alabama and Mississippi during the late 1950s and early 1960s were middle-class white students from the North. When Blacks boycotted segregated buses in Montgomery, Alabama, in 1955 and 1956, Virginia Foster Durr, a wealthy white Southern woman, drove black workers to and from work every day so they wouldn't lose their jobs. Today, people like Morris Dees, a white attorney who gave up a lucrative law practice to devote his life to bringing white supremacists to trial, continue the battle for racial equality and equity (Ayvazian, 2001).

- The movement for gay rights has been bolstered by the participation and support of non-gay allies. PFLAG (Parents and Friends of Lesbians and Gays) is an organization of mostly heterosexuals who provide education and advocate on behalf of gays and lesbians. They speak at churches, schools, and community organizations, describing their commitment to protecting the rights of gays and lesbians. Their impact, which at times has been significant, arises from the fact that they are heterosexuals talking, for the most part, to other heterosexuals (Ayvazian, 2001).

- The current Living Wage Movement is made up of people who seek to require cities and counties to pay their low-wage workers an amount above the federal minimum wage. Initially, the people who were seeking to increase wages were the low-wage workers themselves. They weren't particularly effective in gaining public support. Only when religious organizations, labor groups, and college students got involved did the movement achieve some notable successes. Over the past 10 years, more than 100 cities have passed living-wage laws (Tanner, 2002).

In most cases, it's usually not enough simply for the people who are suffering the most from structural disadvantage to complain about their plight. The movements that are most effective in creating long-term institutional change are the ones that construct a broad coalition of supporters. These are the movements that may not only affect current social arrangements but also help shape future conceptions of race, class, gender, and sexuality.

FICKLE FUTURES

I've always envied television meteorologists. They can make weather-related forecasts, get them flat-out wrong on occasion, and still keep their jobs. In fact, their popularity (and hence their job security) has nothing to do with how accurately they predict the weather.

Arguably, there's more at stake when trying to forecast the future of the job market, race relations, the state of American families, or trends in health care and legal justice than when trying to predict if it's going to snow tomorrow. And yet, discussing the future of some key aspect of society—especially when inequality is part of it—may be even more suspect than predicting the weather. Human behavior is notoriously erratic. So sociologists usually talk about *projections* rather than *predictions*, implicitly acknowledging the impossibility of foretelling the future with any certainty. At best, we can examine past and current patterns and say something about what social life might look like if these patterns continue. With that caveat in mind, let's take a peek at some possible trends regarding social identities and inequalities in the future.

ETHNORACIAL OUTLOOKS

In 1900, Americans lived, for the most part, in distinctly separate racial worlds. In the South, it had only been a little over three decades since slavery was abolished, and a system of official, legally sanctioned segregation maintained unmistakable partitions between races. In the North, the dividers were less formal but no less powerful in maintaining racial boundaries and racial injustice. Few white Americans 100 years ago thought about, let alone questioned, racial arrangements, and Americans of color lacked the power to mobilize social movements and make their concerns heard. It's safe to say that most Americans in 1900 simply took the divided racial landscape of the United States for granted (Wolfe, 2000).

But on other dimensions, Americans in 1900 were actually much less divided culturally than they are today. For instance, whatever differences existed between a black American and a white American, chances were pretty good that both were Christian. Furthermore, they probably spoke the same language. The huge influx of immigrants at that time didn't disrupt that assumption. Many of them, like the Irish, came from countries that already spoke English; others, like Poles and Italians, believed that the only way they and their children would succeed in this country would be to assimilate, shedding the language and customs of the old country (Wolfe, 2000).

To someone living in the early 21st century, however, American society looks far more diverse. We can no longer speak of racial divisions along simple black-white lines. For instance, the racial configuration of the U.S. population has changed dramatically in recent years, due primarily to the unprecedented growth in Latino/a immigrants (Lee & Bean, 2004). Today, one in every eight U.S. residents is Latino/a. By 2035, it's projected that Latino/as will account for one in five residents. And, if current trends continue, by 2100, one in three U.S. residents will identify her/himself as Latino/a (Saenz, 2004). The continuing influx of Latino/a immigrants will virtually ensure that the Spanish language and elements of Latino/a culture will occupy an ever more prominent place in U.S. culture. Expect Latino/a groups to occupy more visible and powerful positions in the government, in the health care system, and in religious institutions as well.

It makes even less sense to talk about today's United States as a Christian country. Between 1990 and 2001, the U.S. Bureau of the Census (2004) reported significant growth in a variety of non-Christian religious groups, including Muslim, Buddhist, Hindu, Unitarian/Universalist, Scientologist, Baha'i, Taoist, New Age, Eckankar, Sikh, Wiccan, Druid, and Santeria. During that same time, many mainstream Christian churches (such as Methodists, Lutherans, and Episcopalians) witnessed little, if any, growth in their memberships. To people who believe that our national strength depends on a common system of moral thought, such religious diversity signifies a weakening of society. To people who believe that the values of tolerance, equality, and respect for difference are what define us as a culture, this growing religious diversity instead symbolizes our strength.

What's especially interesting to me—both as a sociologist and as a citizen of this country—is not simply how many people will be counted as members of particular groups in the future, but how race and ethnicity will be defined and how those definitions will affect cultural values and ethnoracial diversity. It seems to me that the future of diversity in this society can go in (at least) two possible directions. At one end of the continuum of possibilities is what some call a "post-ethnic" or "post-racial" society in which race and ethnicity no longer matter. At the other end is a society in which people make increasingly fine distinctions between and among ethnoracial groups, creating more boundaries than ever.

Evolving a Post-Racial, Post-Ethnic Society One possibility for the future is a society in which traditional racial and ethnic definitions would become obsolete or at the very least irrelevant. Ethnoracial boundaries could simply melt away with increasing numbers of interracial marriages and children born with multiracial, multi-ethnic identities. As one supporter of this projection put it, "we are getting past race the way humans always have: through races melding together" (McWhorter, 2004, p. 255).

The accuracy of such a projection rests, in part, on broader attitudes toward multiracial backgrounds. People who come from multiracial heritages feel less pressure today to claim a single, identifying race label than they once did. They might simply say, "my mother is white and my father is black" and leave it at that (McWhorter, 2004). Indeed, multiracial identities have been endorsed in some respects by the official definer and maintainer of racial and ethnic boundaries, the U.S. Bureau of the Census. Racial and ethnic labels changed with the 2000 census. Instead of simply reporting statistics for "Whites," "Blacks," "Asians," "American Indians or Alaska Natives," "Native Hawaiian or other Pacific Islander," and "Hispanics," the Census Bureau can now provide data for 63 possible racial categories including 6 categories for those who report they are members of exactly one race and 57 categories for those who report combinations of two or more races.

Because of this sweeping change, the Census Bureau urges caution in making historical comparisons among and between racial groupings on phenomena like median income and poverty. The change has other far-reaching implications as well. How can we have meaningful conversations about race relations and racial inequality if we have 63 different racial identity groups? Furthermore, as the number of people with some sort of "combined" identity increases, the mixtures will become more complex. Traditional ethnoracial boundaries may become fainter and less vivid, eventually disappearing entirely. The result could be a society in which race and ethnicity, literally and truly, don't matter. Either they wouldn't be noticed or they wouldn't be associated with character assessments. They wouldn't be predictors of social and cultural achievement and access to opportunities. And they wouldn't determine the quality of people's lives.

If we were to look only at the visible trappings of American popular culture, we might conclude that we already live in a "color-blind"—or at the very least, a color-vision-impaired—society:

> It is quite unremarkable to observe Whites, Asians, or African Americans with dyed purple, blond, or red hair. White, black, and Asian students decorate their bodies with tattoos of Chinese characters and symbols. In cities and suburbs, young adults across the color line wear hip-hop clothing and listen to white rapper Eminem or black rapper Jay-Z. A north Georgia branch of the NAACP installs a white biology professor as its president. . . . Du-Rag kits, complete with bandana headscarf and elastic headband, are on sale for $2.95 at hip-hop clothing stores and family-centered theme parks like Six Flags. Salsa has replaced ketchup as the best-selling condiment in the United States. Companies as diverse as Polo, McDonald's . . . , Walt Disney World, Master Card, Skechers . . . , [and] Giorgio Armani have each crafted advertisements that show a balanced, multiracial cast of characters interacting and consuming their products in a post-race, color-blind world. (Gallagher, 2004, pp. 575–576)

Nationwide surveys consistently show that the majority of Whites feel that members of other racial groups now have equal chances in getting jobs and are doing as well as or better than Whites. As the thinking goes, if personal and institutional discrimination have now been replaced by equality of opportunity, then the path to upward mobility runs directly through one's qualifications, not one's color or ethnicity. Certain groups' lack of success is therefore not a result of any systemic discrimination or ethnoracial barriers but is the fault of individuals who lack the ambition, initiative, or desire to succeed. And those who cite continuing racial discrimination as an impediment to their educational or economic achievement are branded as "reverse racists" whose claims are illegitimate or are accused of "playing the race card" to promote a political agenda. However, all evidence points to some stubborn pockets of discrimination. We must remember that the ability to ignore race—both as an essential component of one's identity and as a primary source of discrimination—always reflects the power and privilege of dominant groups.

I'm somewhat pessimistic about suggestions that race will ever be insignificant and that group boundaries will at some point disappear fully. Even in a country like Brazil, where racial mixing is more common and accepted than it is here, status and privilege are still connected to skin color. In the multi-hued future of the United States, there will still be some people who are considered more deserving (perhaps still on the basis of the lightness of their skin) than others (Cose, 2000).

I'm also pessimistic because, just like those Sneetches I described at the beginning of this chapter, humans have a strong tendency to find criteria for making us-them distinctions. Even if race disappeared, we'd draw influential boundaries on some other dimension. Maybe our distinctions will be based on what people have rather than what they look like. Perhaps resident status—native born versus immigrant—rather than race or ethnicity will someday function as the key construct in distinguishing "us" from "them."

If we look to other cultures, we can see that even something as apparently unimportant as the occupational status of distant ancestors can determine group distinctions and influence everyday life chances. Take, for example, the *burakumin*, the most disadvantaged minority in Japan, who represent about 2% of the population. Their low status dates back to the 17th century, when their role in society was to slaughter animals and dispose of the remains, acts that although necessary for society violated Buddhist principles (Kristof, 1995). The *burakumin* are biologically, religiously, and ethnically indistinguishable from other Japanese. Yet many Japanese people considered them a completely different race and innately inferior. They were forced to wear recognizable clothing and were restricted to living in special villages (the word *burakumin* literally means "people of the hamlet"). *Burakumin* were widely stereotyped as mentally weak, aggressive, impulsive, and dirty (Neary, 1986). Before marrying someone or hiring a new employee, some Japanese would have a detective check the background of a person for *burakumin* ancestors.

In fairness, the treatment and perception of the *burakumin* have improved somewhat in recent years. Today, almost two-thirds say they've never encountered discrimination, although many parents never tell their children that they are *burakumin*. More than 70% now marry non-*burakumin*, and most believe they are treated fairly by the police (Kristof, 1995). The Japanese government has invested large sums of money to improve *burakumin* neighborhoods so they are no longer unlivable slums. It ended these projects in 2002, concluding that enough had been done.

Despite these improvements, the *burakumin* still suffer compared to other Japanese citizens. They have the lowest income and educational attainment of any group in Japanese society and the highest rates of poverty, crime, alcoholism, single parenthood, and welfare dependency. And like some ethnoracial minority groups in the United States, their dependence on government assistance has created resentment from a public that believes they are getting special, undeserved help. Moreover, because many of them still tend to live in segregated ancestral villages, they are singled out for all manner of abuse and discrimination based on their addresses. Even today, families will abruptly terminate engagements if *burakumin* origins are uncovered. In 2004, a Japanese father threw his son's fiancée out of their home because she was found to be a descendent of the *burakumin*. The woman's father said he receives daily hate letters with messages like "You non-humans from the hamlets have blood that is vulgar and tainted" (quoted in Yamaguchi, 2004, p. A18).

Some younger *burakumin* advocate using the socially constructed nature of the stigma as a reason to actively reject it:

> Although we cannot choose our parents or birthplace, we can choose not to be fettered by them; and while not hiding the possibility that we might be labeled *burakumin*, we could positively reject it: I am not a *burakumin* if I say I am not. I might even recognize that my father was a *burakumin* but claim that I am not. (Neary, 2003, p. 285)

Just as arbitrary identities (in this case, the occupational status of bygone generations) can motivate discrimination, so too can they open the door to possible change. Perhaps someday in the United States, multiracial individuals will have the same opportunity to create a society in which ethnoracial identity, though still noticeable, loses its power to determine people's access to important life chances.

Subdividing Race and Ethnicity Another future possibility regarding race—not entirely distinct from the first one—is that instead of a new version of the "melting pot" in which race becomes obsolete, we will experience just the opposite: a growing number of more narrowly defined ethnic or national groups that will seek cultural, social, and legal recognition. In this scenario, we'd have more, rather than fewer, ethnoracial boundaries.

I've been arguing throughout this book that although most scholars (myself included) use broad labels like "Black," "Asian," "White," "Latino/a," and so on, there are numerous within-group subdivisions in each of these categories already—for example, Mexican-Americans and Cuban-Americans within the category "Latino/a." Perhaps in the interests of ethnic pride, each of those subgroups—as well as yet-to-be-defined new ones—will become a distinct social group in its own right. As a result, ethnic communities could become more isolated and insulated than those of the past. Some argue that such a trend is already evident:

> Their ethnic shopping malls, ethnic restaurants and groceries, in-language newspapers, one-country Rotary Clubs, community banks, ethnic movie theaters and other amenities often make it unnecessary to have much contact with the integrated main-stream. The more newcomers arrive from the old country, the larger and more all-encompassing these enclaves—both rich and poor—grow, reducing incentives to make the difficult transition to a mixed neighborhood. Meanwhile, geographic proximity and cheap air travel allow newcomers to shuttle back and forth to their home countries and, in some cases, to maintain dual citizenship and even vote in both places. (Jacoby, 2004, p. 7)

Maybe it's not so far-fetched to suggest that racial distinctions will become more narrow, specific, and personally significant in the future. As an analogy, consider what has happened to the world of "ethnic restaurants" today. In our largest and most ethnoracially diverse cities, it's not enough for an eatery to simply advertise itself as a "Chinese Restaurant" or an "Italian Restaurant" anymore. Instead, it must specify its regional or culinary accent: Hunan, Cantonese, Szechuan, Mandarin Chinese; Northern versus Southern Italian.

Will people in the future be content to identify themselves in terms of traditional broad ethnoracial markers, or will they begin to search for finer distinctions, providing them with a sense of uniqueness that they find lacking now? For example, will it be enough to be "Asian American" or will it be necessary to identify a regional heritage or country of origin, such as Korean American, in order for one to feel a sense of psychological completeness? What will it mean for those who lack or eschew a specific ethnic identity? Will it be desirable to call oneself "plain old American"? The answers to all these questions rest not so much in the private desires of individual people but in the broader cultural attitudes toward race and the relative societal statures of the groups involved.

A serious and perhaps dangerous downside accompanies continued subdividing of race and ethnicity. If a severe and prolonged economic downturn were to develop and competition for scarce economic resources were to become more heated, virulent ethnic prejudices could easily erupt (Jacoby, 2004). A campaign promoting "Americanization" could make all ethnic and racial distinctions grounds for discrimination. We need only examine what has happened in some parts of Europe to see what such a pessimistic vision might look like: "Barred from settling permanently, denied equal rights, largely without access to political power, unable to close the education gap and cut off from the job opportunities that only a college degree or better can open for them, migrants languish at the bottom of the social pyramid in many of the world's most civilized nations" (Jacoby, 2004, p. 9).

In just which direction our ethnoracial future lies is anybody's guess. It's certainly premature to talk about the obsolescence of race and ethnicity. Race-based segregation, poverty, and discrimination will never disappear fully. Indeed, given the growing proportion of Asian Americans and Latino/as in the general population and the continuing economic disadvantage of Blacks, some sociologists have begun to talk about a new racial split in the United States. Instead of the old black/white divide, the one that is now most likely to separate us is a black/nonblack divide (Lee & Bean, 2004).

According to sociologist Eduardo Bonilla-Silva (2004), the United States is already evolving into an even more complex tri-racial system similar to what is found in some Latin American countries with "Whites" at the top, an intermediate category of "honorary Whites" in the middle, and a non-white category he refers to as "collective Black" at the bottom. These categories are not merely racial but include elements of ethnicity and class as well. For instance, "Whites" include assimilated white Latino/as, some multiracials, and urban Native Americans as well as Euro-Americans. "Honorary Whites" include groups that have achieved middle-class status, such as Japanese Americans, Korean Americans, Asian Indians, Chinese Americans, and Arab Americans. "Collective Blacks" comprise groups that languish at the bottom of the stratification system, including African Americans, dark-skinned and poor Latino/as, Filipinos, Southeast Asians, and reservation-bound Native Americans.

Yet it also may be overly gloomy to talk about a future society in which racial divisions become more polarizing than they are now. What we can safely project is that 10, 20, or 50 years from now, racial and ethnic identities and the color lines that divide us will not take the form they take today.

THE FUTURES OF GENDER AND THE SEXUAL DICHOTOMY

It seems a little strange to talk about the futures of sex and gender in the same way that I've been discussing the futures of race and ethnicity. We're not in the midst of a massive redefinition of sex as we are regarding race

and ethnicity. The U.S. Bureau of the Census isn't debating ways to redefine sex categories on the census form. Surely no one would argue that
there won't be men and women in the future or that dichotomous thinking about sex will disappear anytime soon. For that matter, I doubt that
many people would maintain that we're headed toward an androgynous
society in which gender is a meaningless social identifier.

Our ideas about sex and gender differences have changed in the past,
however, and will therefore no doubt continue to change in the coming
decades. The recent trend toward searching for the biological underpinnings to gendered behavior suggests that we might someday rely more
on anatomical and genetic explanations of gendered characteristics than
we do now. At the same time, though, there is increasing awareness that
sex and gender—both as a source of identity and as a set of cultural
expectations—are not fixed and immutable.

In fact, we seem to be in the midst of a transformation in our thinking about female and male identifiers. As you may recall from Chapter 2,
intersexual, transsexual, and transgendered folk have become more visible
and more vocal in their attacks on traditional dichotomous thinking about
sex. They question the categorization of all individuals as either male or
female. The Intersex Society of North America maintains that people who
are intersexual (and their families) suffer not because of gender confusion but because of the social stigma that surrounds any phenomenon that
blurs the line between male and female. The condition is often presented
to parents as a "social emergency" that must be addressed immediately
(Navarro, 2004). It should be noted, however, that although the organization wants intersexuality to become less stigmatizing, it nonetheless
supports dichotomous thinking, officially recommending that intersexual
children be assigned as either male or female—albeit only "after careful
examination and diagnosis" (Chase, 2002, p. 4).

Changes taking place in what is expected of and accepted for males
and females (that is, gender) are more obvious. For a glimpse of the
future of gender, one need look no further than the institution of family.
Fifty years ago, the "normal" family was thought to be one with a female
homemaker and a male breadwinner. Functionalist sociologists claimed
that this family type was ideally suited to meet the needs of individuals
and social institutions (Gerson, 2000). Today, though, fewer than 15% of
American families fit this pattern. Most families today are either dual-
earner, single-parent, reconstituted, or "empty-nest" families. Mothers
are less likely to be the primary caretakers of their children than they
were 30 years ago, forcing them to depend on paid caregivers, friends, or

teachers to fulfill the traditional maternal role. In short, today's American families bear little resemblance to the cultural ideal that existed just a generation ago.

Despite the occasional proposal to change the standard household arrangement in this society, it's likely that the vast majority of the adult population will continue to marry—at least 90%, the U.S. Census Bureau estimates (Coltrane, 1996). Marriage, for all its problems and pitfalls, is here to stay. But when it comes to what people are actually doing in their relationships, we can see some dramatic changes. American men and women are slowly moving toward a blurring of gender expectations and away from traditional notions of wives and husbands, mothers and fathers. Each year, Americans show more accepting attitudes toward women's independence and influence at home and at work. Attitudes about men are changing too. Surveys of high school students over the years show that a growing proportion believe that husbands should take on more household and child care responsibilities. The vast majority believe that wives should expect their husbands to participate fully in these duties. Most adolescent boys expect that when they get married, their wives will work, and more and more of them indicate that they intend to take time off from work after becoming fathers (Coltrane, 1996).

As couples in which both partners work outside the home become the norm, employers will have more and more trouble ignoring employees' desire to achieve balance between their work and family lives. We may see the slow disappearance of the 9-to-5, Monday-through-Friday workweek, an acknowledgment of how employees' needs change through the life course, and the appearance of a more flexible and less gender-specific definition of what it means to be a good worker.

Furthermore, as working families become more common, fewer people will publicly condemn working mothers as negligent parents. Most people today already say that they believe, at least in principle, in the ideal of equal opportunities for men and women. If current trends continue, more people will endorse such a belief in the future.

With regard to the work that takes place *within* households, some sociologists argue that changes in the gender-based division of labor will help to propel us toward equality between men and women at home (Coltrane, 1996). Whenever men take on more of the mundane domestic tasks, the balance of power in the household begins to shift. When fathers take on more child care responsibilities, they begin to develop the sort of nurturing sensitivities traditionally associated with mothers. When parents share responsibilities, children thrive intellectually and emotionally and grow up holding less-rigid gender stereotypes. Of course, not everyone's attitudes will conform to this picture. Nevertheless, household tasks may become less tied to gender in the future.

These changes in the home and the workplace have the potential to transform the meaning of gender in future generations. But we have a long way to go yet, and the road toward true gender equity and equality is not completely free of potholes. As you will recall from Chapter 8, most jobs are still based on the assumption that an employee can and should work long hours without worrying about child care and other household needs. Most employed women continue to work in traditionally "female" occupations and still earn substantially lower wages than men. And the vast majority of women are still responsible for the bulk of the house-work and child care.

Moreover, work still tends to be structured around a male career model: 20 years of schooling, followed by 40 years of employment and then retirement (Skolnick, 1996). This model doesn't work for many women, who must combine work and domestic responsibilities. They often have to step out of the paid labor force to raise a family and return to it later when the children are finally grown.

Most of the changes we've witnessed regarding gender have been a result of alterations in women's educational, occupational, and family lives. And so perhaps the most certain projection I can make regarding the future of gender is that men's position will remain, at least for a while, uncertain. The direction in which society will head rests on how men interpret and respond to the changes they face as a result of changes in women's lives. In the face of women's growing confidence, some men might feel threatened. Men may be more willing to devote more of them-selves to their relationships these days and, for those who become par-ents, more time and energy to the rearing of children. But as long as there continues to be a close relationship between paid work, occupational status, and male identity, they will have trouble abandoning the notion that in order to be "a man," they must be the household breadwinner (Reeves, 2004).

Even if gender becomes less of a determinant of work achievement and family responsibilities than it is today, discrimination is unlikely to disappear entirely. Some sociologists feel, however, that family status rather than gender may become the most potent discriminating charac-teristic among workers in the future. These sociologists argue that the social and economic gap between "career-oriented" workers (those single people and couples who downplay family life in pursuit of career advancement) and "child-oriented" workers (those single parents and couples who downplay careers in the interests of their families) will inevitably widen. They fear that employers concerned about productivity and profits will continue to favor career-oriented workers over both men and women who want to spend more time maintaining their intimate relationships (Hunt & Hunt, 1990). If future employers still assume that the most committed employees are those unfettered by family demands, both women and men who openly express a desire to balance work time with time away from work will risk falling behind occupationally.

THE FUTURES OF "[BLANK]SEXUALITY"

As with future definitions of race, the familiar dividing lines between homosexuality and heterosexuality may prove insufficient to capture the ways that many individuals "do" their sexual lives (Lawler, 2001). As we saw in Chapter 2, many people today consider their sexual orientation fluid rather than permanent, something that can change as their interpersonal circumstances change.

Indeed, the blurring of sexuality has, in some sense, become fashionable. For instance, within the past few years, the term *metrosexual* has gained popularity as a term for straight, urban men who appear gay because of their strong aesthetic sense and attention to style and appearance. The wildly popular British soccer star David Beckham is a heterosexual who paints his fingernails, braids his hair, and poses for gay magazines. It's not clear whether the appearance of the label *metrosexual* represents a new direction in sexual categorization or is simply a clever marketing ploy. Regardless, what's interesting about the label is that it seems to indicate that the suspicion of homosexuality may no longer carry the stigma it once did (St. John, 2003).

Yet it's nearly impossible to imagine a society in which some forms of sexual expression are not privileged over others. The line between the privileged and the stigmatized may shift from time to time, pushing toward greater tolerance at one point and more restrictive and punitive definitions at another. But from a societal perspective, there will always be some forms of sexual orientation that are defined as "good" and "normal" and others defined as "bad" and "abnormal."

In the end, though, the future stature of sexuality or sexual orientation in the stratification system may have less to do with how people achieve sexual pleasure in their private lives and more to do with legal recognition of certain forms of intimacy. In recent years, we've seen the

American definition of family expand beyond traditional parameters. At the same time, there are signs of movement in the opposite direction, like the growing number of state legislatures tightening definitions of marriage and the movement to establish a federal, constitutional ban on same-sex marriage. Whichever way this matter goes, the inclusion of various "nontraditional" relationships under the legal rubric of *family* will be at the forefront of emotional debates for years to come.

For compelling evidence of the growing acceptance of "nontraditional" intimacy, we can look to a most unlikely place: corporate America. Each year, more and more major corporations grant financial benefits to unmarried, same-sex domestic partners. Huge multinational companies are in the business of making profits, not taking public stands on controversial political issues. They don't establish their policies frivolously. Many of these companies have apparently acknowledged that domestic partner policies make good financial sense because they increase workers' satisfaction and hence motivation, productivity, and loyalty. To the extent that an inclusive definition of *family* continues to make good business sense, the list of economically and socially "legitimate" types of families will continue to expand. Perhaps these companies will ultimately put pressure on local, state, and federal legislatures to create laws that parallel their policies. Such action will inevitably influence the manner in which sexual orientation is considered in the future.

STRATIFICATION OUTLOOKS: CLASS DISMISSED?

I don't think anyone—not even the most vociferous advocate of equality and social justice—would predict that we would ever have a society with no distinctions between the very rich and the very poor. In fact, if recent figures are any indication of what's in store (see Chapter 8), we're actually moving in the opposite socioeconomic direction, as the income and wealth gaps between the richest and poorest Americans continue to grow wider. You can feel the resignation in this statement on the topic by prominent sociologist Herbert Gans:

> If joblessness and poverty rise in the future, and no more is done about them than has been the last quarter century, living in America would become a grimmer experience for most people, including even those who can hide in the protected parts of the economy or escape to sheltered parts of the country. (1995, p. 136)

Keep in mind, though, that economic inequality depends on the choices we make as a society: how we regulate corporate and union activity, how we distribute the tax burden, how we choose to invest in education, how we set wages, how we choose to finance health care, how we support children, the elderly, and the disabled, and so on (Hout & Lucas, 2001). We can look to other industrialized countries (Sweden, Norway, the Netherlands) for evidence that societies can in fact reduce the gaps between rich and poor if they so desire. When we assume that class inequality is inevitable, however, we free ourselves from any obligation to do something to reduce it.

Indeed, socioeconomic boundaries may actually become more rather than less relevant in the future. Even today, some sociologists argue that class, and not race, is becoming the great divider in U.S. society in the 21st century. Of course, there's no way to project economic trends with any amount of certainty (just ask economists). What we can anticipate, though, is that as long as we continue both individually and culturally to subscribe to a political ideology and an economic system in which one's socioeconomic status derives from one's competitive achievements, we will always have some people who succeed and some people who fail. Because this ideology forms the basis of our very way of life in this society, it seems unlikely to shrink in importance in the future.

FUTURE INTERSECTIONS

"The weakest link in the chain is indifference to the suffering of others." Harry Belafonte (speech given at DePauw University, 2002)

All of us, to one degree or another, are selfish. I don't mean that we're all greedy or that we never care about other people. I mean that at one time or another, we all get so caught up in our own lives and what's happening to us that we fail to recognize how interconnected our lives are with the lives of others. We sometimes forget that our thoughts and our deeds have an impact on other people. If we happen to occupy a position of advantage and privilege in society, we sometimes don't see our daily ties to the countless unnamed and largely invisible people who provide us with the goods and services we need to sustain our own lives.

Even when we aren't especially advantaged, we sometimes don't see the suffering that other people experience. Most of us have little difficulty seeing our own victimization within larger systems of inequality. What we have a harder time doing is seeing how our thoughts, beliefs, and actions lead to and support other people's subordination and disadvantage. People see the type of subjugation most closely associated with the group to which they belong as being most important and classify other types as less so. For example, according to sociologist Patricia Hill Collins (2003), white feminists are inclined to see their own disadvantage as women quite clearly but fail to see how their skin color privileges them. Likewise, a wealthy gay couple may focus on their own victimization in the prohibition against same-sex marriage but not the myriad other ways that poor people suffer legally and economically, whether they're allowed to marry or not.

Broadening our view to encompass the multiple dimensions of inequality helps us see that we're all dominant and all disadvantaged simultaneously:

> I, for instance, am simultaneously dominant as a white person and targeted as a woman. A white able-bodied man may be dominant in those categories, but targeted as a Jew or Muslim or as a gay person. Some people are, at some point in their lives, entirely dominant; but if they are, they won't be forever. Even a white, able-bodied, heterosexual, Christian man will literally grow out of his total dominance if he reaches old age. (Ayvazian, 2001, p. 610)

Similarly, none of us are ever totally without virtue or vice (Collins, 2003). Meaningful social change can take place only when we realize that there are few pure victims or pure victimizers. All of us derive at some point varying amounts of penalty and privilege from the systems of inequality that frame our lives.

The key to undermining or overcoming disadvantage is to recognize the multiple intersecting dimensions of privilege: race, class, gender, and sexuality, as well as others not directly addressed in this book. Dichotomous, either/or thinking—for example, conceiving of race only in black/white terms—corners us into thinking about groups as opposing forces. This way of framing the world encourages us to see ourselves and others as oppressed/not oppressed or powerful/powerless. If we acknowledge the simultaneity of all of the different social dimensions upon which we are positioned, however, we can see ourselves and others as advantaged in some ways and disadvantaged in others (Collins, 2003).

Dichotomous thinking also encourages a ranking of differences and inequalities. Taking a "my oppression is more oppressive than your oppression" stance—what one sociologist called "the Oppression Olympics"

(Martinez, 2003, p. 624)—dooms us to endless competition for attention and resources and forces us to ignore the similar experiences and similar strategic battles faced by all disadvantaged groups.

In order to move to a new vision of inequality, we must begin to ask different questions. Rather than simply asking who is more disadvantaged than whom, we should first assume that race, class, gender, and sexuality are always present (even though one dimension of identity might be more prominent at any given point) and then ask how they interlock to shape relations of inequality. As an example of this interconnected approach, the National Organization of Men Against Sexism moves beyond the singular issue of gender inequality and defines itself as a "pro-feminist, gay-affirmative, and anti-racist" organization (NOMAS, 2004). The NOMAS mission statement recognizes that, because race and sexual orientation (and class) are so tightly connected to gender in the social systems that create and reinforce inequality, gender inequality cannot be remedied without considering the multiple forms that racial and economic exploitation take (Lorber, 1994).

FINAL THOUGHTS

Some historically disadvantaged groups—women, ethnoracial minorities, sexual minorities—have made amazing advances in the United States in recent years. The racial and ethnic landscape of contemporary society would have been unimaginable to even the most optimistic civil rights activist of the 1960s. Could she or he have possibly envisioned a black woman as secretary of state? Could anyone fighting for the rights of homosexuals in the 1970s ever have imagined a time in which some of the most popular prime-time television shows would feature prominent gay men and lesbians? Could a women's liberationist 40 years ago have ever foreseen a time when women would outnumber men in college?

We can't ignore the fact, though, that real, significant, and debilitating imbalances continue to harm some segments of society while leaving others unscathed. People continue to be born into positions of advantage that they themselves had nothing to do with achieving or creating. We continue to live in a society where distrust of, avoidance of, and even hostility toward those perceived to be different is common. Just as I was finishing up this chapter, our school newspaper printed a story about some young men not affiliated with the university who had been roaming the streets of the campus in a pickup truck shouting racial epithets at students of color. After reading the story, a colleague asked rhetorically,

"What year is this anyway?" Well, it's 2005, and despite all the progress that has been made over the past four decades, such incidents still occur.

Truth be told, I wish I didn't have to write this book. Or more accurately, I wish I could have written it from a distant historical perspective rather than a contemporary sociological one. I wish that social inequality was extinct, a relic of bygone human societies, like the feudal system or traveling minstrel shows or phonograph records. I wish I could have written that all these problems of inequality were in our past, that we've managed to overcome them and people don't suffer so much anymore. I wish that people truly were judged by who rather than what they are. But clearly, we aren't there yet.

As I wrap up this book, I'm left with a curiously empty feeling, as if I still may not have convinced you of the multidimensional nature of social inequality in everyday life. It would have been easier to take the more traditional approach and discuss race, class, gender, and sexuality as distinct, mutually exclusive dimensions of identity and inequality. I could have written a separate chapter on each. The result would have been clear, understandable, nicely organized, and informational. You might have had an easier time summarizing chapters and taking exams. But it would have painted the wrong picture.

And herein lies the dilemma in writing a book about social identities and inequalities. At times, it's been necessary, just to be able to write coherently, to address race, class, gender, and sexuality separately. But that does not mean that they are experienced separately or even that they influence people's lives and the society as a whole separately. People don't live their lives solely as a man, solely as a working-class person, solely as a Latina, or solely as a heterosexual. People have identities on all of these dimensions at the same time . . . and more. Add age, nationality, educational achievement, occupation, political affiliation, physical ability, family status, level of attractiveness, height and weight, religion, geographic area of residence, personality, and any other characteristic that distinguishes some people from others. And add the fact that most dimensions of identity are not dichotomous but are instead endlessly nuanced, as in the subdivisions of Latino/as into Dominicans, Puerto Ricans, Mexicans, and so on. Throughout the book, I've also tried to move beyond just talking about inequality only from the perspectives of those who are "different" (and therefore disadvantaged) to talking about those in the majority who are advantaged—which has traditionally meant men, white people, middle- and upper-class people, and heterosexuals. Now you have an even more complicated picture of how inequalities between people arise and function.

So, in the interests of trying to highlight the intersections of race, class, gender, and sexuality, I've ended up asking more questions than answering them. Instead of simplifying things, I've complicated them. We've seen in this chapter, for example, that social inequality is both resistant to and amenable to change. In the interests of understanding people's hostilities and anger toward "others," I may have inflamed them. There are no definitive, iron-clad answers here as to how or why race, class, gender, and sexuality combine to influence people's lives. But there are questions, lots of them, that I hope make you think about and perceive your life in relation to others differently now than you did before you read this book. If you now pay attention to your own race, class, gender, and sexuality and the intersections between them more than you did before—and if you now understand how tremendously fortunate you are in some ways, and how disadvantaged you are in others—then maybe I've succeeded after all.

INVESTIGATING IDENTITIES AND INEQUALITIES

Organizing for a change: Student groups on campus

Changes in the way we think about race, gender, class, and sexuality don't just materialize out of the blue. More often than not, they are the result of people's concerted efforts to alter conditions that they find unacceptable, unfair, and perhaps even harmful. Practically every college campus in the country has a variety of student organizations that seek to address the interests of historically marginalized groups. On my campus, for example, you can find organizations for African Americans; gay men, lesbians, bisexuals, and transgendered individuals; Latino/as; Asian Americans; and women.

For this exercise, identify all the student organizations on your campus that represent the interests of students from historically disadvantaged groups. Start by gathering some background information (usually available from the Office of Student Affairs or Student Services). Are they chapters of national organizations, or are they exclusively local? How long have they existed on campus? Do they have a mission statement, a charter, or a web site that describes their purpose and overall philosophy? What is their annual operating budget? Are there organizations that once existed on campus but no longer do? What happened to them? Is their disappearance a sign of failure or of success in meeting their goals?

Next, see if you can interview student leaders and faculty sponsors of some of these organizations. Why did they decide to take leadership roles in their organizations? What do they see as the organization's purpose? What do they think have been the organization's most noteworthy accomplishments? What have been the biggest disappointments?

In addition, talk to a few students who are members of some of these groups. Why did they join? What sorts of organizational activities do they participate in? It might also be interesting to talk to some students who are not members of these organizations to get a sense of "outsiders'" perceptions. Do non-members see these organizations as valuable or problematic?

For comparison, you might want to also identify the campus organizations that represent historically advantaged groups (such as College Republicans, Christian student groups, various men's clubs, and so on). How are these organizations similar to and different from the organizations representing historically disadvantaged groups?

Once you've gathered your information, try to draw some conclusions about the utility of such organizations at both local and national levels. Racially, ethnically, sexually, religiously, or politically exclusive groups give members a sense of pride and a feeling of solidarity. But at what point do they reinforce rather than overcome the features that divide us as a society?

REFERENCES

Abrams, K. K., Allen, L., & Gray, J. J. 1993. Disordered eating attitudes and behaviors, psychological adjustment, and ethnic identity: A comparison of black and white female college students. *Journal of Eating Disorders, 14,* 49–57.

Adair, V. 2004. Branded with infamy: Inscriptions of poverty and class in America. In D. M. Newman & J. O'Brien (Eds.), *Sociology: Exploring the architecture of everyday life (Readings).* Thousand Oaks, CA: Pine Forge Press.

Adams, S., Kuebli, J., Boyle, P. A., & Fivush, R. 1995. Gender differences in parent-child conversations about past emotions: A longitudinal investigation. *Sex Roles, 33,* 309–323.

Adler, P. A., & Adler, P. 1998. *Peer power.* New Brunswick, NJ: Rutgers University Press.

Albelda, R., & Tilly, C. 2001. It's a family affair: Women, poverty, and welfare. In S. J. Ferguson (Ed.), *Shifting the center: Understanding contemporary families.* Mountain View, CA: Mayfield.

Alexander, J. C. 2001. Theorizing the "modes of incorporation": Assimilation, hyphenation, and multiculturalism as varieties of civil participation. *Sociological Theory, 19,* 237–249.

Allen, I. L. 1990. *Unkind words: Ethnic labeling from* Redskin *to* WASP. New York: Bergin & Garvey.

Allport, G. 1954. *The nature of prejudice.* Reading, MA: Addison-Wesley.

Alvidrez, J., & Areán, P. A. 2002. Psychosocial treatment research with ethnic minority populations: Ethical considerations in conducting clinical trials. *Ethics and Behavior, 12,* 103–116.

American Association of University Women. 2001. Hostile hallways: Teasing and sexual harassment in school. www.aauw.org/research/girls_education/hostile.cfm. Accessed July 31, 2004.

American Civil Liberties Union. 2004. Sanctioned bias: Racial profiling since 9/11. www.aclu.org/RacialEquality/. Accessed August 1, 2004.

American Psychiatric Association. 2000. *Diagnostic and statistical manual of mental disorders. Fourth edition.* Washington, DC: American Psychiatric Association.

American Society for Aesthetic Plastic Surgery. 2004. Cosmetic plastic surgery research: Statistics and trends for 2001, 2002, and 2003. www. cosmeticplasticsurgerystatistics.com/statistics.html. Accessed July 21, 2004.

American Sociological Association. 2002. Statement of the American Sociological Association on the importance of collecting data and doing social scientific research on race. www.asanet.org/governance/racestmt.htm. Accessed June 18, 2003.

American television, situation comedies. 2004. glbtq: An encyclopedia of gay, lesbian, bisexual, transgender, and queer culture. www.glbtq.com/arts/am_tv_sitcoms.html. Accessed June 17, 2004.

Amnesty International. 2003. U.S.: Death by discrimination—The continuing role of race in capital cases. www.amnesty.org/library/index/engamr510462003. Accessed July 23, 2004.

———. 2004. Death penalty facts. www.amnestyusa.org/abolish/racialprejudices.html. Accessed July 25, 2004.

Anderson, E. 1990. *Streetwise: Race, class and change in an urban community.* Chicago: University of Chicago Press.

Anderson, M. L. 2001. Restructuring for whom? Race, class, gender, and the ideology of invisibility. *Sociological Focus, 16,* 181–201.

Andrews, E. L. 2004. Report finds tax cuts heavily favor the wealthy. *New York Times,* August 13.

Angier, N. 1997a. Sexual identity not pliable after all, report says. *New York Times,* March 14.

———. 1997b. New debate over surgery on genitals. *New York Times,* May 13.

Angier, N., & Chang, K. 2005. Gray matter and the sexes: Still a scientific gray area. *New York Times,* January 24.

Ansell, A. E. 2000. The new face of race: The metamorphosis of racism in the post–civil rights era United States. In P. Kivisto & G. Rundblad (Eds.), *Multiculturalism in the United States.* Thousand Oaks, CA: Pine Forge Press.

Anti-Muslim incidents increase. 2004. *New York Times,* May 4.

Anzaldúa, G. 2003. How to tame a wild tongue. In T. E. Ore (Ed.), *The social construction of difference and inequality: Race, class, gender, and sexuality.* New York: McGraw-Hill.

Arendell, T. 1984. Divorce: A woman's issue. *Feminist Issues, 4,* 41–61.

Arrighi, B. A. 2002. America's shame: Women and children in shelters. In R. H. Lauer & J. C. Lauer (Eds.), *Sociology: Windows on society.* Los Angeles: Roxbury.

Ashford, L. S. 2005. Good health still eludes the poorest women and children. Population Reference Bureau Report. www.prb.org. Accessed April 23, 2005.

Astbury, J. 1996. *Crazy for you: The making of women's madness.* Melbourne: Oxford University Press.

Attitudes toward affirmative action. 2003. *American Demographics,* May.

Averett, S., & Korenman, S. 1999. Black and white differences in social and economic consequences of obesity. *International Journal of Obesity, 23,* 166–173.

Ayvazian, A. 2001. Interrupting the cycle of oppression: The role of allies as agents of change. In P. S. Rothenberg (Ed.), *Race, class, and gender in the United States.* New York: Worth.

Bach, P. B., Cramer, L. D., Warren, J. L., & Begg, C. B. 1999. Racial differences in the treatment of early-stage lung cancer. *New England Journal of Medicine, 341,* 119–205.

Baldauf, S. 2000. A hanging exposes views on race and dating. *Christian Science Monitor,* July 13.

Barbeau, E. M., Krieger, N., & Soobader, M. J. 2004. Working class matters: Socioeconomic disadvantage, race/ethnicity, gender, and smoking in NHIS 2000. *American Journal of Public Health, 94,* 269–278.

Bardaglio, P. 1999. "Shameful matches": The regulation of interracial sex and marriage in the South before 1900. In M. Hodes (Ed.), *Sex, love, race: Crossing boundaries in North American history.* New York: NYU Press.

Beagan, B. 2001. Micro inequities and everyday inequalities: "Race," gender, sexuality, and class in medical school. *Canadian Journal of Sociology, 26,* 583–610.

Bearak, B. 2000. Women are defaced by acid and Bengali society is torn. *New York Times,* June 24.

Becker, E. 2004. Number of hungry rising, U.N. says. *New York Times,* December 8.

Beinart, P. 2003. Blind spot. *The New Republic,* February 3.

Belluck, P. 2002. Doctors' new practices offer deluxe service for deluxe fee. *New York Times,* January 15.

———. 2003. Gays respond: "I do," "I might," and "I won't." *New York Times,* November 26.

Bem, S. L. 1974. The measurement of psychological androgyny. *Journal of Consulting and Clinical Psychology, 42,* 155–162.

Benatar, D. 2003. The second sexism. *Social Theory and Practice, 29,* 177–210.

Benokraitis, N. V., & Feagin, J. R. 1991. Sex discrimination—Subtle and covert. In J. Henslin (Ed.), *Down to earth sociology.* New York: Free Press.

Benson, J. B. 1993. Season of birth and onset of locomotion: Theoretical and methodological implications. *Infant Behavior and Development, 16,* 69–81.

Berger, P. L., & Luckmann, T. 1966. *The social construction of reality.* Garden City, NY: Anchor.

Bergesen, A., & Herman, M. 1998. Immigration, race, and riot: The 1992 Los Angeles uprising. *American Sociological Review, 63,* 39–54.

Bernard, J. 1981. The good provider role: Its rise and fall. *American Psychologist, 36,* 1–12.

BlackHealthCare.com. 2003. Sickle-cell anemia—Description. www.blackhealthcare.com/BHC/SickleCell/Description.asp. Accessed June 17, 2003.

Blau, P. M. 1964. *Exchange and power in social life.* New York: Wiley.

Blumer, H. 1958/2004. Race prejudice as a sense of group position. In C. A. Gallagher (Ed.), *Rethinking the color line: Readings in race and ethnicity.* New York: McGraw-Hill.

Bonilla-Silva, E. 2003. *Racism without racists: Color-blind racism and the persistence of racial inequality in the United States.* Lanham, MD: Rowman & Littlefield.

———. 2004. From bi-racial to tri-racial: The emergence of a new racial stratification system in the United States. In C. Herring, V. M. Keith, & H. D. Horton (Eds.), *Skin deep: How race and complexion matter in the "color blind" era.* Urbana, IL: University of Illinois Press.

Bordo, S. 1999. *The male body: A new look at men in public and in private.* New York: Farrar, Straus, & Giroux.

———. 2003. Pills and power tools. In T. E. Ore (Ed.), *The social construction of difference and inequality: Race, class, gender, and sexuality.* New York: McGraw-Hill.

Bowers, W. J., Steiner, B. D., & Sandys, M. 2001. Death sentencing in black and white: An empirical examination of juror race and jury racial composition in capital sentencing. *Penn Journal of Constitutional Law, 3,* 171–274.

Bowker, L. H. 1993. A battered woman's problems are social, not psychological. In R. J. Gelles & D. R. Loeske (Eds.), *Current controversies on family violence.* Newbury Park, CA: Sage.

Bowles, S., & Gintis, H. 1976. *Schooling in capitalist America: Educational reform and the contradictions of economic reform.* New York: Basic Books.

Boydston, J. 2001. Cult of true womanhood. www.pbs.org/stantonanthony/ resources/culthood.html. Accessed July 10, 2001.

Boykin, K. 1996. *One more river to cross: Black and gay in America.* New York: Anchor Books.

Bragg, R. 1999. Restaurant's added gratuity leads to discrimination claim. *New York Times,* November 10.

Bravo.com. 2004. Queer Eye for the Straight Guy. www.bravotv.com/Queer_Eye_for_ the_Straight_Guy/. Accessed June 28, 2004.

Bridal dowry in India. 2000. National Public Radio. www.npr.org/programs/morning. Accessed June 19, 2000.

Brinkley, J. 2000. C.I.A. depicts a vast trade in forced labor. *New York Times,* April 2.

Brint, S. 1998. *Schools and societies.* Thousand Oaks, CA: Pine Forge Press.

Brodkin, K. 2004. How the Jews became white folk. In D. M. Newman & J. O'Brien (Eds.), *Sociology: Exploring the architecture of everyday life (Readings).* Thousand Oaks, CA: Pine Forge Press.

Bronner, E. 1998. Inventing the notion of race. *New York Times,* January 10.

Brooke, J. 1998. Homophobia often found in schools, data shows. *New York Times,* October 14.

Broverman, I., Vogel, S., Broverman, D., Clarkson, F., & Rosenkrantz, P. 1972. Sex role stereotypes: A current appraisal. *Journal of Social Issues, 28,* 59–78.

Brown, P. 1998. Biology and the social construction of the "race" concept. In J. Ferrante & P. Brown (Eds.), *The social construction of race and ethnicity in the United States.* New York: Longman.

Brown, R. 1986. *Social psychology.* New York: Free Press.

Browne, B. A. 1998. Gender stereotypes in advertising on children's television in the 1990s: A cross-national analysis. *Journal of Advertising, 27,* 8–7.

Brownmiller, S. 1975. *Against our will: Men, women and rape.* New York: Fawcett.

Brunner, B. 2004. Confederate flag controversy. www.infoplease.com/spot/confederate1. html Accessed June 23, 2004.

Budig, M. J., & England, P. 2001. The wage penalty for motherhood. *American Sociological Review, 66,* 204–225.

Bullard, R. D. 2001. Decision making. In L. Westra & B. E. Lawson (Eds.), *Faces of environmental racism: Confronting issues of global justice.* Lanham, MD: Rowman & Littlefield.

Burros, M. 2004. Food pyramid is in for an overhaul. *New York Times,* July 13.

Butsch, R. 1995. Ralph, Fred, Archie and Homer: Why television keeps recreating the white male working-class buffoon. In G. Dines & J. M. Humez (Eds.), *Gender, race and class in media.* Thousand Oaks, CA: Sage.

Butterfield, F. 1999. Eliminating parole boards isn't a cure-all, experts say. *New York Times,* January 10.

———. 2000. Racial disparities seen as pervasive in juvenile justice. *New York Times,* April 26.

Campenni, C. E. 1999. Gender stereotyping of children's toys: A comparison of parents and nonparents. *Sex Roles, 40,* 121–138.

Carey, K. 2005. One step from the finish line: Higher college graduation rates are within our reach. Education Trust Report. www2.edtrust.org/EdTrust/Press+Room/college+results.htm. Accessed January 26, 2005.

Carli, L. L. 1997. Biology does not create gender differences in personality. In M. R. Walsh (Ed.), *Women, men and gender: Ongoing debates.* New Haven: Yale University Press.

Carr, D. 2004. Improving the health of the world's poorest people. *Health Bulletin #1.* Washington, DC: Population Reference Bureau.

Carrington, W. J., & Troske, K. R. 1998. Sex segregation in U.S. manufacturing. *Industrial Labor Relations Review, 51,* 445–464.

Centers for Disease Control. 1999. State-specific maternal mortality among black and white women—United States, 1987–1996. *Morbidity and Mortality Weekly Report, 48,* 492–496.

————. 2003a. Cases of HIV infection and AIDS in the United States, 2002. HIV/AIDS Surveillance Report, Vol. 14. www.cdc.gov/hiv/stats/hasr1402.htm. Accessed June 8, 2004.

————. 2003b. Cigarette smoking–related mortality. www.cdc.gov/tobacco/research_data/health_consequences/mortali.htm. Accessed June 3, 2003.

Charon, J. 1998. *Symbolic interactionism.* Upper Saddle River, NJ: Prentice Hall.

Chase, C. 2002. What is the agenda of the intersex patient advocacy movement? First World Congress: Hormonal and Genetic Basis of Sexual Differentiation Disorders. Tempe, AZ, May 17–18.

Chase-Dunn, C., & Rubinson, R. 1977. Toward a structural perspective on the world system. *Politics and Society, 7,* 453–476.

Chen, D. W. 2004. U.S. seeking cuts in rent subsidies for poor families. *New York Times,* September 22.

Cherry, R. 1989. *Discrimination: Its economic impact on blacks, women and Jews.* Lexington, MA: Lexington Books.

Children Now. 2001. Prime time for Latinos. Report II: 2000–2001 prime time television season. National Hispanic Foundation for the Arts. www.childrennow.org/media/fc2001/latino2001.pdf. Accessed June 17, 2003.

Children's Sentinel Nutrition Assessment Program. 2002. The impact of welfare sanctions on the health of infants and toddlers. http://dcc2.bumc.bu.edu/CsnapPublic/Reports.htm. Accessed June 13, 2003.

Ching, C. L., & Burke, S. 1999. An assessment of college students' attitudes and empathy toward rape. *College Student Journal, 33,* 573–584.

Clark, M. A. 2003. Trafficking in persons: An issue of human security. *Journal of Human Development, 4,* 247–263.

Cloward, R., & Piven, F. F. 1993. The fraud of workfare. *The Nation,* May 24.

Cluster, D. 1979. *They should have served that cup of coffee.* Boston: South End Press.

Coe, R. M. 1978. *Sociology of medicine.* New York: McGraw-Hill.

Cohen, P. N., & Huffman, M. L. 2003. Individuals, jobs, and labor markets: The devaluation of women's work. *American Sociological Review, 68,* 443–463.

Cole, D. 1999. *No equal justice: Race and class in the American criminal justice system.* New York: The New Press.

The College Board. 1998. SAT and gender differences. Research summary RS-04. www.collegeboard.com/repository/rs04_3960.pdf. Accessed July 1, 2004.

Collins, C., & Williams, D. R. 1999. Segregation and mortality: The deadly effects of racism. *Sociological Forum, 14*, 49–23.

Collins, P. H. 1990. *Black feminist thought: Knowledge, consciousness, and the politics of empowerment.* New York: Routledge.

———. 2001. Shifting the center: Race, class, and feminist theorizing about motherhood. In S. Ferguson (Ed.), *Shifting the center: Understanding contemporary families.* Mountain View, CA: Mayfield.

———. 2003. Toward a new vision: Race, class, and gender as categories of analysis and connection. In T. E. Ore (Ed.), *The social construction of difference and inequality.* New York: McGraw-Hill.

———. 2004. Some group matters: Intersectionality, situated standpoints, and black Feminist thought. In L. Richardson, V. Taylor, & N. Whittier (Eds.), *Feminist frontiers.* New York: McGraw-Hill.

Coltrane, S. 1996. *Gender and families.* Thousand Oaks, CA: Pine Forge Press.

Comer, J. P., & Poussaint, A. F. 1992. *Raising black children.* New York: Plume.

Connelly, M. 2004. How Americans voted: A political portrait. *New York Times,* November 7.

Cookson, P., & Persell, C. 1985. *Preparing for power.* New York: Basic Books.

Cooper, M. H. 1998. Environmental justice. *CQ Researcher,* June 19.

Cornell, S., & Hartmann, D. 1998. *Ethnicity and race: Making identities in a changing world.* Thousand Oaks, CA: Pine Forge Press.

Cort, M. A. 2004. Cultural mistrust and use of hospice care: Challenges and remedies. *Journal of Palliative Medicine, 7*, 63–72.

Cose, E. 1993. *The rage of a privileged class.* New York: HarperCollins.

———. 2000. Our new look: The colors of race. *Newsweek,* January 1.

Cowley, G., & Murr, A. 2004. The new face of AIDS. *Newsweek,* December 6.

Coyle, M. 2003. Race and class penalties in crack cocaine sentencing. The Sentencing Project Report #5077. www.sentencingproject.org/policy/mc-crackcocaine.pdf. Accessed June 20, 2003.

Crabbe, C. 2003. France caught cold by heat wave. *Bulletin of the World Health Organization, 81*, 773–774.

Crandall, C. S., & Martinez, R. 1996. Culture, ideology, and antifat attitudes. *Personality and Social Psychology Bulletin, 22*, 1165–1176.

Crenshaw, K. 2004a. Mapping the margins: Intersectionality, identity politics, and violence against women of color. In L. Richardson, V. Taylor, & N. Whittier (Eds.), *Feminist frontiers.* New York: McGraw-Hill.

———. 2004b. Was Strom a rapist? *The Nation,* March 15.

Crime and too much punishment. 1997. *New York Times,* August 3.

Critser, G. 2000. Let them eat fat: The heavy truths about American obesity. *Harper's Magazine,* March.

Crittenden, A. 2001. *The price of motherhood: Why the most important job in the world is still the least valued.* New York: Owl Books.

Crossette, T. 1997. Outsiders in the clubhouse. In D. M. Newman (Ed.), *Sociology: Exploring the architecture of everyday life (Readings).* Thousand Oaks, CA: Pine Forge Press.

Croteau, D., & Hoynes, W. 2000. *Media/society: Industries, images, and audiences.* Thousand Oaks, CA: Pine Forge Press.

Culhane, D., & Metraux, S. 1999. One year rates of public shelter utilization by race/ethnicity, age, sex, and poverty status for New York City (1990 and 1995) and Philadelphia (1995). *Population Research and Policy Review, 18,* 219–236.

Cushman, J. H. 1993. U.S. to weigh Blacks' complaints about pollution. *New York Times,* November 19.

Dang, A., & Frazer, S. 2004. *Black same-sex households in the United States: A report from the 2000 Census.* New York: National Gay and Lesbian Task Force Policy Institute and the National Black Justice Coalition.

Darwin, C. 1971. *The descent of man.* Adelaide, Australia: Griffin Press. (Original work published 1871)

Davey, M. 2004. For 1,000 troops, there is no going home. *New York Times,* September 9.

Davis, J. A., & Smith, T. 1986. *General social survey cumulative file 1972–1982.* Ann Arbor, MI: Inter-University Consortium for Political and Social Research.

Davis, K., & Moore, W. 1945. Some principles of stratification. *American Sociological Review, 10,* 242–247.

Davis-Floyd, R. E. 1996. The technocratic body and the organic body: Hegemony and heresy in women's birth choices. In C. F. Sargent & C. B. Brettell (Eds.), *Gender and health: An international perspective.* Upper Saddle River, NJ: Prentice Hall.

Death Penalty Information Center. 2004. Race of death row inmates executed since 1976. www.deathpenaltyinfo.org/. Accessed July 23, 2004.

Deaux, K., & Kite, M. E. 1987. Thinking about gender. In B. B. Hess & M. M. Ferree (Eds.), *Analyzing gender: A handbook of social science research.* Newbury Park, CA: Sage.

D'Emilio, J., & Freedman, E. B. 1988. *Intimate matters: A history of sexuality in America.* New York: Harper & Row.

DeNavas-Walt, C., Proctor, B. D., & Mills, R. J. 2004. Income, poverty, and health insurance coverage in the United States. *Current Population Reports,* P60-226. www.census.gov/prod/2004pubs/p60-226.pdf. Accessed August 27, 2004.

Denizet-Lewis, B. 2003. Double lives on the down low. *New York Times Magazine,* August 3.

deOnis, M., Blössner, M., Borghi, E., Frongillo, E. A., & Morris, F. 2004. Estimates of global prevalence of childhood underweight in 1990 and 2015. *JAMA, 291,* 2600–2606.

DePalma, A. 1995. Racism? Mexico's in denial. *New York Times,* June 11.

Diekman, A. B., & Murnen, S. K. 2004. Learning to be little women and little men: The inequitable gender equality of nonsexist children's literature. *Sex Roles, 50,* 373–385.

Dieter, R. C. 1998. The death penalty in black and white: Who lives, who dies, who decides. Death Penalty Information Center. www.deathpenaltyinfo.org. Accessed July 25, 2004.

Dillon, S. 2005. Harvard chief defends his talk on women. *New York Times,* January 18.

Dion, K. K., & Dion, K. L. 2004. Gender, immigrant generation, and ethnocultural identity. *Sex Roles, 50,* 347–355.

Dixon, T. L., & Linz, D. 2000. Race and the misrepresentation of victimization on local television news. *Communication Research, 27,* 547–573.

Domhoff, G. W. 1998. *Who rules America? Power and politics in the year 2000.* Mountain View, CA: Mayfield.

Dowd, M. 2000. Nymphet at the net. *New York Times,* June 4.

Down state. 2004. *New Republic,* March 15.

Dugger, C. W. 1999. India's poorest are becoming its loudest. *New York Times,* April 25.

———. 2004. Devastated by AIDS, Africa sees life expectancy plunge. *New York Times,* July 16.

———. 2005. U.N. proposes doubling of aid to cut poverty. *New York Times,* January 18.

Duke, S. B. 1994. Casualties of war. *Reason, 25,* 20–27.

Duster, T. 1997. Pattern, purpose, and race in the drug war. In C. Reinarman & H. G. Levine (Eds.), *Crack in America.* Berkeley: University of California Press.

Dyer, R. 2002. The matter of whiteness. In P. S. Rothenberg (Ed.), *White privilege: Essential readings on the other side of racism.* New York: Worth.

Economic Roundtable. 2000. The cage of poverty. www.economicrt.org/publications. html#recent. Accessed July 28, 2001.

Edin, K. 2003. Few good men: Why poor mothers stay single. In A. S. Skolnick & J. H. Skolnick (Eds.), *Family in transition.* Boston: Allyn & Bacon.

Edwards, C., & Hempel, J. 2003. Coming out in corporate America. *Business Week,* December 15.

Egan, T. 1993. A cultural gap may swallow a child. *New York Times,* October 12.

Ehrenreich, B. 1995. The silenced majority: Why the average working person has disappeared from American media and culture. In G. Dines & J. M. Humez (Eds.), *Gender, race, and class in media.* Thousand Oaks, CA: Sage.

———. 2001. *Nickled and dimed: On (not) getting by in America.* New York: Metropolitan.

———. 2004. Let them eat wedding cake. *New York Times,* July 11.

Ehrenreich, B., & English, D. 1979. *For her own good: 150 years of the experts' advice to women.* Garden City, NY: Anchor.

Eitzen, S. D., & Bacazinn, M. 2003. The dark side of sports symbols. In T. E. Ore (Ed.), *The social construction of difference and inequality: Race, class, gender, and sexuality.* New York: McGraw-Hill.

Elliott, S. 2004. With its Viagra under attack by new rivals, Pfizer chooses a new agency for ads in the United States. *New York Times,* June 30.

Engel, R. S., & Calnon, J. M. 2004. Examining the influence of drivers' characteristics during traffic stops with police: Results from a national survey. *Justice Quarterly, 21,* 49–90.

Enloe, C. 1993. *The morning after: Sexual politics at the end of the Cold War.* Berkeley: University of California Press.

Epstein, C. F. 1988. *Deceptive distinctions: Sex, gender, and the social order.* New Haven: Yale University Press.

———. 1997. The multiple realities of sameness and difference: Ideology and practice. *Journal of Social Issues, 53,* 259–278.

Equal Employment Opportunity Commission. 2003. Sexual harassment charges EEOC & FEPAs combined: FY1992–2002. www.eeoc.gov/stats/harass.html. Accessed June 24, 2003.

————. 2004. Sexual harassment charges EEOC and FEPAs combined: FY1992–FY2003. www.eeoc.gov/stats/harass.html. Accessed July 31, 2004.

Erlanger, S. 2000. Across a new Europe, a people deemed unfit for tolerance. *New York Times,* April 2.

Espiritu, Y. L. 2004. Asian American panethnicity: Bridging institutions and identities. In C. A. Gallagher (Ed.), *Rethinking the color line: Readings in race and ethnicity.* New York: McGraw-Hill.

Evans, L., & Davies, K. 2000. No sissy boys here: A content analysis of the representation of masculinity in elementary school reading textbooks. *Sex Roles, 42,* 255–270.

Fagot, B. I., & Hagan, R. 1985. Aggression in toddlers: Responses to the assertive acts of boys and girls. *Sex Roles, 12,* 341–351.

Farley, R. 2002. Identifying with multiple races: A social movement that succeeded but failed? Population Studies Center Research Report #01-491. Institute for Social Research, University of Michigan.

Farmer, J. 2004. The story. www.sitins.com/story.shtml. Accessed September 10, 2004.

Farmer, R. 2002. Same sex couples face post–September 11 discrimination. *National NOW Times,* Spring.

Fat-phobia in the Fijis: TV—Thin is in. 1999. *Newsweek,* May 31.

Fausto-Sterling, A. 1985. *Myths of gender: Biological theories about men and women.* New York: Basic Books.

————. 2000. *Sexing the body: Gender politics and the construction of sexuality.* New York: Basic Books.

F.B.I. 2003. Hate crimes statistics, 2002. www.fbi.gov/ucr/hatecrime2002.pdf. Accessed July 29, 2004.

Feagin, J. R., & McKinney, K. D. 2003. *The many costs of racism.* Lanham, MD: Rowman & Littlefield.

Feagin, J. R., & O'Brien, E. 2003. *White men on race: Power, privilege, and the shaping of cultural consciousness.* Boston: Beacon Press.

Feagin, J. R. 1991. The continuing significance of race: Anti-black discrimination in public places. *American Sociological Review, 56,* 101–116.

Feagin, J. R., & Feagin, C. B. 2004. Theoretical perspectives in race and ethnic relations. In C. A. Gallagher (Ed.), *Rethinking the color line: Readings in race and ethnicity.* New York: McGraw-Hill.

Feagin, J. R., & Vera, H. 2000. White racism: A case study from the heartland. In P. Kivisto & G. Rundblad (Eds.), *Multiculturalism in the United States.* Thousand Oaks, CA: Pine Forge Press.

Feagin, J. R., Vera, H., & Imani, N. 2000. The agony of education: Black students at white colleges and universities. In D. M. Newman (Ed.), *Sociology: Exploring the architecture of everyday life (Readings).* Thousand Oaks, CA: Pine Forge Press.

Fears, D., & Deane, C. 2001. Biracial couples report tolerance. *Washington Post,* July 5.

Federal Bureau of Prisons. 2004. Quick facts. www.bop.gov/fact0598.html. Accessed August 2, 2004.

Fields, C. B., & Scout, 2001. Addressing the needs of lesbian patients. *Journal of Sex Education and Therapy, 26,* 182–188.

Fields, J. 2003. Children's living arrangements and characteristics: March 2002. *Current Population Reports*, P20-547. U.S. Bureau of the Census. Washington, DC: Government Printing Office.

Fields, J., & Casper. 2001. America's families and living arrangements: March 2000. *Current Population Reports*, P20-357. U.S. Bureau of the Census. Washington, DC: Government Printing Office.

Fine, M., & Weis, L. 2000. Disappearing acts: The state and violence against women in the twentieth century. *Signs, 25*, 1139–1146.

Finlay, B., & Walther, C. S. 2003. The relation of religious affiliation, service attendance, and other factors to homophobic attitudes among university students. *Review of Religious Research, 44*, 370–393.

Firebaugh, G. 2003. *The new geography of global income inequality*. Cambridge: Harvard University Press.

Fischer, M. J., & Massey, D. S. 2000. Residential segregation and ethnic enterprise in U.S. metropolitan areas. *Social Problems, 47*, 40–24.

Fisher, I. 2002. Seeing no justice, a rape victim chooses death. *New York Times*, July 28.

Fleischaker, D. T. 2004. Dead man pausing: The continuing need for a nationwide moratorium on executions. *Human Rights, 31*, 14–18.

Fleury-Steiner, B. 2002. Narratives of the death sentence: Toward a theory of legal narrativity. *Law & Society Review, 36*, 549–576.

Food First. 1998. 12 myths about hunger. www.foodfirst.org/pubs/backgrdrs/1998/s98v5n3.html. Accessed July 19, 2004.

Forbes, H. D. 1997. *Ethnic conflict: Commerce, culture and the contact hypothesis*. New Haven, CT: Yale University Press.

Foucault, M. 1990. *The history of sexuality*. New York: Vintage.

Foundation for Individual Rights in Education. 2004. Free speech. www.TheFire.org/issues/speech.php3. Accessed June 21, 2004.

Fouts, G., & Burggraf, K. 2000. Television situation comedies: Female weight, male negative comments, and audience reactions. *Sex Roles, 42*, 925–932.

Fox, J. A., & Zawitz, M. W. 2002. Homicide trends in the United States. www.ojp.usdoj.gov/bjs/homicide/homtrnd.htm. Accessed July 30, 2004.

Frank, N. 2004. Gays and lesbians at war: Military service in Iraq and Afghanistan under "Don't Ask, Don't Tell." Center for the Study of Sexual Minorities in the Military. www.gaymilitary.ucsb.edu/publications/Frank091504_GaysAtWar.doc. Accessed September 26, 2004.

Frankenberg, R. 2002. Whiteness as an "unmarked" cultural category. In D. M. Newman & J. O'Brien (Eds.), *Sociology: Exploring the architecture of everyday life (Readings)*. Thousand Oaks, CA: Sage.

Freeman, M. 2002. Fewer series feature black-dominant casts. *Electronic Media*, April 15.

Freund, P. E. S., & McGuire, M. B. 1991. *Health, illness, and the social body: A cultural sociology*. Englewood Cliffs, NJ: Prentice Hall.

Friend, T. 1994. White trash nation: White hot trash and the white trashing of America. *New York Magazine*, August 22.

Frohmann, L. 1997. Convictability and discordant locales: Reproducing race, class, and gender ideologies in prosecutorial decisionmaking. *Law & Society Review, 31*, 531–555.

Gallagher, C. A. 1997. White racial formation: Into the twenty-first century. In R. Delgado & J. Stefancic (Eds.), *Critical white studies: Looking behind the mirror.* Philadelphia: Temple University Press.

————. 2004. Color-blind privilege: The social and political functions of erasing the color line. In C. A. Gallagher (Ed.), *Rethinking the color line: Readings in race and ethnicity.* New York: McGraw-Hill.

Gans, H. 1995. *The war against the poor.* New York: Basic Books.

Garfinkel, J. 2003. Boutique medical practices face legal, legislative foes. *Cincinnati Business Courier.* www.bizjournals.com/cincinnati/stories/2003/02/24/focus2.html. Accessed July 12, 2004.

Gasparino, C. 2004. Suing the street. *Newsweek,* December 6.

Gates, A. 2000. Men on TV: Dumb as a post and proud of it. *New York Times,* April 9.

Gates, H. L. 1992. TV's black world turns—but stays unreal. In M. L. Anderson & P. H. Collins (Eds.), *Race, class and gender: An anthology.* Belmont, CA: Wadsworth.

Gaubatz, K. T. 1995. *Crime in the public mind.* Ann Arbor: University of Michigan Press.

Gee, H. 2004. From *Bakke* to *Grutter* and beyond: Asian Americans and diversity in America. *Texas Journal on Civil Liberties & Civil Rights, 9,* 129–158.

Gelles, R. J., & Straus, M. A. 1988. *Intimate violence.* New York: Touchstone.

Gerson, K. 2000. Resolving family dilemmas and conflicts: Beyond utopia. *Contemporary Society, 29,* 180–187.

Giallombardo, R. 1966. *Society of women: A study of women's prison.* New York: Wiley.

Gilligan, J. 2004. Culture, gender, and violence: We are not women. In M. S. Kimmel (Ed.), *The gendered society reader.* New York: Oxford University Press.

Gilliom, J. 2001. *Overseers of the poor: Surveillance, resistance, and the limits of privacy.* Chicago: University of Chicago Press.

Gillis, J. R. 1996. *A world of their own making: Myth, ritual, and the quest for family values.* New York: Basic Books.

Gilman, S. 2004. *Fat boys.* Lincoln: University of Nebraska Press.

Giuffre, P. A., & Williams, C. L. 2000. Not just bodies: Strategies for desexualizing the physical examination of patients. *Gender & Society, 14,* 457–482.

Gladwell, M. 1996. Black like them. *The New Yorker,* April 29, May 6.

A glance at women in the military. 2001. *Associated Press Online,* May 9.

Glater, J. D. 2005. Crime and punishment, the celebrity version. *New York Times,* March 6.

Glaze, L. E., & Palla, S. 2004. Probation and parole in the United States, 2003. Bureau of Justice Statistics Bulletin, NCJ205336. www.ojp.usdoj.gov/bjs/pub/pdf/ppus03.pdf. Accessed July 26, 2004.

Glazer, S. 2003. Mothers' movement. *CQ Researcher, 13,* 297–320.

Glick, P., & Fiske, S. T. 1996. The ambivalent sexism inventory: Differentiating hostile and benevolent sexism. *Journal of Personality and Social Psychology, 70,* 49–12.

Goldberg, J. 1999. The color of suspicion. *New York Times Magazine,* June 20.

Goldberg, S. 1999. The logic of patriarchy. *Gender Issues, 17,* 53–69.

Goldberg, S., & Lewis, M. 1969. Play behavior in the year-old infant: Early sex differences. *Child Development, 40,* 21–31.

Golway, T. 2004. Redrafting America. *America,* August 2–9.

Good, G. E., Porter, M. J., & Dillon, M. G. 2002. When men divulge: Portrayals of men's self-disclosure in prime time situation comedies. *Sex Roles, 46,* 419–427.

Goodnough, A. 2004. Voting rights of Florida felons scrutinized after 2000 election. *New York Times,* March 28.

Goodwin, J. 2003. The ultimate growth industry: Trafficking in women and girls. In E. Disch (Ed.), *Reconstructing gender: A multicultural anthology.* New York: McGraw-Hill.

Gordon, L. 1997. Killing in self-defense. *The Nation,* March 24, 25–28.

Gould, S. J. 1981. *The mismeasure of man.* New York: Norton.

———. 1984. Similarities between the sexes. *New York Times Book Review,* August 12.

Graham, L. O. 1999. *Our kind of people: Inside America's black upper class.* New York: HarperCollins.

Granfield, R. 2005. Making it by faking it: Working-class students in an elite academic environment. In S. J. Ferguson (Ed.), *Mapping the social landscape.* New York: McGraw-Hill.

Gray, H. 1995. Television, black Americans, and the American dream. In G. Dines & J. M. Humez (Eds.), *Gender, race and class in media.* Thousand Oaks, CA: Sage.

Greenhouse, L. 1993. Court, 9–0, makes sex harassment easier to prove. *New York Times,* November 10.

Greenhouse, S. 2004. If you're a waiter the future is rosy. *New York Times,* March 7.

Greenhouse, S., & Hays, C. L. 2004. Wal-Mart sex-bias suit given class-action status. *New York Times,* June 23.

Griffin, S. 1986. *Rape: The power of consciousness.* New York: Harper & Row.

Gross, J. 2004. Splitting up boys and girls, just for the tough years. *New York Times,* May 31.

Gross, L. 1994. What is wrong with this picture? Lesbian women and gay men on television. In R. J. Ringer (Ed.), *Queer words, queer images.* New York: NYU Press.

———. 1995. Out of the mainstream: Sexual minorities and the mass media. In G. Dines & J. M. Humez (Eds.), *Gender, race and class in media.* Thousand Oaks, CA: Sage.

Grossman, C. L. 2003. Public opinion is divided on gay marriages. *USA Today,* October 6.

Gusfield, J. 1963. *Symbolic crusade.* Urbana, IL: University of Illinois Press.

Hacker, A. 1992. *Two nations: Black and white, separate, hostile, unequal.* New York: Scribner's.

———. 1994. White on white. *New Republic,* October 31.

Hagan, J. 2000. The poverty of a classless criminology: The American Society of Criminology 1991 presidential address. In R. D. Crutchfield, G. S. Bridges, J. G. Weis, & C. Kubrin (Eds.), *Crime readings.* Thousand Oaks, CA: Pine Forge Press.

Halbfinger, D. M., & Holmes, S. A. 2003. Military mirrors a working-class America. *New York Times*, March 30.

Hale-Benson, J. E. 1986. *Black children: Their roots, culture, and learning styles.* Provo, UT: Brigham Young University Press.

Hall, J. D. 1995. "The mind that burns in each body": Women, rape, and racial violence. In M. L. Anderson & P. H. Collins (Eds.), *Race, class, and gender.* Belmont, CA: Wadsworth.

Hall, S. 1995. The whites of their eyes: Racist ideologies and the media. In G. Dines & J. M. Humez (Eds.), *Gender, race and class in media.* Thousand Oaks, CA: Sage.

Hamer, D., & Coupland, P. 1994. *The science of desire.* New York: Simon & Schuster.

Hamilton, D. L. 1981. *Cognitive processes in stereotyping and intergroup behavior.* Hillsdale, NJ: Erlbaum.

Hamilton, J. A. 1996. Women and health policy: On the inclusion of women in clinical trials. In C. F. Sargent & C. B. Brettell (Eds.), *Gender and health: An international perspective.* Upper Saddle River, NJ: Prentice Hall.

Hamilton, L. 2005. Mixed record of sustaining aid beyond disaster relief. *Indianapolis Star*, January 17.

Haney López, I. F. 1996. *White by law: The legal construction of race.* New York: NYU Press.

Hantzis, D. M., & Lehr, V. 1994. Whose desire? Lesbian (non) sexuality on television's perpetuation of hetero/sexism. In R. J. Ringer (Ed.), *Queer words, queer images.* New York: NYU Press.

Harris, D. R., & Sim, J. J. 2002. Who is multiracial? Assessing the complexity of lived race. *American Sociological Review, 67*, 614–627.

Harris, G. 2003. If shoe won't fit, fix the foot? Popular surgery raises concern. *New York Times*, December 7.

Harrison, P. M., & Karberg, J. C. 2004. Prison and jail inmates at midyear 2003. Bureau of Justice Statistics Bulletin, NCJ203947. www.ojp.usdoj.gov/bjs/pub/pdf/pjim03.pdf. Accessed July 25, 2004.

Hartmann, K., Viswanathan, M., Palmieri, R., Gartlehner, G., Thorp, J., & Lohr, K. N. 2005. Outcomes of routine episiotomies. *JAMA, 293*, 2141–2148.

Hays, S. 1996. *The cultural contradictions of motherhood.* New Haven, CT: Yale University Press.

———. 2003. *Flat broke with children: Women in the age of welfare reform.* New York: Oxford University Press.

Helms, J. E. 1993. *Black and white racial identity: Theory, research, and practice.* Westport, CT: Praeger.

Henderson, A. F. 1979. College age lesbianism as a developmental phenomenon. *Journal of American College Health, 28*, 176–178.

Henderson, J. J., & Baldasty, G. J. 2003. Race, advertising, and prime-time television. *The Howard Journal of Communication, 14*, 97–112.

Henwood, D. 2001. Wealth report. *The Nation*, April 9.

Herdt, G. 1994. *Third sex, third gender: Beyond sexual dimorphism in culture and history.* New York: Zone Books.

Herek, G. M. 2000a. The psychology of sexual prejudice. *Current Directions in Psychological Science, 9*, 19–22.

————. 2000b. Sexual prejudice and gender: Do heterosexuals' attitudes toward lesbians and gay men differ? *Journal of Social Issues, 56,* 251–266.

Herrnstein, R. J., & Murray, C. 1994. *The bell curve: Intelligence and class structure in American life.* New York: Free Press.

Hill, M. E. 2002. Skin color and the perception of attractiveness among African Americans. *Social Psychology Quarterly, 65,* 77–91.

Hill, N. E. 1997. Does parenting differ based on social class? African American women's perceived socialization for achievement. *American Journal of Community Psychology, 25,* 67–97.

Hill, S. A. 1999. *African American children: Socialization and development in families.* Thousand Oaks, CA: Sage.

Hill, S. A., & Sprague, J. 1999. Parenting in black and white families: The interaction of gender with race and class. *Gender & Society, 13,* 480–502.

Hillier, L., & Harrison, L. 2004. Homophobia and the production of shame: Young people and same sex attraction. *Culture, Health, and Sexuality, 6,* 79–95.

Hines, R. I. 2001. African Americans' struggle for environmental justice and the case of the Shintech plant: Lessons learned from a war waged. *Journal of Black Studies, 31,* 777–789.

Hochschild, J. L. 1995. *Facing up to the American Dream: Race, class, and the soul of a nation.* Princeton: Princeton University Press.

Hollander, J. A., & Howard, J. A. 2000. Social psychological theories on social inequalities. *Social Psychology Quarterly, 63,* 338–351.

Holmes, S. 1999. Blacks sue, saying hotel discriminated. *New York Times,* May 21.

————. 2000. New policy on census says those listed as white and minority will be counted as minority. *New York Times,* March 11.

Hooks, G., & Smith, C. L. 2004. The treadmill of destruction: National sacrifice areas and Native Americans. *American Sociological Review, 69,* 558–575.

Hosenball, M. 1999. It is not the act of a few bad apples. *Newsweek,* May 17.

Hout, M., & Lucas, S. R. 2001. Narrowing the income gap between rich and poor. In P. S. Rothenberg (Ed.), *Race, class, and gender in the United States.* New York: Worth.

Howard, J. A., & Hollander, J. 1997. *Gendered situations, gendered selves.* Newbury Park, CA: Sage.

Howell-White, S. 1999. *Birth alternatives: How women select childbirth care.* Westport, CT: Greenwood Press.

Hu-DeHart, E. 1996. Beyond black and white: A conversation with Evelyn Hu-DeHart. www.jhu.edu/~igscph/spr96ehd.htm. Accessed January 7, 2005.

Hughes, D., & Chen, L. 1997. When and what parents tell children about race: An examination of race-related socialization among African American families. *Applied Developmental Science, 1,* 200–214.

Hulbert, A. 2004. *Raising America: Experts, parents, and a century of advice about children.* New York: Vintage Books.

Hull, K. E., & Nelson, R. L. 2000. Assimilation, choice, or constraint? Testing theories of gender differences in the careers of lawyers. *Social Forces, 79,* 229–264.

Human Rights Watch. 2001. Caste discrimination: A global concern. www.hrw.org/reports/2001/globalcaste. Accessed June 16, 2004.

Hunt, J. G., & Hunt, L. L. 1990. The dualities of careers and families: New integrations or new polarizations? In C. Carlson (Ed.), *Perspectives on the family: History, class, and feminism.* Belmont, CA: Wadsworth.

Hyde, J. S. 1984. How large are gender differences in aggression? A developmental meta-analysis. *Developmental Psychology, 20,* 722–736.

Iceland, J., Weinberg, D. H., & Steinmetz, E. 2002. Racial and ethnic residential segregation in the United States: 1980–2000. Census 2000 Special Report, CENSR-3. Washington, DC: U.S. Government Printing Office.

Income gap of poor, rich widens. 2004. CBSNews Online. www.cbsnews.com/stories/2004/08/13/national/main635936.shtml. Accessed August 18, 2004.

Initiative Media North America. 2003. Proprietary study reveals TV networks winning African American viewers. *IMsight News, 2,* 1–2. www.im-na.com/news/img/IMsightsv2n4.pdf. Accessed August 1, 2003.

Institute for Policy Research. 2002. Housework in double-income marriages still divides unevenly. *Institute for Policy Research News, 24,* 1–2. www.northwestern.edu/ipr/publications/newsletter/iprn0212/housework.html. Accessed August 2, 2003.

Institute of Medicine. 2003. Unequal treatment: Confronting racial and ethnic disparities in health care. National Academy Press. www.nap.edu/books/030908265x/html/. Accessed July 19, 2004.

Jackson, J. L. 2004. Birthdays, basketball, and breaking bread: Negotiating with class in contemporary black America. In L. D. Baker (Ed.), *Life in America: Identity and everyday experience.* Malden, MA: Blackwell.

Jackson, S. 1995. The social context of rape: Sexual scripts and motivation. In P. Searles & R. J. Berger (Eds.), *Rape and society.* Boulder, CO: Westview Press.

Jacobson, L. 2004. Poll of teachers finds two-tiered system. *Education Week,* May 19.

Jacoby, T. 2004. Defining assimilation for the 21st century. In T. Jacoby (Ed.), *Reinventing the melting pot.* New York: Basic Books.

Janofsky, M. 1998. Maryland troopers stop drivers by race, suit says. *New York Times,* June 5.

Jenness, V. 2002. Coming out: Lesbian identities and the categorization problem. In D. M. Newman & J. O'Brien (Eds.), *Sociology: Exploring the architecture of everyday life (Readings).* Thousand Oaks, CA: Pine Forge Press.

Johnson, A. G. 2001. *Privilege, power, and difference.* New York: McGraw-Hill.

Johnston, D. 2002. Big names but no authority to prosecute. *New York Times,* July 10.

Jones, N. A., & Smith, A. S. 2001. The two or more races population: 2000. *Census 2000 Brief,* C2KBR/01–6. www.census.gov/prod/2001pubs/c2kbr01-6.pdf. Accessed September 22, 2004.

Jost, K. 2000. Racial profiling. *CQ Researcher,* March 17.

Joyce, A. 2004. Wal-Mart bias case moves forward. *Washington Post,* June 23.

Kanter, R. M. 1977. *Men and women of the corporation.* New York: Basic Books.

Karraker, K. H., Vogel, D. A., & Lake, M. A. 1995. Parents' gender stereotyped perceptions of newborns: The eye of the beholder revisited. *Sex Roles, 33,* 687–701.

Katz, J. N. 2003. The invention of heterosexuality. In T. E. Ore (Ed.), *The social construction of difference and inequality: Race, class, gender, and sexuality.* New York: McGraw-Hill.

Kaufman, G. 1999. The portrayal of men's family roles in television commercials. *Sex Roles, 41,* 439–458.

Kaw, E. 2002. "Opening" faces: The politics of cosmetic surgery and Asian American women. In D. M. Newman & J. O'Brien (Eds.), *Sociology: Exploring the architecture of everyday life (Readings).* Thousand Oaks, CA: Pine Forge Press.

Keister, L. A., & Moller, S. 2000. Wealth inequality in the United States. *Annual Review of Sociology, 26,* 63–81.

Keith, V. M., & Herring, C. 1991. Skin tone and stratification in the Black community. *American Journal of Sociology, 97,* 760–778.

Kennedy, R. 2002. *Nigger: The strange career of a troublesome word.* New York: Pantheon.

Kershner, R. 1996. Adolescent attitudes about rape. *Adolescence, 31,* 29–33.

Kessler, S. J., & McKenna, W. 1978. *Gender: An ethnomethodological approach.* Chicago: University of Chicago Press.

———. 2003. Who put the "trans" in transgender? Gender theory and everyday life. In S. LaFont (Ed.), *Constructing sexualities: Readings in sexuality, gender, and culture.* Upper Saddle River, NJ: Prentice Hall.

Kessler-Harris, A. 1982. *Out to work: A history of wage-earning women in the United States.* New York: Oxford University Press.

Khalema, N. E., & Wannas-Jones, J. 2003. Under the prism of suspicion: Minority voices in Canada post–September 11. *Journal of Muslim Minority Affairs, 23,* 25–39.

Kibria, N. 2004. College and notions of "Asian American": Second-generation Chinese and Korean Americans negotiate race and identity. In L. D. Baker (Ed.), *Life in America: Identity and everyday experience.* Malden, MA: Blackwell.

Kilborn, P. T. 1999. Bias worsens for minorities buying homes. *New York Times,* September 16.

Kilbourne, J. 1992. Beauty and the beast of advertising. In P. S. Rothenberg (Ed.), *Race, class and gender in the United States.* New York: St. Martin's Press.

Kimmel, M. 2004. *The gendered society.* New York: Oxford University Press.

Kinsey, A. C., Pomeroy, W. B., & Martin, C. E. 1948. *Sexual behavior in the human male.* Philadelphia: Saunders.

Kinsey, A. C., Pomeroy, W. B., Martin, C. E., & Gebhard, P. H. 1953. *Sexual behavior in the human female.* Philadelphia: Saunders.

Kirby, D. 2004. Party favors: Pill popping as insurance. *New York Times,* June 21.

Klein, F. 1990. *The bisexual option.* New York: Harrington Park Press.

Klinenberg, E. 2002. *Heat wave: A social autopsy of disaster in Chicago.* Chicago: University of Chicago Press.

Knott, A. 2004. Lobbyists bankrolling politics. Center for Public Integrity. www.publicintegrity.org/bop2004/report.aspx?aid=273. Accessed August 7, 2004.

Knuckey, J., & Orey, B. D. 2000. "Symbolic racism in the 1995 Louisiana gubernatorial election." *Social Science Quarterly, 81,* 1027–1035.

Kochhar, R. 2004. The wealth of Hispanic households: 1996–2002. Pew Hispanic Center Report. www.pewhispanic.org/index.jsp. Accessed October 18, 2004.

Koeppel, B. 1999. Cancer Alley, Louisiana. *The Nation,* November 8.

Kohlberg, L. A. 1966. A cognitive-developmental analysis of children's sex-role concepts and attitudes. In E. Maccoby (Ed.), *The development of sex differences.* Stanford, CA: Stanford University Press.

Kohn, H. 1994. Service with a sneer. *New York Times Magazine,* November 6.

Kohn, M. L. 1979. The effects of social class on parental values and practices. In D. Reiss & H. A. Hoffman (Eds.), *The American family: Dying or developing.* New York: Plenum.

Kokopeli, B., & Lakey, G. 1992. More power than we want: Masculine sexuality and violence. In M. L. Anderson & P. H. Collins (Eds.), *Race, class and gender: An anthology.* Belmont, CA: Wadsworth.

Kolata, G. 2004a. Experts set a lower low for cholesterol levels. *New York Times,* July 13.

———. 2004b. "Normal" blood pressure may still be too high. *New York Times,* November 10.

Kollock, P., Blumstein, P., & Schwartz, P. 1985. Sex and power in interaction: Conversational privileges and duties. *American Sociological Review, 50,* 34–46.

Kornreich, J. L., Hearn, K. D., Rodriguez, G., & O'Sullivan, L. F. 2003. Sibling influence, gender roles, and the sexual socialization of urban early adolescent girls. *Journal of Sex Research, 40,* 101–110.

Kosinsky, J. 1965. *The painted bird.* Boston: Houghton Mifflin.

Kozol, J. 1991. *Savage inequalities: Children in America's schools.* New York: Harper-Perennial.

Kristof, N. D. 1995. Japanese outcasts better off than in past but still outcasts. *New York Times,* November 30.

Kulik, D. 2000. Gay and lesbian language. *Annual Review of Anthropology, 29,* 243–285.

Lacey, M. 2004. A decade after massacres Rwanda outlaws ethnicity. *New York Times,* April 9.

Lakoff, G. 2004. Kerry was framed. www.alternet.org/election04/19768. Accessed September 3, 2004.

Lakoff, R. 1973. Language and women's place. *Language and Society, 2,* 45–80.

———. 1995. Cries and whispers: The shattering of the silence. In K. Hall & M. Bucholtz (Eds.), *Gender articulated: Language and the socially constructed self.* New York: Routledge.

Lalasz, R. 2004. World AIDS Day 2004: The vulnerability of women and girls. Population Reference Bureau Report, November. www.prb.org. Accessed December 1, 2004.

———. 2005. Full-time work no guarantee of livelihood for many U.S. families. Population Reference Bureau Report, January. www.prb.org. Accessed January 19, 2005.

Lamont, M. 1995. Money, morals, and manners. In D. M. Newman (Ed.), *Sociology: Exploring the architecture of everyday life (Readings).* Thousand Oaks, CA: Pine Forge Press.

Landesman, P. 2004. The girls next door. *New York Times,* January 25.

Lang, S. 1998. *Men as women, women as men: Changing gender in Native American cultures.* Austin: University of Texas Press.

———. 2003. Lesbians, men-women, and two-spirits: Homosexuality and gender in Native American cultures. In S. LaFont (Ed.), *Constructing sexualities: Readings in sexuality, gender, and culture.* Upper Saddle River, NJ: Prentice Hall.

Lareau, A. 2003. *Unequal childhoods: Class, race, and family life.* Berkeley: University of California Press.

Larew, J. 2003. Why are droves of unqualified, unprepared kids getting into our top colleges? Because their dads are alumni. In K. E. Rosenblum & T. C. Travis (Eds.), *The meaning of difference: American constructions of race, sex and gender, social class, and sexual orientation.* New York: McGraw-Hill.

Lawler, S. 2001. Introduction: The futures of gender and sexuality. *Social Epistomology, 15,* 71–76.

Leap, W. 1996. *Word's out. Gay men's English.* Minneapolis: University of Minnesota Press.

LeBesco, K. 2004. *Revolting bodies? The struggle to redefine fat identity.* Amherst, MA: University of Massachusetts Press.

Lee, J., & Bean, F. D. 2004. America's changing color lines: Immigration, race/ethnicity, and multiracial identification. *Annual Review of Sociology, 30,* 221–242.

Lee, S. M. 1993. Racial classifications in the U.S. Census: 1890–1990. *Ethnic and Racial Studies, 16,* 75–94.

Lee, S. M., & Edmonston, B. 2005. New marriages, new families: U.S. racial and Hispanic intermarriage. *Population Bulletin, 60,* 1–36.

Lee, V., & Marks, H. M. 1990. Sustained effects of the single-sex secondary school experience on attitudes, behaviors and values in college. *Journal of Educational Psychology, 82,* 578–592.

Legman, G. 1941. The language of homosexuality: An American glossary. In G. W. Henry (Ed.), *Sex variants: A study of homosexual patterns.* New York/London: Hoeber.

Leland, J. 2004. Why America sees the silver lining. *New York Times,* June 13.

Lemire, E. 2002. *Miscegenation: Making race in America.* Philadelphia: University of Pennsylvania Press.

Leonard, A. S. 2003. The gay rights workplace revolution. *Human Rights,* Summer.

Leonhardt, D. 2002. Blacks' mortgage costs exceed whites' of like pay. *New York Times,* May 1.

Lepkowska, D. 2004. Model minority tag hides Asian drop-out problem. *Times Educational Supplement,* May 7.

Lester, W. 2005. Poll: 29% in U.S. give tsunami aid. *Indianapolis Star,* January 8.

Letellier, P. 1996. Gay and bisexual male domestic violence victimization. In L. K. Hamberger & C. Renzetti (Eds.), *Domestic partner abuse.* New York: Springer.

LeVay, S. 1991. A difference in hypothalmic structure between heterosexual and homosexual men. *Science,* August 30, 1034–1037.

Levine, H., & Evans, N. J. 2003. The development of gay, lesbian, and bisexual identities. In K. E. Rosenblum & T. C. Travis (Eds.), *The meaning of difference.* New York: McGraw-Hill.

Lewin, T. 2001. Women's health is no longer a man's world. *New York Times,* February 6.

Lewis, G. B. 2003. Black-white differences in attitudes toward homosexuality and gay rights. *Public Opinion Quarterly, 67,* 59–79.

Lichtblau, E. 2003. Bush bans racial profiling, with exceptions for security. *New York Times,* June 17.

———. 2004. Cracker Barrel agrees to plan to address reports of bias. *New York Times,* May 4.

Lieberson, S. 1980. *A piece of the pie: Blacks and white immigrants since 1880.* Berkeley: University of California Press.

Limited black slots on TV. 2000. *New York Times,* February 26.

Lippmann, L. W. 1922. *Public opinion.* New York: Harcourt Brace Jovanovich.

Liptak, A. 2004a. Bans on interracial unions offer perspective on gay ones. *New York Times,* March 17.

———. 2004b. Ex-inmate's suit offers view into sexual slavery in prison. *New York Times,* October 16.

Loe, M. 2001. Fixing broken masculinity: Viagra as a technology for the production of gender and sexuality. *Sexuality & Culture,* 5, 97–125.

Lorber, J. 1994. Dismantling Noah's ark: Gender and equality. In J. Lorber (Ed.), *Paradoxes of gender.* New Haven, CT: Yale University Press.

———. 1998. *Gender inequality: Feminist theories and politics.* Los Angeles: Roxbury.

———. 2000. *Gender and the social construction of illness.* Walnut Creek, CA: Altamira Press.

Lowes, R. 2002. How unhappy are women doctors? In R. H. Lauer & J. C. Lauer (Eds.), *Sociology: Windows on society.* Los Angeles: Roxbury.

Lucal, B. 1999. What is means to be gendered me: Life on the boundaries of a dichotomous gender system. *Gender & Society,* 13, 781–797.

Lyall, S. 2004. In Europe, lovers now propose: Marry me, a little. *New York Times,* February 15.

MacDonald, K., & Parke, R. G. 1986. Parent-child physical play: The effects of sex and age on children and parents. *Sex Roles,* 15, 367–378.

Macgillivray, I. K. 2000. Educational equity for gay, lesbian, bisexual, transgendered, and queer/questioning students: The demands of democracy and social justice for America's schools. *Education and Urban Society,* 32, 303–323.

MacMillan, R., & Gartner, R. 1999. When she brings home the bacon: Labor-force participation and the risk of spousal violence against women. *Journal of Marriage and the Family,* 61, 947–959.

Mantsios, G. 1995. Media magic: Making class invisible. In P. S. Rothenberg (Ed.), *Race, class and gender in the United States.* New York: St. Martin's Press.

Marger, M. 1994. *Race and ethnic relations.* Belmont, CA: Wadsworth.

Markowitz, L. 2000. A different kind of queer marriage. *Utne Reader,* September–October.

Marmor, J. 1996. Blurring the lines. *Columns,* December.

Marmot, M. 2004. *The status syndrome: How social standing affects our health and longevity.* New York: Times Books.

Married households rise again among blacks, Census finds. 2003. *New York Times,* April 26.

Marshall, B. L. 2002. "Hard science": Gendered constructions of sexual dysfunction in the "Viagra Age." *Sexualities,* 5, 131–159.

Martin, C. L., & Ruble, D. 2004. Children's search for gender cues. *Current Directions in Psychological Science,* 13, 67–70.

Martinez, E. 1998. *De colores means all of us: Latina views for a multi-colored century.* Cambridge, MA: South End Press.

———. 2003. Seeing more than black and white: Latinos, racism and the cultural dividers. In T. E. Ore (Ed.), *The social construction of difference and inequality.* New York: McGraw-Hill.

Marx, K., & Engels, F. 1982. *The communist manifesto.* New York: International Publishers. (Original work published 1848)

Massey, D., & Fischer, M. J. 1999. Does rising income bring integration? New results for Blacks, Hispanics, and Asians in 1990. *Social Science Research, 28,* 316–326.

Mastrilli, T., & Sardo-Brown, D. 2002. Pre-service teachers' knowledge about Islam: A snapshot post September 11, 2001. *Journal of Institutional Psychology, 4,* 159–173.

Mathews, L. 1996. More than identity rides on a new racial category. *New York Times,* July 6.

Matsuda, M. J. 1993. Public response to racist speech: Considering the victim's story. In M. J. Matsuda, C. R. Lawrence III, R. Delgado, & K. Williams Crenshaw (Eds.), *Words that wound.* Boulder, CO: Westview.

Mauer, M. 1999. *Race to incarcerate.* New York: The New Press.

Maume, D. J. 1999. Glass ceilings and glass escalators: Occupational segregation and race and sex differences in managerial promotions. *Work and Occupations, 26,* 483–509.

Mayberry, R., Mili, F., & Ofili, E. 2000. Racial and ethnic differences in access to medical care. *Medical Care Research & Review, 57,* 108–146.

McCain, F. 1991. Interview with Franklin McCain. In C. Carson, D. J. Garrow, G. Gill, V. Harding, & D. Clark Hine (Eds.), *The Eyes on the Prize civil rights reader.* New York: Penguin.

McCloskey, D. 1999. *Crossing: A memoir.* Chicago: University of Chicago Press.

McCormick, J. S., Maric, A., Seto, M. C., & Barbaree, H. E. 1998. Relationship to victim predicts sentence length in sexual assault cases. *Journal of Interpersonal Violence, 13,* 41–20.

McIntosh, P. 2001. White privilege: Unpacking the invisible knapsack. In P. Rothenberg (Ed.), *Race, class, and gender in the United States.* New York: Worth.

McLeod, J. D., & Owens, T. J. 2004. Psychological well-being in the early life course: Variations by socioeconomic status, gender, and race/ethnicity. *Social Psychology Quarterly, 67,* 257–278.

McLoyd, V. C., Cauce, A. M., Takeuchi, D., & Wilson, L. 2000. Marital processes and parental socialization in families of color: A decade review of research. *Journal of Marriage and the Family, 62,* 1070–1094.

McMichael, P. 1996. *Development and social change: A global perspective.* Thousand Oaks, CA: Pine Forge Press.

McNeil, D. G. 2004. When real food isn't an option. *New York Times,* May 23.

McVey, G., Tweed, S., & Blackmore, E. 2004. Dieting among preadolescent and young adolescent females. *Canadian Medical Association Journal, 170,* 1559–1561.

McWhorter, J. 2004. Getting over identity. In T. Jacoby (Ed.), *Reinventing the melting pot.* New York: Basic Books.

Mead, M. 1963. *Sex and temperament.* New York: William Morrow.

Media Awareness Network. 2005. Gender stereotyping. www.media-awareness.ca/english/parents/video_games/concerns/gender_videogames.cfm. Accessed January 8, 2005.

Media Report to Women, 2003. Boxed in: Women still outnumbered behind scenes and on screen in prime time. www.mediareporttowomen.com/issues/314.htm. Accessed June 30, 2004.

Meertens, R. W., & Pettigrew, T. F. 1997. Is subtle prejudice really prejudice? *Public Opinion Quarterly, 61*, 54–71.

Mendez, T. 2004. Separating the sexes: A new direction for public education? *Christian Science Monitor*, May 25.

Merton, R. 1949. Discrimination and the American creed. In R. M. MacIver (Ed.), *Discrimination and national welfare.* New York: Harper & Row.

———. 1957. *Social theory and social structure.* New York: Free Press.

Messner, M. 2002. Boyhood, organized sports, and the construction of masculinities. In D. M. Newman & J. O'Brien (Eds.), *Sociology: Exploring the architecture of everyday life (Readings).* Thousand Oaks, CA: Pine Forge Press.

Meyer, I. H. 1995. Minority stress and mental health in gay men. *Journal of Health and Social Behavior, 36*, 38–56.

Michael, R. T., Gagnon, J. H., Laumann, E. O., & Kolata, G. 1994. *Sex in America: A definitive survey.* Boston: Little, Brown.

Millman, M. 1980. *Such a pretty face.* New York: Norton.

Mintz, S., & Kellogg, S. 1988. *Domestic revolutions.* New York: Free Press.

Mishel, L., Bernstein, J., & Allegretto, S. 2004. *The state of working America: 2004/2005.* Economic Policy Institute. Ithaca, NY: Cornell University Press.

Mitford, J. 1993. *The American way of birth.* New York: Plume.

Modelminority.com. 2003. About ModelMinority.com: A guide to Asian American Empowerment. www.modelminority.com. Accessed June 19, 2003.

Mokhiber, R. 1999. Crime wave! The top 100 corporate criminals of the 1990s. *Multinational Monitor*, July–August, 1–9.

Molloy, B. L., & Herzberger, S. D. 1998. Body image and self-esteem: A comparison of African-American and Caucasian women. *Sex Roles, 38*, 631–643.

Mom's market value. 1998. *Utne Reader*, March/April.

Monteith, M., & Winters, J. 2002. Why we hate. *Psychology Today, 35*, 44–52.

Moore, R. B. 1992. Racist stereotyping in the English language. In M. L. Anderson & P. H. Collins (Eds.), *Race, class and gender: An anthology.* Belmont, CA: Wadsworth.

Morgan, M. 1982. Television and adolescents' sex role stereotypes: A longitudinal study. *Journal of Personality and Social Psychology, 48*, 1173–1190.

———. 1987. Television sex role attitudes and sex role behavior. *Journal of Early Adolescence, 7*, 269–282.

Morgan, R. 1996. *Sisterhood is global.* New York: The Feminist Press at the City University of New York.

Morrongiello, B. A., & Hogg, K. 2004. Mothers' reactions to children misbehaving in ways that can lead to injury: Implications for gender differences in children's risk taking and injuries. *Sex Roles, 50*, 103–118.

Moss, R. F. 2001. The shrinking life span of the black sitcom. *New York Times*, February 25.

Mulkern, A. C. 2004. Canada offers preview of gay-marriage impacts. *Denver Post*, July 4.

Murguia, E., & Telles, E. E. 1996. Phenotype and schooling among Mexican Americans. *Sociology of Education, 69*, 276–289.

Murphy, D. E. 2004. Imagining life without illegal immigrants. *New York Times*, January 11.

Murphy, M. L. 1997. The elusive bisexual: Social categorization and lexico-semantic change. In A. Livia & K. Hall (Eds.), *Queerly phrased: Language, gender, and sexuality.* New York: Oxford University Press.

Nagel, J. 2003. *Race, ethnicity, and sexuality: Intimate intersections, forbidden frontiers.* New York: Oxford University Press.

Nanda, S. 2003. Hijra and Sādhin: Neither man nor woman in India. In S. LaFont (Ed.), *Constructing sexualities: Readings in sexuality, gender, and culture.* Upper Saddle River, NJ: Prentice Hall.

Nasar, S., & Mitchell, K. B. 1999. Booming job market draws young black men into the fold. *New York Times,* May 23.

National Alliance to End Homelessness. 2005. Frequently asked questions. www.endhomelessness.org/disc/index.htm#three. Accessed June 8, 2005.

National Association for Single-Sex Public Education. 2004. Single-sex education. www.singlesexschools.org. Accessed July 10, 2004.

National Center for Health Statistics. 2003. Health, United States, 2003. www.cdc.gov/nchs/products/pubs/pubd/hus/trendtables.htm. Accessed September 23, 2004.

National Center for Policy Analysis. 2000. Stock ownership is becoming widespread. www.ncpa.org/oped/bartlett/jan2400.html. Accessed July 31, 2003.

National Committee on Pay Equity. 1999. The wage gap: 1998. www.feminist.com/fairpay. Accessed July 1, 2000.

National Eating Disorders Association. 2004. Statistics: Eating disorders and their precursors. www.nationaleatingdisorders.org. Accessed July 21, 2004.

National Fair Housing Alliance. 2004. 2004 fair housing trends report. www.nationalfairhousing.org. Accessed August 31, 2004.

National Institute of Mental Health. 2001. Eating disorders: Facts about eating disorders and the search for solutions. NIH Publication #01-4901. www.nimh.nih.gov/publicat/eatingdisorder.cfm. Accessed July 21, 2003.

National Low Income Housing Coalition. 2003. Out of reach 2003: America's housing wage climbs. www.nlihc.org/oor_current/. Accessed October 27, 2004.

Navarro, M. 2003. Census reflects Hispanic identity that is hardly black and white. *New York Times,* November 9.

———. 2004. When gender isn't a given. *New York Times,* September 19.

Neary, I. 1986. Socialist and Communist party attitudes towards discrimination against Japan's Burakumin. *Political Studies, 34,* 556–574.

———. 2003. *Burakumin* at the end of history. *Social Research, 70,* 269–294.

Netzhammer, E. C., & Shamp, S. A. 1994. Guilt by association. Homosexuality and AIDS on prime-time television. In R. J. Ringer (Ed.), *Queer words, queer images.* New York: NYU Press.

Newman, C. 2000. The enigma of beauty. *National Geographic,* January.

Newman, D. M. 2004. *Sociology: Exploring the architecture of everyday life.* Thousand Oaks, CA: Pine Forge Press.

NOMAS. 2004. The National Organization of Men Against Sexism. NOMAS statement of principles. www.nomas.org/sys-tmpl/principles2/. Accessed September 9, 2004.

Nord, M., Andrews, M., & Carlson, S. 2003. Household food security in the United States, 2002. U.S. Department of Agriculture, Food Assistance and Nutrition

Research Report #35. www.ers.usda.gov/publications/fanrr35/fanrr35.pdf/. Accessed July 19, 2004.

Northridge, M. E., Stover, G. N., Rosenthal, J. E., & Sherard, D. 2003. Environmental equity and health: Understanding complexity and moving forward. *American Journal of Public Health, 93,* 209–214.

O'Brien, J. 1999. *Social prisms: Reflections on everyday myths and paradoxes.* Thousand Oaks, CA: Pine Forge Press.

O'Brien, M., & Huston, A. C. 1985. Development of sex-typed play behavior in toddlers. *Developmental Psychology, 21,* 866–871.

Omi, M., & Winant, H. 1992. Racial formations. In P. S. Rothenberg (Ed.), *Race, class and gender in the United States.* New York: St. Martin's Press.

Onishi, N. 2001. On the scale of beauty, weight weighs heavily. *New York Times,* February 12.

———. 2002. Globalization of beauty makes slimness trendy. *New York Times,* October 3.

Ordover, N. 1996. Eugenics, the gay gene, and the science of backlash. *Socialist Review, 26,* 125–144.

Orfield, G., & Yun, J. T. 1999. Resegregation in American schools. *Harvard Civil Rights Project Report.* Cambridge, MA.

Organ Procurement and Transplant Network. 2004. National data. www.optn.org/latestData/rptData.asp. Accessed July 18, 2004.

Ortner, S. B. 1996. *Making gender: The politics and erotics of culture.* Boston: Beacon Press.

———. 1998. Identities: The hidden life of class. *Journal of Anthropological Research, 54,* 1–17.

Out athletes. 2003. www.outsports.com/outathletes.htm. Accessed January 25, 2005.

Padavic, I., & Reskin, B. 2004. Moving up and taking charge. In L. Richardson, V. Taylor, & N. Whittier (Eds.), *Feminist frontiers.* New York: McGraw-Hill.

Parenti, M. 1996. The make-believe media. In M. J. Carter (Ed.), *Society and the media.* New York: HarperCollins.

Parker, S., Nichter, M., Nichter, M., Vuckovic, N., Sims, C., & Ritenbaugh, C. 1995. Body image and weight concerns among African American and white adolescent females: Differences that make a difference. *Human Organization, 54,* 103–114.

Parsons, T. 1951. *The social system.* New York: Free Press.

Parsons, T., & Bales, R. F. 1955. *Family, socialization and interaction process.* Glencoe, IL: Free Press.

Pattillo-McCoy, M. 1999. *Black picket fences: Privilege and peril among the black middle class.* Chicago: University of Chicago Press.

Paul, A. M. 2004. Taming your mood swings. *Shape Magazine,* July.

Payer, L. 1988. *Medicine and culture.* New York: Penguin.

Pear, R. 2000. Studies find research on women lacking. *New York Times,* April 30.

Pear, R., & Kirkpatrick, D. D. 2004. Bush plans $1.5 billion drive for promotion of marriage. *New York Times,* January 14.

Pearce, D. 1979. Gatekeepers and homeseekers: Institutional patterns of racial steering. *Social Problems, 26,* 325–342.

Perez-Peña, R. 2003. Study finds asthma in 25% of children in central Harlem. *New York Times,* April 19.

Perlez, J. 1998. A wall not yet built casts the shadow of racism. *New York Times,* July 2.

Perlin, S. A., Sexton, K., & Wong, D. W. S. 1999. An examination of race and poverty for populations living near industrial sources of air pollution. *Journal of Exposure Analysis and Environmental Epidemiology, 9,* 29–48.

Peters, M. F. 1988. Parenting in black families with young children: A historical perspective. In H. P. McAdoo (Ed.), *Black families.* Newbury Park, CA: Sage.

Peterson, R. R. 1996. A re-evaluation of the economic consequences of divorce. *American Sociological Review, 61,* 528–536.

Peterson, S. B., & Lach, M. A. 1990. Gender stereotypes in children's books: Their prevalence and influence in cognitive and affective development. *Gender and Education, 2,* 185–197.

Pettit, B., & Western, B. 2004. Mass imprisonment and the life course: Race and class inequality in U.S. incarceration. *American Sociological Review, 69,* 151–169.

Phelan, J., Link, B. G., Moore, R. E., & Stueve, A. 1997. The stigma of homelessness: The impact of the label "homeless" on attitudes toward poor persons. *Social Psychology Quarterly, 60,* 323–337.

Phillips, K. 2002. *Wealth and democracy.* New York: Broadway Books.

Pieterse, J. N. 1995. "White" negroes. In G. Dines & J. M. Humez (Eds.), *Gender, race and class in media.* Thousand Oaks, CA: Sage.

Piper, A. 1992. Passing for white, passing for black. *Transition, 58,* 4–32.

Political correctness. 2004. Wikipedia on-line encyclopedia. http://en.wikipedia.org/wiki/Political_Correctness. Accessed June 18, 2004.

Population Reference Bureau. 2002. Racial and ethnic differences in U.S. mortality. www.prb.org. Accessed July 15, 2004.

———. 2004a. The wealth gap in health, May. www.prg.org. Accessed July 15, 2004.

———. 2004b. 2004 world population data sheet. www.prb.org/pdf04/04WorldDataSheet_Eng.pdf. Accessed August 24, 2004.

Porter, E. 2004. Hourly pay in U.S. not keeping pace with price rises. *New York Times,* July 18.

Potts, A., Grace, V., Gavey, N., & Vares, T. 2004. "Viagra stories": Challenging erectile dysfunction. *Social Science and Medicine, 59,* 489–499.

Probe into race link with homelessness. 2002. *Community Care,* September 19.

Queen, R. 1997. I don't speak spritch: Locating lesbian language. In A. Livia & K. Hall (Eds.), *Queerly phrased: Language, gender, and sexuality.* New York: Oxford University Press.

Quinion, M. 2004. Chav. www.worldwidewords.org/topicalwords/tw-cha2.htm. Accessed January 10, 2005.

Quinney, R. 1970. *The social reality of crime.* Boston: Little, Brown.

A radical assault on the Constitution. 2004. *New York Times,* July 24.

Raffaelli, M., & Ontai, L. L. 2004. Gender socialization in Latino/a families: Results from two retrospective studies. *Sex Roles, 50,* 287–299.

Rankin, S. R. 2003. Campus climate for gay, lesbian, bisexual, and transgender people: A national perspective. National Gay and Lesbian Task Force. www.thetaskforce.org/downloads/CampusClimate.pdf. Accessed September 22, 2004.

Ransom, E. I., & Elder, L. K. 2003. Nutrition of women and adolescent girls: Why it matters. Population Reference Bureau, July. www.prb.org. Accessed July 15, 2004.

Reeves, R. 2004. Men remain stuck in cages of their own creation. *The New States-man,* August 16.

Reiman, J. 2004. *The rich get richer and the poor get prison.* Boston: Allyn & Bacon.

Reinisch, J. M., Rosenblum, L. A., Rubin, D. B., & Schulsinger, M. F. 1997. Sex differences emerge during the first year of life. In M. R. Walsh (Ed.), *Women, men and gender: Ongoing debates.* New Haven, CT: Yale University Press.

Relethford, J. H., Stern, M. P., Caskill, S. P., & Hazuda, H. P. 1983. Social class, admixture, and skin color variation in Mexican Americans and Anglo Americans living in San Antonio, Texas. *American Journal of Physical Anthropology, 61,* 97–102.

Rennison, C. M. 2003. Intimate partner violence, 1993–2001. United States Bureau of Justice Statistics Crime Data Brief. NCJ197838. Washington, DC: U.S. Government Printing Office.

Rennison, C. M., & Welchans, S. 2000. Intimate partner violence. United States Bureau of Justice Statistics Special Report. Washington, DC: U.S. Government Printing Office.

Renzetti, C. M., & Curran, D. J. 2003. *Women, men, and society.* Boston: Allyn & Bacon.

Report on Black America finds college gender gap. 2000. *New York Times,* July 26.

Research findings affirm health of women hinges on reform on clinical research. 2003. *Women's Health Weekly,* August 14.

Reyes, L., & Rubie, P. 1994. *Hispanics in Hollywood: An encyclopedia of film and television.* New York: Garland Press.

Richardson, L. 1997. An old experiment's legacy: Distrust of AIDS treatment. *New York Times,* April 21.

Richardson, L. 2004. Gender stereotyping in the English language. In L. Richardson, V. Taylor, & N. Whittier (Eds.), *Feminist frontiers.* New York: McGraw-Hill.

Rimer, S. 2002. Suspects lacking lawyers are freed in Atlanta. *New York Times,* June 4.

Rimer, S., & Arenson, K. W. 2004. Top colleges take more blacks, but which ones? *New York Times,* June 24.

Risman, B., & Myers, K. 1997. As the twig is bent: Children reared in feminist households. *Qualitative Sociology, 20,* 229–252.

Robinson, R. V., & Bell, W. 1978. Equality, success and social justice in England and the United States. *American Sociological Review, 43,* 125–143.

Rodriguez, C. E., & Cordero-Guzman, H. 2004. Placing race in context. In C. A. Gallagher (Ed.), *Rethinking the color line: Readings in race and ethnicity.* New York: McGraw-Hill.

Roediger, D. R. 1998. *Black on white: Black writers on what it means to be white.* New York: Schocken.

Roehling, M. V. 1999. Weight-based discrimination in employment: Psychological and legal aspects. *Personnel Psychology, 52,* 969–1017.

Rogmans, W. 2001. The rich and the poor. *Injury Control and Safety Promotion, 8,* 129–130.

Romero, M. 2004. Life as the maid's daughter: An exploration of the everyday boundaries of race, class, and gender. In D. M. Newman & J. O'Brien (Eds.), *Sociology: Exploring the architecture of everyday life (Readings).* Thousand Oaks, CA: Pine Forge Press.

Romesburg, D. 1997. Thirteen theories to "cure" homosexuality. www.law.harvard. edu/students/orgs/lambda/1_13theo.html. Accessed January 11, 2005.

Rose, M. 2004. *The mind at work: Valuing the intelligence of the American worker.* New York: Viking.

Rosenbaum, D. E. 2003. Race, sex, and forbidden unions. *New York Times,* December 14.

Rothenberg, P. 1992. *Race, class, and gender in the United States.* New York: St. Martin's Press.

———. 2000. *Invisible privilege: A memoir about race, class, and gender.* Lawrence: University of Kansas Press.

Rothman, B. K. 1984. Women, health and medicine. In J. Freeman (Ed.), *Women: A feminist perspective.* Palo Alto, CA: Mayfield.

Rothman, B. K., & Caschetta, M. B. 1999. Treating health: Women and medicine. In S. J. Ferguson (Ed.), *Mapping the social landscape: Readings in sociology.* Mountain View, CA: Mayfield.

Rothschild, N. 1990. *New York City neighborhoods.* New York: Academic Press.

Rothstein, R. 2002. Linking infant mortality to schooling and stress. *New York Times,* February 6.

Ruane, J. M., & Cerulo, K. A. 1997. *Second thoughts.* Thousand Oaks, CA: Pine Forge Press.

Rubin, J. Z., Provenzano, F. J., & Luria, Z. 1974. The eye of the beholder: Parents' views on sex of newborns. *American Journal of Orthopsychiatry, 44,* 512–519.

Rubin, L. 1990. *Erotic wars: What happened to the sexual revolution?* New York: Harper Perennial.

———. 1994. *Families on the fault line.* New York: Harper Perennial.

Rubinstein, S., & Caballero, B. 2000. Is Miss America an undernourished role model? *Journal of the American Medical Association, 283,* 1569.

Russell Sage Foundation. 2000. Multi-city study of urban inequality. www.russellsage. org/special_interest/point_5_residential.htm. Accessed May 31, 2000.

Sabo, D. 2003. Masculinities and men's health: Moving toward post-Superman era prevention. In E. Disch (Ed.), *Reconstructing gender: A multicultural anthology.* New York: McGraw-Hill.

Sadker, M., & Sadker, D. 2002. Failing at fairness: Hidden lessons. In S. Ferguson (Ed.), *Mapping the social landscape.* New York: McGraw-Hill.

Sadker, M., Sadker, D., Fox, L., & Salata, M. 2004. Gender equity in the classroom: The unfinished agenda. In M. S. Kimmel (Ed.), *The gendered society reader.* New York: Oxford University Press.

Saenz, R. 2004. Latinos and the changing face of America. Population Reference Bureau. www.prb.org. Accessed September 4, 2004.

Salant, J. D. 2002. A richer congress. www.commondreams.org/headlines02/ 1225–02.htm. Accessed August 7, 2004.

Samuels, A. 2004. Smooth operations. *Newsweek,* July 5.

Saulnier, C. F. 2002. Deciding who to see: Lesbians discuss their preferences in health and mental health care providers. *Social Work, 47,* 355–365.

Schmitt, E. 2004. Military women reporting rapes by U.S. soldiers. *New York Times,* February 26.

Schnittker, J. 2004. Social distance in the clinical encounter: Interactional and sociode-mographic foundations for mistrust in physicians. *Social Psychology Quarterly, 67,* 217–235.

Schooler, C. 1996. Cultural and social structural explanations of cross-national psychological differences. *Annual Review of Sociology, 22,* 323–349.

Schultze, S. 2004. Campaigns condemn political flier; Paper aimed at black voters falsely states voting rules. *Milwaukee Journal Sentinel,* October 30.

Sciolino, E. 2004. Spain mobilizes against scourge of machismo. *New York Times,* July 14.

Scott, L. D. 2003. The relation of racial identity and racial socialization to coping with discrimination among African American adolescents. *Journal of Black Studies, 33,* 520–538.

Screen Actors Guild. 2002. Casting data report: 2001. http://new.sag.org/sagWebApp/index.jsp. Accessed August 1, 2003.

Scull, A., & Favreau, D. 1986. A chance to cut is a chance to cure: Sexual surgery for psychosis in three nineteenth century societies. In S. Spitzer & A. T. Scull (Eds.), *Research in law, deviance and social control (Vol. 8).* Greenwich, CT: JAI Press.

Sedney, M. A. 1987. Development of androgyny: Parental influences. *Psychology of Women Quarterly, 11,* 311–326.

Seelye, K. Q., & Elder, J. 2003. Strong support is found for ban on gay marriage. *New York Times,* December 21.

Seidman, S. 2004. *Beyond the closet: The transformation of gay and lesbian life.* New York: Routledge.

Seldes, G. 1985. *The great thoughts.* New York: Ballantine.

Senate Judiciary Committee. 1993. The response to rape: Detours on the road to equal justice. www.inform.umd.edu/EdRes/Topic/WomensStudies/GenderIssues/Violence+Women/ResponsetoRape/full-text. Accessed January 18, 2001.

Seuss, Dr. 1961. *The Sneetches and other stories.* New York: Random House.

Sexual harassment statistics in the workplace and in education. 2004. http://womensissues.about.com/cs/goverornews/a/sexharassstats.htm. Accessed July 31, 2004.

Shah, A. 2004. Causes of poverty: Poverty facts and statistics. www.globalissues.org/TradeRelated/Facts.asp?p=1. Accessed November 11, 2004.

Shakin, M., Shakin, D., & Sternglanz, S. H. 1985. Infant clothing: Sex labeling for strangers. *Sex Roles, 12,* 955–964.

Shanker, T. 2004. Inquiry faults commanders in assaults on cadets. *New York Times,* December 8.

Shanklin, E. 1994. *Anthropology and race.* Belmont, CA: Wadsworth.

Shipler, D. K. 2004. *The working poor: Invisible in America.* New York: Knopf.

Shoemaker, N. 1997. How Indians got to be red. *American Historical Review, 102,* 625–644.

Shugart, H. A. 2003. She shoots, she scores: Mediated construction of contemporary female athletes in coverage of the 1999 US Women's soccer team. *Western Journal of Communication, 67,* 1–31.

Shweder, R. A. 1997. It's called poor health for a reason. *New York Times,* March 9.

Sidel, R. 1990. *On her own: Growing up in the shadow of the American Dream.* New York: Penguin.

Siegel, R. B. 2004. A short history of sexual harassment. In C. A. MacKinnon & R. B. Siegel (Eds.), *Directions in sexual harassment law*. New Haven, CT: Yale University Press.

Signorielli, N. 1990. Children, television, and gender roles. *Journal of Adolescent Health Care, 11,* 50–58.

Silberstein, F. B., & Seeman, M. 1959. Social mobility and prejudice. *American Journal of Sociology, 60,* 258–264.

Silverglate, H. A., & Lukianoff, G. 2003. Speech codes: Alive and well at colleges. *Chronicle of Higher Education, 49,* B7–B8.

Simmons, R. 2002. *Odd girl out: The hidden culture of aggression in girls.* Orlando: Harcourt.

Skolnick, A. 1996. *The intimate environment: Exploring marriage and the family.* New York: HarperCollins.

Smith, C. S. 2002. Risking limbs for height and success in China. *New York Times,* May 5.

Smith, D. 1997. Study looks at portrayal of women in media. *New York Times,* May 1.

Smith, D. E. 1993. The standard North American family: SNAF as an ideological code. *Journal of Family Issues, 14,* 50–65.

Solomon, J. 1996. Texaco's troubles. *Newsweek,* November 25.

Spencer, M. E. 1994. Multiculturalism, "political correctness," and the politics of identity. *Sociological Forum, 9,* 547–567.

Sperling, S. 1991. Baboons with briefcases: Feminism, functionalism, and sociobiology in the evolution of primate behavior. *Signs, 17,* 1–27.

St. Jean, Y., & Feagin, J. R. 1998. *Double burden: Black women and everyday racism.* Armonk, NY: M. E. Sharp.

St. John, W. 2003. Metrosexuals come out. *New York Times,* June 22.

Staggenborg, S. 1998. *Gender, family and social movements.* Thousand Oaks, CA: Pine Forge Press.

Stanley, A. 2005. TV's Busby Berkeley moment. *New York Times,* January 30.

Stanley, L. 2002. Should "sex" really be "gender"—or "gender" really be "sex"? In S. Jackson & S. Scott (Eds.), *Gender: A sociological reader.* London: Routledge.

Staples, B. 1999. The final showdown on interracial marriage. *New York Times,* July 6.

Staples, R. 1992. African American families. In J. M. Henslin (Ed.), *Marriage and family in a changing society.* New York: Free Press.

Stein, R., & Connolly, C. 2004. Medicare changes policy on obesity. *Washington Post,* July 16.

Steinberg, J. 2003a. The new calculus of diversity on campus. *New York Times,* February 2.

———. 2003b. Not all of them are pre-med. *New York Times,* February 2.

Stephan, C. W., & Stephan, W. G. 1989. After intermarriage: Ethnic identity among mixed-heritage Japanese-Americans and Hispanics. *Journal of Marriage and the Family, 51,* 507–519.

Stolberg, S. G. 1998. Live and let die over transplants. *New York Times,* April 5.

Strom, S. 2003. In middle class, health benefits become luxury. *New York Times,* November 16.

———. 2005. U.S. charity overwhelmed by disaster aid. *New York Times,* January 13.

Strong, P. T. 2004. The mascot slot: Cultural citizenship, political correctness, and pseudo-Indian sports symbols. *Journal of Sport and Social Issues, 28,* 79–87.

Sullivan, C. M., Tan, C., Basta, J., Rumptz, M., & Davidson, W. S. 1992. An advocacy intervention program for women with abusive partners: Initial evaluation. *American Journal of Community Psychology, 20,* 309–332.

Sunwolf, & Leets, L. 2004. Being left out: Rejecting outsiders and communicating group boundaries in childhood and adolescent peer groups. *Journal of Applied Communication Research, 32,* 195–223.

Super, C. M. 1976. Environmental effects on motor development. *Developmental Medicine and Child Neurology, 18,* 561–567.

Survivor stories. 2001. Protection Project. www.protectionproject.org/main1.htm. Accessed July 28, 2004.

Swarns, R. L. 2004a. "African American" becomes a term for debate. *New York Times,* August 29.

———. 2004b. Hispanics resist racial grouping by census. *New York Times,* October 24.

Sweeney, G. 2001. The trashing of white trash: *Natural Born Killers* and the appropriation of the white trash aesthetic. *Quarterly Review of Film and Video, 18,* 143–155.

Tahan, R. 1997. Realtors to receive cultural training. *Indianapolis Star,* November 16.

Talbot, M. 2002. Men behaving badly. *New York Times Magazine,* October 13.

Tannen, D. 1990. *You just don't understand: Women and men in conversation.* New York: William Morrow.

Tanner, J. 2002. Living wage movement. *CQ Researcher, 12,* 769–792.

Tauber, M. A. 1979. Parental socialization techniques and sex differences in children's play. *Child Development, 50,* 225–234.

Tavris, C. 1992. *The mismeasure of woman.* New York: Touchstone.

Tavris, C., & Offir, C. 1984. *The longest war: Sex differences in perspective.* New York: Harcourt Brace Jovanovich.

Telles, E. E., & Murguia, E. 1990. Phenotypic discrimination and income differences among Mexican Americans. *Social Science Quarterly, 71,* 682–696.

Thomas, C. B., & Healy, R. 2003. Conduct unbecoming. *Time,* March 10.

Thomas, W. I., & Thomas, D. 1928. *The child in America.* New York: Knopf.

Thompson, H. S., Valdimarsdottir, H. B., Winkel, G., Jandorf, L., & Redd, W. 2004. The group-based medical mistrust scale: Psychometric properties and association with breast cancer screening. *Preventive Medicine, 38,* 209–219.

Thompson, M. S., & Keith, V. M. 2004. The blacker the berry: Gender, skin tone, self-esteem, and self-efficacy. In D. M. Newman & J. O'Brien (Eds.), *Sociology: Exploring the architecture of everyday life (Readings).* Thousand Oaks, CA: Pine Forge Press.

Thompson, T. L., & Zerbinos, E. 1995. Gender roles in animated cartoons: Has the picture changed in 20 years? *Sex Roles, 32,* 651–673.

Thomsen, S. R., Weber, M. M., & Brown, L. B. 2002. The relationship between reading beauty and fashion magazines and the use of pathogenic dieting methods among adolescent females. *Adolescence, 37,* 1–18.

Thorne, B. 1995. Girls and boys together . . . but mostly apart: Gender arrangements in elementary schools. In D. M. Newman (Ed.), *Sociology: Exploring the architecture of everyday life (Readings).* Thousand Oaks, CA: Pine Forge Press.

Thornton, M. C. 1997. Strategies of racial socialization among black parents: Main-streaming, minority, and cultural messages. In R. Taylor, J. Jackson, & L. Chatters (Eds.), *Family life in Black America*. Thousand Oaks, CA: Sage.

Thornton, M. C., Chatters, L. M., Taylor, R. J., & Allen, W. R. 1990. Sociodemographic and environmental correlates of racial socialization by black parents. *Child Development, 61*, 401–409.

Thurlow, C. 2001. Naming the "outsider within": Homophobic pejoratives and the verbal abuse of lesbian, gay, and bisexual high-school pupils. *Journal of Adolescence, 24*, 25–38.

Tittle, C. R. 1994. The theoretical bases for inequality in formal social control. In G. S. Bridges & M. Myers (Eds.), *Inequality, crime, and social control*. Boulder, CO: Westview.

Tjaden, P., & Thoennes, N. 2000. Extent, nature, and consequences of intimate partner violence. National Institute of Justice Report #NCJ 181867. www.ncjrs.org/pdffiles1/nij/181867.pdf. Accessed October 12, 2004.

Toner, R. 2004. Money, politics, and four rich men. *New York Times*, July 11.

Tonry, M. 1995. *Malign neglect*. New York: Oxford University Press.

Trebay, G. 2004. The subtle power of lesbian style. *New York Times*, June 27.

Tuller, D. 2004. Gentlemen, start your engines? *New York Times*, June 21.

Tumin, M. 1953. Some principles of stratification: A critical analysis. *American Sociological Review, 18*, 387–393.

Tyre, P. 2005. House calls. *Newsweek*, February 7.

Udry, J. R. 2000. Biological limits of gender construction. *American Sociological Review, 65*, 443–457.

Uggen, C., & Blackstone, A. 2004. Sexual harassment as a gendered expression of power. *American Sociological Review, 69*, 64–92.

Uggen, C., & Manza, J. 2002. Democratic contraction? Political consequences of felon disenfranchisement in the United States. *American Sociological Review, 67*, 777–803.

Ulrich, L. T. 1990. *A midwife's tale: The life of Martha Ballard, based on her diary, 1785–1812*. New York: Knopf.

UNAIDS. 2004. 2004 report on the global AIDS epidemic. www.unaids.org/bangkok2004/report.html. Accessed July 20, 2004.

United States Bureau of Justice Statistics. 2001. The sexual victimization of college women. BJS Press release. www.ojp.usdoj.gov/bjs/pub/press/svcw. pr. Accessed January 28, 2001.

———. 2002. Sourcebook of criminal justice statistics, 2002. www.albany. edu/Sourcebook/1995/pdf/t526. Accessed August 2, 2004.

———. 2003. Criminal victimization in the United States, 2002 statistical tables. NCJ200561. www.ojp.usdoj.gov/bjs/pub/pdf/cvus02.pdf. Accessed July 28, 2004.

United States Bureau of Labor Statistics. 2004a. The employment situation: October 2004. www.bls.gov/news.release/pdf/empsit.pdf. Accessed November 18, 2004.

———. 2004b. Time-use survey—First results announced by BLS. USDL04-1797. www.bls.gov/tus/. Accessed September 15, 2004.

———. 2004c. Women in the labor force. Report #973. www.bls.gov/cps/wlf-databook.htm. Accessed September 23, 2004.

United States Bureau of the Census. 2002. Historical poverty tables. Table 6. www.census.gov/hhes/poverty/histpov/hstpov6.html. Accessed August 9, 2004.
———. 2003a. Historical income tables. Table H-1. www.census.gov/hhes/income/histinc/h0101.html. Accessed August 18, 2004.
———. 2003b. Statistical Abstract of the United States. www.census.gov/prod/www/statistical-abstract-03.html. Accessed September 16, 2004.
———. 2004. Statistical Abstract of the United States, 2004–2005. www.census.gov/prod/www/statistical-abstract-04.html. Accessed December 15, 2004.
United States Conference of Mayors. 2003. Hunger and homelessness survey. www.usmayors.org/uscm/hungersurvey/2003/onlinereport/HungerAndHomelessnessReport2003.pdf. Accessed August 23, 2004.
United States Department of Health and Human Services. 1994. Transracial adoption. http://naic.acf.hhs.gov/pubs/f_trans.pdf. Accessed September 22, 2004.
United States Department of Justice. 2001. Criminal victimization in United States, 1999 statistical tables. NCJ 184938. www.ojp.usdoj.gov/bjs/pub/pdf/cvus99.pdf. Accessed January 28, 2001.
United States Department of Labor. 2003. Household data, annual averages. Table 39. www.bls.gov/cps/cpsaat39.pdf. Accessed August 18, 2004.
———. 2004. Characteristics of minimum wage workers: 2003. Table 1. www.bls.gov/cps/minwage2003tbls.htm. Accessed August 23, 2004.
United States Department of State. 2002. Victims of Trafficking and Violence Protection Act 2000: Trafficking in persons report. www.state.gov/documents/organization/10815.pdf. Accessed July 28, 2004.
United States General Accounting Office. 2003. Women's earnings: Work patterns partially explain difference between men's and women's earnings. GAO Report 04-35. Washington, DC: U.S. Government Printing Office.
United States Sentencing Commission. 2004. Fifteen years of guidelines sentencing: An assessment of how well the federal criminal justice system is achieving the goals of sentencing reform. www.ussc.gov/15_year/ 15year.htm. Accessed November 27, 2004.
U.S. English, Inc. 2004. About the issue. www.us-english.org/inc/official/about/. Accessed June 25, 2004.
Valenti, C. 2002. Crime and punishment. ABCNews.com. http://abcnews.go.com/sections/business/DailyNews/corporatepunishment_020807.html. Accessed August 1, 2004.
Van Auken, B. 2004. Iraq crisis spurs call for US military draft. World Socialist Web Site. www.wsws.org/articles/2004/apr2004/draf-a22.shtml. Accessed August 7, 2004.
Van Ausdale, D., & Feagin, J. R. 2001. *The first R: How children learn race and racism.* Lanham, MD: Rowman & Littlefield.
Vanek, J. 1980. Work, leisure and family roles: Farm households in the United States: 1920–1955. *Journal of Family History, 5,* 422–431.
Vidal de Haymes, M., & Simon, S. 2003. Transracial adoption: Families identify issues and needed support services. *Child Welfare, 82,* 251–272.
Vojdik, V. K. 2002. Gender outlaws: Challenging masculinity in traditionally male institutions. *Berkeley Women's Law Journal, 17,* 68–122.
Wade, N. 2002. Race is seen as real guide to track roots of disease. *New York Times,* July 30.

Waldman, A. 2003. Broken taboos doom lovers in an Indian village. *New York Times,* March 28.

Walker, R. 2004. The pain principle. *New York Times,* June 27.

Ward, L. M. 2003. Understanding the role of entertainment media in the sexual socialization of American youth: A review of empirical research. *Developmental Review, 23,* 347–389.

Warshaw, R. 1988. *I never called it rape.* New York: Harper & Row.

Waxman, S. 2004a. Hollywood's he-men are bumped by sensitive guys. *New York Times,* July 1.

———. 2004b. Using a racial epithet to combat racism. *New York Times,* July 3.

Webber, T. 2004. Illnesses hit blacks hard. *Indianapolis Star,* July 11.

Weber, L. 1998. A conceptual framework for understanding race, class, gender, and sexuality. *Psychology of Women Quarterly, 22,* 13–32.

Weber, M. 1970. *From Max Weber: Essays in sociology* (H. H. Gerth & C. W. Mills, Eds.). New York: Oxford University Press.

Weil, E. 2005. Heavy questions. *New York Times Magazine,* January 2.

Weinberg, M. S., Williams, C. J., & Pryor, D. W. 2003. Becoming bisexual. In P. A. Adler & P. Adler (Eds.), *Constructions of deviance: Social power, context, and interaction.* Belmont, CA: Wadsworth.

Weiss, J. 2000. *To have and to hold: Marriage, the Baby Boom and social change.* Chicago: University of Chicago Press.

Weitzman, L., Eifler, D., Hodada, E., & Ross, C. 1972. Sex-role socialization in picture books for preschool children. *American Journal of Sociology, 77,* 1125–1150.

Weitzman, N., Birns, B., & Friend, R. 1985. Traditional and nontraditional mothers' communication with their daughters and sons. *Child Development, 56,* 894–898.

West, C., & Zimmerman, D. 1987. Doing gender. *Gender & Society, 1,* 135–151.

White, J. E. 1997. Multiracialism: The melding of America. *Time,* May 5.

Wildman, S. M., & Davis, A. D. 2002. Making systems of privilege visible. In P. S. Rothenberg (Ed.), *White privilege: Essential readings on the other side of racism.* New York: Worth.

Wilgoren, J. 2003. Governor assails system's errors as he empties Illinois death row. *New York Times,* January 12.

Wilkins, D. E. 2004. A tour of Indian peoples and Indian lands. In C. A. Gallagher (Ed.), *Rethinking the color line: Readings in race and ethnicity.* New York: McGraw-Hill.

Will, J., Self, P., & Datan, N. 1976. Maternal behavior and perceived sex of infant. *American Journal of Orthopsychiatry, 46,* 135–139.

Williams, B. 2004. The "n-word." Minnesota Public Radio. http://news.minnesota.publicradio.org/features/2004/06–28_williamsb_nword/. Accessed October 14, 2004.

Williams, C. 2004. Still a man's world: Men who do "women's work." In D. M. Newman & J. O'Brien (Eds.), *Sociology: Exploring the architecture of everyday life (Readings).* Thousand Oaks, CA: Pine Forge Press.

Williams, G. H. 1995. *Life on the color line: The true story of a white boy who discovered he was black.* New York: Dutton.

Williams, J. A., Vernon, J. A., Williams, M. C., & Malecha, K. 1987. Sex role socialization in picture books: An update. *Social Science Quarterly, 68,* 148–156.

Williams, L. 1991. When blacks shop bias often accompanies sale. *New York Times,* April 30.

Williams, P. J. 1997. The hidden meanings of "Black English." *The Black Scholar, 27,* 7–8.

———. 2004. Uncommon ground. *The Nation,* April 5.

Williams, W. L. 1992. *The spirit and the flesh: Sexual diversity in American Indian culture.* Boston: Beacon Press.

Williamson, R. C. 1984. A partial replication of the Kohn-Gecas-Nye thesis in a German sample. *Journal of Marriage and the Family, 46,* 971–979.

Wilson, W. J. 1980. The declining significance of race. Chicago: University of Chicago Press.

———. 1987. *The truly disadvantaged: The inner city, the underclass and public policy.* Chicago: University of Chicago Press.

———. 2003. Jobless ghettos: The social implications of the disappearance of work in segregated neighborhoods. In T. E. Ore (Ed.), *The social construction of difference and inequality: Race, class, gender, and sexuality.* New York: McGraw-Hill.

Wines, M. 2004a. As AIDS continues to ravage, South Africa "recycles" graves. *New York Times,* July 29.

———. 2004b. Women in Lesotho become easy prey for H.I.V. *New York Times,* July 20.

Winter, G. 2003. Ruling provides relief, but less than hoped. *New York Times,* June 24.

———. 2004. Long after Brown v. Board of Education, sides switch. *New York Times,* May 16.

Wise, T. 2002. Membership has its privileges: Thoughts on acknowledging and challenging whiteness. In P. S. Rothenberg (Ed.), *White privilege: Essential readings on the other side of racism.* New York: Worth.

Witt, S. D. 1997. Parental influence on children's socialization to gender roles. *Adolescence, 32,* 253–260.

Wolfe, A. 2000. Benign multiculturalism. In P. Kivisto & G. Rundblad (Eds.), *Multiculturalism in the United States.* Thousand Oaks, CA: Pine Forge Press.

Wood, N. 2005. Eight nations agree on plan to lift status of Gypsies. *New York Times,* February 6.

World Bank. 2003. Global poverty monitoring. www.worldbank.org/research/povmonitor. Accessed August 24, 2004.

———. 2004. Report predicts 30-year growth record. World Bank DevNews Media Center. www.worldbank.org. Accessed November 29, 2004.

World Health Organization. 1995. World health report 1995—Executive summary. www.who.int. Accessed June 23, 2001.

Worsnop, R. 1996. Getting into college. *CQ Researcher,* February 23.

Wright, E. O. 1976. Class boundaries in advanced capitalist societies. *New Left Review, 98,* 3–41.

Wright, E. O., Costello, C., Hachen, D., & Sprague, J. 1982. The American class structure. *American Sociological Review, 47,* 709–726.

Wright, E. O., & Perrone, L. 1977. Marxist class categories and income inequality. *American Sociological Review, 42,* 32–55.

Xiao, H. 2000. Class, gender, and parental values in the 1990s. *Gender & Society, 14,* 785–803.

Yamaguchi, M. 2004. In Japan, feudal stigma persists; Burakumin class still encounters bias. *Washington Post*, July 18.

Yang, A. 1997. Trends: Attitudes toward homosexuality. *Public Opinion Quarterly, 61,* 477–507.

Yardley, J. 2000. Studies find race disparities in Texas traffic stops. *New York Times,* October 7.

Yllo, K., & Straus, M. A. 1990. Patriarchy and violence against wives: The impact of structural and normative factors. In M. A. Straus & R. J. Gelles (Eds.), *Physical violence in American families*. New Brunswick, NJ: Transaction.

Young, L. M., & Powell, B. 1985. The effects of obesity on the clinical judgments of mental health professionals. *Journal of Health and Social Behavior, 26,* 233–246.

Your most private sex questions. 2004. *CosmoGirl Magazine*. May.

Zeller, T. 2004. Of fuzzy math and "food security." *New York Times,* January 11.

Zhang, S. D., & Odenwald, W. F. 1995. Misexpression of the white gene triggers male-male courtship in Drosophila. *Proceedings of the National Academy of Sciences, 92,* 5525–5529.

Zwicky, A. M. 1997. Two lavender issues for linguists. In A. Livia & K. Hall (Eds.), *Queerly phrased: Language, gender, and sexuality.* New York: Oxford University Press.

Excerpt from "The hidden life of class" by Ortner, S.B. in *Journal of Anthropological Research, 54*, pp. 1–17. Copyright © 1998. Reprinted with permission of University of New Mexico, Department of Anthropology.

Excerpt from "What it means to be gendered me: Life on the boundaries of a dichotomous gender system" by Lucal, B. in *Gender & Society, 13*, pp. 781–797. Copyright © 1999 Sociologists for Women in Society. Reprinted by permission of Sage Publications, Inc.

Excerpt from "A different kind of queer marriage" by Markowitz, L. in *Utne Reader*, September–October, 2000, p. 24. Reprinted with permission.

Excerpt from "Double Lives on the Down Line" by Denizet-Lewis, B. from *The New York Times Magazine*, August 3, 2003, p. 31. Copyright © 2003, Benoit Denizet-Lewis. Reprinted by permission.

Excerpt reprinted by permission of the author, Michael Quinion, World Wide Words, http://www.worldwidewords.org.

Excerpt reprinted by permission of the Foundation for Individual Rights in Education. www.thefire.org.

Excerpt from "Black Like Them" by Malcolm Gladwell from *The New Yorker*, April 29, May 6, 1996. Reprinted by permission of the author.

Excerpt from "African American becomes a term for debate" by Swarns, Rachel, L. from *The New York Times*, August 29, 2004. Copyright © 2003 by The New York Times Co. Reprinted with permission.

Exhibit 5.1 excerpted from "Campus climate for gay, lesbian, bisexual, and transgender people: A national perspective" by Rankin, S. R. Reprinted with permission from The Task Force, www.thetaskforce.com.

Excerpt from "Addressing the needs of lesbian patients" by Fields, C.B. & Scout in *Journal of Sex Education and Therapy, 26*, 2001: p. 182. Reprinted by permission of the American Association of Sex Educators, Counselors, and Therapists (AASECT).

Excerpt from "Narratives of the death sentence: Toward a theory of legal narrativity" by Fleury-Steiner, B. from *Law & Society Review, 39*, 2002: pp. 562 & 570. Reprinted by permission of Blackwell Publishing Ltd.

Excerpt from "Survivor Stories: Maria." Reprinted by permission of The Protection Project, www.protectionproject.com.

Excerpt from "Causes of poverty: Poverty facts and statistics" from www.globalissues.org. Copyright © 1998–2005 Anup Shah.

Excerpt from "Imagining life without illegal immigrants" by Murphy, Dean E. from *The New York Times*, January 11, 2004. Copyright © 2004 by The New York Times Co. Reprinted with permission.

Photos Credits

positive differences in, 10
pride in, 9–10
slurs about, 75
socialization, 117–122
stereotypes, 95–96
subdivision of, 319–321
use of term, 28
violence motivated by, 178–180, 230
Whites' sense of own, 164–165
working class assumptions of, 100
ethnoracial, use of term, 28
Europeans
  racial classification started by, 43
  same-sex marriage of, 237
  "white" as blanket term for, 43
expectations, creating, 152, 153
Extreme Makeover, 92, 101

fairness, equality *v.*, 305
false consciousness: situation in which
    people in the lower strata of society
    come to accept a belief system that
    works to their disadvantage, 24
families
  future of, 322–323, 326
  gender roles in, 162, 322–323
  homeless, 278–279
  name importance in, 27, 28–29
  socialization in, 108–132
Family & Medical Leave Act of 1993,
    193, 253
Family Matters, 96
family trees, social mobility identified
    through, 29
fashion, homosexuality and, 97
FBI, crime statistics from, 230, 244
Feagin, Joe, 165–167, 176, 303–304
females. *See also* motherhood
  African American, colorism among,
    170–171
  African American, in media, 95
  African American, in workplace,
    298, 303–304
  aggressive, 136–137, 163
  biological inferiority of, 161–163,
    216–217

bullying by, 136–137
closet homosexual, 62–63
communication differences with, 13
communication patterns of, 84–85
discrimination against, institutional,
    180–181, 297–304
dual expectations from, 91–92
earnings for, median annual, 285–286
future roles of, 322–324
gender norms violated by, 116–117
HIV/AIDS contracted by, 207–208
intimate violence against, 258–265
Jewish, in media, 95
language biased against, 78–79
laws for rights of, 253–254
medicalization of, 216–220
mothering stereotypes of, 154–156
normality standard for, 17
separate spheres ideology of, 297–301
sexual exhibition of, 90–93
sexual harassment of, 253, 254–255
sexual orientation socialization for,
    125–126
sick role privileges for, 194
in single-sex schools, 135
slurs used for, 76, 116
in sports, 92, 116
teacher behavior toward, 134–135
television networks for, 89
as tomboys, 116
trafficking, 256–258
weight concerns of, 93, 201–202
World War II life for, 7, 298–299
femininity
  19th century ideals of, 66, 161, 297–298
  atypical, 55
  biological predisposition to, 109–111,
    162–163
  degradation of, 162–163
  media reinforcement of, 91–93
feminist movement, 66
feminist perspective: a theoretical
    perspective that focuses on gender,
    more so than class or socioeconomic
    status, as the most important source
    of conflict and inequality in social
    life, 26–27

Montgomery, Alabama, social
  movements in, 313
moral boundaries, between social
  classes, 50
Morocco, rape viewed in, 260
motherhood. *See also* parenting
  class and race influence on, 131–132
  good, stereotyping, 154–156
  single, 286–288
MTV, 100
Mulattos, 32, 44
The Mullets, 101
multiculturalism: a way of thinking that
  emphasizes the importance of
  maintaining the cultural elements
  that give society variety and
  make groups different from one
  another, 83
  future of, 316–318
  panethnic labels used for, 83
  prejudice from, 158
Multiethnic Placement Act of 1994, 119
multiracial identities, 45–46, 47*f*
Mundugumor culture, 110
Murray, Charles, 165
Muslims
  gender socialization by, 134
  prejudice against, 5–6, 156–157, 230
  racial profiling of, 241
My Wife and Kids, 95, 96

NAACP (National Association for the
  Advancement of Colored People)
  plastics plant supported by, 214
  slurs used by, 77
NABSW (National Association of Black
  Social Workers), 119
nadle (androgynous people), 57
National Association for the
  Advancement of Colored People.
  See NAACP
National Association of Black Social
  Workers. *See* NABSW
National Association of Realtors, 183
National Crime Victimization Survey,
  241, 259

National Eating Disorder Association,
  201–202
National Fair Housing Alliance, 182
National Longitudinal Study on
  Adolescent Health, 46
National Organization of Men Against
  Sexism. *See* NOMAS
National Origins Act of 1924, 7
National Survey of Black Americans, on
  colorism, 171
Native Americans
  adoption of, transracial, 120
  androgyny sex recognized by, 57
  colorist prejudice of, 169
  discrimination against, institutional,
    6, 181
  environmental regulations of, 213
  ethnoracial labels used for, 79–80
  government recognition of, 80
  graduation rate of, 295
  historical categorization of, 44
  mascots derived from, 86
  parenting by, 131
  political correctness for, 86–87
  prejudice against, 160, 161
  racial socialization of, 118
  as "red men," 43
  variation among, concealment of, 82
Navajos, androgyny recognized by, 57
Navratilova, Martina, 290
NBC, 100
Nepal, caste-based discrimination
  in, 48
New Guinea, gender socialization study
  in, 110–111
New Jersey, human trafficking in, 257
New York
  California *v.,* 148–149
  everyday life in, 148–149
  schools in, 141, 142
New York Times, 97
New Yorker (Jew), 80
news
  ethnoracially-biased, 95–96
  lower class portrayed by, 102
newspapers, for-profit nature of, 100
Nigeria, beauty viewed by, 198

Public Health Service, Tuskegee study
    by, 215
public schools, private v., 141–142
Puerto Rican Americans, as single
    mothers, 287–288
Puerto Rico, racial categories in, 42

Quadroons, 44
queer, as self-label, 81
Queer Eye for the Straight Guy, 97
quiet bias, 174–175

race: a category of individuals who are
    believed to share common inborn
    biological traits, such as skin color;
    color and texture of hair; and shape
    of eyes, nose, or head
    biological inferiority of, 160–161
    classification created by, 43
    conflict perspective applied to, 26
    death penalty influenced by, 249–252
    death rates by, 211f
    diseases distributed by, 40–41, 207
    economic inequalities by, 273–274,
        275–276, 275f, 280–284
    female bullying influenced
        by, 136–138
    gender socialization's influence on,
        120–122
    government rules defining, 44–45
    harmony between, 96–97, 316–318
    health care influenced by, 210–216
    historical categorization for, 44
    HIV/AIDS statistics by, 207
    identities by, 40–46, 117–122
    importance of, 175–178
    income trends by, 275f
    institutional discrimination by, 6, 7,
        181, 182–183, 292–297
    intelligence correlated to, 160, 165
    justice influenced by, 239–243
    language biased by, 79–80
    lower class socialization and, 131–132
    media portrayal of, 94–97, 101
    miscegenation and, 233–236

obesity influenced by, 200–202, 200f
parenthood, single, influenced by,
    286–288
physical v. experiential characteristics
    of, 41–42
poverty statistics by, 154, 276–277
prejudice against, 160–161
prisoner population by, 246–249, 246f
social class influence on, 120–122
social class v., 67
socialization, 76, 117–122, 137–143
as socioeconomic slang, 42, 43
stereotypes, 95–96
subdivision of, 319–321
transformation of, 31–32
use of term, 28
variations, 40–41
white male perceptions of, 165–167
working class assumptions of, 100
workplace discrimination by, 292–297,
    303–304
racial profiling, 96, 177–178, 241–243
racial transparency: a state of being in
    which whiteness is unremarkable and
    unexamined, 18, 163–167
Raffaelli, Marcella, 114
ranking. *See* **stratification**
rape, 259–262
Raytheon and Lockheed, 291
real estate industry, racial discrimination
    by, 182–183
The Real World, 95
"red men," 43
Reiman, Jeffrey, 245
religion. *See also specific religions*
    changes in diversity of, 315
    hiding, 150
    holidays and, 73
    institutional discrimination by, 292
    prejudice based on, 5–6, 148–150,
        156–157, 229
    racial socialization enforced by, 118
residential segregation, 182–183
restaurant industry, racial discrimination
    in, 292–293
retail industry, racial discrimination in,
    186–187